Praise for *Imagine a City*

'A journey around both the author's mind and the planet's great cities that leaves us energised, open to ~~new~~ ~~experiences~~ and ready to re~~turn~~'

'*Imagine a City* . . . will e~~ngage~~ ~~compa~~red in recent years for th~~e~~

'Evocative . . . Lyrical . . . At the keyboard Vanhoenacker has danced, and on his pages there is tumbling mirth indeed'
Boston Globe

'A moving account of personal unbelonging'
The Times

'Vanhoenacker is exceptionally well travelled and an exceptionally curious and widely read observer . . . He doesn't waste an hour and with every return his engagement with each city deepens . . . Superb'
Times Literary Supplement

'*Imagine a City* is really about home . . . A variation on the *Great Expectations* narrative, with our young hero feeling uncomfortable where he grows up, flying the nest for a series of transformative experiences but discovering he can never quite leave home nor fully return'
Spectator

'What makes Mark Vanhoenacker's *Imagine a City* such a joy is that this is a travel book entirely rooted in modernity and globalisation . . . but which nonetheless retains the wide-eyed wonder not so much of a nineteenth-century explorer as of a medieval pilgrim'
Asian Review of Books

'More personal than *Skyfaring*, but with the same reassuringly precise and perceptive voice'
Financial Times

'An enriching memoir of how a sensitive, introverted boy's yearning for escape and acceptance found its fulfilment in the life of an airline pilot . . . A touching survey of human dreams and endeavours and a hymn to the quiet pleasures of returning, in the flesh or in memory, to the intimate geography of one's hometown'
Patrick Gale

MARK VANHOENACKER

Mark Vanhoenacker flies the Boeing 787 for British Airways and is the author of the international bestsellers *Skyfaring* and *How to Land a Plane*. A regular contributor to the *New York Times* and the *Financial Times*, he has also written for *Wired*, *The Times*, the *Los Angeles Times*, the *Atlantic* and *Popular Science*. He worked in business before starting his flight training in 2001. Described as 'a poet of the skies' (*Spectator*), Mark changes how readers view the world.

ALSO BY MARK VANHOENACKER

Skyfaring
How to Land a Plane

MARK VANHOENACKER

Imagine a City

A Pilot's Love Letter to the
World's Greatest Cities

VINTAGE

1 3 5 7 9 10 8 6 4 2

Vintage is part of the Penguin Random House group of companies
whose addresses can be found at global.penguinrandomhouse.com

Penguin
Random House
UK

First published in Vintage in 2023
First published in Great Britain in hardback by Chatto & Windus in 2022
First published in the United States by Alfred A. Knopf in 2022

penguin.co.uk/vintage

Printed and bound in Great Britain by Clays Ltd, Elcograf S.p.A.

The authorised representative in the EEA is Penguin Random House Ireland,
Morrison Chambers, 32 Nassau Street, Dublin D02 YH68

A CIP catalogue record for this book is available from the British Library

ISBN 9781529112023

Penguin Random House is committed to a sustainable
future for our business, our readers and our planet. This book
is made from Forest Stewardship Council® certified paper.

And I fled from the old city
Fled underneath the thorn bush
Fled into the night sky
Fled underneath the damp earth
Where I passed through a doorway
And found you sitting at the kitchen table and smiling

Nick Cave

Contents

IMAGINE A CITY

PROLOGUE

CITY OF MEMORY

Pittsfield and Abu Dhabi

PITTSFIELD

I'm thirteen. It's after school. I'm in my room, at my desk. I look out of the window over the drive and towards the garage. It's late autumn and it's almost dark outside. There's frost in the corners of the window and snow is falling.

I look across the room, at the light-up globe on my dresser. I go to it, flip the switch on its cord and watch as the darkened sphere turns blue in the failing light and starts to shine as if it were in space.

I return to my desk. I sit down, pick up my pencil with my left hand and rest its tip on the sheet of graph paper. I love aeroplanes and cities and so, not for the first time, I've drawn a simple map of the world. I'll draw a line that begins in one city and ends in another. But which city to start from?

I set down the pencil and look around my room again – at my model aeroplanes perched on my dresser, on my desk and next to my old Snoopy on my bookcase. There's a green-and-white Lockheed TriStar and a mostly white McDonnell Douglas DC-9. On the plane I assembled most recently, a grey DC-10, I notice that the decals aren't attached very well. Maybe, I think, I could have done a better job, but these decals are a pain. You have to soak them in a bowl of water until they loosen from their backing, then align them on the aircraft's fuselage or tail without tearing them, even as they're drying out and curling up. Sometimes I ask myself if I really like assembling model aeroplanes; maybe I only like having the aeroplanes afterwards.

The flagship of these models is a Boeing 747 in the blue-and-white colours of Pan Am. On a December night two decades or so from now, an hour before I pilot an actual 747 for the first time, from London to Hong Kong, I'll walk around the plane to conduct the preflight inspection and when I look up at its sail-like, six-storey tail fin I'll recall this model, and this window by my desk, and the view it offers from a house that by then will be the home of someone else.

I look back down at the page. Now, where . . . ?

I could start from Cape Town. A cape with a town on it. From this far – from Pittsfield, the small, upland Massachusetts city where I was born – Cape Town is only that, a name.

Or I could begin in an Indian city. New Delhi – the capital, I'm reminded by the star that marks its location on the globe that's shining on my dresser.

Or Rio de Janeiro, whose name comes from a bay that an explorer mistook for a river on the first day of a now-long-gone new year. I pause to consider if that can be right. Is that how Dad explained the city's name to me after I told him how much I liked it? Dad lived in Brazil for years before he moved to New England. He'll be home from work soon. I'll wait until I see the red brake lights of his grey Chevy station wagon as he drives carefully through the snow that will muffle the car's noise on the drive below my window, and then I'll go downstairs and ask him to tell me again about the City of the River of January.

I could start in Rio. It wouldn't be the first time. But the best thing about today is the snow. So the air route I draw this afternoon should depart from a cold place. Boston or New York, perhaps.

Boston, our nearest big city and the state capital, is where my parents met. It's about two and a half hours east of Pittsfield. I visit Boston once or twice a year, on day trips with school or my family – to the science museum, the aquarium or my favourite skyscraper (which is blue, as is nearly everything I like best). From its observation deck you can look east towards Boston's airport and listen to a radio tuned to the voices of the pilots flying to and from it.

Boston, then. I'll start in Boston.

Today's destination, meanwhile, is not a real city; rather, it's the city I've liked to imagine since I was maybe seven years old. Its location changes occasionally, as does its name. But no matter where I draw it or what I call it, it's the same city to me.

My city is where I travel to when I'm sad or worried, or when I don't wish to think about what I don't like about myself, such as the fact that I'm unable to pronounce the letter *r*, and therefore many words, including my own name. It's also where I go when I want to escape my dawning awareness that I'm gay. A few months ago, for example, the youth group my brother and I attend, the one that gathers on the second floor of a church here in Pittsfield, held a session about 'human development'. We were invited to write on cards any questions we didn't want to ask out loud. One of the leaders collected the cards and a few minutes later read my question to the group: Is there a way to not be gay? He paused, and finally answered: I don't know of a way. Instead, he said, it's something people come to accept about themselves. And when I realised that he was looking at me, and how much I feared what he might say next, I turned my eyes away from his, and towards the lights of my imaginary city.

I also like to go to my imaginary city at more ordinary times: when I'm doing things I don't enjoy, such as washing up or raking leaves; when, in school, I get bored or lose track of what the teacher is saying; or when it's late and the house is quiet and dark but I can't sleep and so I look out of my bedroom window and I see how blue the night is and that it has started to snow, and when I lie back down and close my eyes I see the same snow falling past the towers of my city.

Now the lights from Dad's car appear on the drive and shake over the garage doors as I pick up the pencil again. I make two small

circles on the map and write a name by each. I draw the line that
curves between them and then I go downstairs.

ABU DHABI

A young woman finishes an uneven rendition of Gloria Gaynor's
'I Will Survive' and hands back the mic.

A few minutes later, Jane, a late-middle-aged woman with
shoulder-length curly brown hair, picks it up. I'm terrible at karaoke
but an enthusiastic supporter, and as she reaches the stage I applaud
and try to shout the loudest.

Jane is one of the cabin crew from my flight from London today.
She worked in the forward cabin, the one nearest to the flight
deck. She came up for a chat with me and the captain on her break
between the two passenger meal services, when we were crossing
the Black Sea coast of Turkey and the sun was setting. Later, she
came back to the cockpit with two cups of strong tea as the hazy
green lights of Baghdad filled the long side window that ran past my
right shoulder, and she returned again as we sailed down the Gulf's
skies and crossed near one glowing city after another, and over the
petroleum complexes that themselves resemble whole cities. Then,
in the terminal in Abu Dhabi, after touchdown, Jane and I spoke
once more, about the views we'd each had of this desert metropolis,
which sprawled on the coast like the Milky Way on a beach holiday,
as we made a slow circuit above and landed, having reversed direction, facing back towards London.

Nothing we talked about, though, has prepared me for what happens when she starts to sing. Jane's voice is so rich it seems to change
the air in the room. Entire tables of friends or colleagues fall silent
as they turn and see that she has not only the voice, but also all the
right moves: she twists the cable that isn't trailing from the cordless
mic; one moment she makes eye contact with a member of the audi-

ence, and the next she looks up into a smoky light as if her muse is beckoning from within its beam.

She starts a second song, John Lennon's 'Imagine', and I take out my phone to make a video to send home to my husband. Then I watch and listen as she finishes and the crowd erupts. Jane hands the mic to the next person and returns to a festive welcome and expressions of disbelief and vicarious pride from our table. When she was young, she explains with a smile, she worked as a showgirl in Las Vegas. Then she came home to England to raise a family. Several decades later, she decided to see the rest of the world.

Before too long we all return to our hotel. My room is on a high floor, maybe the twenty-fifth. It's late now, but I'm on London time and I know it won't be easy for me to sleep yet. I walk to the nearly floor-to-ceiling windows and slide open the successive waves of curtains that I'd struggled to figure out how to close earlier. I turn down some of the lights, to dim the images of the bed and minifridge that repeat over the nightscape beyond the glass.

As I look out through the reflections that remain, I try to retrace the decisions and circumstances that led to my first visit to Abu Dhabi, many years ago. My parents divorced when I was sixteen; Dad remarried a few years later. After high school, I left Pittsfield for university in a town only an hour or so away, over the hills to the east. Later, I moved to England for graduate school. Two years after that I was due to go to Kenya as part of my graduate studies, and I returned to Pittsfield to visit Mom beforehand (while I'd been in England, Dad and my stepmother had sold the old house in Pittsfield and moved south, to Raleigh, North Carolina). At the end of my visit, Mom took me to the bus station and waved me off, smiling – in order not to appear sad, it seems now – as the bus rolled away along the first metres of my first trip to Africa. Late the next night I landed in Abu Dhabi, on a layover en route to Nairobi.

I'd never been to the Middle East before, let alone to Arabia, and, though my stay here in Abu Dhabi would be measured only in hours, I'd looked forward to it with the enthusiasm of someone who had spent most of their life dreaming about aeroplanes and journeys to cities as distant from home as this one. I remember a yellow rain of lights as I pressed my face to the jet's window on the final approach; gusts of a new kind of heat on the airbridge; tiles on a curved ceiling, in a shade of blue that was close to perfection; and the wonder, to me, of Arabic script on the advertisements along the walkways. Nothing else.

I left the graduate programme that had taken me to Kenya once I was certain that I wanted to become an airline pilot. I moved to Boston for the first time, to work at a management consultancy in order to save money for my flight training. Three years later I moved to Kidlington, near Oxford, England, to start my pilot course, after which I moved to a shared house near Heathrow to start my flying career. In those early years I flew a narrow-body Airbus jet on short-haul routes to cities all across Europe. Eventually I retrained on the Boeing 747, the iconic airliner I'd dreamed of flying since I was a little kid. In my eleven years on the 747 fleet, I travelled to many of the world's largest cities, but never to Abu Dhabi.

Not long ago I retrained again, to fly the 787, and it was in the cockpit of one of these newer and smaller jets that I finally returned to this city. Now I've flown here several times as a pilot, on trips that typically include around twenty-four hours off 'down-route', that is, on the ground but away from home. That's time enough to sleep, to study the latest updates to our manuals, to file my scheduling requests for the following month (Johannesburg? Chennai? Another Abu Dhabi?), to exercise while I listen to music or catch up on a podcast, or to wander out to see something of the city, in the company of my colleagues or on my own.

From the tower of our hotel I look down to the nearby streets. Many Gulf cities have long histories as small coastal settlements. As major metropolises, though, all of them are new.

Close by is a broad avenue lined with shops and framed by rows of apartment and office buildings, perhaps twenty storeys high. The avenue is lit to a snowy brilliance even at this hour, while the road that runs parallel to it is herringboned by side streets dense with what look like large single-family homes, an incongruously cosy sight from my high and anonymous room. Further away is a cluster of skyscrapers, many of which are capped with beacons. Between these red-lit points, my eyes follow the zigzag line that is like a signature of the city's creators.

I yawn and ponder if it might soon be time for bed. Abu Dhabi, meanwhile, doesn't appear to be sleepy: the roads below are still busy, a common sight in Gulf cities, where summer nights are so much more pleasant than summer days, while during Ramadan public life may seem to begin only after sunset. I watch the skyscrapers and construction cranes twinkle as if in an effort to communicate, and I think of David Leavitt's *The Lost Language of Cranes*, maybe the first novel I read that presented gay characters. The friend who gave the book to me when I was perhaps eighteen had said little to me about it. I thought it would be about the birds, and perhaps Japan, where I knew they were revered enough to be painted on the tails of planes; rather, the book's title follows from the story of a small child who saw a construction crane from his window, and came to treat its sounds and movements as a language.

I check my phone: it's sunny in Pittsfield; my husband, Mark (we share a name), has enjoyed the clip of my colleague singing; my aviation-focused weather app reports strong south-westerly winds at Heathrow. If I'm not going to sleep I might as well iron my shirt. Nearly a day remains until I'll button it on for the flight home, but I can complete the preparations now. I can press it carefully and hang it in the closet, with my epaulettes and name badge in place, and my ballpoint pen in the little vertical pocket next to the main front pocket, another aviation checklist complete.

I extend and latch open the legs of the squeaky board. As I move to plug the iron in, I'm struck by the sight of the desk in front of the windows, silhouetted by the glowing towers behind it. It reminds me, suddenly, of the desk by the window of my childhood bedroom, and of the many versions of my imaginary city that I envisioned or drew there.

I cross the room and sit down at the desk. I look down at the small metal plate on which an arrow indicates *qibla*, the direction of Mecca. From this marker I can estimate the initial direction of the great circle route – the shortest distance over the surface of a sphere – that would run from Abu Dhabi back to London; it's not so different from the heading that a pilot might initially follow, if any pilot ever has, to journey from Abu Dhabi to Pittsfield.

And at this desk I remember that for many years I've wanted to write about what cities have meant to me.

I want to record my journey from one city, my small hometown, to so many real cities that are each a thousand times more fascinating than anything I imagined as a child. And I want to be open about myself as I write this, even if it's not always easy. I know that's the only way to try to understand my deep love for the hometown I was once so keen to leave.

I have other, more matter-of-fact reasons to write this book. Most pilots love their job and tend not to want to retire when the rules say we must. When my days and nights of flying are finished, I want to be able to remember all I can about the cities I saw. In addition, while years may remain before my retirement, I'd like to share now what I love best about many of these cities – not only with my family and friends, but with readers who might not travel as often, as far, or in as extraordinary a manner as a pilot does.

And *extraordinary* is the right word. Long-haul airline pilots today are given an experience of cities that no one else in history has ever had. Two decades into my career – in an age in which it often seems that the urbanised future of our civilisation is taking form directly before my eyes – my experience of cities as a pilot remains a source of deep fascination to me, one that's distinct from my love for flight itself.

During a single flight we may cross above dozens of cities, most memorably after dark. On some journeys the lights of a sleeping and apparently silent settlement beneath us – one that, if it doesn't have a major airport, we may not be able to name without consulting our navigation charts – suggest Coleridge's ancient mariner, passing 'like night, from land to land', and the fragility and even the loneliness of what an observer arriving in our orbit might regard as only one more of the universe's strains of bioluminescence. On other flights, when I see a gathering of dim lights stitched into the far-below floor of a Siberian or Nigerian or Iranian night, I'm struck instead by a sense of warmth, even intimacy, and by the possibility that I'm looking down on an evening much like the most peaceful ones of my Pittsfield childhood.

Then we descend. If we do so at daybreak, the returning light allows us to see how wilderness, farmland, inhospitably steep terrain, or thousands of miles of open ocean give way to our destination: one of the largest cities in history, perhaps, which has grown through its own long centuries, and which now, on this latest of its mornings, and in the last twenty minutes of our journey, expands to fill the jet's windscreen with a map-like view of its awakening streets.

After we land, we have the opportunity to repeat or deepen a set of urban experiences that are, again, like those of no one else. Our stays in cities – in so many cities! – are typically short but frequent; carefully arranged around our legal responsibility to rest, but also freedom-giving and time-bending; as shallow a traveller's experience as we might sometimes be grateful for, or as fine-grained as our interests and the length of our down-route stay (twenty-four hours is common for long-haul pilots, more than seventy-two is not) might allow.

The most remarkable effect of visiting cities in this manner, time and time again, year after year, is that each begins to take on a curious sense of familiarity. Indeed, in some cities this familiarity is so powerful and deceptive that I've struggled to remind myself: I am not from here. This city is not mine.

Los Angeles, for example, is a place whose name first captured my imagination as a child, and that I longed to someday see. After I trained to fly the 747, I began to fly there regularly. Then for a few years I did not, and when I returned for the first time after this gap I asked myself how many times I'd flown there in total. Fifteen, perhaps? I checked my logbook and it was thirty-nine. Now it's more than fifty, which (if each stay was forty-eight hours; some have been longer) means that I've spent more than three months in the city – long enough that when I'm in LA, waiting for a coffee or stuck in traffic, it's easy, momentarily, to imagine that I've always lived there.

Then I fly away. And when I meet someone from Los Angeles elsewhere in the world, I may be excited to talk to them, in part because I feel that we have their well-named metropolis in common, until I catch myself: that feeling can't be right; I have it about too many cities for it to be true of any of them.

São Paulo is another city I've visited more times than I can count without consulting my logbook. I've walked and run many miles in Ibirapuera Park; I've spent hours people-watching from the window seats of cafés and buffet restaurants near Avenida Paulista; I've saved up errands from home merely for the adventure of getting a watch strap replaced in a South American megalopolis; I've visited the cathedral, the observation deck of the tower that resembles the Empire State Building, the food market full of fruits and fish that are foreign to me, and the stunning, stunningly named, railway terminal: Estação da Luz, Station of Light. In São Paulo, indeed, I'll often find myself overtaking tourists on staircases and crowded pavements as surefootedly and half-exasperatedly as I might at home. Then, on that same afternoon, perhaps, I leave. And a few days later I'll catch myself walking like that someplace else.

The first time I landed in Mumbai – indeed, it was the first time I set foot in India – I had only twenty-four hours there. I was excited, of course, but I was also surprised to notice how relaxed I was about my plans for my first day in a new city and country. The reason, I slowly realised, was that I already knew that I'd return to Mumbai again and again, whether or not I wished to, and that each time I'd be free to explore the city as closely as each short stay allowed, to decide if I loved it, and even to pretend to be a little at home in it; or, in contrast, to behave – if the monsoon rains threatened, or I was tired, or I had an episode of a favourite TV show to catch up on – as if I was hardly in Mumbai at all.

My years of experiencing cities in this manner have had three distinct effects. The first is that the familiarity – albeit deceptive – I associate with individual cities has gradually expanded until it blankets the entire urban planet. Today, if someone asks if I've been to a particular city, it may take me a moment to set aside my impression that I've been more or less everywhere.

And it's important that I set aside that impression, because even pilots do not go everywhere. In 2018, the United Nations published a list of the 548 cities with a population of more than one million. The figures for some cities include only those within the city limits, while for others the total encompasses a much more expansively drawn urban region. (The challenge of choosing a city's most meaningful boundaries echoes that of merely defining a city, whether in legal terms or in our everyday language. The Town of Cary, North Carolina, near to where my father and stepmother retired, is four times the size of the City of Pittsfield – in Massachusetts, a state where settlements ruled by citizen meetings are towns, and those governed by a council and perhaps a mayor are cities. While in England, the designation of cities is a royal matter; it's commonly said that an English city must have a cathedral, but my husband's hometown, the City of Southampton, does not.)

Setting aside such questions, as I looked down the United

Nations' list of 548 large cities I was surprised to discover that – even if I include cities I've flown to and from without ever setting foot beyond the airport, and those I've visited as side trips from other cities, or on personal journeys – I've been to only around a quarter of these.

Nor do the cities I've been to constitute anything like a representative sample. Around sixty of the cities on that list are in India, a country that I might have presumed to know a little about after dozens of visits in the years following my first morning in Mumbai. In fact, I've been to only five Indian cities, and I was shocked to realise that I did not recognise the names of Thrissur, Salem, Tiruchirappalli, or of dozens of others. More than 120 of those 548 cities are in China. I've been to four.

Such figures underscore the increasing demographic supremacy of the urban planet – more than half of us already live in cities and by 2050 more than two-thirds may do so – as well as its heterogeneous and predominantly non-Western character. It's humbling, and perhaps reassuring, too, to realise that even long-haul pilots may see so little of it.

For each individual pilot, however, the experience of the many cities he or she does encounter may remain an almost overwhelming wonder. Hence the second effect of encountering cities as only a pilot might: I've come to categorise cities not only geographically, but with respect to certain features or qualities – rivers, skyscrapers, old walls – that are appealing or meaningful to me.

Now, at 1 a.m. and from this high floor, I look down on Abu Dhabi and I think of what's most memorable about the hours since we touched down and drove in. This capital, I could say, is a city of towers, such as the many I can see from the one I'm so high up in; or it is a city of nights, given that the only hours at which I've ever landed in or departed from Abu Dhabi are those of darkness; or one of light, given how brightly it shines when I recall it from far away.

I began to categorise cities in this manner unconsciously. I recognised I was doing so only after years of flying, and then I found myself unsure of where the instinct came from. It may reflect my total reliance, when I was small, on the most obvious elements and structures of cities in order to assemble my imaginary one. Or maybe it's only a matter of convenience, or necessity, for anyone who sees more cities than one person is meant to. Perhaps I adapted it, at least in spirit, from Italo Calvino's *Invisible Cities*, one of my favourite books, which is organised on similar (though also mathematical) principles. And of course, there's the compelling tradition of epithets that we still deploy to speak of such places as the City of Angels, the City of Gardens, the City of Sails and the City That Lit the World.

But I suspect my most memorable encounter with this manner of describing cities occurred in my early twenties, when I read my father's writings, which he arranged in terms of the many cities he had known in the course of a life that spanned four continents. So the chapters of his autobiography, for example, bear such subtitles as 'The City of the 365 Churches' and 'The City of the Bicycles'.

Whatever its origins, I find that this way of thinking about cities isn't without its pleasures. The greatest of these is that I know Dad would have liked it. Another is that while it highlights the individuality of cities, it also clarifies how much they have in common. There are, after all, many cities of towers, and many of light.

The possibility that cities share so much more than we might at first imagine they do, and that we might even think of them as nearly grammatical arrangements of forms such as parks, libraries, intersections and houses of worship, might help to explain the third long-term effect of my travels as a pilot: as I get older, I'm astonished by the ever-intensifying power of the world's cities – including some of the largest metropolises on Earth, and many of those most foreign to me – to return my thoughts and my heart to my small hometown.

I know that my relationship with Pittsfield isn't straightforward.

Growing up there, I learned to hide so much about myself, and to dream about shining, faraway places: one imaginary city so perfect that kids there were untroubled by what troubled me; and many real cities where I believed that I might find the right girl, and even learn to speak to her in a language that contained no *r*, or only a kind of *r* that I could pronounce. Then, when I was a little older, I dreamed of finding a city where I believed that being myself (by which I mostly meant being gay, but not only that) would occur effortlessly, as the practically physics-ordained result of my motion along the line that connected Pittsfield to the life I imagined in that other place.

But after I left Pittsfield, I learned that many of my difficulties had accompanied me. And I began to understand, as well, that it was Pittsfield itself – the loving family, friends and neighbours who mostly remained there; its teachers, librarians and Scout leaders; the folks who helped me save for a summer homestay in Japan and then for college, such as the subscribers to the newspaper I delivered and the generously tipping customers at the diner I worked at, not to mention the family circumstances that allowed me to keep whatever money I earned; and even the city's infrastructure, such as the runway I rolled down on my first flying lesson, and, finally, one of the well-maintained roads that run out from the city – that had made my long-imagined departure possible.

Today, though my parents are no longer alive, I return to Pittsfield often. Many people I love remain there, and many of its places remain important to me. I've long dreamed of a retirement very near Pittsfield, one in which almost every day Mark and I will visit the city's library, or one of its cafés or wildlife reserves; but I also worry that it might never feel quite right to live again within the city's limits.

Indeed, my relationship with my hometown offers my most repetitive lesson in how two opposed feelings might coexist. After I left home, I came out. I found good friends, work that I love and Mark. When I'm in Pittsfield now, I can occasionally see how instinctive it was – when it came to disliking things, or running from them – to confuse my hometown with myself, and I can't quite believe I'm at ease in both. At other times, even in middle age and with my husband at my side, I find that I'm still uncertain about myself in the streets I know best.

And, increasingly, when I'm far away from Pittsfield, I understand that my perceptions of every other city are still shaped by it.

Sometimes I think Pittsfield acts like a lens, its particular dimensions and qualities governing how I see all other settlements. At other times it feels more like a map I carry, one I unfold over every new place: when I'm planning a stroll in Bangalore, for example, and I realise I'm assessing a distance of half a mile in terms of the walk from my childhood home to my high school, or when I pause atop the staircase of a New York subway station and try to orient my perspective on the intersection to the view from the desk in my old bedroom, in order to figure out which way is east.

But mostly I think that Pittsfield's role in my life is like that of a first language, one that I've no choice but to turn to when I'm trying to make sense of other places – as linguists, sorting and describing the world's languages, must themselves deploy one particular language to do so. I think it's this singular quality of hometowns, as much as my complicated feelings about my own, that explains why Pittsfield is always with me, especially in the cities that are most different or distant from it.

One day, after landing in Kuala Lumpur, I decided to jump on a bus to the city of Malacca, whose name was the only one I recognised on the departures board at the busy airport bus station. I reached Malacca not long after dark, found a room and then went out for a walk. A narrow side street I followed turned into a bridge across the Malacca River, where I paused to try to see which way the river ran, and in which direction the Strait of Malacca and the Indian Ocean might therefore lie, as only hours ago my flight from London had crossed that ocean's north-eastern reaches.

On that warm night, as I stood above Malacca's narrow river, which shimmered with multicoloured light from the promenades as brightly as if oil burned on its surface, I tried to calculate what time it must be in Pittsfield, and I thought of the Housatonic River that runs through my city, and the glass-like shelves of ice that winter forms along its banks. I thought, too, of the etymology of *metropolis*, mother city, and of all the ways in which a hometown is like a mother tongue, as there in Malacca the curves of my first river returned to me as easily as a turn of phrase.

To anyone who says that we can never go home again, I reply – with all the years of evidence that only a pilot could gather – that we can't ever leave it. When the Italian patriot Giuseppe Garibaldi decided to flee the Eternal City, he reassured those who would accompany him: *Dovunque saremo, colà sarà Roma*; Wherever we may be, there shall be Rome. I can't remember anything of the city I was in when I first read these words – not whether it was ancient or modern, low-rise or many-towered, nor whether I was seated by a hotel room's desk or in a subway train or on a shaded park bench. I know only that as I recall them now, in the smallest hours of this night in Abu Dhabi, I think of home.

I stand up from the desk and walk to the windowpane. I look through the reflections of the lights in the room behind me, across to the skyscrapers and down again to the road. I draw the curtains, brush my teeth, set my alarm and climb into bed. I'll start early, before the heat builds. I'll get a coffee and then I'll walk.

CHAPTER I

CITY OF BEGINNINGS

Kyoto, Salt Lake City,
Milton Keynes, Cairo and Rome

IN MY LATE THIRTIES I came across the epic poem *Paterson,* by William Carlos Williams. In an introductory note, Williams describes its premise: that 'a man in himself is a city, beginning, seeking, achieving and concluding his life in ways which the various aspects of a city may embody – if imaginatively conceived – any city, all the details of which may be made to voice his most intimate convictions'.

It's not that I've ever knowingly felt like a city. But if it's true that each of us is like a city, then it might also be true that each city is like a person. And so I like to think of Pittsfield – its streetlamps strung like nerves, its thoughts idling in the layer of reflective air on the roads on August afternoons, or its memories falling slowly through the grey-to-black depths beneath the ice on its lakes in January – and of who it might be.

And if a city is like a person, then I can understand better why we might speak of them as mothers: as Mecca and Asunción are each known as the Mother of Cities, and Cape Town is the Mother City; and as Kipling remembered his first city ('Mother of Cities to me, / For I was born in her gate'), in his poem 'To the City of Bombay', in which he also described an individual's attachment to their hometown as like that of 'a child to the mother's gown'.

It explains, indeed, why we might speak of a city's aspects in such human terms: its spirit and its soul (an idea at least as old as Plato); its heart, arteries, lungs and bones; its sisters; and even its spouse, as Jeddah is known as the Bride of the Red Sea, and as Venice has loved – and been loved by – her waters, into which each year the doge, or the mayor, now, still ritually casts a wedding band. It explains how it is that we can love one city so deeply that when we close our eyes we may picture its upturned face, or try to imagine what the sky was like on its first day.

PITTSFIELD

I'm walking away from my middle school across a muddy playing field. A dear friend of my parents has already developed the tradition of relating how, at one Thanksgiving – celebrated in her home, no less – I walked past her chair and muttered, 'Worst Thanksgiving I've ever had!' I was, she reports, three years old.

Now, at twelve, I say to myself: worst middle school I've ever had. Rich – the friend with whom I build treehouses, hang out in the woods, or search for the smooshed remains of coins we've laid in the path of the freight trains that roll through Pittsfield – is moving to Connecticut. Rich's dad, who has a sports car and likes me well enough to take me shooting occasionally, works for General Electric, the multinational corporation that provides most of Pittsfield's best jobs, and he has been promoted to a role at the company's headquarters.

I'll be sad to lose Rich. Middle school is tough and he's tough, too, and much better liked than I am. Unlike me, nobody calls Rich a nerd or a geek or accuses him of being gay. No one would dare make fun of his speech impediment if he had one, and no one makes fun of mine when Rich and I are together. No kids ever give Rich a day, time and place on which they will beat him up, which is the appointment I'm facing today.

After my last class, I got my coat from my locker and started carefully north across this field. My stomach has been turning since yesterday. What will happen will happen, I say to myself. I've been in this situation before and once I told Mom about it. After I made her promise not to call the school she told me it was important to stand up and fight.

My brother has given me advice, too. On most days for several years, starting when he was seven or eight and I was five or six, we used to have the non-serious fight that Mom and Dad called our 'Daily'. Sometimes the Daily took place indoors, sometimes in a pile of leaves or atop a snow fort we'd built in the yard. My brother always won, so as I walk I try to remember what he told me. I'll do my best.

I continue to step carefully. One foot after the other. Now I'm in the middle of the field – the right place and time – but the kid who threatened me is not here. What I don't yet realise is that he has almost certainly forgotten his words – if he ever meant them at all – even as they altered my week, my month.

I pass by a few other kids, but not the one I fear is waiting for me. I know not to look back and I know not to run. (One foot after the other.) I reach the north side of the athletic field and start up the steep street that begins across from it.

A few minutes later, I'm at the top of my own road and as I start down its gentle hill I start to breathe more easily. I reach and open our unlocked kitchen door, put down my book bag, make a hot chocolate in our just-installed first microwave and fill a bowl with Doritos. I bring my snack upstairs to the desk in my room. Before I start my homework I take a blank piece of paper and write the name of my imaginary city in small capital letters at the top. Then I start to draw it, as if for the first time: the rails curving in from the countryside, the two runways, the straight lines of new streets.

KYOTO

Dave and I lie on our adjacent but not-quite-touching futons and let the smoke from our cigarettes swirl above our heads. They're Seven

Stars brand; seven's my favourite number, but only because it features in the designations of many aeroplanes. A Walkman lies on the mat between our futons and we're each using one of its earphones. We're listening to Enigma, music of a sort that's entirely new to me this summer and that inspires the slow figure eights we draw in the darkness above us, as each cigarette leaves a glowing contrail that doesn't quite fade before the music guides our embers back around.

It's August and we're in the last days of a high school summer homestay programme in Japan. It's taken me two years to save for it and it's been worth every hour I spent washing dishes at my restaurant job and trudging through snow on subzero winter mornings on my paper route.

There are about a dozen of us on the trip. Most of us are seventeen, like me, and about to start our final year of high school. We spent a few days in Tokyo – the largest city that has ever existed, I was amazed to learn – and then a month in Kanazawa, on Japan's west coast. Each of us lived with a Japanese family (mine named their new puppy Mark II; a few years from now, when I go to Japan in college and visit them, this dog – though I only knew him for a few of his earliest and most impressionable days – will shake and leap with joy when I re-enter his house), and every weekday we met for language classes. Now, before flying home, we have this brief trip to Kyoto, only us and our chaperone, Meg, an American graduate student who recently wrote in large, underlined letters across one of my diary's final pages what she says I must always remember: *No matter where you go, there you are.*

I like these words, even though I'm not sure I understand them. Does she mean that you should try to be fully present wherever you go? Or that – contradictorily, it seems to me – even the furthest journey won't allow you to escape yourself?

Today, though it is my first day in the city of Kyoto, more and more of my thoughts have been centred on faraway Pittsfield, where I have no choice but to return to a few days from now. Mom and Dad divorced last year. Mom left Pittsfield and then came back; she's buying a little house a few streets away from the family home where Dad, my brother and I still live. For now there are awkward dinners at the new, round glass table in her small apartment along the road that leaves Pittsfield to the south.

Meanwhile Dad is dating someone I expect he'll marry. She is kind to me but it will be years before I'm half as kind in return. For now she and I at least have aeroplanes in common: her first husband, who is no longer alive, was a private pilot. He learned to fly at Pittsfield Municipal Airport, where I've taken my first flying lessons. She tells me about her own love of flying, and shares stories such as the one about the time her husband flew her from Pittsfield down to New York and got permission to land their single-engine Cessna 172 at two minutes past 8 p.m. on the longest runway at JFK.

I'm happy to talk about any aeroplane or about Kennedy's schedule of landing charges (twenty-five dollars before eight o'clock but only five dollars after, she relates), but this doesn't change the fact that my parents' divorce is as hard for me as its causes are mysterious. Going away – as I have this summer – makes it easier, so much so that there have even been times when I briefly forgot that it ever happened.

Japan's distance also allows me to see my hometown more clearly. For the first time I understand that on the one hand there are countless cities like Pittsfield. On the other, the name of where you are born – a detail so significant that in other ages it might form part of the name you passed to your descendants – is fixed forever.

And it's occurred to me, also for the first time, that for my parents Pittsfield must once have seemed an unlikely place to have come to call home. Especially to Dad, who was born in a small town in the Belgian province of West Flanders and trained in the city of Bruges to become a Catholic priest. He left Belgium to work in what was then the Belgian Congo, before moving across the ocean to spend a decade working in three large Brazilian cities.

Mom's journey to Pittsfield was more direct but still, to me, implausible. She was born in a small town in the anthracite coal country of Pennsylvania. All four of her grandparents were born in Lithuania and while Mom grew up speaking mostly English, throughout her life she could easily summon many Lithuanian words. As a young adult she became a member of a Catholic lay missionary group outside Cincinnati, Ohio. This organisation dispatched her to Paris and planned to send her on to Indonesia. Instead, she decided to leave the organisation and move to Boston.

In the spring of 1968, Dad, who had been struggling with his faith for years, stopped in Boston on his way from Brazil to Belgium; an interracial ecumenical association had invited him to speak in Roxbury about the social and economic justice projects that he and fellow priests had initiated in the Brazilian city of Salvador. Mom attended and invited Dad to dinner the next evening. They exchanged addresses, but Dad understood (incorrectly, and perhaps due to his difficulties with conversational American English) that Mom already had a boyfriend, one more reason he assumed they would never meet again after he resumed his journey to his homeland.

In Belgium, Dad sought out the Bishop of Bruges in order to tell him that he had decided to leave the priesthood (there was no excuse, he later wrote, for 'leading a life that was no longer mine'). His superior, Dad recorded in his notes, insisted on three further meetings over several months, and turned to the arguments that 'St Thomas Aquinas had moulded in the thirteenth century' to reassure him of God's existence, but these failed to alter Dad's decision.

America, Dad felt, promised a new start, and with friends already in Boston, including Mom – they'd been writing back and forth – he crossed the Atlantic once more. Mom met him at Logan Airport. The next year they married. They remained in Boston for several years, and then moved to Burlington, Vermont, where they adopted my brother, who was born in João Pessoa, one of the metropolises in which Dad lived during his decade in Brazil ('the easternmost city of the Americas', as he titled his notes on it). Soon after, Dad got a job in Pittsfield, a city neither of my parents had ever seen, though they had honeymooned elsewhere in the Berkshires. I was born in the late spring after their first winter in Pittsfield.

Here in Japan, the other students are from cities such as Atlanta, Tampa, San Francisco, Chicago and New York. Only one of these new friends had heard of Pittsfield before, and I experience this – as much as I do the fact that they didn't know me before, either – as freedom. I needn't tell them about the speech impediment I only recently put behind me. I believe that several of them suspect I'm gay, but none of them express this in the form I've most often heard it, as an intended insult. I needn't tell them about my parents' divorce, nor about the short history of most of my friendships back home, the ones I describe to them in terms that suggest they're all but lifelong.

I've dreamed of gaining this distance from Pittsfield for much of my life. So one aspect of this dream's fulfilment is entirely unexpected: when I look back at my life from the far side of the Pacific Ocean, I discover that while I'm worried about returning – to high school, to my divorced parents, to the city that part of me can't wait to leave again – it's also true that I love my hometown.

This contradiction takes the form of affectionate jokes with the other students about Pittsfield. In fact, this Pittsfield banter has become my 'thing' over the course of the summer, and I've never had a thing before: there's a password you need to travel over the mountains into Pittsfield, I say, and a special visa, too. A new friend from the Bronx laughs and asks if there's even a special handshake. Yes, I tell her, and there's a dialect I could switch to if I wanted, but then you wouldn't catch a word I say. (Already I'm able to joke about not being understood.)

Among the friends I've made this summer I'm particularly close to Dave. Dave likes aeroplanes almost as much as I do. He's funny and we laugh a lot, and whenever our group is required to break into pairs – to complete language exercises, to take seats on a bus, or to be roommates, like in this inn – we choose each other. He tells me about California, where he's from, and I tell him about Pittsfield, not only with wisecracks but through my ham-fisted efforts to explain what it's actually like there: how the hills look, when the first snow might fall, what kind of trouble my brother gets up to, who my small gang of friends are, you wouldn't believe the crazy things we've done, one time this, one time that.

In the nearly dark room in this quiet inn the next song starts and Dave and I each light another cigarette. As I do so I recall a classmate in Pittsfield, and the time his sister told their mother, as we all stood eating Ritz crackers in their kitchen, that she thought I was gay. Their mother put one hand on my shoulder to reassure me: Oh, don't pay any attention to her. Do you think I'd let you sleep over if I thought that were true?

Suddenly, in this Kyoto inn, I sense the approach of a feeling that I realise I did not leave in Pittsfield. (No matter where you go, there you are.) I don't yet know to call it shame, but I do know that I want to think about something else.

If not my imaginary city – I'm seventeen; it's a childish thing that I should leave behind, I should leave it behind – then Kyoto. Before we arrived, I studied a map of this mountain-ringed city and tried to make sense of the waterways, temples and shrines so densely marked on it. Meg has explained that Kyoto's name might sound unfamiliar to us, but the meaning of the two characters that compose it in Japanese could hardly be more straightforward: 'capital' and 'city'. I'm fascinated, as well, by the city's age and, simultaneously, by the fact that for practically all of the earth's existence, there was no city here. Did Kyoto have a first day?

I lean back on my futon and when I look up it's as if a simple sketch of my guidebook's fold-out map repeats in my vision. Our cigarettes burn and turn. Sometimes I start to forget where I am and then Dave speaks and I picture the map of Kyoto above me, and it's as if the city itself is waiting for me to answer.

Now there's silence, except for the crackling as one of us inhales, and I try to imagine that there's no ceiling to the room, no roof to this inn, and that our cigarettes are swirling against the stars of Japan's sky; or that I'm up there, too, looking down on the lights, and on ourselves, as we lie on these futons, these beds that are all but on the floor, a height at which, at home, only shoes sleep. Then Dave says something about a buddy of his, a story about that friend's girlfriend, and in this near-darkness we could be anyone, anyplace.

SALT LAKE CITY

London, the North Atlantic, Greenland and around 2,000 miles of Canada are behind us. We'll arrive in Los Angeles in a few hours, in darkness.

For now we're roughly keeping pace with the near-dusk, and the continent-dividing Rockies practically fill the width of my forward window. Wyoming is below; a few minutes ago, from the right side of the cockpit, I saw Yellowstone and then the Grand Tetons, a range of mountains so cartoonishly jagged that, even from a perspective as clear as that which a 747's cockpit offers, it's hard to believe they're real.

Colorado is in sight, as well, and when I realise how badly I'm humming John Denver's 'Rocky Mountain High' I stop to check that my headset intercom, which would transmit this directly to the captain's ears – both captains and first officers are pilots and do roughly the same amount of flying, but the captain has additional managerial responsibilities, and ultimate legal authority, as commander of both the aircraft and its crew – is definitely turned off.

When I was growing up, Dad worked in the Pittsfield offices of the state government, whose headquarters are in Boston, on the opposite side of Massachusetts. I understood that Boston, therefore, was where Dad's most stressful phone calls originated, and that our state capital was the seat of a power unattenuated by a distance that within Massachusetts could hardly be greater. Because Boston told us to, Dad might respond with a sigh, as he tried to prepare dinner while I asked question after question to unpeel the layers of his workday.

The idea that Boston might have desires of its own, and the ability to direct even those who were far from it, overlapped with the most arresting fact I learned about it in high school: that both the city, and the nation whose independence it helped secure, might be identified with the City upon a Hill, the image that the Pilgrim father John Winthrop found in the Sermon on the Mount:

'Ye are the light of the world. A city that is set on an hill, cannot be hid.'

As a teenager I couldn't believe that a city as familiar as Boston – in the sense that Dad went to meetings and eye doctor appointments there, and my own visits to the city were already growing so numerous as to be indistinct – could be associated with words as grand as those.

Later, when I lived in Boston, I found the association of that beloved but ordinary metropolis with an unseen or imagined one – in particular, with a metaphorical or divine city that embodies all the eventual perfection we might believe in or hope for – a little disheartening, especially when I learned that of the three hills prominent enough to give Boston its early name, Trimountain, two were long ago levelled, and the third (despite its providential title, Beacon Hill) much lowered. The City on a Hill epithet wasn't much consolation, either, on the occasions I was nearly blown to a stop by the wind that howled through a dystopian concrete plaza I crossed on the way to work, after I'd waited too long for one of the wheezing, ancient subway trains that never came.

Now, high over south-western Wyoming and to the right of the

747's nose, a city starts to roll into view. I've never been to Salt Lake City, though I've seen it often enough from above. Someday, I hope, I'll visit, and at this in-between hour it seems right to ask how its valley would have looked to the first humans to come upon it. They might have arrived from the north-west, perhaps, rather than from the east, as Mormon settlers did millennia later, or from the north-east, as my plane comes to the valley's skies tonight.

Salt Lake City is marked out by its light, as well as by the terrain that gives way to it and the sudden absence of snow. As it shines from within the darkness that fell first on Utah's lower elevations, I wish I could learn to recognise the pattern of its red-yellow gridded lines as easily as I can read the cool-blue letters, KSLC, near the circle that marks the city's airport on our navigation screens.

In global terms, Salt Lake is still a newish city. The Mormon pioneers laid it out with reference to the Plat of the City of Zion, an urban plan that Joseph Smith had drawn up far from here, and to which he had added such instructions as 'When this square is thus laid off and supplied, lay off another in the same way, and so fill up the world in these last days.' The metropolis was known as the New Jerusalem, and also as the City of the Saints, an epithet that formed the title of a book by Richard Francis Burton, the fabled nineteenth-century explorer who came by stagecoach to the settlement now shining below our 747 in order to add one more to the list ('Memphis, Benares, Jerusalem, Rome, Meccah') of holy cities he knew.

Tonight, caught between the brilliance of the sunset over the west and the lights gathered below our wings, I'll call Salt Lake City this: the high city; the new city; the city of the reddening peaks; the most striking city I've seen. And, from above the crimson snow on the mountains that guard its eastern approaches, and then, a few minutes later, as we bank into a gentle turn almost directly above its palmistry of lit streets, it's not hard to believe that in two hundred years, in two thousand years, the city's children will still learn the words attributed to Brigham Young, and to the moment he first looked out on the valley whose darkening sky the navigation lights of our jet are crossing: 'It is enough. This is the right place.'

MILTON KEYNES AND CAIRO

I've been dozing. I'm in my twenties, I've been living in England for only a few months, and when I last awoke on this half-empty inter-city bus it was dark out and I was confused, because we were driving through a town in which the straight-running thoroughfares, modern buildings and general spaciousness looked so American to me that for a moment it was as if I'd never crossed the ocean.

Later this evening I'll tell one of my housemates about the place I woke to. He'll laugh, maybe a little unkindly – at me or the city, I can't tell – as he explains that I was in Milton Keynes, a city-sized town of around a quarter million people, I'll learn, that was first laid out only in the late 1960s.

It's a new town, he'll tell me, a new city, in effect, and as he speaks I'll remember a book, *Imagined Communities*, by Benedict Anderson, that was assigned in a university class. The book (and this is all I will easily recall of it) includes a discussion of the names of new cities of this sort: *New* York (or indeed *Nieuw* Amsterdam), *New* Orleans (*Nouvelle* Orléans), *New* London, etc., and when I encountered these familiar city names, all together in the course of a page or two, I realised that I had never before broken them apart.

Years from now, after I've become a pilot, my housemate's words – *a new city* – will often come to my mind involuntarily, when the jet I'm flying emerges from the clouds above the parallel and numbered streets of a roomy metropolis on the west coast of North America, say, in the same week in which I returned from an Asian megacity that might be multiples older and denser, and whose earliest days might be mythical or lost.

But the idea of a new city will strike me most forcefully whenever

I overfly an obviously modern settlement that lies near or forms part of an ancient one. Along the Nile, for example, on flights on clear and dry winter nights, I'll sip my tea as I look across metropolitan Cairo at the new cities shining from within it like electrified engineering schematics, or like new sets of Christmas lights, plugged in to be tested before they're pulled from the plastic scaffolding on which they come neatly arrayed. Later I'll look up their names: one is simply New Cairo; another, New Heliopolis; while several bear such unique names as Sixth of October or Fifteenth of May – like recent birthdates, it's easy to believe, rather than commemorations of historical events, so new do their patterns of streets appear to be.

ROME

On a cool February morning my husband and I are in Vatican City, circling the centre of St Peter's Square. Mark is taking photographs and I'm stepping between the oval markers in the stonework that display the names of the winds, such as the Scirocco, the Tramontana and the Ponente, that arrive from different directions and in different seasons.

Arranged here as if on a compass, these markers form a stylised version of the chart known as a 'wind rose'. Those who design airports rely on wind roses in order to align new runways favourably, and pilots may consult them in order to familiarise themselves with an airport's weather patterns. The wind roses that I may scroll to on a cockpit-mounted tablet computer don't feature personifications of winds, such as the Old Man Winter–style blowy faces that here in Rome I'm carefully stepping over or around, but with their arrangements of straight lines, complete circles and fragmented arcs, they, too, appear to be as much artistic as scientific constructions.

As Mark and I complete our loop and stop, I think, as well, of the direction in which Pittsfield lies from here; of the absence of fabled winds in my hometown, as far as I know; and of all that Dad, as a former priest, would have been able to tell me about this square and the basilica above it, from which blessings are periodically offered *urbi et orbi*, to the city and to the world.

My parents have been gone for some years now. Nevertheless, Mark and I still return to the Berkshires and Pittsfield often, not least because there remain in the city members of the 'Berkshire gang', the group of families I grew up with. In the Berkshire gang, those of my parents' generation are like aunts ('Worst Thanksgiving I've ever had!') and uncles to me, and their children are my extra siblings. Three of the four families lived across the street from each other or in adjacent houses early on; and Mom, in her last years, after her divorce from Dad, and once her health and finances meant that she could no longer live alone, shared the home of one of my aunts. Even now, in my late forties, when we all still gather for Christmas, Thanksgiving and important birthdays, the presence of these old friends is so warm and familiar that I sometimes forget that my parents have not, in fact, only briefly stepped out of the room.

Among the Berkshire gang, almost everyone of my parents' generation grew up in deeply religious environments. Indeed, in addition to Dad, several others had also been priests or nuns before their faith altered. This shared religious background, as much as ordinary neighbourliness and the similar ages of us kids, was the foundation of the collective friendship that turned us into an extended family.

And I was struck, growing up, when my parents and their friends observed the life of the church that many of them were no longer really a part of, to hear them sometimes speak about Rome exactly as Dad spoke about his bosses in Boston – Rome can't allow that, they might say, or, Well, Rome will have to find a balance – and in this way I came to understand that Rome, too, might act like a person.

After I grew up, left Pittsfield and became a pilot, I flew to Rome dozens of times, and I was often pleased to note on the flight computers that the city's latitude, despite its much warmer climate, was within a degree of Pittsfield's. On a typical journey we'd take off from Heathrow and turn south-east. We'd say good-bye to the last British controller somewhere over the Channel, talk to our journey's first French controller even as we were still climbing, then a Swiss controller as we drank our tea above the snowcapped serrations of the Alps, and finally a series of Italian controllers as we overflew their country's scenic west coast and began our descent. We'd touch down, taxi in, park and complete the shutdown checklist, and if it happened to be a breezy day in the Eternal City the silvery blades of the cooling engines would slow but never stop.

And I would not leave Rome's airport. Indeed, I might not even leave my seat. Once the arriving passengers had disembarked, departing ones would board and we'd fly away from the navigation beacon whose coding, OST, is a very-high-frequency shout-out to Rome's ancient port at Ostia. We'd make our best time for London and, if my journey to Rome had started early enough, I'd be home for dinner.

Only now, in my forties, have I had the opportunity to come here – to the city that Ovid declared coterminous with the world – as an ordinary traveller, with Mark. A few days ago we stepped out of Rome's Termini station, bewildered by the brightness of the teeming morning that the night train from Munich had so deftly snuck us into. In the hours since, we've drunk our coffees standing up, as we watch the locals do; we've nearly been run down on an ill-advised walk along the edge of a fast, narrow and pavement-free portion of the Appian Way; we've taken several guided tours, afraid of how much we might otherwise miss; we've joked that everything, especially the laminated menu at the pizza restaurant we visit and revisit, must be a palimpsest.

Among all this, I've been particularly struck by my encounters with the city's emblem, a gold crown above a maroon shield on which +SPQR is written: *Senatus Populusque Romanus*, the Senate and People of Rome. So I began to look for it everywhere, and to consider it all the more marvellous an ancient acronym when I found it in so many ordinary and even unsavory places in the modern city, on the sides of buses and shared bicycles, for example, but also on the grates that cover drains.

Equally remarkable is an image that, like SPQR, you can't walk far in Rome without encountering: that of a wolf with two boys. The story of the she-wolf, and of the twin brothers she saved, is memorably recounted by Livy in his history of Rome, *Ab Urbe Condita*, or *From the Founding of the City*.

In Livy's telling, the scheming Amulius seized the throne that was rightfully his brother's. He killed his brother's sons and consigned his niece, Rhea Silvia, to a virgin priesthood, a role that might have been expected to prevent the birth of potential rivals for the throne he occupied. 'But the Fates were resolved', Livy writes, 'upon the founding of this great City', and Rhea Silvia gave birth to Romulus and Remus (and claimed that Mars was their father). Amulius ordered that the twin brothers be put in the Tiber. The river had flooded and the king's servants left the boys in a basket; the waters receded and a she-wolf, who came down to drink, 'turned her steps towards the cry of the infants, and with her teats gave them suck so gently'.

So the brothers survived. Later, from their troubled fraternal relationship – and thanks also to augury, the interpretation of the behaviour of birds – the Eternal City rose:

> Romulus and Remus were seized with the desire to found a city in the region where they had been exposed and brought up. . . . Since the brothers were twins, and respect for their age could not determine between them, it was agreed that the gods who had those places in their protection should choose by augury who should give the new city its name, who should govern it when built. Romulus took the Palatine for his augural quarter, Remus the Aventine.

Remus is said to have been the first to receive an augury, from the flight of six vultures. The omen had been already reported when twice that number appeared to Romulus. Thereupon each was saluted king by his own followers, the one party laying claim to the honour from priority, the other from the number of the birds. They then engaged in a battle of words and, angry taunts leading to bloodshed, Remus was struck down in the affray. . . .

Thus Romulus acquired sole power, and the city, thus founded, was called by its founder's name.

PITTSFIELD

On a March day I'm standing in a graveyard old enough not to have a proper car park, so I pulled up on the grass outside its gate. It seemed wrong, especially when I imagined carriages where my rented Nissan stands now, and scenes of funerals from period dramas (the steaming breath of the horses, the women all in black, the grim-faced men holding their tall hats), but there's nowhere else to park, and the frozen ruts indicate I'm not the first driver to stop there.

The cemetery, roughly square, is enclosed by a stone wall that's collapsed in places and, I conclude from a few beer cans wedged into the gaps, intentionally pulled down in others. On the west side of the cemetery two trees form parts of the wall, as if its builders chose to borrow from their strength, or save on materials, and all these years later my eyes contentedly follow their riff on this most New England of lines: stone, rough bark, stone again.

Snow shelters in the deep shadows to the north of the wall and the larger grave markers, but it'll melt soon. As I drove here I listened to the radio, and after the weather forecast came an interview with several Berkshire farmers. They said that the conditions – frosty nights and thawing days – are almost ideal for placing the taps in the maples; that as the season unrolls their sap will change and be refined into syrups of deepening colour and intensifying taste; that there's one late and dark grade you may encounter only rarely, because it's not popular among pancake lovers. I know I won't retain these new maple facts but still, as I listened to the voices of the farmers, I had the feeling that, after all, the world will be okay.

The street this graveyard stands on, Williams Street, is one of those I know best in the world. It's much busier than it was when I used to bike along it as a kid, though Pittsfield's population is now smaller. Past the cemetery was a turkey farm, a four-generation family establishment we'd visit in the run-up to Thanksgiving, but not only then. Up the mountain to the east of the cemetery the Christmas tree farm remains, where you can still stagger through snowy fields to cut your own.

On Williams Street two battered green posts mark the beginning and end of a measured mile, as if, as I once thought, Pittsfield had its own versions of such units. On one of its side streets lived Mrs Johnson, my English teacher in my last year of high school. A tear comes to my eye now as I step among the headstones and recollect the glasses that hung from a chain around her neck when she was not wearing them, and the day she whirled around from the chalkboard, when she heard a comment I had not, and snapped: There'll be no homophobia in my classroom.

Williams Street is also memorable to me for its nearness to Canoe Meadows, a nature reserve whose land originally served Native Americans as a burial ground, which the Mohicans would continue to visit for some time after European settlement, pulling their birch canoes out of the river and inspiring the site's English name. Now, decades later, when I jog or ski through or drive past Canoe Meadows, I sometimes think that my brother and I must have retained some fragment of this story when we decided to scatter a portion of Dad's ashes in the river there, and when we did the same with some of Mom's ashes two years later.

Pittsfield is in the north-central part of Berkshire County, in the far west of Massachusetts. Only one town lies between it and the New York State line: Hancock, formerly a Shaker settlement and once known – echoing a bygone name of Baghdad, and the name of La Paz, too – as the City of Peace, and also as Jericho, as the Berkshire hills were said to resemble those that shelter that distant place.

My first city lies in a valley, at an elevation of around 300 metres. Following the height chart of the world's cities as a pilot might, its airport stands a little higher than Ouagadougou's, and a little lower than Geneva's. Pittsfield is surrounded by hills that are dotted with lakes, farms and much smaller settlements. Otherwise forest runs out from it to as far as the eye can see, though it turns out these woods aren't as ancient as I once liked to think; in the nineteenth century much of the primeval forest had been turned to pasture, or into the charcoal that could supply the county's iron and glass works with the temperatures that ordinary wood could not. The forests have regrown; in ecological terms, I often struggle to remember, they are still young.

Pittsfield's population peaked in the 1960s, near 60,000. It was around 50,000 when I was little and it's heading now towards 40,000, the number it last possessed in the 1920s.

Pittsfield may be a small city and one relegated, despite its plentiful and loyal Red Sox fans, to one of Boston's outermost orbits. Still, it has reasons to be proud. A 1791 bylaw, enacted 'for the Preservation of the Windows in the New Meeting House', is America's first known reference to the national pastime, and as baseball's origins are obscure, a less scrupulous citizenry would certainly get away with claiming their hometown as the sport's birthplace. In 1811 Pittsfield held the first American agricultural fair. In the early 1850s Herman Melville wrote *Moby-Dick* in his farmhouse here. In 1859, the town hosted the nation's first intercollegiate baseball game.

Pittsfield is also where the practical electrical transformer was perfected in the late nineteenth century. One 4,000-kilowatt model, built here in 1893, was said to have been the world's largest machine, while in 1921 an artificial lightning bolt of one million volts was generated in the city. And Pittsfield, skilled in electricity and so often thigh-deep in snow, is where night skiing made its world debut in 1936, on a slope that rises from the site of a former mink farm. Bousquet Mountain has produced more than its share of Olympians, not because it's especially challenging but because, rather, it's unusually accessible – being within the city limits and inexpensive – and as a result many Pittsfield kids could ski there most every winter afternoon or evening.

Such a severe climate delayed the European settlement of what would become my hometown (one early Dutch mapmaker ominously wrote *Win-ter-berg-e*, winter mountains, across this otherwise blank region of his map), as did border disputes between Massachusetts and New York, and conflicts with those whom one of my high school history books still referred to in the early 1990s as 'red men', 'heathens' and 'the painted'. Nevertheless, by the early 1740s, three men of European descent – whose surnames, Livingston, Stoddard and Wendell, are affixed, respectively, to the streets on which stand my family's first house, the office of the paediatrician who looked after me and my brother and the public library – had acquired title to the land on which the future city would rise.

In 1752 the first families took up residence in the log cabins that the original wave of settlers had prepared for them. The next year the General Court of Massachusetts granted the 'Proprietors of the Settling-lots in the Township of Poontoosuck' – a Mohican name that means 'the haunt of winter deer' – the all-important right to levy taxes. In 1761 the town was incorporated in honour of William Pitt ('the Elder', as we now know him), the British official who 'by his vigorous conduct of the war against France, had made himself the idol of all parties in New England'.

Thirteen decades later, when its population had grown to around 17,000, Pittsfield's citizens agreed to give up the traditional New England form of government by town meeting, and became a city.

The snow that fell as dawn broke on 5 January 1891 was understood to be 'a benediction from above'. A few hours later, Judge James M. Barker addressed the gathered populace. Among his first words was the term that recalls the observations of birds that midwifed Rome's bloody foundation: 'We are at home. We meet under happy auspices.'

Indeed, no one could accuse Judge Barker of shying from the day's import: 'The old order is about to pass, the footfall of the new City as she comes to take her appointed place and assume her allotted work approaches!' After the grand speeches a ball was held at the Academy of Music. The 800 guests, among whom both 'matronly dignity' and 'masculine stability' were said to be well represented, were serenaded by 25 musicians and lit by a star formed of 42 lights and '1,000 candle power strong'. Supper arrived after midnight and the dancing continued past four in the morning.

Drawn so strongly to every Pittsfield story, I sometimes enjoy trying to calculate the significance of these celebrations. (For how long did Pittsfield remain the world's newest city? A day? A week?) And in particular I love to imagine the hour of their conclusion: the new-fangled, yellowy light falls through the academy's doors and casts shadows of the danced-out citizenry as they sway out onto the snow; the bitter cold takes their breath and waters their eyes as they step or ride further into the surrounding darkness; while far to the east, the light of the new city's first dawn rises from the ocean, crosses the forearm of Cape Cod and strikes the dome of Boston.

I'm slightly disappointed, however, to have found little in these stories that's mysterious or mythical. Perhaps it's that the details are too well documented, or perhaps they have lacked sufficient centuries to season into legend. After all, as Livy wrote, 'It is the privilege of antiquity to mingle divine things with human, and so to add dignity to the beginnings of cities.'

Still, when it comes to origin myths, it's never too late to create new ones.

For Pittsfield, framed by its famously picturesque hills, a more fable-like foundation story might be formed from the city's setting. In his speech for Pittsfield's inauguration, Judge Barker said, 'Just how much the fact that Rome sat upon a throne of beauty helped her to rule the world we may not know.' From the Eternal City he then drew a line nearly due west to the newborn one that lay before him: 'Who shall say how beauty of situation, fine scenery, and a healthful and invigorating climate have helped us hitherto, and how they shall hereafter aid to stimulate and ennoble thought and life.' A myth rooted in a particular arrangement of hills, lakes and waters would emphasise Pittsfield's impressive natural context; it would also remind us that all cities – so often built along rivers, or on natural harbours so faultless as to seem fated, or at the intersections of roads or railway tracks themselves steered by topography – are sculpted by nature before they are by people.

A creation myth of Pittsfield could also turn, Rome-like, on its wolves, which at the time of my hometown's foundation remained a terrifying presence in this part of New England. Bounties were paid for their scalps, and one early matriarch of the settlement, known in her golden years for her high manners and 'fine, erect form' had once, when still a young wife, heard her family's sheep 'rushing wildly' against the door of the cabin. On opening it she found a 'huge, gaunt and hungry wolf in eager pursuit' and shot it dead.

Or a Pittsfield mythmaker might turn for inspiration to the story of Sarah Deming, who arrived here aged twenty-six in 1752, riding pillion on the horse of Solomon, her husband. She knew war, sacrifice and the birth of not only her town but of a nation (her son Noadiah is one of three Demings listed in Pittsfield's records of Revolutionary Service). When Sarah died, aged ninety-two, in 1818, she was Pittsfield's oldest woman, and surely the last of its settlers to depart from the earth.

Here in this cemetery on this cold March day, I walk up to the four-sided white monument that marks her grave. As I shiver and stuff my hands into my pockets, and fidget with the rental car's clunky key chain, I remember playing in Deming Park, and how, as a high school student, I would cross Deming Street at least twice every weekday. But I knew none of her story then, in part because I never stopped to read her epitaph, though it's still perfectly legible on the obelisk before me, which my brother and I must have biked past many hundreds of times: A MOTHER OF THE REVOLUTION AND A MOTHER IN ISRAEL.

As I return to the cold car, start it and steer left onto Williams Street, I try to imagine THE MOTHER OF PITTSFIELD carved in the marble, in the same script as the rest. I can't quite imagine, however, the legend that might depart from the handful of facts known of Sarah Deming's life; nor can I guess how she might have told her story, or that of the birth of the city that would grow up mostly to the west of her grave.

Alternatively, we might come up with many myths to explain Pittsfield's beginning, and let time choose from among them. As I head towards my favorite downtown café I pass by Canoe Meadows again, and the nearness of its unthawed waters reminds me of a winter night when I was maybe seven. My brother and I were in our backyard in our snowsuits, having our Daily, when he chased me onto what we called the goldfish pond, though we never had goldfish; it was swampy in summer and solid ice in winter. Or so I thought until that night, when I fell through.

Looking back, the water was perhaps only half a metre deep, but that was more than enough to terrify me. In my cold and suddenly lowered position I thought I was about to die or to get into serious trouble – or both, somehow. I scrambled ahead, breaking through one great pane after another, until my brother grabbed me and lifted me out. As we ran back I was shaking, my coat and clothes were heavy, the yard was blue-white in the near-darkness, and our house appeared to be made only of light.

That evening's events took place at around the age when I began to think a lot about cities. So let me try this for the origin myth of Pittsfield, or of the city that I imagined so often in the years that followed:

On a clear winter night two brothers went out on a pond, long after they should have been in bed. There were no wolves, but there was a sort of augury: a cardinal flew over the ice, its crimson barely perceived in the near-darkness by the elder brother, while at that moment the younger brother saw something glint ahead of him. He went closer, but it was only the moon's reflection, and as he realised this he fell through. His older brother pulled him out and carried him back to the house, where under heavy blankets they both slept more deeply than they ever had before, watched over by faces on which worry and the light of the fire flickered. Soon after the start of this long night's sleep the new city formed, and the first of its centuries began to unroll in the air that crackled between them, in the course of the dream they shared.

And as for which of the two brothers would be remembered as the city's founder, well, let's say they fought constantly about that, and much else, as brothers will.

CHAPTER 2

CITY OF DREAMS

Liverpool and Brasília

YEARS AGO, when I was in my early twenties, long before I ever saw anything of Dallas, I dreamed about it on several successive nights. In these dreams I was walking along the edge of a busy, fast-flowing road. The lane markings were illuminated from within the asphalt, and the road curved and sloped gently upwards towards a cluster of skyscrapers that grew larger as the dream and the road continued. As I walked, I looked up at a sign on which this artery's name was backlit: NORTH DALLAS TOLLWAY.

In terms of my imaginings of an ideal, shining city, these dreams could hardly have been less subtle. (Indeed, I wasn't aware of ever having returned to a dream before.) I didn't think about them again for years, however, until I first flew to Dallas as a pilot. After we landed and went through immigration and customs, our crew bus pulled away from the terminal and proceeded from one wide road to another, until I saw a sign ahead, not for the North Dallas Tollway, but for the Dallas North Tollway, which we turned onto and followed in the direction of our hotel.

Later I told a friend from Dallas about how I'd had more than one dream about a highway that I didn't know her city did, in fact, possess, and we laughed at the similarity between the dreamed and real names. Surely, we speculated, I must have encountered the real one – in a newspaper, on the TV news, or maybe even on *Dallas,* the soap opera – but not remembered doing so. And then for some reason it had stayed with me, encoded, in a jumbled form, by a line of dutiful neurons, though perhaps, as the years turned, their voltage began to fade a little, and some even began to grow uncertain of what they stood for, until the night I flew to Dallas and came upon the real road.

My middle-school maths teacher looks out across the silent classroom but no one raises their hand. I berate myself: I think I know the right answer – 90 degrees – it's only that I don't want to say it, because *degrees* has an *r* in it and *r* is a sound I still can't make.

I used to have not only an *r* problem but an *s* one, too. The *s* one resolved a few years ago, maybe when I was ten; Mom is a speech therapist and worked with me on it. But the *r* problem is as difficult for me as ever, and I don't want to work with Mom on it because we tried a couple of times and it didn't help, and now I don't even want to talk about it.

My *r* problem causes me no end of worry. In particular, people often can't understand my first name, which I have to say often, especially at the start of each school year, or when there's a substitute teacher, and in any number of otherwise routine situations. Mack? Mike? folks guess, surely unaware of the nausea that is rising in me at every such moment.

Sometimes I have to repeat my name. Sometimes, when I'm extremely nervous, I have to write it down, or find a reason to do so in advance. (A tip if you should ever need permission to go to the bathroom from a substitute teacher who doesn't know you: write out a permission slip before you go up to their desk, and then you don't have to say your name. They might even thank you for being helpful.)

Situations that require me to say my first name are the most challenging, because there's no other word I can use in its place. Nevertheless, I worry about almost all conversations with those who haven't known me since I was small, so much so that I sometimes prepare my sentences in advance, in order to choose words that have fewer *r*'s, and above all to avoid short ones with an *r* at the start.

Whenever this worry lifts, I can begin to understand how much it otherwise dominates my thoughts. On the first day of sports day-camp last summer, the first counsellor to greet me introduced himself as Mark. So when he asked me my name I realised I could answer easily, even casually: same as you. Then the counsellor laughed, and I did, too, briefly free. (It's a moment I'll recall seventeen years or so from now, on a late spring day in London, when my future husband first introduces himself.)

Other kids sometimes report that they have trouble understanding Dad, especially if he answers when they phone the house. In contrast, I don't hear his supposedly thick Flemish accent at all. From this I understand that, in the same way, my brother doesn't perceive my *r*'s as abnormal or absent, and one of the reasons I'm so grateful for him is that I can speak to him using any words I like.

If my speech impediment makes me more attached to my brother, and to being inside our home, where I can speak most easily, it's also one of the reasons I tend to look to places far from Pittsfield. My fast-growing love of foreign languages, for example, comes largely from the realisation that I can more or less pronounce a Spanish *r*, for example, a sound that is completely different from the American one. There are even places, Dad has explained, where an *r* might be replaced with what sounds to me like an *h* – in the Brazilian Portuguese pronunciations of the names of the cities of Rio as 'hee-o', for example, and Recife, which Dad knew well in his years in Brazil, as 'heh-ceefee'. So there are places, I think, that I could choose to go to as soon as I grow up; there are cities where speech and life will be effortless.

But for now, here in this middle-school classroom, my teacher – one whom I'd previously thought of as kind – again asks us for an answer. I rebuke myself further – *Come on, Mark* – and finally put up my hand. My teacher calls on me and I give my version of the correct answer. Ninety deg-leees? he repeats, with a smile. Well, I think I know what you mean, he adds, quickly, as I look down at my graph paper, place one hand on my forehead to hide my eyes, and fire up a daydream of someplace else.

LIVERPOOL

On a rainy night in 2002 the three of us – a flight instructor, a fellow trainee and I – lift off from our small training airport north of Oxford and bank right, towards Liverpool.

My fellow cadets and I started our visual flight training in Arizona last autumn, only weeks after 9/11, and completed it a few months ago, in the first weeks of 2002. We returned to England to learn how to fly on instruments, in clouds, without sight of the earth and the wayfinding clues it offers, a task to which this gloomy night could hardly be better suited. Soon after takeoff from Kidlington's soaked runway the world is replaced by a textureless black that flashes to a cottony grey when it's pierced by the aircraft's lights.

My instructor, seated next to me, is a long-retired 747 pilot of the very old school. His arms are usually crossed, unless he's actually flying. Once, when I asked him, in an effort to make conversation, if it might be a pleasure to return to down-and-dirty light-aircraft flying like this after so many years on the lofty flight deck of the 747, he scowled and sighed. Finally he gestured at my fellow trainee in one of the rear seats, and said to us: Well, Mark, I could be by a pool in Singapore with people who laugh at my jokes, or I could be flying on this cold night with the likes of you and your little friend here.

Another night, on a tricky approach, I told him in the most measured, let's-find-a-solution tone I could manage: I need you to stop yelling at me so that I can do my best. He huffed and exclaimed with a Jack Nicholson you-can't-handle-the-truth roar: Your best? Your best? Maybe your best isn't good enough!

But, my fellow trainees and I suspect, it's largely an act, especially as he gets every one of us right through our exams. It's after the last of these exams, a few months from now, that Mom will mail an envelope from Pittsfield to Oxford. She often sends me cards, letters, or clippings of articles or sermons on topics she's enjoyed. (I'll have left the flight school by the time the last of these arrives in Oxford, and so a friend will collect it from my pigeonhole. This friend will forget to give the letter to me, and it will end up packed away in a box with her logbooks until she discovers it more than a decade later, long after Mom has died. My friend will then give me the still-sealed envelope and I'll carry it in my flight bag for several years. I'll find comfort in the anticipation of further words from Mom – and I'll occasionally speculate that no letter, in all of history, has ever travelled further – until curiosity gets the better of me and I finally decide to open it, and I read her congratulations on my becoming a licensed pilot.)

Recently Mom has been drawn to Carl Jung, and from afar, via our correspondence, she's been trying to interest me in his writings and his interpretations of archetypes and dreams. She might have had better luck if she'd suggested to me that the image of an ideal city – to the extent it's arisen in many individuals, societies and circumstances – was a good example of an archetype. And it certainly would have helped her cause if she'd told me about Jung's dream of a city that he never saw:

> It was night, and winter, and dark, and raining. I was in Liverpool. With a number of Swiss – say, half a dozen – I walked through the dark streets. I had the feeling that there we were coming from the harbour, and that the real city was actually up above, on the cliffs. . . . When we reached the plateau, we found a broad square dimly illuminated by street lights, into which many streets converged. The various quarters of the city were arranged radially around the

square. In the center was a round pool, and in the middle of it a small island.

In the cockpit now, on the dark night of my first trip to Liverpool and under my instructor's thundercloud gaze, I follow a connect-the-dots sequence of radials towards the city, as if they were long, nearly invisible wires running from one navigation beacon to the next through the murk of this English night. Soon we're on our final approach, extending the flaps and landing gear for a westerly landing at the airport that was recently renamed after John Lennon, and whose interior features a statue of Lennon and a plaque with lyrics – 'Above us only sky' – from his song 'Imagine'.

But I won't have time to find those words tonight, nor to see the spot by the terminal where a yellow submarine will someday be parked, or anything else of the city, aside from a tilting star field of amber lights when at last we break through the lowest-lying cloud. This one's a touch-and-go, my instructor reminds me as we emerge. I guide the small twin-engine propeller plane onto the airport's sole runway. Before there's time to begin to slow down, I open the throt-tles. The engines roar and the plane lurches as the propellers bite the air anew. I pull the control column back. The streaming runway lights fall away, I raise the landing gear, and as we climb into the mist the world again goes dark.

BRASÍLIA

A land that's new to me streams past the aeroplane's windows: deep green in the tropical sun, dotted with crimson-orange patches where the earth lies freshly cut. Almost perfectly straight roads diffuse into roundabouts and then re-form to continue their runs across the savannah. The land is all but flat, so there's no reason it should look elevated, but it does, and it is: the plateau that the city stands on is around two-thirds of a mile high.

Brasília is a city that's long fascinated me from afar. First, because it's the capital of the country of my brother's birth (and the land to which he, who is Indigenous, is often inclined to look when he experiences racism in New England). In addition, when our dad lived in Brazil he visited the city during its construction and was deeply moved by what he saw. There are further reasons for the city's appeal to me: Brasília is shaped like a cross, an east-facing bird, or, in the eyes of many, an aeroplane; and this was not only a planned city but a dreamed one, having appeared in a priest's vision, decades and thousands of miles from the time and place in which it finally arose.

When my brother and I were in high school, Dad took painting classes and at some point he decided to design a coat of arms for what he described as the American branch of our family. For the motto that would appear on it he chose 'Tanto Faz', a Brazilian expression that he translated as 'It does not matter', and which he explained like this:

> It does not mean I would be indifferent in important matters. But people don't have to worry about small things that are not exactly the way I like them.

In the heart of his emblem he arranged several symbols: a small version of the coat of arms of his Belgian hometown; a cardinal, a bird unknown in Belgium but easy to spot in Pittsfield in winter, when its red feathers were often the only brightness in our snow-bound backyard; and an irregular diamond with bent-in sides. In his notes on the back of the canvas he described this diamond as 'roughly the shape of the pillars of the Palace of the Alvorada' and also as the emblem of Brasília.

The Palácio da Alvorada, Brazil's presidential residence, is therefore my first stop in Brasília – I've flown here as a tourist, during an especially long trip as a pilot to São Paulo – and a few hours after touchdown a minibus drops me off outside it. The glass, steel and reinforced concrete palace rises, if such a low and long building can be said to do so, in a green and spacious lakeside district outside the city centre. When it was completed in 1958, a sign reads, it was the first permanent building in Brasília; today it's only one of the city's many modernist masterpieces designed by the architect Oscar Niemeyer.

I walk towards the wire security fence. Along it hang decorative metal plates, each with a large diamond cut out in the shape that I first saw on Dad's easel in Pittsfield. Through the fence I can see marble-clad pillars of the same shape, fronting the distant palace. Dad was drawn to this form, but to me the name of the palace is even more stirring: Palácio da Alvorada, the Palace of Dawn. I repeat it to myself, in English and as well as I can in Portuguese.

I can't go inside the palace today, it seems, so there's nothing to do but wander outside. As I do so waves of the feeling I call place lag – a bewilderment and astonishment at where I find myself, as if not only our sense of time, but our deep sense of place, too, requires a period of adjustment in the aftermath of a journey enacted at the speed of an aeroplane – wash over me. Like jet lag, place lag diminishes as you stay on in a place, but so peripatetic has my adult life been that I suspect my place lag only ever truly lifts when I'm in Pittsfield, where its absence, then, is nearly as disconcerting.

A rhea, an ostrich-like South American bird, strolls past under a rainbow that has formed near one of the distant downpours, and I have again the realisation that has no business still surprising me after so many trips to so many tropical cities: that I could watch years turn and never see all the leaves fall, or snow come to rest on bare branches; that, mostly, the air would feel to me as it does now.

Brasília, unlike Pittsfield, is a city of publicly accessible fruit – there's even an app to help you locate the free fruit you want, or to share reports of what you find – including *abacate* (avocado) and *manga* (mango), whose trees I wouldn't recognise aside from their fruit, and several, such as *ingá* (ice cream bean), *jaca* (jackfruit), *jamelão* (Java plum) and *monguba* (Malabar chestnut), not even then.

Young men and women are laughing as they shake a *goiabeira*, a guava tree. One of the guys calls out to me and offers me a guava. I know I should be spontaneous, a traveller of the right school, one who doesn't hesitate when, on their first day in a city, a stranger pulls a piece of fruit down from a tree and offers it in his upturned hand. But I'm not sure how to eat it, or if I'll like it, and I'm tired, and while I know Dad would have taken it, I thank the man and decline.

∽

I've had a long sleep, a huge breakfast of pastries and several delicious Brazilian coffees. No guavas. Now, on my first full day in the city I'm standing outside the Cathedral of Brasília (it's officially known as the Metropolitan Cathedral of Our Lady of Aparecida, a reference to the patron saint of Brazil, and to the statue of a Black Madonna found by three fishermen in a Brazilian river in 1717), and I'm turning my phone this way and that, and then raising it to the horizon, giving the appearance, surely, that I'm snapping new photos rather than pondering one a half century old.

Years ago, not long after Dad died, I found a photo he'd taken in the 1950s in Trafalgar Square, on his first visit to a city he wouldn't return to until after I moved there early in the next century. There were pigeons, a red bus, crowds, all of it as if from a film set, and so little had changed, it seemed, when I walked through the square after his death and tried to find the spot on its west side from which he'd taken it. Along with his photographs, I also inherited boxes of slides from his years in Africa and Brazil. I treasured the idea of these but rarely the reality, as I didn't own a slide projector and it was tedious to take them out, one by one, and squint while holding the corners of their lapsed and miniaturised world up to a window or a bright wall.

Then, on Christmas morning a few years ago, I opened a gift: a book, full of prints of all Dad's slides from Africa and Brazil, which Mark had secretly scanned in over the course of several months, while also managing to transcribe, and then translate online, Dad's antiquated Flemish penmanship from their frames.

In the first image, now heavily scratched, Dad pointed his camera east towards Brasília's National Congress. Perhaps the most recognisable of the city's grand architectural works, the complex features twin white towers – conjoined by a bridge halfway up – that rise above two white semispheres, a bowl and an inverted bowl, one for each house of Brazil's legislature.

On the right of Dad's slide is an hourglass-shaped arrangement of curving white ribs that, at the time, he could still see through, but that would become the cathedral I stepped out of a moment ago. Another Niemeyer masterpiece, and one to which Liverpool's Metropolitan Cathedral is often compared, the interior features angels suspended on steel cables in a volume defined by its ribs and by the glass between them, over which wave-like green and blue patterns run. I was struck, as well, on the floor below the angels, by several beautifully curved, light-hued wood structures that I briefly thought I could imagine in a high-end furniture catalogue – modernist confessionals, I belatedly realised. Outside the cathedral, and above me now, are four bells, gifts from Spain, mounted on a tall metal stand; three are named for Columbus's ships and the fourth is named Pilarica, in honor of Our Lady of the Pillar, believed by some to be the first apparition of Mary, in Spain in AD 40, even as her earthly life continued on the other side of the Mediterranean.

The Brazilian writer Clarice Lispector wrote that this city was built with 'space calculated for clouds'. As any aeroplane-shaped city should be, a pilot might add; and Brasília appears to be making good use of its space: behind the bells, storms are rising in real time, billowing up in great doomy folds that are more complicated, vertiginous and fast-altering than I've ever seen in the cooler skies of Pittsfield or London, and as I try to calculate the upwind direction in which it would be safest to fly around them, I have the rare sensation of being content on the ground.

In a country defined by its crescent of coastal settlements and major metropolises arcing around a much emptier interior, the audacity of Brasília's foundation, around 600 miles inland from the Atlantic, can hardly be overstated. It's as if in the middle of the twentieth century the United States had moved its capital hundreds of miles west from Washington, to a barely populated version of Kentucky.

The construction of a new capital in the interior of Brazil had first been envisioned in the eighteenth century; its satisfying name was proposed later, in the early 1820s, by José Bonifácio de Andrada e Silva, a leading light of Brazil's independence movement. The new capital was constitutionally sanctioned at various points, but it wasn't until the 1950s that President Juscelino Kubitschek made its construction a campaign promise. Completed in only forty-one months, Brasília was designed both to open a new frontier and to serve as a unifying, more central locus of economic growth for a vast nation: 'Integration through interiorisation', said Kubitschek, whose capital-building credentials, the anthropologist Caroline S. Tauxe notes, would be likened to those of Peter the Great, the pharaoh Akhenaten and Romulus.

James Holston, author of *The Modernist City*, a fascinating book about Brasília, describes the city as 'the most complete example ever constructed' of modernist architecture and planning, and an echo, at least, of Le Corbusier's vision for idealised cities. The lead planner was Lúcio Costa, while the city's best-known landmarks are the predominantly white concrete temples to modernism of Oscar Niemeyer.

Brasília is defined by its two axes. Imagine the arced north-south axis as a bow, and the straighter east-west axis as its drawn arrow. The east-west avenue is known as the Eixo Monumental, the Monumental Axis. Many work here – in its twenty-eight sectors dedicated to the bureaucratic functions of the Brazilian state – but, in accordance with the rules of the city's master plan, no one lives here. Alongside the axis's central green area, in which Americans may not be able to stop themselves from seeing echoes of Washington's National Mall, run busy roads (originally planned without progress-hindering traffic lights) and ministries, monuments, plazas, offices of state and the cathedral before me.

The other axis, the Eixo Rodoviário, the Highway Axis (sometimes referred to as the Residential Axis), features lines of *superquadras*, superblocks, that contain roughly ten apartment buildings and several thousand people each, not to mention schools, parks and shops. The two axes cross at a transportation hub.

Far more than with most cities – even gridded ones – the hand of a master designer is obvious. Some see a bird in the city's shape, and when I fly over Brasília at night, there is indeed something of a phoenix to it, one that has completed its self-immolation so recently that the road-like lines along which its bones ran still glow in the ashes.

Costa himself specified that the shape of his city was that of the cross, but many see an aeroplane. It's little use looking to Niemeyer to settle the cross-versus-aeroplane aspect of the debate: he was an atheist who was afraid – despite his love of clouds, which he described as 'the cathedrals of Saint-Exupéry' – to fly. A cross or an aeroplane? Dad's life, and therefore much of mine, was shaped by both.

To me, unsurprisingly, the likeness of early drawings of Brasília to an aeroplane's engineering diagram is unmistakable. But then, what else might a pilot see, especially in the light of such bold aeronautical allusions as the name of the *Plano Piloto,* the Pilot Plan, Costa's blueprint for the city; the term *asas*, wings, for the halves of the Highway Axis; and Brasília's motto – has any city a better one? – *Venturis ventis,* To the coming winds.

When I contacted James Holston for help in interpreting one of Dad's slides, he asked if my father had in fact been in an aeroplane when he took the now-scratched image, so high was his vantage point above the new city. It wouldn't have been out of character: in 1965, when Dad arrived to work in Salvador, Brazil's first capital, he hired a pilot to help him survey the informal and economically disadvantaged neighbourhoods in which he was about to work. Holston told me that the kinship between Brasília and flight was compelling even before the city's completion: aviation fulfilled 'the modernist idealisation of new technology and, above all, speed', he wrote, and paired well with the nation's socioeconomic ambition of 'leaping over stages of slow development to get to an imagined and radiant new future'.

In the Southern Hemisphere winter of 1961, Yuri Gagarin, the first human to go into space, came to Brazil to receive the National Order of the Southern Cross, the highest honour Brazil bestows on foreigners. When he saw Brasília he had the sensation that he was 'disembarking on a different planet, not on Earth'. For anyone who has ever imagined a city that does not exist, Brasília is both breathtaking and confounding. It suggests that a dream that's simultaneously monumental and finely detailed one night became concrete, and has been left here for us to awaken to, and to tend in the light; or that, at least when it comes to cities, the distinction between dreams and reality has never been clear.

∽

Here in the crypt I step aside to allow several elderly women to pass. They nod to me and make the sign of the cross as they near their city's most treasured relic: a fragment of the right arm of Giovanni Melchiorre Bosco, the Italian saint known in Brazil as João Bosco, or Dom Bosco. The relic resides in an urn in the *santuário*, sanctuary, that is named for him.

Dom Bosco was born near Turin in 1815. He became devoted to the care of children, and in 1859 he founded the order known as the Society of Saint Francis de Sales to ameliorate the conditions of underprivileged and dislocated youth at a time of economic upheaval. He found magic to be a particularly effective way to connect with kids. (In 2002, a Salesian priest presented a magic wand to Pope John Paul II, along with a petition asking that Dom Bosco be declared the patron saint of stage magicians.)

Dom Bosco never visited Brazil, a fact that makes his dream on the night of 30 August 1883, of a journey across the country's Central Plateau in the company of an angelic guide, all the more spellbinding:

> I saw the bowels of the mountains and the depths of the plains. . . .
> I saw numerous mines of precious metals. . . . Between the fifteenth
> and the twentieth degrees of latitude, there was a long and wide
> stretch of land which arose at a point where a lake was forming.
> Then a voice said repeatedly: . . . there will appear in this place the
> Promised Land, flowing with milk and honey. It will be of inconceivable richness.

Dom Bosco died in 1888, unaware of the accuracy of his auguring, both in terms of the location of Brasília (which stands between the fifteenth and sixteenth degrees of south latitude) and the date of its construction (his dream included the prophecy that it would come true within three generations, and it did so about seventy-five years later). He was even correct about the lake: Paranoá Lake is one of the city's most prominent features. (The lake is artificial, however, and those who created it were presumably well aware of his foretelling.) In 1957, a shrine to Dom Bosco became the first masonry structure erected in the new capital. In 1962, Our Lady of Aparecida and Dom Bosco (who was canonised in 1934) were named the city's patron and co-patron saints, and by 1970 the sanctuary in which I'm standing was completed.

I'm not surprised to find myself moved by the remains of a saint in the very city whose arising he foretold. Even so, the sanctuary itself is a joy, I think, as I leave his relic, climb the stairs and return to what is essentially a large cube, lined with thin lancet-like windows that run from the floor and narrow to a Gothic point at the five-storey-high ceiling. These windows are composed of patterns of small squares of glass, in white and in twelve hues of blue, made by a Belgian glassmaker in São Paulo and evocative, in some panels, of an evening sky, and in others of a starry night one.

I take a seat and watch as tourists and worshippers come and go. This is not only the bluest interior I've ever seen, but one of the most peaceful places I've ever spent a quiet hour. I'll return here on my last day in the city, to observe a Mass.

For now, I don't need to close my eyes to imagine another city, one as faultless as Brasília was intended to be. It's a city in which not every window is blue, of course, but let's say there was a period of around eight decades in which only the recently invented wonder of bright blue glass was permitted in the windows of new churches: a gift to those who love blue, as well as to students of ecclesiastical architecture, who have it so easy when it comes to identifying the works of the age.

∽

E.T.'s expression is fixed but he can't be unpleased by the lushness of this park, and by the sunlight that sifts through the canopy of trees as I pedal fast enough to summon something of a cooling breeze.

The stuffed-toy version of Hollywood's famous alien belongs to Vívian, and she's brought him along just for fun. I haven't thought about the film in years, and I'm reminded of how much I liked it as a kid, especially when we stop to take photos – of E.T., the bike basket, a palm – as if for a poster for a new version of the film, on which a tropical sun will hang where the full moon did.

I'm lucky to have friends in several of the US cities that I fly to regularly, as well as friends or family in a handful of European cities, and a few that are further afield – an old pen pal in Sydney, relatives in Cape Town, a childhood friend in Singapore. It's a joy, of course, to see someone you know for a walk or dinner when work has called you to the far side of your world; and so, whenever a room-service menu or a pillow tempts me to cancel such a plan, I try to remember that I might never in my life have seen many of these folks again, had I not become a pilot.

I didn't know a soul in Brasília. But most of Dad's cohort of Belgian-born priests stayed in Brazil, left the priesthood, married Brazilians, and had children who now form a network of cousins, of sorts, to my Brazilian-born brother and me. Eduardo, the last survivor among the Belgians with whom Dad worked in Brazil, and the one who arranged my brother's adoption, is ninety now, and lives in Salvador, 700 miles north-east of Brasília. Eduardo writes notes to me and my brother that are like no others we ever receive: he urges my brother to remember his roots in Brazil; he sends me birthday wishes that read, in their entirety: 'I thank God for your life.' In a recent email he offered me pointers for my visit to Brasília, and reminisced to me about the sense of astonishment that he and Dad never quite shook after they came here from Belgium, 'from a cold and nebulous continent to this bright luminous tropical world'. And thanks ultimately to Eduardo, one of my cousins soon put me in touch with his university friend, Vívian, who wrote to say that she would be happy to send some tips on Brasília, and to show me around a little, too.

Last night, Vívian took me to a district of restaurants along the shore of Paranoá Lake, on which she sometimes goes rowing while capybaras swim alongside her. She remarked on her favourite elements of the city's art scene (music, graffiti, theatre, circus) as well as on Brasília's particular diversity in an already diverse nation – a result of how many people arrived from all over Brazil to help build the 'Capital of Hope' they then never left, and of how many new people are always coming to the seat of power of one of the world's most populous countries. As we spoke I watched people stroll past us under the palm trees – couples, groups of friends and far more multigenerational families than you'd likely see in the UK or US at such a late hour – chatting and tapping on their phones as the lights of their city reflected from the surface of its prophesied lake.

Now, on the following morning, Vívian, E.T. and I are cycling through the Parque da Cidade, the City Park. Another Niemeyer design, it's similar in size to New York's Central Park and runs to the west of, and parallel to, the city's south wing. It's as fine a park as any I've seen, with its own lake as well as gently curving paths for joggers and cyclists, and plentiful facilities for most every sort of outdoor recreation.

I love the park but I'm struggling to pedal on in the sun and the heat, and to blink through my shellacking of high-strength sunscreen. If this were a film, I can't help thinking, E.T. would notice my frustration right about now, and beatifically deploy his powers to aid our propulsion. I'm hungry, too, a realisation that comes as it does so often when I'm jet-lagged: late, but with additional force. So I'm glad when Vívian suggests we stop at a *barraquinha*, a food stand, for savoury *pastéis*, fried, rectangular pastries, and *caldo de cana*, sugarcane juice that a man – in his sixties, perhaps, with a deeply weathered face – presses while I chew on a fibrous chunk of cane he passes to me, a gift to welcome me after he's asked Vívian where I'm from. He hands us the cool juice and the hot, oil-soaked pastries and we head to a nearby table.

As we sit in front of the stand, Vívian tells me more about the differences between Brasília's original, planned urban area, in which only a small portion of the metropolitan area's population now lives, and all that's since grown up around it. She talks about the strength of various religious practices in the city, and I tell her a story from Dad's time in Brazil, and about his observation – in lay clothes, in the district of Salvador known as the Lower City – of a trance-filled service of Candomblé, a Brazilian-born religion that blends West African traditions brought here by enslaved persons, and also incorporates elements of Roman Catholicism. Vívian tells me that Brasília is known for its skies, at sunrise and sunset in particular but also more generally, because the land is so flat and the city so spread out. Of the sky above the city, she says to me: You see more parts of it.

Vívian and I finish our meal and get back on our bikes. We cycle past Praça Eduardo e Mônica, Edward and Monica Square. Vívian tells me the name of the square comes from a song, 'Eduardo e Mônica', by Legião Urbana, Urban Legion. That's a great name for a band, I think, as Vívian tells me that they were one of the most successful groups ever in Brazil; the lead singer, Renato Russo, who died from AIDS-related complications in 1996, was compared to Bob Dylan for his lyrics and his powers of storytelling.

'Eduardo e Mônica' chronicles the love between a couple whose first date took place in this park. They fell for each other despite all their differences; they are, in the lyrics' Brazilian terms, like beans and rice. The names are changed but the lovers in the song are real people, Vívian says; they were friends of Russo and she believes they're still together.

As Vívian and I cycle back to her apartment, I repeat her city's name to myself. I like how each syllable dissolves into the next, at least when Brazilians pronounce it. And – a globe-spinning kid might ask – shouldn't all capitals be given a version of their nation's name? While we wait at a traffic light Vívian asks if I'm still thirsty, and so after we cross we stop for coconut water at a roadside stand. This blade-wielding vendor, too, asks Vívian where I'm from, and gestures to offer me the choice of a plastic cup, or a straw with which to drink directly from the coconut he strikes with a practised flash. I ask for a straw.

Back at Vívian's building we chain the bikes on the parking deck and head up to her apartment. She'd thought of a restaurant, and with the day's heat in mind had suggested I bring a change of clothes for after our ride. So she waits on the couch in the living room while I go to her bathroom to shower. As I close the door and carefully rest the folded towel she gave me on the sink, I'm struck again by the kindness of someone I met only yesterday, and by how she's separated by only a few degrees from Dad, who saw the construction of the city that stands around us. I step into the shower and turn on the tap. The capital's water runs over me, the sunscreen melts into my eyes, and for the half second of pain after I close them it's as if I've never lived anywhere else.

CHAPTER 3

CITY OF SIGNS

Los Angeles, New Orleans,
Boston and Keeler

IMAGINE THE VIEW, around dusk, from the camera of a low-orbit satellite moving above a densely settled part of the world, and how this perspective allows us to watch a web of glowing cities, each flat and etched as finely as circuitry, turn towards us with the silent inevitability of the planet itself.

Such a view reminds me of the life any of us might make in one of those cities, and of the ordinary hour in which we might walk home, say, after a meal with a friend, and stop for some bread and milk, and then, when we turn the key and set down our groceries and switch on a lamp, we fail again, as we almost always must, to imagine the illumination of which we form part, between the lifeless rock beneath the city and the airless void above.

Horizontally, too, a relative darkness surrounds every city, one composed of much smaller settlements, farms and wilderness – all the regions that, at night, and from above, appear dimmer, if not entirely black. I like to think about the roads that run through these lands, and the signs that stand along them, signs that bear the city's name, but which late at night may go unread for hours, and are perhaps not even lit until the headlights of a car sweep over them.

Each river has a watershed, the territory throughout which rain and melted snow descend to it; and similarly, each city has a region composed of all the hinterlands and provinces in which it's signposted. Watersheds are illustrated most clearly on topographic maps, which suggest how we might envision a city's name-shed, too: we could mark on a map every sign that points to a metropolis, and then connect these in a series of rough halos. Rippling out like contour lines, these would chart the field of the city's gravity, and reveal the direction in which a traveller through the region would most naturally find themselves drawn.

It's an autumn afternoon, maybe in my final year of high school. Class has finished for the day and I'm walking up East Street to Pittsfield's public library.

The official name of the library is the Berkshire Athenaeum. For years, I'll think of this term, *athenaeum*, as unique to Pittsfield, as naturally as I'll fail to see within it the name of the goddess Athena, or the name of the distant city of which she's the patron, though these could hardly be more clearly spelled out by the black metal capital letters that form the sign on the library's red-brick façade.

My ignorance of the roots of the library's name will persist into my twenties, until I see a reference to another athenaeum, one from ancient Rome, which, I'll learn with surprise, was *the* athenaeum: the academy and intellectual repository founded by the emperor Hadrian, who also reinvigorated the city of Athens. For now, though, I know of only Pittsfield's athenaeum (Latin motto: *Optima seculorum in secula servare*, To protect the best of the ages for the ages); indeed, it's one of the buildings I know best in the world.

Our athenaeum's two entrances, from two parallel streets, arrive on different levels. One entrance leads to the lower floor and the children's section. It's near a library return chute, where, when I was little, books released from my hands would land with a satisfying but – given the care with which I had been taught books should be handled – worrisome thud. Right inside, past the water fountain, is the checkout desk, one of the few places where, in my memory, Mom will always be twice my height.

The library's other entrance, from the next street to the west, leads to the upper floor and the adult section. If I come here on my lunch break I typically sit by the north windows, which, depending on the season, offer a view into leafy branches or down onto snowy streets. In winter, I'll often leave my coat on while I read, despite the nearby radiators, as waterfall-like blasts of cold air run down the tall windows and over me. It's a sensation that will return to me years later when I'm studying meteorology as part of my pilot's course and the instructor urges us to stop thinking of air as a continuous mix: instead, we're to think of parcels of it, moving in relation to other parcels.

In these years I am already dreaming of becoming a pilot, and so on many weekday visits to the athenaeum, I fill out a form to request the latest issues of *Aviation Week*. Today, though, I bring a large atlas to a desk. I sit down and open it to a page at random. As I do so, I lean back in the library's simple wooden chair, and wince as I think – as I still will decades from now at such moments – of another wooden chair, which stood around the table in our dining room at home.

I do a lot of my homework at that dining table, and I often used to lean back in one of the chairs that are, along with the table, my parents' only treasured pieces of furniture. Mom had always warned me not to – correctly, it turned out, because as I leaned back one day after school, the aft two legs broke off, the back of the chair split and I dropped to the floor.

I ran to find my brother.

Right, he said, calmly. (This is the stressful moment I'll think of years from now, when I first watch the body disposal scene in the film *Pulp Fiction*.) He pointed out that there were six chairs but only four of us, and, unless my parents invited at least two guests for dinner, which didn't happen often, the extra chairs lived in different corners of the basement. In that case who would miss one immediately, or have reason to blame me when they finally did? We only needed to dispose of the one I'd broken, he calculated. So we took the remains of the chair up to the attic and placed them on the newspaper he spread on the floor to catch the sawdust, under the naked bulbs that hung from the pitched ceiling. I held each large piece firm as my brother worked quickly with Dad's red-handled hacksaw. Then we wrapped it all in rubbish bags and set these in the bin on the street only minutes before our parents reached home. The perfect crime, until perhaps six months later, after my parents had turned the house upside down and spent several hours phoning all the friends and neighbours who might have borrowed a chair. I looked across at my brother's narrowing eyes, mouthed a 'Sorry', and cracked.

Our dining room was special to me long before I made it a crime scene. When I was younger, Dad and I often browsed our family atlas at the table there. Back then, a city was almost nothing more to me than its name, and I loved some names much more than others. Seoul, and its easy elision with *soul*. Las Vegas, which I thought referred to multiple examples of the bright star Vega, not to a Spanish word for meadows, which made an already mellifluous name so pleasing that decades later, if I find myself walking through Las Vegas to get a haircut or a burrito and I stop to wait for a light to change, and I look down and scuff my sensible forty-something pilot shoes through a burned-up pool of dust, I'll understand that some part of me is standing in the other Las Vegas, the starry one that a mistranslated name once conjured.

Here in the athenaeum other names come to me as I dare to lean back: Lisbon, Lisboa. Nairobi. Geneva – Genève in French and Genf in German, Dad told me. Tokyo, the Eastern Capital. Beijing, the Northern Capital.

Now I close my eyes and it's as if I'm not in the library, but seated at home, at the dining room table. It's a few years ago and our atlas is open and I am not leaning back in my chair because Dad is there next to me. Riyadh is an agreeable name, we decide; I love the *r* even if I have trouble saying it. Toronto – three short *o*'s, but the middle

one different – has a good rhythm. And despite my speech impediment I'm okay with Toronto's central *r;* I'm sure that if I had to say
the city's name, context would lead anyone to add the sound I cannot. Den Haag, The Hague – The Hedge, Dad explains. The next
time I alter the name of my imaginary city, I'll remember: If you can
call a city The Hedge, then you can call a city anything you like.

And Los Angeles, of course. Among all the city names printed
on the pages Dad and I are turning, not only is it my favourite, but
I'm struck by how vast its position reveals the US to be: the city
appears to be nearly as far from us as Europe, and neither Dad nor
Mom has ever seen it.

36,000 FEET ABOVE THE MOJAVE DESERT,
190 MILES FROM LA

With Las Vegas behind us I look through the forward, right-hand
window of the cockpit, west towards the sunset that's almost complete. I remove my sunglasses and zip them into the front pocket of
my flight case.

In 1770, the Barcelona-born military engineer Miguel Costansó –
a member of an expedition that passed where Los Angeles would
shortly begin to rise – described the Southern Californian peaks
that 'furnished us points and determined places which served as
landmarks to ascertain our position'. Today, our 747's computers
are automatically tuning the navigation beacons nearest us, while
we need only look ahead, to where a snow-trimmed curtain of rock
and forest appears to have been raised, out of modesty, or with a
director's eye for suspense, around the city once known as El Pueblo
de Nuestra Señora la Reina de los Ángeles, the Town of Our Lady
the Queen of the Angels.

Los Angeles was founded in 1781. David Kipen, in *Dear Los Angeles*, an anthology of writings about his native metropolis, records

that a late-nineteenth-century traveller compared the city's air to that of 'Old Egypt', and marvelled that nowhere else had he 'seen any such sunlight, transparency and luminousness of atmosphere as characterise the days here in Southern California'. Today the air is less pure, of course, but there's still a golden gentleness to the light in and above the city. Then, when night falls, this softness gives way to a brilliant, cut-glass clarity. When I arrive here around dusk, as we will today, it's easy to think: *Here is our shining city*, and just in time, as the continent's edge rolls into sight and the sun lowers in my eyes.

Los Angeles really does shine. It's physically large – for some time it was the largest city in the world by area. It's also profligately lit, though even a dimmer metropolis would stand out against the desert, mountains and dark ocean that cradle it. Passengers who fly in after sunset, their cameras clicking as they descend towards the map-like sheet of illumination that scrolls beneath the wings, might be surprised by how long this view has been so memorable. In 1946, for example, Eleanor Roosevelt, en route to visit her grandchildren in Pasadena, wrote that 'the most impressive time to fly in to Los Angeles is at night, when all the lights are on and the city lies below you like a multi-colored heap of jewels'.

Now I look far ahead to the lights gathered upon the land's and the day's end. From our current altitude and distance they appear almost continuous, even whole, and I'm reminded of a conversation I once had with a man from California about my love for Los Angeles. He wasn't at all surprised that someone from New England would be as dazzled as I am by the city. Keep in mind, though, he added, that very little that you can say about LA is true. I asked him what he meant. He replied: Well, it's only from the air that it's one place.

An air traffic controller instructs us to 'contact the Los Angeles Center' on the next of its many frequencies. I greet the subsequent controller, who replies: 'Descend when ready via the ANJLL arrival', a reference to the locally tuned (ANJLL, angel) name of the STAR, or Standard Terminal Arrival Route, that many aircraft approaching the city from the north-east will follow.

The plane banks gently and I turn, also, to look practically straight down on the coal-black floor of the Mojave National Preserve. The architectural historian Reyner Banham wrote that San Francisco was made by waves of settlers who arrived by sea, while those who formed Los Angeles came mostly by land. Indeed, Los Angeles began fourteen or so miles inland, a location that – in the absence of a port, or trams and cars to speed you to the surf – you wouldn't necessarily call coastal. In the early 1900s, and despite such advances, a New York newspaper could still print that Los Angeles 'can never be a great business center because it is too far away from the ocean'.

Before we roll out of our turn I look right, to Interstate 15, the highway whose lanes our south-westerly flight path now roughly parallels. Tonight, it appears more brightly red than any other road I've seen, and it takes me a moment to realise – in this time-scrambling job it can be hard to remember such ordinary facts – that it's Sunday evening. What I and everyone else on the starboard side of the plane can see, then, is not only the tail-lights of the cars on the motorway. It's the brake lights, too, of thousands of motorists returning to LA from a weekend away, along with other travellers, surely, who are about to become the newest Angelenos. In the open desert below our descending 747 they press on their brake pedals to slow or stop, and form and brighten the river of bottlenecked light that winds through the evening to the city ahead.

NEW ORLEANS, 1,894 MILES FROM LA

Over a drink at a crowded restaurant in New Orleans, less than two miles from an interstate that could take us straight to downtown Los Angeles, a friend's eyes light up as he describes two signs he saw many years ago, on the California coast, not long after he moved from England to California. He was driving along, thinking about how much he still felt like a stranger to America, when he realised that the road, and the continent as well, were about to end. One sign pointed left to Los Angeles and the other right to San Francisco. That was it, he says with a smile; nothing else.

In return, I tell him about the first sign for Los Angeles that I ever encountered as a driver. At university, long before I ever visited LA, I made a friend from the city. Lea and I talked easily, and about almost everything. Her mother is Native American, and much about Lea's perspective on history and culture echoed my brother's. And I was grateful to realise that to her it was the most ordinary thing in the world that I'm gay.

Sometimes, as Lea and I got to know each other, I'd tell her about Pittsfield, which she hadn't heard of before she met me, and which lay only over the hills from the university she'd travelled across the continent to attend. I preferred to talk about her hometown, however. She told me about LA's weather and traffic and how the mountains, sometimes even snowcapped, loom above the apparent ends of so many roads. She confirmed that you can indeed surf and ski in the same day, but she suspected that almost no one ever does. As a teenager Lea loved to sing and to play the guitar, sitting alone or with friends on her city's piers and beaches after school, all of which sounded to me like scenes from a film.

A few years after I graduated I went to Los Angeles for the first time, to stay with Lea and her mother. By then her mother had moved to the San Fernando Valley, where, they explained, though they had moved across the Santa Monica Mountains, which seem such a natural frontier, they were, in fact, still within the city limits.

When it was time to go to bed on my first night in Los Angeles, Lea's mother asked if I wished to sleep inside or outside. I was surprised by a question that in western Massachusetts could only be a weary joke – depending on the season – about mosquitoes, bears, or the cold. Outside, I replied. So she made up the four-poster in the backyard, and on my first night in Los Angeles I slept under the stars as the moon cast long shadows of the resting limbs of an exercise machine – it was outside, too, in a choice spot on an elevated terrace – across the lawn.

The next morning, after breakfast, Lea had gone out to do errands, and her mother – a psychotherapist – said to me: Why, you look like you want to go for a drive. No one had ever said that to me before, though perhaps, I thought, it's a common diagnosis in Los Angeles. She was right, anyway, and I told her so with a laugh, and added that she must be very good at her job. She suggested a place for me to get a fancy coffee, and then a route she thought I'd enjoy through the nearby mountains. She offered me my choice of her two cars, which had vanity number plates to the effect of MTHR ERTH and FTHR TIME. I walked out into Lea's quiet neighbourhood, got into one – FTHR TIME, maybe – and drove it carefully away.

Wherever in the world I find them, I'm drawn to signs that point to a city but do not mention its name, because from where such a sign stands no other could be intended. In Toronto's international airport a simple sign, next to an arrow, states: TRAIN TO CITY. Years ago, through a gap in the curtains of a bus leaving an airport in India, I was struck to see a sign that featured only the word CITY, while similar signs, around Cape Town, are marked, in Afrikaans and English, STAD/CITY. Such signs remind me of how, as teenagers, my brother, his friends and other cool kids in Pittsfield would speak of 'the city', which everyone took to mean not Albany, Hartford, or Boston, our state capital, but New York, though it was the furthest of these.

Los Angeles, however, is such a fine name that I only ever want to see it spelled out. A few minutes after I left Lea's house on that long-ago day, I stopped at a red light near an entrance to a freeway, where I realised that for the first time in my life I was nearly underneath a sign that points to Los Angeles. I looked up, immobilised by the new intensity of the spell my favourite city-name had so often cast, until someone behind me saw the light had changed. They honked and honked again. I waved a sorry, set my coffee down in the cup holder, and started into the morning.

BOSTON, 2,980 MILES FROM LA

An hour after landing we're at our crew hotel near Back Bay station. Some of my favourite trips as a pilot are to this city I once lived in, and so, after a shower and a cursory unpacking, it's with a familiar spring in my step that I head out of the hotel and up Dartmouth Street en route to have pancakes at a café I know well.

On my way I'll make a detour in order to pass by my first apartment in Boston. I lived there when I started my office job here, before I moved to England and became a pilot. It was a fourth-floor, five-person share within a few blocks of the apartments where Mom and Dad each lived before they got married. I didn't know this when I chose it, but I liked the serendipity, and I'm happy to be reminded of it when I walk these streets.

As I wait at a light at the corner of Dartmouth Street and Huntington Avenue I look across to the public library, towards its reverential inscriptions –

THE PUBLIC LIBRARY OF THE CITY OF BOSTON · BUILT BY
THE PEOPLE AND DEDICATED TO THE ADVANCEMENT
OF LEARNING A.D. MDCCCLXXXVIII

– and its heavy black sconces, so suggestive of a medieval weapon or a crown.

Do I love Boston? When I'm in the city (motto: *Sicut Patribus Sit Deus Nobis*, God Be with Us as He Was with Our Fathers) I often recall what I know of my parents' new starts here, and of their lives in neighbourhoods that would also become familiar to me when I was a young adult.

'The City on a Hill' aside, I'm not moved by Boston's epithets (the 'Athens of America' is somehow both immodest and lacking in confidence, while chief among the problems with 'Hub of the Universe' is that it seems improbable). Nevertheless, when I lived here I quickly grew to feel pride in a city I couldn't be certain I would ever leave: when I sat on a bench outside the old church in Copley Square and stared at the image of its stone structure that shimmered on the glass wall of the Hancock Tower; when I tried to excuse the subway's failings because its staff are so kind and because, after all, it was the country's first; or whenever I walked through the Public Garden and thought of a black-and-white photo of Mom, taken there in the late 1960s. That photo is reason enough to love this city deeply: it reminds me that Mom was young here, and on a summer day she laughed and posed beneath a weeping willow.

When I'm here I also can't help but remember a lot of my favourite scenes from the television show *Cheers*. The show was a fixture of the Thursday evenings of my Pittsfield childhood; indeed, for my brother and me, it was often the highlight of our week. I found it very funny, of course, and I liked that the seafood restaurant above the bar was named Melville's (after the author associated with both the sea and Pittsfield, I presumed), and also that in the episode in which the psychiatrist Frasier Crane encourages several anxious fliers to think of their happy place, that place is the Berkshires. To me the show and its theme song also stood for the warmth and acceptance that I believed a large city might offer. And when I watched the show (especially the episode that featured the gang's response to the visit of a gay former Red Sox player) it never occurred to me that it could have been set in a city other than the one in which the biggest road near my hometown ended.

Indeed, in this pedestrian-scaled part of the city it's easy to forget that the road towards Pittsfield – the Massachusetts Turnpike, or Interstate 90 – runs beneath you, underground, and as the light changes and I look left and start to cross into Copley Square, it's nearly as easy to miss the single-lane down-ramp that leads onto the highway booming through the tunnel below.

On a sign above this ramp is a downward-pointing arrow and a city's name: NEW YORK. I must have walked past this sign hundreds of times, but it still strikes me as curious. New York, after all, is more than 200 miles away by road, and nowhere near Interstate 90, which runs instead towards Worcester, the second-largest city in Massachusetts, and Springfield, the third largest, and then – after it passes near Pittsfield – on to Albany, Cleveland, Chicago and Seattle. Indeed, given Boston's position near the nation's north-east corner, practically any American city might be reasonably signposted here. Perhaps the sign illustrates the effects of the Big Apple's asymmetric gravity on the imaginations of even proud Bostonians; or perhaps a traffic study concluded that New York was the most common reason for Bostonians to leave town.

Whatever its story, it's this curious Boston sign for New York that I'll think of when I first encounter the term *control city*, used by transportation engineers for the city on a sign that indicates the direction of a road. On a long road the control city changes as you move along it, a process that continues until the road ends, either at the junction with another road, or upon its arrival in the final control city.

Where you join Interstate 90 near Pittsfield, you're offered the choice of westbound lanes, signed to Albany, or eastbound lanes, signed to Boston. The window seats of the buses that transport air crews after landing sometimes offer views of even more arresting examples. Leaving King Khalid International Airport, there are enormous signs for Riyadh, of course, but at a certain point we reach a junction where signs would lead us north-east to Dammam, or south-west to Makkah, or Mecca. Riyadh, then, is the control city that guides us south-east along the road from the airport; Dammam and Mecca are the control cities on the road we meet.

A road's control cities are often among those listed on distance-to-go signs, too. When I was little and my family drove from the Berkshires to Boston, I liked to look out for the miles-to-Boston signs – I once knew all their numbers – as the highway widened and grew busier. (I remembered those journeys and the particular excitement of their staccato countdown when I read *Boom Town*, by Sam Anderson, and learned that in the early decades of Oklahoma City an enthusiastic leader was careful not only to formalise the auspicious 'city' in its name, but also to raise miles-to-go signs far out on the roads, hoping to conjure the new city's majesty from the anticipation he scaffolded across the land.)

As a kid I never questioned where in Boston, exactly, such distances were measured from. Later, however, I came to often recollect those family drives east along the turnpike as I've set out to walk through a city until I reach its navel-like zero-mile point: Rome's Milliarium Aureum, the Golden Milestone, of which Plutarch wrote; the Nihonbashi, the Japan Bridge, in Tokyo; or the location, west of the station called Charing Cross in London, of the final cross raised to mark the path of the thirteenth-century funeral procession of Queen Eleanor.

High above all roads, meanwhile, a more literal notion of control cities will resonate with pilots, as we progress through the air traffic regions into which the world's skies are divided. These often bear the names of major cities, and so controllers might instruct a pilot to 'contact now the Atlanta Center', for example, followed – in the order in which a westbound flight might encounter them – by Memphis, Fort Worth, Albuquerque, and finally the Los Angeles Center.

KEELER, 207 MILES FROM LA

I wake up early in the simple house I've rented, a house that – the furnishings, the lace curtains over the sink, the small table, suitable for one or two, in the middle of the kitchen – reminds me a little of my grandmother's home in Pennsylvania.

I turn on a light. I make coffee and drink my first cup standing up. I try to imagine that I'm much older and that this is my routine in this, my house; that every morning I wake up well before dawn, at least in winter, and walk along the carpeted hall from the bedroom to the kitchen, where I put a saucepan on the hob.

I sit at this kitchen table for the first and last time in my life and flip through the news on my phone. After my breakfast I wash my coffee cup and rest it at an incline to dry on the side of the sink. I take my bag outside, walk down the steps and close the gate with the NO TRESPASSING sign on it.

The skies have cleared during the night and I can see the first line of mountains between here and Death Valley. It runs between the outlines of the nearby trees and the stars, in a series of scribbled arcs edged by the lightning-blue rind of the arriving day. My car is glazed in ice, and without a scraper – not standard issue for cars rented in Long Beach, I realise, as I feel around the rear footwells and come up empty – I must wait for it to warm and melt itself clear.

I close the door and turn the key. The engine starts roughly, and I remember the Pittsfield mornings when I sat in the dark-grey light and the eerie silence of the back seat of a snow-entombed car, while Mom or Dad stomped around outside, brushing the snow from it as if they were painting the day on. I turn a dial on the climate-control panel far into the red zone. Gradually the air from the vents clears a blooming pattern from the windshield, until I turn on the wipers and they sweep the wet sheets of remaining ice onto the drive.

I flew into Los Angeles a few days ago. When I first began to fly there, I explored it as deeply as I might any city that was largely new to me. As the years went on, though, I started to occasionally leave the city to explore its surroundings. Sometimes I'll bring a van full of colleagues out to a hiking spot in a state or national park. If I'm by myself, I might drive out to Daggett, to stretch my legs on a section of Route 66, Steinbeck's Mother Road, to be startled by spiders large enough to have facial expressions, and to stare as perhaps only a pilot might at the wooden arrows on a post that point towards Detroit, Tokyo and Hong Kong. I might drive on, through the settlement known as Bagdad, to Amboy – 'the ghost town that ain't dead yet' – to watch from the town's café as light aircraft taxi past the window en route to the nearby runway, or to ponder how an official-looking, accent-free sticker marked LEGION ETRANGERE, the Foreign Legion, ended up on a pyramidal chunk of concrete that lies in the dirt.

This is an even longer work trip than usual, so I decided to spend a night out of town. After stopping for a couple of hikes in Death Valley, I drove west, through the mountains that tower above one of the hottest places on Earth, past snowploughs and signs that warn of the need for chains in snowstorms. In the late afternoon I arrived on the eastern side of the Owens Valley, and found my way to Keeler (home to sixty-six people in 2010) and to this small house.

Keeler was once a lakeside town with a pier, but the lake is long gone. I walked all around the town before I went to bed last night, setting one dog barking after another. The streets, of cracked asphalt or dirt and gravel, are lined with dry and golden grasses that murmured in the wind that never ceased to blow across the lake bed. Some of the town's homes appear to be abandoned, with rusted-out or even overgrown vehicles nearby, and I passed a swimming pool that contained only dust. From other homes, however, I could hear televisions and smell wood fires. This used to be a ghost town, but it's coming back, a woman told me, as we spoke beneath a layer of clouds that almost met the snowline on the mountains.

Now in the near-darkness my headlights show up far down this mostly straight and flat road, and scatter from its rimed surface. I'm heading south-east, along the valley's edge, but soon I'll turn south-west, across the valley, towards the town of Olancha. To the sides, the peripheral glow of the headlights reveals saltbush scrub and dried tumbleweed, caked in a thick, ghostly frost that's as grey as ash. I thought I knew frost but I've never seen it like this. It's the result, a friend will later tell me, of an ice fog known as *pogonip*, a Native American term.

I near the western side of the valley and the junction with Route 395, the road that runs down the eastern edge of the Sierra Nevadas, and is sometimes known as El Camino Sierra, the Sierra (or Mountain) Highway. As I approach the junction, I see two signs for Los Angeles. The first comes a short distance before the intersection and the other stands on its far side.

In 1860, a botanist 'in camp at Los Angeles' wrote that 'all that is wanted naturally to make it a paradise is water, more water'. By the end of the nineteenth century, the city had essentially run dry and might have never grown much beyond its then population of around 200,000 were it not for the Belfast-born William Mulholland, who became a sailor at fourteen and arrived in Los Angeles in his early twenties. He began his career in the city as a *zanjero*, a ditch tender; later, his talent for water-channelling would be likened to that of the engineers of ancient Rome.

In 1904, Mulholland and Fred Eaton, a former mayor of Los Angeles, rode hundreds of miles north from the city along a wagon road, past the graves of unlucky travellers and the bleached bones of horses, and into this valley, which was originally the home of the Paiute people known as the Eastern Mono. By the end of the nine-teenth century, farmers had diverted much of the water that melted out of the snowy High Sierras in order to create a flourishing agricultural industry. Mulholland passed through Olancha, the town I'm arriving in now, and soon after was dazzled by the brightness of the water he found in a realm that the Los Angeles–born historian Remi Nadeau, in his book *Los Angeles: From Mission to Modern City*, characterised as 'like the land of milk and honey after the flight from Egypt'.

In all that clear water Mulholland saw what his adopted metropolis required – 'If you don't get the water now, you'll never need it', he would later warn Angelenos – and he saw, too, that, so high up, it would not need to be pumped; gravity, and the deceit that has made this thread of the history of Los Angeles legendary, would bring it down. The result was the Los Angeles Aqueduct, at the time the world's longest, built by around 5,000 labourers and financed by millions of dollars in bonds approved by the voters of the city it would transform. Angelenos came to the official opening with tin cups to drink from, and when the water began to flow, Mulholland exclaimed: 'There it is. Take it!'

Los Angeles took it and the city grew explosively – indeed, its size became a joke, as residents took photos of themselves with NOW ENTERING LOS ANGELES CITY LIMITS signs they installed in distant locales. 'You could trek to the Himalayas and still never escape', as David Kipen put it.

The aqueduct laid the groundwork for what became known as the water wars, carried out with an urban-rural fury that inspired armed standoffs, bombings and the hurling of the city's construction equipment into the river. Los Angeles won, it hardly needs to be said, and grew to be the nation's second-largest city, while the dried bed of Owens Lake became the nation's single largest source of particulate pollution. And so the historian Nadeau would be able to describe the Owens Valley, in terms suggestive of a Roman hinterland, as a 'tributary province to the city it helped to build'; the writer Wallace Stegner could characterise Los Angeles, in hydrological terms, as cantilevered 'out over empty space'; and Mulholland, the former ditch tender, would be awarded an honorary degree from the University of California, Berkeley on which was written *Percussit saxa et duxit flumina ad terram sitientum*, He broke the rocks and brought the river to the thirsty land.

I pull over before the first sign for Los Angeles, turn off the engine and remove the key in order to stop the music. In the sudden quiet I look north, to where patches of fog rest on the dusty lake bed, and then south, along the road that follows the mountains. Flying above so much of the world I've grown accustomed to seeing highways, waterways and railways crossing deserts or cultivated lands on their way to the often ancient cities from which they radiate. At such moments I'm reminded of physics lessons, and a teacher's use of the image of a bowling ball on a trampoline to illustrate how mass distorts space-time; and of biology class, as well, as I consider whether it's more apt to describe a city's effect on its surroundings as like that of the blood vessels of a tumour or the roots of a tree.

The car's engine starts to click as it cools. When I left the little house in Keeler, the temperature was –2 degrees Celsius, according to the rental car's digital display. Here in Olancha, around fifteen miles across the valley and at the junction with Highway 395, near where icy air masses sliding off the peaks of the High Sierras might first touch down, it's –8. I get out to stretch my legs and wait for the sun to rise.

My feet crunch on the frozen soil as I walk in the direction of the junction and the mountains above it. I stop and then look north, past Fremont cottonwoods dressed in their winter gold and motionless against the calm sky. Cows are lowing in a field by the road, behind a barbed-wire fence, and I wonder in something like Mom's voice if they mustn't be cold. Beyond them a carpet of mist covers the bed of the lake that Los Angeles took. There are no cars on this road, aside from mine. On 395, the road that this road meets, the trucks sound like distant fighter jets until at last they trundle into view, spaced out in intervals long enough for me briefly to stop asking myself – as I still do, even at my age – what someone might think of me, without even a lit cigarette to help explain why I'm standing alone on the side of the road.

In Calvino's *Invisible Cities* we may read Marco Polo's description, to Kublai Khan, of walking through a wilderness towards the city of Tamara, a journey on which 'rarely does the eye light on a thing, and then only when it has recognised that thing as the sign of another thing'.

In such a manner, Calvino suggests, the thirteenth-century Venetian traveller might have steered the imagination of the Mongol emperor. Today, and in a manner not necessarily more prosaic, the principles of the signs that direct American motorists are described in the federal document known as the *Manual on Uniform Traffic Control Devices*.

For example, in Section 1A.02: 'Principles of Traffic Control Devices', we learn that:

> *To be effective, a traffic control device should meet five basic requirements:*
> *A. Fulfill a need;*
> *B. Command attention;*
> *C. Convey a clear, simple meaning;*
> *D. Command respect from road users; and*
> *E. Give adequate time for proper response.*

I walk towards the first of the two signs for Los Angeles and stop. I love signs because of the contrast between how indirectly their power functions and how considerable that power can be. Even the newest and best-lit road signs, after all, only ever stand for something and someplace else; and this purpose, already oblique, seems to grow even more beguilingly insubstantial as GPS-based navigation obviates the names and the arrows that so many signs still raise.

Here, however, as close as I may have ever stood to such a large road sign, the detail of the object itself strikes me. The apparently racetrack-like rounded corners, I realise, are formed by white, reflective and slightly raised strips, and not by the sharp-cornered metal they curve over. The white arrow that points to Los Angeles is more gently drawn than I expected: the three points that form the triangular arrowhead are smoothed off, and the side that joins the upper and lower vertices to the arrow's shaft is slightly indented. The white, black-bordered symbol that frames the road number and is meant to resemble a shield has been generously expanded, as if for a heavy-set knight, to incorporate the large 3, 9 and 5 of the road we meet.

The front, meanwhile, is covered in bolts that go through to brackets on the unpainted, pattern-swirled back, which are themselves mounted on two thick, square wooden posts as golden as the trunks of the living trees that stand around them. These bolts are a marring of the sign's face, really, from this close, but like the trompe l'oeil corners, it's surely never mattered to any passing motorist; the sign does what a sign should.

I see, too, that the sign's sturdiness depends, as of course it must, on more than a hint of heft. In our imagination or dreams, a sign requires only two dimensions. What towers above me, in contrast, is not a surface, but a mass, with edges thick enough for long crystals of frost to crisscross as they grow. For a moment the sign is sturdy enough to lay over a ditch and trust that it might hold me; then I blink and again it's flat, and only an indication of somewhere else, all but alone and feeling, perhaps, like nothing to itself.

I step back, in search of a distance from which these two aspects might balance. How many ordinary signs, for so many cities, must there be in the world? Someone designed this sign; someone cut and painted it; someone drove it here and stood in the saltgrass to pound it into California.

Arrows used on guide signs to indicate the directions towards desig-

nated routes or destinations should be pointed at the appropriate angle to clearly convey the direction to be taken. There are so many kinds of knowledge, so many kinds of work that fill so many different lives. And for once I'm astonished, not by how easily the real world and its cities might apparently be perfected, but by the fact that anything practical ever gets built at all.

Ahead of me, at the top of the T-junction, stands another sign, the one that indicates the distance to Los Angeles. The letters of the city's name fill much of its span. *The lateral spacing to the vertical borders should be essentially the same as the height of the largest letter.* I half close my eyes and try to imagine what it might feel like to come across this sign on a winter morning as still as this one, to have been lost and then to read the name of the city for the first time.

I walk past the sign and look up, past the bare branches of the cottonwoods, into the nearest of the High Sierra's frozen naves. *The background of all guide signs that are not independently illuminated shall be retroreflective.* The silent gap between two speeding trucks passes like a light over where I'm standing, and for a moment the warmth of Los Angeles is as unimaginable as spring.

Here, around 200 miles north of the cathedral named Our Lady of the Angels, whose consecrating cardinal spoke of 'our great city of many cities', and of families on the move, and truck drivers, and bells that the lonely might hear, I realise that I'm shivering, and that I haven't packed right. I might know better, I think; a traveller from New England should. I walk back to the car, start the engine and turn up the heat and the music. I roll to the line and turn left.

CHAPTER 4

CITY OF PROSPECTS

Shenandoah, Zürich,
Hong Kong and Pittsburgh

IMAGINE A COASTAL CITY, surrounded by mountains on three sides, and the most important road that leads to it. This road twists and rises up the slopes, but gently, as such a wide road must. As it climbs, digital signs advise drivers to check their brakes, and warn of any snow or ice at the higher elevations to come, where the worst winter storms may close the highway for hours, diverting motorists to the jams that then form on the lower and longer routes.

When at last the gradient of the mountain becomes too much for even such a skilfully engineered highway to climb, the road, still five or six lanes in each direction, plunges into a tunnel that curves and slopes slightly downwards as it passes through the heart of the mountain. This tunnel is meticulously maintained, and its lane lines – which will never be obscured by snow, except in the first few metres near the entrances – are lit with small, flush bulbs that run off into the darkness, as elementally as they might in an early video game.

Footage from within the tunnel, accompanied by music in a minor key, often appears in films set in the city to which the road leads: say, a couple drives home from a party as the curving-away lights flicker over their faces, and from their continued silence we're meant to understand that the technologies of tunnelling and lighting may change but we do not.

When the highway at last emerges on the city side, it's still perhaps 100 metres above sea level, near the top of a valley – whose built-up slopes evoke the Mid-Levels, the steep, escalator-accessed hillside neighborhoods from which Hong Kong's skyscrapers rise most precariously – where it shoots onto a cable-stayed bridge above the valley floor that briefly continues to drop away from it.

At this moment travellers are presented, all at once, with a memorable view of two distinct gatherings of skyscrapers – much as Midtown and Downtown appear to be separate cities when Manhattan is viewed from a distance – while a third stands on the far sides of the bridges that illuminate the harbour, beyond the slowly shifting constellations formed by the lights of ferries. So fine is this view that in the tunnel's last quarter of a mile the speed limit reduces, lane changes are not permitted and signs warn drivers: EYES ON THE ROAD! Not on the city.

I walk down the steps of my high school and pause while I decide. Left on East Street, towards the athenaeum? Or straight across the same street to the state office building where Dad works?

I'm sixteen, a junior. At Pittsfield High School juniors and seniors are allowed to leave school at lunchtime. We typically head to Dunkin' Donuts (my favorite), a hot dog restaurant (such restaurants are unusually popular in Pittsfield, I'll realise only once I've left), or a pizza or burger joint, all of which offer tasty alternatives to the repetitive meals in the school's cafeteria.

Even if I've brought my lunch from home, I sometimes leave school to eat it. If I go to the library to spend my lunchtime reading, I'll eat my sandwich on the way. Today, though, I decide I'll have lunch with Dad at his office. I cross East Street and the car park from where, on an afternoon at the end of this year and in five centimetres of unforecasted snow, my driving test will start. I pass the signs for the ground-floor Registry of Motor Vehicles, enter through a side door and take the lift up to Dad's floor.

Dad is generally a joyful guy but whenever I walk in, he looks up from his desk with an easy smile that suggests I'm a particularly welcome break from whatever he's doing, and also that he won't ever ask me why I'm not with the other kids. I sit on the guest's side of his desk, as if, we often joke, we're about to have a very formal meeting, and we each unwrap the sandwiches we made on the kitchen counter this morning.

Allowing for the walk from and back to school, we have only twenty minutes or so together. The rest of Dad's time in this office, when I'm not here, is mysterious to me. I know he organises services for the state's mental health-care programmes, but I don't understand what this means he actually does. What does anyone in an office do, from one minute to the next?

Sometimes he talks about group or community homes, in which a number of individuals reside together in a supervised setting. I know a little about these, at least, because one of them was on my first paper route, and there was always a man at its door waiting to greet me (an aide on a night shift, Dad explained), which was unusual at 6 a.m., especially in the darkness of winter, as was the invariably lit main room, which I gradually came to understand was different from a regular living room that belonged to one family, but wasn't quite like a hotel lobby, either.

I love two things about Dad's office. One is his rubber plant, which grew so high that he positioned it in the corner, beneath the hole in his ceiling left by an unfinished maintenance project, through which it eventually grew into the office above. Decades from now, long after his job has been terminated in a restructuring, and even after his death, whenever I drive by his building I'll enjoy imagining the plant continuing to grow, its branches turned to curious angles to allow the light-seeking leaves to spread themselves against the dusty windowpanes, while elsewhere its roots break through plaster, entwine with and then short out the electrical wiring, briefly downing distant networks, as if in a children's story about the unstoppability of nature, maybe, or about how even rules-minded adults might find joy in occasionally colouring outside the lines.

The other thing I love about Dad's office is that it's on a high floor. As I finish my sandwich I go to stand for a moment, as I almost always do on these visits, by his south-facing window. I look to the right, through the bare treetops towards the fourteen-storey downtown hotel that is Pittsfield's tallest building, and out to the hills beyond. Then I take a breath and look down and across the street, onto the entrance of my high school, and when I see other kids not walking but running up the steps towards its heavy doors, I know that it's time for me to go.

SHENANDOAH

I'm ten, maybe, and in the back seat with my brother, who's twelve or so. Mom is driving the last miles between Pittsfield and Shenandoah, her hometown, in Pennsylvania's anthracite coal country, which occupies a neat, bowl-like indentation in some of the most continuously undulating countryside I'll ever encounter.

As an adult, Mom's hometown is the only place I'll think about – erroneously but contentedly – whenever I encounter a new recording of the song 'Shenandoah'. The town – more precisely a borough, of around 5,000 – is small but surprisingly dense, with the gaps between some homes narrow enough for a kid to try to climb spread-eagle between them, or no gap at all. It's unlike any other town I've seen, and it adds to my sense that while Dad may be foreign born, Mom comes from the more different place.

Tonight, as always, I'm looking forward to a particular view that comes near the end of the journey from Pittsfield when, as we crest the last hill, the yellow glow of the town will suddenly fill the windscreen, a perspective that is closely bound to all my imaginings of how a city, at night, might momentously appear. When I'm older I'll think that this pairing didn't make sense, so small is Shenandoah, and then I'll remember that, aside from Pittsfield, I had not yet seen a single other place so often from above and after dark.

In a few minutes we'll be at Grandmom's house, from which she sends cards, addressed in a script so fine that it seems more etched than inked, to 'Master Mark'. Her house, like her mining hometown, is like no other I'll ever know. Downstairs, coal is delivered through a dedicated low door at the front that leads directly to the basement, where it lands near corrugated, silvery washboards and a hand-cranked clothes wringer that my brother and I turn as we dare and double dare each other to place our fingers nearer.

Upstairs, the coal fuels a kitchen stove used for cooking – often the filled dumplings called pierogies (handmade by Grandmom, or those of Mrs T's, a Shenandoah-based brand) and the sausages known as kielbasa, all of which we cart back to Pittsfield by the bagful – but also for heating, and so, from October to April, Mom explains to us, the stove remains continuously lit.

In the dining room is a dark, polished cabinet on which a platter holds little rolls of Certs mints, Assorted Fruit flavour, that my brother and I sometimes steal; we reason that it's not only more lucrative but safer to steal an entire roll. Years later, a thickly iced cake – perhaps for a cousin's wedding – will be on this cabinet and I'll watch from the corner of the room as Grandmom runs her finger along a portion of its circumference, raises the icing she's collected to her lips, looks up to see me and makes a 'Shhh . . .' as she winks and walks away, in the only act of indulgence that I'll ever associate with her.

This town, I won't realise until I'm an adult, and then only gradually, is Mom's Pittsfield; and this small house must be the one that some part of her always lived in, as I'll recall how on subzero Berkshire mornings she would turn on our ordinary electric oven and crack its door open a few centimetres, to make the kitchen cosier than the rest of the house as she prepared our breakfast.

Now our car isn't far from Shenandoah. We pass under the line of lights – like Christmas all year, I always think – that runs along a coal conveyer that hangs above the road. Only seconds remain until we make it over the last hill, and I lean towards the front seat, where Mom is steering, in order not to miss the basin of Shenandoah's light as it opens to us. I try not to blink – the view lasts only a moment – and then I relax back in my seat as the engine's noise changes and we start downhill. The glow of Shenandoah turns into its individual streets, and finally into Mom's old one. As she eases to a stop I look up to see Grandmom standing on her porch, and both her hands are on its black metal railing, and her face is tight as she looks down at us, as if she has worried all evening about the length of our journey, and had stepped out again to scold the darkness in which we drove.

ZÜRICH

The German-made van in which my crew is travelling purrs through the bright afternoon, from the airport into the roughly mile-long Milchbuck Tunnel that runs south, under a hillside, and into the city.

After I first came through this tunnel, on my first trip to Zürich in my first year of flying short-haul European routes from London, I remarked to friends on how immaculate it appeared, almost as if it were a corridor in a warehouse or factory, and I joined colleagues in joking that it suggested more the chandeliered passage a Bond villain might construct than something a highway should roar through.

By any measure it's a fine public work. As we near its end, however, I'm braced for the familiar disappointment as we emerge, because when we do so we're already in the heart of Zürich. What I long for is what I often imagined as a kid: for a city that's been concealed by the hills that shelter it to appear suddenly; but of course, such a view would come most easily from the middle or the top of a hillside, and climbing is exactly what this magnificent tunnel has been built to spare us.

PITTSFIELD

I brake as our headlights scan over the trunks of ghostly birches on the outside of the bend. I'm driving with Desirae, a friend who lives a couple of blocks away from me.

This road up to the hill towns south-east of Pittsfield is fun – it begins mostly with curves – and it offers us the chance to leave our hometown, an experience we're keener than ever to practise in our final months there. It's 9 or 10 p.m., but this is our last year of high school and our parents no longer worry much about where we go, or when.

Desirae's house is on my paper route and she delivers the news whenever I cannot – while I was in Japan last summer, for example. We'll be friends long into our adult lives; three decades from now she'll be working in Islamabad when I first fly to the city as a pilot. On a quiet evening there we'll look at each other across her uneven table and shake our heads and smile: two old friends from the Berkshires, and our dinner of chicken and rice in her little apartment in a youthful capital near the foothills of the Himalayas.

As we drive up and out of Pittsfield we light a cigarette to pass between us, and so even though it's cold I lower the front windows in Dad's car and then I turn up the volume so that the song – about boys from one London district meeting girls from another – is louder than the wind. Neither of us has any idea what it means to be a West End girl, but we affirm all the same that Desirae is Pittsfield's version of one. Another song starts, titled 'It's a Sin'. I suspect that 'it' refers to being gay but I don't ask Desirae if she agrees; instead I make our usual joke about not stopping.

Then, as always, I turn Dad's car around and as we begin to glide down – that's how it feels, so steep are the roads from these practically centreless hill towns – we're both waiting for the spot at which we know we'll see Pittsfield's lights sifting through the dark fingertips of the bare trees. There aren't many lights, of course, and the forest, and the slopes and curves of the road, mean that even this view is always incomplete, but we love it all the same.

Now. Right where we expected it, night-Pittsfield isn't a revelation, nor would anyone mistake it for downtown Boston, let alone Manhattan. For a moment, however, we're high enough, far enough and late enough to see something of our city in light. I turn the music even higher as sparks from our second cigarette fly out the window, catch in the slipstream and corkscrew into the darkness behind us. Desirae lets out a whoop and reaches across the steering wheel to extract the cigarette from my fingers, and when almost all the lights of Pittsfield have disappeared beneath the treetops I know we're nearly home.

HONG KONG

The sun goes down as we start our descent on the arrival routing that pilots from Europe follow most often as they near Hong Kong.

This city was the destination of my first-ever flight as a 747 pilot, and each subsequent approach is a pleasing echo of that journey, the most thrilling of my life. Our local navigation charts depict radio beacons, and even now, after so many trips, their names – Tung Lung, Lung Kwu Chau, Siu Mo To – underline how far I am from home. One name, though, Cheung Chau, is surprising because it's familiar. For a few years in my early teens I corresponded with a pen pal, Lily, who lived on Cheung Chau island. Lily and I have long since lost touch, but I still remember her street's name and even her house number, as well as the tissue-thin pale blue aerogrammes that I would regularly post to an island of the city I'm bound for tonight.

Lily must be middle-aged now, like me. Probably she still lives in Hong Kong, perhaps even on Cheung Chau, I think, as the 747's navigation computers tune the beacon named for her home island and automatically decode the Morse code identifier it transmits.

Tonight it's humid and warm – typical for Hong Kong, Lily might have written as we described our hometowns to each other in our first letters – and clouds obscure most of the cityscape, but their denseness appears pure black rather than grey, thanks to the contrast formed by the city lights that appear nearly everywhere mist does not.

When I was young, my measure of a city's greatness was based on its skyline, as straightforwardly as if all the world's towers were bars on a graph. Indeed, as an adult, when I first travelled to a number of European cities, I was bewildered by the comparative absence of skyscrapers; it had never occurred to me that any city's inhabitants might embrace such a shortcoming.

Beloved or not, a skyline is a city's most obvious characteristic from a distance (while from within a city it's so often the observation deck on one tower that allows you to best appreciate the scene formed by the others). Even today, when I'm in the back of a taxi, or an airline crew bus, especially one entering a city that's new to me, I feel twitches of the muscle memory of lowering myself in my seat, as I did on drives with my parents into Boston or New York, in order to see the towers better as we got among them.

Which city has the greatest skyline? Certainly, my favourite individual skyscraper is the Boston one previously known as the John Hancock Tower. Designed by Henry Cobb, a partner of I. M. Pei, New England's tallest building is by day a dream of blue, cloud-mirroring glass; at night the contrast of its lit and dark offices forms a perpendicular puzzle of light. My parents often took my brother and me to visit its observation deck when we were kids – it was the Boston treat I asked for most often – and later, when I got my corporate job in Boston, my first Christmas office party took place atop it, a few weeks before I actually started work. It was a lavish, catered and casino-themed affair, and I concentrated on not talking about the jets bound for the airport we could see below us; instead I tried to memorise the names of everyone I met, and to do my best to appear relaxed in my new navy suit, fresh from the old-school men's shop in downtown Pittsfield.

Since I became a pilot, I've seen far more skylines than I ever dreamed I might, and I've also had the opportunity to watch them change. Dubai's skyline gets more magnificent by the month, it seems, and there's something about Miami's that always moves me from the cockpit; I once thought it was only the particularly clear view we're given of its seafront towers right after takeoff from the city's east-facing runways, but on a recent trip I was stunned by how much it had grown since I last saw it. Years ago, on a trip to Chicago, I chatted in a shop with a French couple, architects who had come to the city only to see its skyscrapers, and from them I understood that – from a professional or historical perspective – the skyline of Chicago might be the most interesting on Earth.

And then there is Hong Kong.

The city is home to some of the world's most densely populated urban spaces, and to an array of towers made all the more breathtaking at night by the slumbering shadows of the city's steep mountains and the heaving, light-braiding surface of its storied harbour.

One measure of skylinearity, to coin an awkward term, is the number of buildings that reach at least 150 meters – corresponding to a modern, spaciously ceilinged office building of around thirty-five storeys, or around half an Eiffel Tower. In April 2021, Hong Kong had 482 of these, far more than any rival, according to the Council on Tall Buildings and Urban Habitat. Shenzhen, which borders Hong Kong, was second, with 297; New York ranked third, with 290. Indeed, of the leading twenty cities on this list, nine are in China and only four – New York, Dubai, Chicago and Toronto – are not in East Asia.

Tonight, with only a few minutes remaining before touchdown in Hong Kong, we bank our 747 left and left again and now there'll be no further turns: we're lined up with a runway that we can't yet see.

Soon only one cloud, its matte-black silhouette as cleanly edged as a sail, is all that remains between us and the city it almost entirely obscures. We skim its tops, descend into the heart of its all-obscuring mist, and then, a moment later, as suddenly as if a switch has been thrown, we emerge beneath it. Anyone watching the world's lushest and highest electric forest sprawl beneath the left wing could be forgiven for concluding that there's no reason to imagine a greater one; while here in the cockpit there's hardly time to take in the cityscape before it fractures into the shimmer of its surrounding waters, and so we look where we must, straight ahead and across the waves, to the line of lights that guide us west to the airport island.

PITTSBURGH

We're over the upland forests of western New England, about 400 miles north-east of Pittsburgh, when the captain, in reference to our earlier conversation, asks me where, exactly, I am from: It's around here, right?

I look down at the navigation screen, then point across the cockpit, through the window to his left, in the direction of a cirrus-blanketed city we can't see. There, I say, with an emphasis on my hometown's second syllable: I'm from Pittsfield, about thirty miles that way.

I've never been to Pittsburgh before, but I've always felt connected to it. It's not that Mom is from Pennsylvania (her hometown is near the other side of the state). Rather, the kinship, and some confusion, too, derives from the similarity between its name and that of my hometown. Both were christened in honour of the British statesman William Pitt; both take their motto, *Benigno Numine*, By

Divine Providence (or By the Favour of Heaven), and the inspiration for their official seals, from his family's coat of arms.

This kinship is asymmetrical, of course; the population of metropolitan Pittsburgh is around fifty times that of Pittsfield proper. Indeed, Pittsburgh is so well known, and Pittsfield so not so, that some of Dad's Belgian family once believed we lived there. One cousin came to spend a summer with us when he was a teenager, and was visibly disappointed by the size of the city we took him to after we'd picked him up at New York's JFK Airport. When I first began to travel and had reason to tell people where I came from, I learned that almost no one had heard of Pittsfield and they sometimes assumed I'd said Pittsburgh, and if our interaction was likely to be brief, and I was too lazy to correct them, then I might enjoy imagining I was, in fact, from Pittsfield's much larger cousin.

A few minutes later it's time to start our descent. We touch down in Pittsburgh, park, complete our paperwork, and then start to find our way through the terminal to our bus – often the most confusing part of flying to a city for the first time, and one that we sometimes joke should be practised, as so much else is, in a simulator beforehand. I get a seat near the front and watch as the driver steers us past signs bearing the numbers – 376, 79 – of interstates that are new to me. It's early evening when we leave the airport, and I'm struck, as I had been throughout the approach and landing, by how green the surroundings are of this city made famous by its industry. Most of what I see around me is forest, and in this way, at least, nearing Pittsburgh is like nearing Pittsfield.

I've been excited for weeks about my visit here and so I've been reading up on the city. I was most struck to learn that Pittsburgh, in a foundation as auspicious as any, arose at the intersection of three rivers: the Ohio, the Allegheny, and the Monongahela.

Born near so much water, it seems no less inevitable that Pittsburgh has come to be known as the City of Bridges. There are at least

29 river crossings, and around 450 bridges of every sort (for comparison, New York and Hamburg each claim more than 2,000 bridges, while Venice is said to possess 400 or so canal crossings). Pittsburgh also has large hills, up which, from the middle of the nineteenth century, 'inclines', or cable railways, were constructed to pull cars of freight, coal and commuters along grades too steep for conventional trains.

As our bus rolls through my first Pittsburgh evening, I plan out tomorrow: I'll ride up one of the still-operational inclines, echoing my first-ever day in Hong Kong, when I rode the Peak Tram up Victoria Peak for a view of that distant but also mountainous and watery city; I'll walk back down to the Golden Triangle, the downtown core where two of the city's rivers meet to form its third; then, in the evening, I'll join the entire crew at a baseball game, the Pittsburgh Pirates versus the Chicago Cubs, where I'll recall with increasing urgency an instruction I'll have paused to read in a church earlier in the day: 'Pray for us and for the Steel City.'

But for now, as our bus continues and our surroundings grow more developed, there's still no sign of the metropolis that we'll see triumph tomorrow, 18–5. There's no baseball park, no skyscrapers, not one river – let alone three – and as the forests stream past I remember again my Belgian cousin en route to Pittsfield, and his confusion at the sight of so many trees so late in his journey.

Now, in the fast-falling light, I see a hillside ahead. I barely have time to consider how the road will go around it before we enter the Fort Pitt Tunnel. The forest on the hillside, aside from the tunnel's entrance, appeared all but unbroken, and I assume that beyond the tunnel's end there will be some miles yet until Pittsburgh's centre. Or that the tunnel will run into the city itself, the buildup unseen, and we'll emerge into the fully formed metropolis from below.

Less than a minute later I see the end of the tunnel approaching. It's hard to make sense of the illumination that lies beyond, and then I realise that the lights are those of skyscrapers; and that, rather than their bases, I'm staring at their middle or upper floors.

Since I was a teenager I've enjoyed imagining the most compelling ways a city might reveal itself, all at once, to those approaching it. Now, when I suddenly see how such a moment might work best, there's no time to fire up my phone's camera because the towers of Pittsburgh are glittering and tilting and so quickly drawing near that I let my phone fall to the seat as we sail out into a dusk transfigured by the city's light, over treetops and onto the upper deck of a yellow bridge that crosses high above one of the three rivers and then gently descends, when at last it must, to the streets below.

PITTSFIELD

Mark and I stop to pick up three sandwiches and two bags of cider doughnuts. Then we drive to the base of Bousquet Mountain, the alpine ski area near Pittsfield's airport. It's early September and here in the Berkshires, at least, the summer heat has broken; it's a clear, dry and windy day, and the upper reaches of the hills around us are lit by the first sparks of autumn.

My brother rarely comes to Pittsfield unless we're meeting. Today he'll come on his own – the second bag of cider doughnuts is for his wife, who's coaching basketball today – and we're lucky to have even him. He works in a bike shop and throughout the warmer months everyone wants new bikes, or repairs to old ones.

Mark and I get out and wander in the car park. In my pockets are a phone with a western Massachusetts area code, which I sought out long after I'd left the region, and a card for a Pittsfield-based bank account I've kept open since I was six or seven, when the bank, thanks to the popcorn vendor who parked his old-fashioned red wagon outside, was by far the best-known among Pittsfield's youngest savers; also in my pockets are a card that unlocks the gates of an airport car park in London, and a handful of coins from countries on three continents. As we wait for my brother we once again talk, half seriously, about spending our old age in the Berkshires, and I understand that I'm pulled, as I so often am, by three familiar desires: to be in Pittsfield, my first city; to live near it, but not quite in it; and to look back on Pittsfield from the sheltering anonymity of a megacity on the furthest side of my world.

My brother's car pulls up in a cloud of late-summer dust. Through the rear window I see spokes, wheels, a bright silver frame. Our hike, the athletic highlight of my week, is nothing to him in terms of exercise; after it he'll go for a long ride around much of Berkshire County. He loves bikes as much as I do planes (we're something like the Wright brothers, we joke). But he's also prone to grisly cycling-related injuries – a brake cable punctures his palm, a tumble from a mountainside trail exposes bone – and I always worry when I'm about to see him.

He seems okay, though, when he gets out of the car. We hug and then I offer him our can of insect repellent. Mosquitoes circle and veer – there hasn't been a hard frost yet – but under this Pittsfield mountain and the beacon that identifies its heights to nearby pilots, I sense something of autumn, and I stuff a hooded sweatshirt in my backpack in case I'm cold.

The three of us start to walk up Drifter, the most forgiving of the trails here. I skied a little when I was young, but never as well as the kids who earned the distinctive ski-patrol or high school team jackets, nor half as well as my brother. My memories of this mountain are mostly of other kids racing past, and of my brother slowing to shout guidance from behind the face masks and goggles that protected us from the most bitter Pittsfield nights.

We leave the ski run behind and follow freshly painted bright-blue rectangular blazes onto a newly cut trail into the woods. The direct light disappears, the trail steepens, the wind sighs through the canopy, and we come to the first of the rough stone stairways that have been cut into the mountainside where the slope of the trail would otherwise be too steep. We climb the stairs and walk on, through stands of maple, oak, shagbark hickory and beeches, and under a number of saplings that half fell in a recent storm and now lean above the trail, lodged in the slingshot-shaped forks of other trees at simultaneously pleasing and worrying angles.

We reach the base of an inclined clearing, marked by two almost conical cairns. We cross it and wind our way up the far side, to an overlook that faces south. It's not the most spectacular Berkshire view, but it's well framed, both by the trees in the foreground and by the wavelike contours of the land below.

Across the intervening bowlful of Berkshire sky we can see Monument Mountain, atop which Herman Melville sheltered from a thunderstorm in the company of Nathaniel Hawthorne in August 1850. A month later Melville bought a farm in Pittsfield, one with a great hearth against which he'd rest the harpoon he'd repurpose as a poker. Beyond and to the right of Monument Mountain is Mount Everett, its name once indistinguishable to me from that of Mount Everest, when I was small and I heard my parents planning a hike or a picnic. Somewhere far past it are the skyscrapers of New York, while above us and to our right, hidden by the ridge, stands the fire tower my brother and I sometimes hike up to on another trail. When we were kids you could climb not only to its base but all the way up it, to a view from an inland lighthouse that was briefly our own.

This is a decent view, but we think we know the way to a better one. We head back into the woods above the clearing, then make our way along the ridge, towards the top of the ski runs. We pass a telecom tower. I completed a portion of my flight training in Phoenix, Arizona, and on certain flights I was required to steer near the grove of masts atop South Mountain, which I liked because that is also the name of a hill in Pittsfield, not far from this one. The transmitters on that Phoenix peak were so powerful that music from commercial stations sometimes broke through into aviation frequencies, a reminder, as if one was needed as the ridge and its towers grew in the tiny aircraft's forward window, that it was time to turn away.

We pass the shed where the stretchers used to rescue injured skiers are stacked, and the ski patrol's warming cabin, and the rubble that's all that remains of an old chairlift's mountaintop bull wheel and terminal hut. As we walk further north, what Melville called the 'Most Excellent Majesty' of Mount Greylock rises, and a few dozen metres further Pittsfield itself emerges in the low between Greylock's massif and the hill we're on. It's around here that skiers immediately off the chairlift would first gain speed, and I exhale sharply as I recollect the bright sting of another season's winds, and the numbness that bloomed on whatever was exposed of my face.

We reach a rough wooden picnic table and sit on its weathered top, to escape any ticks in the grass, and to improve the view. I pass around our sandwiches. A little charred wood and ash are piled on the ground near the city side of this table. Someone built a fire here, at night, surely, and sat by its light and Pittsfield's; some evening we, too, could do that. I look to my brother, who's looking down to town; to Mark, who's so far from his own childhood home in the port city of Southampton; and out across Pittsfield as a small, silvery plane crosses the green, bound for the airport, just out of sight below us, where I took my first flying lessons in high school.

From here, as from the cockpit of an overflying airliner, the most distinctive feature of Pittsfield's cityscape is Building 100. An enormous, off-white, rectangular structure where electrical transformers were once assembled and tested, it's now the most prominent monument to the city's great age of manufacturing. From it I follow an unseen street, whose name is lost to me, west to a clutch of downtown steeples and the tall hotel, not far from my high school, where my senior prom was held.

I try but I can't see anything of the line made by either branch of the Housatonic, the river that Mark and I recently canoed on. Its environmental recovery remains the subject of frequent articles in the *Berkshire Eagle*, the newspaper that I once delivered and still subscribe to, though only online, so that sometimes, when I can't sleep in my blacked-out crew hotel room in Chennai or Beijing or Muscat, I dial it up on my phone and the glowing news from home lights a portion of my pillow.

I look north, to where the city's resurgence is embodied by a café that Mark and I have grown to love, and by various quirky businesses, including a clock-repair shop whose antiquated sign – to say nothing of its shelves of dusty cuckoo clocks – is like something from a bewildering dream. Not far away is a tavern that serves the best fries, and a thriving theatre company, and beyond it is the red-brick-and-concrete hospital where I was born, and where Mom passed away.

I take a doughnut – made with a dash of cider from the orchard on the far slope of this ridge, and quite a bit more than a dash of sugar and cinnamon from more distant places – and pass the bag to Mark and my brother. No one can eat just four, my brother and I often joke. Or I might say: these right here are the reason I come home.

I look out again and blink at the sea of green. I know the trick of these trees: their ability, in this season at least, and along angles like those of my gaze, to conceal whatever lies beneath them. Their upper branches hide so many of Pittsfield's smaller structures, including most of its homes, and give rise to the illusion that there is even less city than there is. I know this, but still I can't stop thinking: *there is so much green.* There is so much, and it's not hard to imagine what a little more rain, a few more minutes in the light of a more direct sun, or a further dusting of the right minerals might do: how we might then climb the mountain to find the forest whole again.

I got warm as we hiked, but now, almost motionless, and exposed to the wind as it gusts over this summit, I'm cold for what must be the first time in months. I think ahead to the first snow, and I imagine the silence it will bring, and how it, too, will hide the city when it falls.

I release Mark's hand as we start to gather our things. He and my brother are laughing about a scene in a show they both like, and as they climb down off the picnic table and start to walk, I reach into my backpack for my bunched-up sweatshirt. It takes me a moment to find its sleeves and in the wind I struggle to pull it on. Once I've done so, I open my eyes, and the city is briefly so bright that I raise my hand to shield them. Then I scramble off the sun-warmed table and look around for my husband and my brother. I jog through the weeds to catch them and together we descend.

CHAPTER 5

CITY OF GATES

London, San Francisco
and Jeddah

IMAGINE A LARGE CITY, in which only a few of its old gates remain. The best-preserved of these have been incorporated into larger and more recent structures, and so on the concourse of a train station, under the gleaming glass-and-steel vault of an atrium through which the lights of skyscrapers can be seen rising until they disappear into the clouds, you might find an ancient stone arch and a tower, with a plaque to identify them and explain, for example, their roles in a siege on which the city's story turned. Commuters and travellers have found that these ruins, which weather will never touch again, form a convenient meeting place amid the station's bustle, while children love to run along the recessed lights that show the wall's old path as it curved away from the gate and tower, across what's now the well-trafficked, nightly-polished marble floor of the train hall, as if an electrified version of the city's motto – which is, I like to imagine, similar to the most stirring fragment of Madrid's: *Mis muros de fuego son*, My walls are made of fire – has become real.

Let's say, also, that in the distant past the city's gates were closed at night, except for the most heavily guarded, which, therefore, over time, became known as the Midnight Gate. The Midnight Gate was dismantled along with the city walls at the start of the last century, but it survives in the name of a metro station, and a neighbourhood that's now one of the most desirable for young apartment hunters. Indeed, though the gate is gone, the district surrounding its former position is better known than ever, thanks to its name, which is so easily deployed – in poems, novels and songs, and in TV shows and films – to evoke both the round-the-clock vitality of the modern metropolis and the condition of an apprehensive or sleepless evening within it. Nevertheless, few train passengers will think of the name's origin when they hear: 'The next station is Midnight Gate. The doors on the right side will open.'

If you're a motorist, meanwhile, using the screen of your smartphone to navigate into town, you might hear 'Pass the Midnight Gate' followed by 'then continue on . . .' and the name of the road that will carry you in. As you approach, the image of the long-gone gate will appear, becoming larger and larger until it flies off to the left, right and top of the screen as you pass over the point that still bears its name. Beyond, the colour of the road on your screen will change, from grey to green, to indicate that this is the old city, the first city, and that if its walls still stood you would now be safe within them.

I'm running on a road outside Pittsfield that climbs nearly straight up a densely forested hill. A deer runs off, a family of turkeys approaches the lawn of the last house, and a dark something or other – a raccoon? a porcupine? – parallels my path and rustles through the remains of last year's fallen leaves.

It's high summer and I'm soaked in sweat. I run up and on. Not long after I cross the broken line where the asphalt road crumbles into a dirt one I reach the top of the hill, where there are two gates. The gate on the left bars vehicles from a road that leads down to a reservoir, but it's easy enough to follow the little path – a smile path, they're sometimes called, thanks to their parenthetical shape – that the steps of others have worn around it. The gate on the right lies across what was once a rough road, and which, over the years since its maintenance ceased, has grown practically indistinguishable from any other Berkshire forest trail.

I place my hand on the right-hand gate. I know that in a moment, several mosquitoes will find me. I know I won't stay long but it feels good to rest on the cool metal bars. My pulse thrums in my fingers as they press. This couldn't be more unlike the city gates I've seen on my recent work trip to Jeddah, yet the same noun somehow covers both, and I calculate what time it is on the western coast of Saudi Arabia, and consider how much hotter it must be there, even in the city's smallest hours. I think, as well, of the wildlife reserve that this trail leads to, and of Mr Oltsch, the high school biology teacher who taught us the degree to which life depends on cell membranes or walls for much of what matters most: the holding off of entropy and invaders; but regulated access for raw materials, energy and signals.

I lean a little more into the coolness of the gate and look over to the lock that bolts it across this path. If I had to choose my three favourite city gate-names, I would probably pick these from Jeddah, London and Copenhagen: the Mecca Gate, Moorgate and Nørreport. The gate in front of me, meanwhile, is surely unnamed, I think, as I let go of its crossbar, wipe the hand it's chilled across my forehead, and turn. From here the trees are mostly below me, and I blink to change them all to towers as I start to run down.

LONDON

On the Northern Line, on my way to King's Cross, I hold my bags between my legs so that I can free my hands and raise my fingers to my ears as the train approaches the first of the two worst screeches in the tunnel between Camden Town and Euston stations.

I close my eyes and I imagine a city whose trains do not make noises like these. I open them again and gaze across the carriage at the Northern Line map and at two names on it, each a welcome euphonic distraction: Highgate and Moorgate.

When I was very young and I drew maps of my imaginary city, its edges were often rough or indistinct. As I grew older, they became clearer and more prominent, perhaps as I first learned about the existence and historical importance of walled cities. And perhaps, as I unquestioningly continued to locate all my hopes for a chance to be myself more easily in distant cities, I began to appreciate that a place that could offer such protection would itself need protecting.

In *Invisible Cities,* Calvino writes: 'What line separates the inside from the outside, the rumble of wheels from the howl of wolves?' The walls and gates of cities must have arisen from pressures as fundamental as those that drove the evolution of cells. But as cities grew – and survived, thanks in part to their ramparts, into ages in which sieges and invasions were receding concerns – they have tended to take down their walls. The stones might have been useful for other structures, while the paths of demolished walls often became roads, especially ring roads.

Today, when the gates or walls of most cities are fragmented artefacts, or gone entirely, the ancient promise of safety within a city's boundaries may live on, and take forms as varied as we are. And so archetypal are gates that notions of them may affect us where few or no examples remain, and even where they have never been built. (The mayors of many American cities that have never been walled, for example, may bestow keys that open nothing on those they wish to thank or acclaim.) For me, the sense of both greatness and protection that gates conjure remains so beguiling that whenever I see a map of a city, especially those European and Asian ones old enough to have needed walls, my eyes are drawn to gate-names first, if they're in English, or if there's a fragment of the language that I can recognise: *porte; puerta; tor*; or, in Simplified Chinese 门, and in Japanese 門, the characters that signify what they resemble.

In this manner, in so many cities, gates live on in names of neighbourhoods, streets, churches and stations, each an indication of where a portal – perhaps to an older and smaller incarnation of the current metropolis, or to a mere castle or palace within it – no longer stands. Not all London gate-names are equal, though, I think, as the carriage lurches and howls and I imagine sparks swirling up from the wheels and rails into the darkness that our train disorders. Moorgate is particularly striking, due to the eeriness I associate – thanks to Sherlock Holmes – with moors, and also, surely, to the engagingly straightforward name of the street, London Wall, that runs so near to Moorgate Station. Ludgate is also a fine London gate-name, as are Aldersgate and Cripplegate, which travellers will encounter near the equally fortification-evoking Barbican.

London once had a Newgate, as did Newcastle; and as Tunis, Cairo and Jerusalem still do. Aside from Moorgate I like the London name Bishopsgate best, partly because of the religious majesty it embodies, but mostly because it's now also the name of a thoroughfare, permitting modern addresses such as '78 Bishopsgate', which (like those on Piccadilly, Whitehall, or the Strand) are all the statelier to me for not having 'street' or 'avenue' appended. And I love London's gate-names all the more when they appear alongside 'without', used in its otherwise antique sense of 'outside', such as in St Botolph-without-Bishopsgate, a church named for a patron saint of wayfarers as well as for an ancient gate to this capital.

At King's Cross I alight and wait for a Circle Line train. This line has three gate-names: Moorgate, Aldgate and Notting Hill Gate, which, like Highgate, is named for a tollgate, not for a passage through London's former walls.

I was first transfixed by the name of King's Cross from Pittsfield, when I heard a Pet Shop Boys song about the station and its neighbourhood. While in another of their songs I heard another station name – the Finland Station, not in Finland, but in St Petersburg, I learned – which lodged even more deeply in my mind. I loved the idea of naming one place for another, and I was reminded of the confusion and wonder once induced in me by the name of New York's Pennsylvania Station, which seemed to reference a place so different from the city it allowed us to enter.

The style of naming one place for another has long proved popular for gate-names, too. Aurangabad, India's 'City of Gates', is said once to have had fifty-two, and one that still stands is named for Delhi, the distant city it faces. Both Delhi and Lahore have a gate named for Kashmir, each opening in the direction of that region; Jerusalem has its Damascus Gate and its Jaffa Gate. Sometimes the gates of two cities have mirrored one another: on Hamburg's transport map I can ponder the position of the station named for the city's Berlin Gate, while Berlin, in turn, once had a Hamburg Gate.

In Ghent a Bruges Gate once stood, while in Bruges, where Dad studied, a Ghent Gate still does.

Traditionally, many cities closed their gates at night, a precaution that calls to mind why walls were first needed, and what the darkness beyond them once meant. Copenhagen's Nørreport, for example, was once the sole gate left open after midnight, when a traveller could only enter the city upon paying a fee to the watchman. In some eras Jeddah's gates would close at sunset, except the Customs Gate, which would stay open one hour later, and the Mecca Gate, which would stay open for two; during Ramadan, however, when many daylight activities are restricted, both would remain open until midnight. Seoul's gates (six examples of which still stand, along with much of the city's wall, to which an entire marvelous museum is devoted) were closed during the nightly curfew; their opening and closing were announced by the ringing of a bell that's now struck on New Year's Eve, as if to open the coming year.

My Circle Line train nears Paddington Station and I, along with almost everyone else encumbered by luggage, prepare to disembark. I pull my bag upstairs and make my way to platform 7. I step onto the train to Heathrow, then pause, turn around and look up into the internal sky of the London portal I know best. The haziness in the upper reaches of what's far too grand to refer to as the 'train shed' has disappeared, along with most of the old diesel trains, but on a foggy morning, or if, at night, you squint, it's easy enough to recall it.

The doors of the carriage *beep-beep-beep* and start to close. I stow my bags and find a window seat on the right-hand side of the train. Among the businesspeople and the young travellers with backpacks, I spot someone wearing a uniform identical to mine. He's no one I know, but still, I return his hardly perceptible nod. Then I turn away towards the window, where the clarity of my reflection startles me, and then helps me to straighten my tie as the train rolls out of the city.

SAN FRANCISCO

I wander north-west towards Golden Gate Park. I still have a few flyers and so every few blocks, whenever I pass a group of homeless people in a park or talking around a bench, I stop to chat and hand them one.

The explorer John C. Frémont dubbed the strait that leads into San Francisco Bay the Chrysopylae, the Golden Gate, to evoke the Chrysoceras, the Golden Horn – the name the Greeks gave to the waterway at the heart of Byzantium. (Perhaps he also knew of Constantinople's Golden Gate, which opened onto the Via Egnatia, the great road that led in the direction of Rome.)

On some early maps and documents, Frémont's English translation of Chrysopylae appears secondarily, or parenthetically, as if he intended a future in which we would call the crossing the Chrysopylae Bridge. Whether in Greek or English, however, the name 'Golden Gate' must be hard to improve on. And yesterday, as our 747 banked above the dusty-vermilion towers of the eponymous span, which rise from the whitecaps torn from the steel water by the same blustery west wind that our navigation computers had had to account for in order to calculate the heading that would guide us between successive waypoints, it occurred to me once again that there may be no finer natural gateway to a city anywhere in the world.

When I was young, in my mind I designated other kids as happy or sad, though *extrovert* and *introvert* might have been more precise words for what I meant. Henry, who lived a few streets from me and who, as a teenager, became close to the Berkshire gang, was both happy and an extrovert, with an infectious laugh and a gentleness that's obvious in his smile in the photo on the flyers. He had a fun time in high school, which is to say he got into trouble now and then, but he was – everyone, even the teachers and school officials he sometimes frustrated, would agree – a good kid. After university Henry fell in love with a young woman and moved to San Francisco, where he got a job working with computers.

A few years later, though, his life began to fall apart, in part because of drug abuse. He lost his job and gave away his possessions. His relationship ended. Soon he was homeless. Meanwhile, Henry's mother and brother tried to guide him into accommodation and treatment, but he would not be persuaded.

My father had always been particularly fond of Henry, and in 2004, only days before Christmas, he flew out to San Francisco to look for him. It was the sole time Dad used the discounted standby tickets that I, a newly employed pilot, could offer him. Once there, Dad, aged seventy-three, spent a week or so asking about Henry in shelters and community centres; in parks; and on the street, especially in the Castro, where Henry had often hung out. Eventually Dad found him at a free meal service at the Metropolitan Community Church. In the following days they went for bagels, to a Chinese restaurant and to a public library. At night Henry slept on a cot in Dad's room in a motel near the edge of Mission Dolores. Dad described their last meal together in his diary:

> For supper he chose the Bombay Indian Restaurant at 2217 Market Street. The waiter took two more pictures of the two of us and with many hugs and thank-yous, we said goodbye.
>
> It was a cold evening. We had seen empty cardboard boxes put out by the merchants and he was going to put a few layers of the corrugated stuff under his sleeping gear to keep the ground chill out. He no longer had a sleeping bag or a tent but in his duffel bag he had a blanket and more warm clothing. I told him not to forget the black bag with his empty soda cans, exchangeable for money, that he had hidden in the bushes the day before. He knew exactly where he had left it. I walked towards the motel and he disappeared in the opposite direction.

Three months later, Dad, aged seventy-four and otherwise in good health, died from a stroke that occurred after a routine stent placement procedure. Two years after his death I began to fly the 747 and to visit San Francisco regularly, a city I then barely knew, but whose promise, especially for gay folks, had long appealed to me. Over the years, however, Henry's life has reminded me of what else it can mean to lose yourself in a city so far from your first one; and often, as I laughed with colleagues en route to dinner after our flight, I'd be shaken to realise how easily I might forget to examine the faces of the younger homeless men we passed. On other trips, I'd post flyers, or look for Henry in shelters, parks, or on the street, but I was never as good at this as Dad was, and years would pass before I finally found him.

JEDDAH

I put down my cup of tea and toggle the transmit switch. Good night, Athens, I answer, followed by the new frequency that the last Greek controller on this route has given us. I tap the new frequency into the keypad and speak again: Cairo, Cairo, good evening.

London to Jeddah is always an overnight flight for me, which can make it hard to keep in mind – as cups of tea, invisible aerial borders and midnight come and go – that it's one of the shortest routes a London-based pilot of wide-body airliners might fly. The handover from Greek to Egyptian controllers takes place when Crete is barely behind us and the lights of vessels off Alexandria are almost in sight, and from the cockpit so close do these civilisations appear, one to the other, that I'm no longer surprised by all the Greek terms – papyrus, hieroglyph, sarcophagus, pyramid, even – we rely on to speak of Egyptian antiquity.

Egypt itself now turns into view, in the illuminated form of the north-flowing Nile's broad delta here, which – at 1 a.m., 2 a.m. – shines up in the diffuse glow of settlements that pour out in the shape of a fan. As we pass over Alexandria and continue south, following the river's flow in reverse, this cone of light narrows with the water, until the dense glow of Cairo floods across the darkness. Leaving the capital behind, life clings to the unseen Nile ever more tightly, and it grows all too easy for an aerial observer to mistake the curve of illuminated communities below for the river itself.

Soon afterwards we pass near Luxor – formerly Thebes, or Hundred-Gated Thebes, to distinguish it, as Homer did, from Thebes of the Seven Gates, in mainland Greece – and then we turn more sharply east, towards Egypt's Red Sea coast. And now, while still in Egyptian airspace, we start our descent for Jeddah. The thinnest edge of the eastern sky begins to lighten, while in the starry blackness straight above there's no hint yet of the coming day. Towards the slowly colouring horizon we race out over the water, steering – sometimes, on a cloudless night, it's as simple as this – to the lights on the far shore.

The first aircraft to bring Mecca-bound pilgrims to Jeddah touched down in 1938, according to Angelo Pesce, the historian and author of *Jiddah: Portrait of an Arabian City*. That aeroplane was named *Buraq*, Lightning, after the winged, horse-like creature said to have transported Muhammad to Jerusalem. In our unnamed jet we complete our crossing of the Red Sea and bank north over the still-quiet streets. The runways here are aligned not only with the wind but also with the coastline, and as we descend the city's seafront flows past us in the left-side cockpit window. To our right is Mecca, and the rest of Arabia, and the point in the mountains from which the sun is about to rise.

Jeddah, with around four million inhabitants, is Saudi Arabia's second-largest city. It's the country's commercial centre, and is said to exhibit an outgoing coastal cosmopolitanism that contrasts with staid Riyadh, the capital, which lies around 500 miles inland from Jeddah – a distance comparable to that between Detroit and New York.

Over the centuries its name has taken many Romanised forms: Jeddah, Jiddah, Jedda, Gidá, Gedda, Jidda, Djeddah, Djuddah, Juddah, Djudda, or Zida. Sometimes Dsjidda or Judá. Even Guida, Grida, or Zidem. Such diversity draws attention to Jeddah's age and importance: foreigners have long had reason to speak the city's name, and to try to write it.

The name is commonly said to derive from the Arabic word for grandmother, an etymology entwined with associations between Jeddah and Eve that date at least to the tenth century, and that were centred on the tomb, located north-east of the city, that was said to be her resting place. There are other explanations for the city's name, however. In the eleventh century, the Arab geographer al-Bakri wrote that 'the *juddah* of a sea or a river is that part of the land adjacent to it', while Pesce collects other possible meanings recorded by travellers over the ages, including *'way, road,* this city being the road leading to the House of God', that is, to Mecca. Or the city's name might mean 'rich', a 'plain wanting water', or 'seashore', all of which ring accurately, if less evocatively, in the ear of the modern visitor.

The early history of Jeddah is lost, though in its first centuries, whenever they were, it surely had a population of only a few hundred people – 'at best a fishermen's hamlet', in the words of Pesce. In the second century AD, Ptolemy did not mention Jeddah, but he did note the two settlements we now know as Mecca, about 50 miles to the east, and Medina (meaning simply 'city', it's in fact a shorthand for a formal name that means 'the Luminous City'), about 250 miles to the north.

Settlers from Persia are credited with the construction of Jeddah's first walls, in the sixth century, and therefore the city's first gates. Uthman ibn Affan, Muhammad's son-in-law and the third caliph to rule after his death in Medina in 632, sought a port for Mecca that would offer more security from pirates than the landing south of Jeddah then in use. Having bathed in the sea here, and so enjoyed it that he invited 'his followers to join him', he designated the fledgling city the official port of Mecca. Since then Jeddah has served as a point of transit for those for whom a journey to Mecca required a ship; and there grew to be many such pilgrims as the Muslim world expanded, an expansion furthered in part by the thriving commercial routes that, in turn, made a long-distance pilgrimage a reasonable proposition.

In the early sixteenth century, the rise of Portuguese military and commercial power in the Indian Ocean, enabled by the newly opened route around southern Africa, threatened not only Jeddah's trading profits but the city itself. Jeddah, therefore, had reason to rebuild its walls, and did so not long before Portugal's first attempt to sack the city, in April 1517. In the same era Jeddah, like Egypt and much of the Red Sea, fell under the Ottoman Empire's formal control (in which it mostly would remain, in one form or another, until the days of Lawrence of Arabia and the foundation of the modern Saudi state in the twentieth century). From the seventeenth century the subsequent rise of the Netherlands and England as maritime powers further diminished its trading fortunes. Nevertheless, in the eighteenth century – when Jeddah's walls had so decayed that in places they could be ridden over on horseback – the British East India Company maintained a warehouse here, and in the nineteenth century, according to a guide written for the company's employees, the merchandise here included cardamom, turmeric, musk, quicksilver, sandalwood and saltpetre.

For modern visitors, also, Jeddah has much to offer. The city has many outdoor sculptures, including works by Mustafa Senbel, Henry Moore and Joan Miró. It's home to the world's tallest fountain, which fires water more than 300 metres into the sky, at a speed of hundreds of miles per hour, forming, at night, a brilliantly lit plume that drifts across the darkness as it tumbles back down to the sea.

From beneath the great fountain the city spreads its long, skyscraper-adorned arms along the shore of the Red Sea. Jeddah's Corniche – a term that generally refers to a coastal road cut into the edge of a cliff, but which many Gulf cities use to describe a seafront promenade – is among my favourites in all of Arabia. Its most appealing segments are lined with cycle paths; soaring white sun shields that, like the pilgrim terminal at the airport, evoke the lines of both sails and desert tents; and food stands that crowd the edges of the generously irrigated greenery on which large, multigenerational family groups sprawl to picnic after sunset.

In addition to 'The Bride of the Red Sea', Jeddah was also known as 'The Town of the Consuls', or 'The Town of Consulates', a reference to the increasing attention foreigners gave the city and region, and to the privileges that they sometimes enjoyed here, even while much of the rest of Arabia remained a difficult place for outsiders to travel through.

Jeddah's most common nickname, however, is also, to me, its most distinctive: 'The Gate to Mecca'.

Above all, it's unusual to hear one city so candidly clothe itself in the holiness and distinction of another. More prosaically, Jeddah stands at two natural gateways. Long, jagged reefs, ideal for slicing open the hulls of vessels, line much of the Red Sea's coast, as did, in former times, bandits who might rob or murder the survivors of any shipwreck who managed to make it to shore. Nevertheless, an opening – difficult to find and to navigate except by local pilots – leads through the reefs to the safety of Jeddah's harbour. Ibn Jubayr, a Valencia-born Muslim who was caught in a storm off Jeddah on his way to Mecca in the 1180s, recorded his admiration and gratitude for the sailors who 'would enter the narrow channels and manage their way through them as a cavalier manages a horse that is light on the bridle and tractable'.

The second gateway is on land: over millennia, erosion through the mountains that rise to the east has carved a path from Mecca down to the sea. It seems foreordained that a city would rise where these two gates in the sea and the mountains align; and that the city would be built with stones quarried from the ancestors of those same reefs.

SAN FRANCISCO

As I steer my California-plated rental car north across the Golden Gate Bridge, I enjoy the thought that to other motorists I might appear to live here; they might assume that I'm a Californian who has crossed this bridge a thousand times or more, and that I'm therefore as unsurprised as they are to find the near tower draped in fog, while its sibling stands clear.

Yesterday, I arrived on my latest 747 trip to San Francisco. This morning, I'm on my way to see Henry, who I've learned is in a psychiatric hospital north of the city. His mother reminded me that today is his birthday, so after I picked up the car I got a couple of ridiculously large and brightly decorated cupcakes from a supermarket bakery.

The morning light is canary yellow and the temperature is in the high teens as I emerge from the mist. It's above 30 as I park at the hospital. I give my name. I reach into my wallet to retrieve my driver's licence, and catch sight of the top of the laminated card with the phone number that as a pilot I can call free of charge, from any city on Earth, to speak with a doctor – a privilege that, thanks to its global effectiveness, including in places where quality medical care is inaccessible to many residents, is not only more reassuring but also more telling than any other I know. I once had to call this number from Mexico City, and an hour or so later, though it was the middle of the night, a specialist who also held an academic position at a medical school knocked on the door of my hotel room. He wore a full, dark suit, carried an old-fashioned medical bag, and solemnly handed me his card.

I show my driver's licence to the guard. He notes its details and goes away, then returns to say that Henry doesn't want to see me. I've come a long way, I tell him, and I ask if in his experience it's worth waiting a while and asking Henry again. It's up to him, says the guard with a shrug, as if to say, Who else would it be up to? I want to cry and I wish, more strongly than I have in a long time, that Dad was here. Dad would know what to say and do next.

After a moment I ask the guard if I can leave the cakes with him to give to Henry. Not allowed, he says. I look down at the oversized cupcakes, unmarred in their rigid and perfectly clear plastic boxes. I ask the guard if he would like them. I can't take those, he says, suddenly sitting up straighter, and so I carry them back out into the day's heat. I place them next to me on the passenger seat and then find my way back to the highway, the bridge and the city.

JEDDAH

My phone's alarm fills my hotel room. I turn it off, take out my earplugs and walk across the room towards the light breaking onto the carpet through the folds in the bottom edge of the curtains.

I pull them back and stare at the windows and the glass door that leads to my small balcony. They're dripping wet and for a moment I blink and think: *It rained? Here in Jeddah, it rained?* It's not rain, though, but condensation: so heavily cooled is the hotel, and so humid the air outside, that – like a can of soda when you take it out of the refrigerator on a summer afternoon – the building collects condensation. The droplets run down in increasingly thick streams, until, by the time they reach the lower floors, the effect on the windows is like that of rain.

The climate crisis is so urgent that it can be hard to remember that some places, though they are growing hotter, have always been, in the traveller al-Maqdisi's laconic tenth-century description of Jeddah, 'very hot'. In high summer, Jeddah's heat reminds me of those August moments in New York when you might wince or raise your hand to shield your face as you walk past the air-conditioning outlet of a hulking, right-up-against-the-pavement building; only in Jeddah it can seem that the entire metropolis is subject to that same hair-dryer-like blast.

As well as the heat, another reason for me to linger indoors today is that it is the middle of Ramadan, and so the meal I'd like to have out in the city must wait until after sunset. I go to the gym – where I realise that no one on the adjacent treadmills is even drinking water – and then I return to my room to read and to write a little. After a while, I stand, stretch and walk out onto the narrow balcony.

My room faces east, away from the seafront and the towers – mostly other hotels – that rise along it. The view is dominated by white, beige and rust-coloured low-rise buildings, and by minarets, a communications tower, a mall, palm trees and golden-brown mountains. If I squint a little and set aside the humidity and almost all the minarets, it could be Phoenix.

The Mecca pointer on the desk reminds me of the waypoint named ISLAM in our aircraft flight management computers, the one we can dial up on the far side of the world when a passenger asks the cabin crew for the direction in which to pray. Today, in Jeddah, I'm as close as I've ever been to the city itself. Dusk won't be long now, I think, and as the peaks between this city and Mecca turn to rose and crimson I head downstairs and walk out into the street.

The Renaissance scholar Nicholas of Cusa, in a kind of thought experiment on the nature of perception and creation, described how we might each construct a world entirely within our imaginations, using only the information that we gather through our senses, which he likened to the gates of a city: 'The cosmographer is a perfect living being with senses and intellect, and his inner city has five gates, namely the senses. The messengers of the whole world enter these gates, and they bring messages of the world's disposition.'

Five senses, five gates. In 1050, there were two gates to Jeddah, according to the Persian writer and traveller Nasir Khusraw: 'one towards the east and Makkah and the other towards the west and the sea' – surely the minimum for a port that also served a holy city in the interior. In the thirteenth century the Damascus-born geographer Ibn al-Mujawir counted four; in the late sixteenth century, an African enslaved by the Portuguese recorded three; an 1851 Ottoman map depicts seven; and Laila al-Juhani, a Saudi novelist, recently wrote of nine – the Mecca, Yemen and New Gates, and six further city gates that give onto the sea – in her novel *Barren Paradise*:

> You know already that the things we love have greater power to bewitch us; but doubt spurs us to walk far, to run sometimes, and you've run through the alleys of Jeddah to the point of love. And now here you are at the edge of the sea. . . . Swim out just a little way from the beach, from Jeddah and her nine gates, each guarded by two sentries who ask every comer for the password. Each gate has a password; sea, open your waves, clouds, open your eyes. Jeddah, open your gates.

Darkness falls as I reach the outskirts of Jeddah's old town. The air cools, prayer calls echo and at the traffic lights smiling boys and young men run up to the cars and hand out loosely tied clear plastic bags containing the traditional fast-breaking gifts of dates and water. Perhaps because I'm so obviously a visitor, I'm offered more of these than I can hold and, hungry after my run, I devour the sticky dates, amazed as always that something so natural can be so sweet.

Outside a mosque hundreds of men are sitting on the ground, eating, drinking water and laughing. And soon, along the side of a busy, multi-laned road, I come to a gate. It's a large and formidable-looking stone fortification that's suggestive, to me, of a slice of a curtain wall around a castle. It's formed of two rounded bastions, topped with loopholed parapets, on either side of a lancet arch that forms an entrance perhaps seven metres high. I walk through the gate and then I cross the road to the dirt-surfaced portion of a large traffic island, where reconstructed fragments of Jeddah's wall stand beneath palm trees and bright lights. I ask a passerby to take a photograph of me, and then I thank him and walk on.

The district I now enter, in which only one out of every hundred Jeddah inhabitants now resides, is called Old Jeddah or the Old Town in English, and in Arabic, simply, Al Balad, the Town. It forms a startling anachronism within the modern, highway-framed metropolis, as if the cupped hands of one era are unsure of what to do with the relics they hold of another. Indeed, its labyrinthine layout still largely adheres to a pattern that dates at least to the sixteenth century, and that reflects, perhaps above all, the severity of the city's climate. Streets – many of which, like the runways at Jeddah's airport, are aligned with the north-west direction of the predominant wind – are narrow enough to help shield residents from the sun, while the upper floors of the tall houses along them could catch any breeze, which, along with the difference in temperatures between the floors, is said to induce a comforting draft through the houses.

The minaret of Jeddah's al-Shafi'i Mosque is estimated to be 900 years old, and the city's oldest building is said to be a warehouse that dates from the 1200s. The most famous structures of the old city, however, are its hundreds of nineteenth-century *roshan* tower houses, named for the city's distinctive take on a bay window that is common in the Middle East. These ornate structures – carved from hardwoods that were imported, as was all timber here, and selected for their resilience to humidity, heat and insects – extend out over the street, expanding the living and sleeping areas of the homes, and allowing for ventilation while preserving privacy. In Jeddah, one floor's roshan may connect with the next, forming something like an entire new façade, one whitewashed or painted in pastels, and featuring carvings that often reflect Asian traditions brought to Jeddah by generations of traders and, of course, pilgrims.

As I pass through the gate the lights of the shops, opening now for the evening's trade, don't reach high onto these darkened buildings, and I ask myself how it is that so much of Old Jeddah has survived the waves of wealth and planning that have overwritten the histories of so many Gulf settlements. Now, in this era in which many of these same Gulf cities are elaborately showcasing what remains of their pre-oil past, much of Old Jeddah appears unpolished and ungentrified. Shops and stands selling groceries and cheap plastic wares jostle cheek by jowl with mosques, traditional cafés and houses that appear to be only hours away from collapse. Cats chase one another through the shadows of seemingly abandoned construction sites as I turn from a poorly lit alley into a lane too narrow for a car, and then onto a crowded and slightly brighter street that leads me beneath neon signs and strings of multicoloured bunting, and past a sequence of ornately carved sky-blue teak doors. Jeddah's original wall may be gone, but the old town still feels like a self-contained world.

I come by accident, the only way I reach anywhere in Old Jeddah, it seems, to the western edge of the old city, and to Bab al-Furda, the Port Gate, which despite its name stands not by the sea – such is the scale of the modern city's westward reclamation and expansion – but in a neighbourhood dominated by jewellery, watch and perfume stores, and several shopping malls. The gate is a four-legged, vertically oriented stone rectangle with a semicircular arch cut through it. Tastefully spotlit, and with a pedestrian crossing leading right into it, it seems an entirely ceremonial rather than a military construction, one designed only to conjure the majesty of the boundary that its previous incarnations helped to command. In front of it are signs similar to those I've seen on a hundred Massachusetts crossings; they announce in stern English, but not in Arabic, that 'state law' requires vehicles to stop for pedestrians.

I send a few photos of gates to Mark. Having grown up in Southampton – from where John Winthrop and his fellow Pilgrims set off to cross the sea and become 'as a citty upon a hill' – notions of walls and gates are scattered across the landscape of his childhood. The bus that Mark and his brother took as kids to get home from the centre of Southampton left from a stop near remnants of their city's walls, and within sight of the twelfth-century Bargate. Mark's mum, Jean, would always distinguish between Above Bar, the street that is home to the shops she liked best, and the area she called Below Bar, south of the gate, within the path of the old wall, and on the way to the ruins of that port city's Watergate.

I turn from Jeddah's Port Gate back into the old city. Henry Rooke, a British major who visited in the late eighteenth century, wrote about Jeddah's 'always full' coffeehouses, and described 'the common people there drinking their dish of coffee together, as ours would their pot of beer at an alehouse'. At a café I order a karak tea, made here with condensed milk, cardamom, cinnamon and cloves. There is Zamzam water for sale, which is collected from a well in Mecca and is a traditional present brought home by pilgrims. The man behind the counter insists I accept a bottle as a gift, and we get to talking.

Like many who live in the old town, he's not Saudi-born; rather, he's a long-term immigrant from Nubia, in southern Egypt. I don't learn if he arrived on pilgrimage and stayed, but he would hardly be the first to do so; by one reckoning most inhabitants of Jeddah are the descendants of pilgrims or traders who arrived and never left. He asks why I'm in Jeddah. I tell him I'm a pilot, and that I flew from London and crossed over his home region in Egypt, in fact, the previous night. He doesn't want to discuss aeroplanes or Nubia, however. He assumes I am both English and a sports fan and wants to talk about the cricket and about Manchester United.

I take my tea into the café's seating area. I find a table, set my bag down on it and walk to the front of the room. I read a framed copy of a 1926 article from a French magazine, whose author describes the delicate architecture of Jeddah (*la Ville de la Grand'Mère*, the City of Grandmother) as unstained by modern or European constructions, but also sadly lacking in grand public monuments, such as the fountains *qui sont la gloire du Caire ou de Damas*, which are the glory of Cairo and Damascus. A glass case along the wall holds an old telephone, oil lamps and a Koran that I'm told is 600 years old. I buy a few of the postcards on a stand only because in the course of my several dozen visits to Saudi Arabia, they are the only ones I have ever seen for sale.

On the far wall of the seating area is an annotated aerial black-and-white photograph, from around 1940, in which the final incarnation of Jeddah's city wall still stands. Also visible on it are the Medina Gate, several mosques, a prison, seawater condensers, the Egyptian Legation, the British Legation and the Bab al-Jadid, the New Gate, which was built in the early twentieth century to allow cars into the city for the first time – indeed, inside the city can be seen at least one vehicle.

In the photograph – despite the car, and the perspective on the city that only an aeroplane could have offered – Jeddah appears to be ancient, and little more than a village, or, given the wall that dominates the view, a castle, protecting its inhabitants from their seaborne enemies and the desolation of the desert. Indeed, it's not hard to pair this image with the earliest known drawing of the city, by a sixteenth-century Portuguese scrivener who accompanied the city's would-be destroyers. In this drawing the prominent wall surrounds a dense semicircle of structures that constitute the entirety of the settlement. *Judá* is written in the drawing's top-left corner; the

Portuguese fleet, some of its vessels under sail and others under oar, masses offshore. What's portrayed is so elemental, so archetypal, that the drawing suggests, as Calvino might, that there has only ever been one city, whatever the names or structures we may know it by in the real world; it suggests, too, that a fastness on which so much depends must once have endured odds like those a Portuguese seafarer documented 500 years ago: this fleet, here, has come to destroy that city, there, the one beneath the wind-whipped banners that fly from the turrets on its wall.

I leave the café and make my way to a square in the heart of the old city, the main features of which are a tree, a captured Portuguese cannon with a cat asleep on it, and Jeddah's most famous building: Bayt Nassif, Nassif House. Completed in 1881, the seven-storey house was the tallest structure in the city until 1970, and its stairs, it's said, are wide enough to allow camels to carry their cargoes directly to the fourth-floor kitchen.

The tree in the square is a neem, of the mahogany family. Reportedly planted in the late nineteenth century, this is said to be the oldest tree in Jeddah; indeed, by some accounts, it was the only tree in Jeddah until 1920. These days, the city boasts innumerable palms along its roadways and seafront, and heavily irrigated landscaping is as common as its costs are unimaginable, but the underlying starkness of this city on the edge of the Arabian sands is far beyond what the word *desert* might lead anyone familiar with the scrubby or cactus-dotted terrain of Arizona or California to expect. This is a city of which, in the eleventh century, one visitor wrote that there is no 'vegetation at all', while another, in the sixteenth century, recorded that 'the land does not produce one single thing'.

Tonight, I take a seat beneath the neem, listen for a while as its boughs shimmer with what sounds like ten thousand birds not quite at rest, and recall the story that several Jeddawis – as inhabitants of Jeddah are known – have told me about it. A pilgrim who travelled from Morocco to Mecca, via Jeddah, wished to express his gratitude to the owner of the house nearby, who had given him food and gifts. The pilgrim did not know the address, so he posted his letter to 'The house near the tree, Jeddah', and that, in those days, was enough. Indeed, in a city of a single tree, there was no other house it could be.

Months later, at home, I'll hope that such an address might still suffice, and I'll send a letter addressed in English and, with help, in Arabic, to 'The House by the Tree, Jeddah, Saudi Arabia', with a note to the museum that now occupies the 106-room structure. A few months later my letter will be returned, unopened; there are too many trees in Jeddah, now.

I stand and leave the square and its still-dozing cat. I walk past the eastern edge of the old town, to where the Mecca Gate, its large central arch flanked by two smaller arches, stands between a cemetery and the Old Mecca Road, in a plaza that's laid with polished stones that catch the gaudy lights of nearby businesses, and inset with dark-red examples of the eight-pointed stars, formed by two concentric squares, one rotated 45 degrees with respect to the other, that are a recurring element of Islamic art and design.

This is not the original Mecca Gate, nor is this its original location; it was moved east and rebuilt during the modernisation of the city that included the demolition of the city's last wall, in 1947, which allowed a ring road to assume its former path, and inaugurated the frenetic expansion of the city whose rigid frontiers had hardly altered over the preceding four centuries.

The markets around the gate's former position, where pilgrims would stop to buy provisions for their journey on to Mecca, were once legendary for their congestion and cosmopolitanism. Tonight, every few minutes, small groups of young men, laughing and chatting – I rarely see women walking here, though more recently I've started to see a number of them driving – pass through the gate with their plastic shopping bags. At one point, when I briefly have the plaza to myself, I walk in through one arch and then back out through the other. *I'm within Jeddah, I'm without it*, I say to myself, as huge cars with bright headlights careen around the plaza and race off into the suburbs or to Mecca itself, and to hours and rooms beyond my imagining.

I walk back through the gate and make my way to a branch of Albaik, a chain of fast-food chicken restaurants that is a Jeddah institution. It's like every other fast-food restaurant I've been to, except that it's tastier than most, and there are separate queues for men and women. I go to my line; I stare at the English menu and its familiar numerals, the ones described as Arabic, though they're nothing like the ones often used in Saudi Arabia. When it's my turn I order a spicy chicken sandwich and a fizzy drink, for ten riyals. I fumble with the banknotes from my wallet, and shuffle through and turn them over until I find a '10' I can recognise. With the line behind me in mind, I apologise to the cashier, but he smiles and shakes his head, and says to me, in English: Welcome, and please do not worry.

SAN FRANCISCO

A few months ago Henry called his brother and left a brief voicemail. He's using his social worker's phone, he said. We dial the number two dozen times over the next month but there's never any answer. We try everything we can think of, but no agency or authority will give us information that Henry doesn't want us to have.

I have only a few months left on the 747 before I start my training for a new kind of plane, the 787. And so the work trip I'm on now might well be my last to San Francisco, as it's not a route the 787 currently flies. This possibility is an unwelcome reminder of the painful paradox in the way in which I experience cities: frequently enough to occasionally search for someone like Henry, but not enough to contribute in a meaningful or ongoing way to his life, or to that of the city in which he must survive.

So for this – perhaps final – trip a friend and I made up another round of flyers, and once again I'm nearing Golden Gate Park with only a few left in my hand. Before I enter the park I stop to speak to a group of young homeless people.

In foreign countries I'm often struck – when on a bus, for example, I listen to young people chatting in a language I don't understand about a video playing on one of their phones, or when I stare at a billboard or television advertisement because I can't even understand what the product is – by a dizzying awareness of how each particular country, each particular city, even, constitutes its own entire world, a whole I could dedicate the rest of my life to inhabiting and learning about, yet perhaps never begin to feel truly at home in.

I like to think that it's important for these worlds to be better connected, and that increasingly they are: by history and stories; by immigrants and travellers; by computers and – if it's not too prideful to say this – by aeroplanes. In San Francisco, however – where I'm often reminded how, for a period of time when Henry was young, this city embodied the unfolding reality of his dreams: a girlfriend, an apartment, a job – I may have two less-hopeful thoughts: that there are many worlds even within one city; and that Henry may be in San Francisco, but he's no longer in the San Francisco that I can see.

Nevertheless, when I walk around with flyers and tape I realise that most people here want to help me. And then I may be reassured by the possibility of connection, and by a version of an appreciation I'll later recognise in the words of the writer Jan Morris, 'that in every row of houses, almost anywhere, in any country, decent people are living, only waiting to laugh, cry and be kind'.

The homeless men I've spoken to over the years are almost invariably kind. They study Henry's picture at length. They repeat his name as if to be sure, or perhaps some have difficulty reading the smaller text on the flyer in their hands. They show the flyer to nearby folks, or suggest I walk with them to the far side of the street to reach someone else who they think might help. They may take an extra copy, one that I'll later encounter taped up in a place where I myself didn't think to post one – near the doorway to the public toilets at the north-west corner of Mission Dolores Park, for example – and I'll stare at it for the second or two it takes me to fathom how on earth it might have gotten there.

At the end of our conversations, they often mention where, after all, they might once have seen Henry, though to be honest they can't be sure. Sometimes I worry that their desire to help, and not to let me walk away without so much as the name and general direction of the place I should look next, may even lead me astray. Then I remember that many years have passed since anyone from Pittsfield last found Henry, and I realise how foolish it would be for me to follow anything but their advice.

Today, one of the group of homeless men I've been speaking to – he's thin, blond, a version of Henry in his twenties – steps away from the rest. He takes one of my last flyers and studies the photo. Then he looks me in the eye and swears that he'll find Henry and that he'll call me when he does. I can't share his certainty, but it's a comfort all the same.

I caution him again about how long ago the heavily pixelated photo of Henry was taken. Then I thank him and head into the park. A month from now, after I've left San Francisco for the last time in the cockpit of a 747 – after we've rolled down the southernmost of the two western-facing runways, lifted into the distinctive Bay Area headwind that diminishes rather than strengthens as we climb, and banked over the Golden Gate as we set course for London – he'll text me, but only a couple of times until this new line, too, goes silent: *Don't worry*, he'll write; *I'm looking, I'm looking.*

CHAPTER 6

CITY OF POETRY

Fargo, Venice,
London and Delhi

TWILIGHT IN DELHI

To my eye the pleasures of the world are nothing but dust.
Except for blood, what else flows in the guts?

Turned to dust, the wings are now a spent force;
they might even blow away on the winds.

Who is this coming towards us with the very face
of heaven, his path strewn with roses, not dust?

I should have been kind to myself, even if she wasn't.
How I have wasted my breath for nothing!

The mere thought of spring makes them drunk;
what had the tavern doors and walls to do with it?

I am ashamed of the violence of my own love.
In this ruined house how I had hoped to be a builder!

Today our verses, Asad, are only an idle pastime.
What's the use of flaunting our talent, then?

– Mirza Asadullah Khan Ghalib (1797–1869)
(translated by R. Parthasarathy)

I'm in the back seat, listening, as Mom steers our station wagon through downtown and explains to a visiting relative next to her in the front that while most American towns have a Main Street, the Pittsfield street that serves as such is, in fact, called North Street.

After she parks the three of us get out and walk to England Brothers, Pittsfield's grand downtown department store. Mom has an errand on the ground floor and afterwards we go to an elevator, in order to reach the toys on the fourth floor. Above the elevator is a semicircle, like the top half of a clock face, that indicates the car's position. The hand unwinds to the left, a bell sounds and the uniformed operator slides open the scissor gate and motions us in.

England Brothers, or England's, as generations of locals have known it, was founded in 1857 by the Bavarian brothers Moses and Louis England. The first Berkshire store to have an elevator or escalator, England's was described on postcards as 'a "big" city department store in the heart of the Berkshires'. The store's erstwhile slogan, 'It Wouldn't Be North Street Without England Brothers', echoes my own schoolboy sense of its importance, especially in terms of visits to Santa and the talking reindeer named Robert (whose words were those of an unseen employee), and the scoping-out of Christmas presents.

On this day in the early 1980s, I'm too young to see what Mom must: that this store, which to Pittsfield has been as lively and constant as a heart, is already in decline. Finally, in 1988, on Dad's fifty-seventh birthday, England Brothers will close, dealing a dreadful blow to the city's downtown.

The area's first out-of-town shopping centre will open seven months later (one autumn day after school I'll take the new bus route out to it, and I'll walk past the shops that line what to me is the marvel of an indoor street, a car-free thoroughfare that need never be snowploughed or sanded). Ten years after that, the old England Brothers building will be demolished, but the store's distinctive sky-blue boxes, with their logo composed of three strung-together black lamps, will surface now and then in my life well into the next century, until the corners of the last, in which Mom wrapped in white tissue the Christmas ornaments Dad made, break down and I throw the remains away.

England Brothers is such a fixture of my childhood that later I'll find it hard to believe that the only location I ever knew it to inhabit, 89 North Street, was not its first; in fact, the store moved there only in 1891. That is the same year, fittingly, in which Pittsfield officially became a city, and Moses England must have encountered – at the city's inauguration, or on the front page of the newspaper – the poem in which General Morris Schaff, a West Point graduate, Civil War veteran and historian, paired the hopes of the world's newest city with a warning about the fate of the Eternal one:

A WORD TO PITTSFIELD
ON HER CHANGE FROM TOWN TO CITY GOVERNMENT

Proud town! Aloft in splendor thou hast borne
Supreme through languid peace and war's red flame
The refulgent glory of a spotless name.
That radiant gem by queenly Rome was worn
Till civic change; and then – Lo! hear her mourn
From Cato's grave! – its light was quenched. . . .

Ian parks his car but neither of us reaches to open a door. We've bought coffees at Dunkin' Donuts – I've only recently started drinking it – and brought them to the lake.

In the glassed-in silence after Ian turns off his Volkswagen's engine I remember that I barely know him. I'm sixteen; Ian is nineteen and already in university. In the year we shared at Pittsfield High we had no classes together, and saw each other only in the halls. But after he graduated he wrote me a letter, the out-of-the-blue start to a correspondence that led to today's meeting.

I thought I knew awkwardness, but today I'm discovering great new heights. I sip my coffee and look away from Ian, down through the pines towards the beach where my family came for barbecues and swims when I was younger. Ian's car is the most obvious safe topic and so I decide to talk about how excited I'll be to learn to drive over the coming months. He asks if I want to try a little. Let's not go nuts, he says, as if reconsidering his offer. Let's not go on the street.

I don't even have my learner's permit yet and as we swap seats I imagine us careening down the boat ramp into the lake, and I picture the scandalised headlines in the newspapers I won't be alive to deliver. I turn on the engine, reverse and manoeuvre his car slowly around the car park. It's good. This is going to be fun. I park and turn off the engine.

We get out and walk towards the water. I tell Ian about my love of swimming, at the little beach before us and also at the YMCA's summer swimming and sports complex, up a side road we can see on the other side of the lake's outlet. In some years my family bought a summer-long membership there, but many families could not afford this. At the front desk was a dot-matrix printout of all the members, and each day the receptionist would strike off names as the members arrived. It was common, if you had a sibling on the list who wasn't with you, to sneak in a classmate or neighbour instead. Once my brother and I were dropped off to swim with a few friends. We gave our names and the clerk looked between us and scoffed: Don't even try – no way you two are family. It's one of a series of such stories I'll think of in the years to come, as my brother and I talk more openly about our childhoods, and especially after our parents are gone, when we'll be brought much closer by two seemingly contradictory realisations: that in the same small place – in adjoining bedrooms, no less – we both struggled with deep senses of unbelonging; and yet Pittsfield was a very different city for each of us.

Looming over the glass-still water is the massif of Mount Greylock. Ian and I can't yet know how many times we'll go up there together in the next few years, in the course of something more than a friendship. For now maybe we talk about how many English teachers have told us that the mountain, so often clad in snow and ice, suggested to Herman Melville not only the shape but the colour of the whale in his masterpiece, *Moby-Dick*.

Melville spent years on the ocean, then others in the quiet of Pittsfield – where he wrote, in one of the low, creaky rooms that tour guides have led me through on several school trips, that 'I have a sort of sea-feeling here in the country, now that the ground is all covered with snow' – but he was no stranger to large cities. He was born in New York and died there, too. In between he travelled widely, and he wrote easily – about Liverpool and Rome; the gate through which pilgrims left Cairo for Mecca; and 'the Parthenon uplifted on its rock first challenging the view on the approach to Athens'.

As far as I know Melville never mentioned Pittsfield in verse. He did, however, write a poem about the lake whose shoreline Ian and I now stop at, and from which we both look straight out. And perhaps the poem 'Pontoosuc' ('Crowning a bluff where gleams the lake below, / Some pillared pines in well-spaced order stand . . .') counts as a Pittsfield mention after all, as its title recalls not only the lake's name but the 'Township of Pontoosuck', as Pittsfield was first incorporated.

Ian and I step away from the water's edge and find a picnic table set beneath the pines that still pillar this hillside above Pontoosuc. We talk more and drink our coffees. Then we stand and walk back down to the beach, across it, and onto a short trail that leads into greenery along the shore. I tell him about my parents and their separation, and my hopes of going to Japan next summer. It's easier for me to think of going so far, I tell him, because, actually, I don't have a girlfriend at the moment, and anyway, I can't wait to leave Pittsfield for good. He gestures – to indicate all of Pittsfield or only these lakeside trees, I'm not sure – and tells me that leaving isn't everything, and that he's happy we are here.

〜

Mr Peirce, my English teacher from a few years ago, announces: Let's go to the dome, it's the end of the year; in fact, for you guys it really is the end.

He's right; we'll graduate from high school in a matter of weeks. 'Our Home Under the Dome' is my school's motto, and it's an apt one: I'm not alone in confessing that when I was little I didn't realise our city's imposing downtown high school was distinct from the Capitol in Washington.

We follow Mr Peirce through the halls, a half dozen or so of us, to a door we've never before been allowed to pass through. He has a key, or he's borrowed one from the caretaker. As we climb a staircase the sense that rules are falling away is as thrilling to me as the prospect of seeing our city from above.

We step out from the dusty gloom of the stairwell, into a realm cooled by its higher wind and dominated by the blinding whiteness of the columns. I rest my hands on the balustrade and gaze across the street at Dad's office. He could see me, I'm pleased to realise, if he happened to look up from his desk. I look down the street towards the public library and the stately old buildings that line Park

Square. I turn south-east, to where I try to see our house through the trees.

Mr Peirce is asking who's going to leave Pittsfield, and for where, and he's talking with a smile about the literary kudos of our city, as if he's not quite joking about the possibility that while we are together above Pittsfield he might convince more of us to stay.

He doesn't bring up the poet Elizabeth Bishop, who came to Pittsfield several times to visit a boyfriend, a city native named Bob Seaver. (Perhaps because Mr Peirce knows that in 1936, after Bishop declined his proposal of marriage, Seaver sent her a card care of the Hotel Chelsea in New York – 'Go to hell, Elizabeth' – and then shot himself.) Nor does he mention Oliver Wendell Holmes Sr, whose former estate still stands on Holmes Road and who, in 1850, delivered a poem at the dedication of Pittsfield's new cemetery (perhaps because Mr Peirce considers its tone – 'Angel of Death! extend thy silent reign!' – unsuited to young people, especially on a bright spring day only a few weeks shy of their graduation).

Mr Peirce does, though, tell us a story about Henry Wadsworth Longfellow, who, in 1837, met Frances Elizabeth Appleton in Switzerland. Later, they would spend part of their honeymoon at Elm Knoll, the Pittsfield house that had belonged to his wife's grandparents. It was on this first visit to one of Pittsfield's most imposing homes that Longfellow encountered the timepiece that inspired 'The Old Clock on the Stairs':

> . . . There groups of merry children played,
> There youths and maidens dreaming strayed;
> O precious hours! O golden prime,
> And affluence of love and time!
> Even as a miser counts his gold,
> Those hours the ancient timepiece told, –
>   'Forever – never!
>   Never – forever!'

Elm Knoll, Mr Peirce tells us, was built in 1790. But then in 1929, he explains, the house was knocked down, in order that our domed school could rise in its place.

FARGO AND VENICE

Kirun and I have been driving west all through the short summer night, and the sky begins to lighten in the rearview mirror as we cross into North Dakota and the city of Fargo. We've been working in Chicago, before our final year of university. It's been a chance to get to know the city better, and to look up at the thirty-eight-storey skyscraper known as the Pittsfield Building (so named by the estate of Marshall Field, the founder of the Chicago department store, who was born in western Massachusetts, and whose first job, at the age of seventeen, was at a dry goods store on North Street in Pittsfield). Now we have a few days free before we go back to school, so yesterday, not quite in time to beat the Windy City's evening rush hour, we got in a borrowed pickup truck and pulled onto the highway.

Interstate 90 is a road anyone from Massachusetts might think they know well. It's a long road, however – indeed, it's the longest of America's interstates – and its Midwestern miles are all new to me. We broke with 90 on the outskirts of Tomah, Wisconsin, joined Interstate 94, and followed it north-west to Minneapolis and on to North Dakota's largest city. Now, near daybreak, we're hungry and tired. We pull off the highway and within a few minutes we're lost in residential Fargo. It's maybe 5:30 a.m. when we stop on a suburban street of well-tended, middle-class homes.

We turn off the engine and roll down the windows. After the towers of Chicago and our hours of speed and darkness on the highway, we're both bewildered to find ourselves stationary on this still-lifed street. It's a new day, but we have not slept; it's a new city, but nothing, aside from the number plates of the cars in the drives, helps me distinguish this avenue from dozens like it in Pittsfield. My eyes follow the pavement from one Fargo home along to the next, in the sleepy, nearly underwater rhythm that might be familiar to anyone who once carried newspapers from house to house on many dark and snowbound mornings. Most of the upstairs windows are still curtained. No one is walking, cycling, or driving; no garage doors stand open, displaying workbenches or garden tools hanging from nails; no leaf blowers buzz; no kids shout as they play kick the can.

My long friendship with Kirun, which we've subsequently cemented with occasional journeys like this, began one night in our first days of university. We went to a loud party, then left it to talk more easily outside, but from where we could still hear the music and the voices through the open windows. I came out to her a week or two later, in her room, down the hall and around the corner from mine. I'd barely told anyone else, and so it was a stressful conversation for me, but it needn't have been, I later learned, because she had already guessed.

Now, in Fargo, I don't know that a decade from now it will be Kirun, not me, who will be at Mom's side at the end. I'll say to the gathering of family and friends in Mom's Pittsfield hospital room: I'm going to look for some food; I'll be right back.

Then Mark and I will leave and minutes later Mom will pass on. Maybe she heard you were stepping out, the nurse will say to me when we return. It's often like that. It can be hard for them to let go.

Kirun is already an accomplished poet but she doesn't yet know that poetry will be her life's work. I want to be a pilot, but I have no idea how that might come about. I took some flying lessons in high school but it was too expensive to do more. Meanwhile, Kirun is teaching me about poetry. This summer she introduced me to the work of Anne Sexton, starting with her poem about Icarus and flight called 'To a Friend Whose Work Has Come to Triumph'.

Kirun knows me well, I thought, as I read: 'larger than a sail, over the fog and the blast / of the plushy ocean, he goes'.

I loved, too, Sexton's poem '45 Mercy Street' (and the lyrics – 'the dreams all made solid' – of the song by Peter Gabriel that it inspired). Most of the poem's meaning was dark, and lay further than I could see, I suspected, but I liked that in my edition of Sexton's work, the poem followed an epigraph that explained that a *hegira* is an important journey. The poem also introduced me to the idea that a poet could be so tightly bound to a city – in this case Boston, where I'd not yet lived, but which had always featured so brightly in the stories of how my parents met, and of their early lives together. And as I read about holding matches up to signs, though 'the street is unfindable for an / entire lifetime', I recognised my own familiar desire to seek something in a city, however poorly I defined that search's object.

We start the car and find a diner for breakfast. A few days from now, after we've left the diner, Fargo, and North Dakota, I will tell Kirun about my imaginary city, the one I'd created as a child. Telling her will be harder than coming out had been. Afterwards I'll think: *Well, that's it; I have no more secrets.*

A few weeks later, she will give me a book that's new to me: *Invisible Cities*, by Italo Calvino. She'll write a note in the front that refers to our shared fascination with cities, whether real or imagined ones, and she'll use multiple paper clips to attach a card to the back cover, to conceal the blurb. (I won't ever remove it and so I can't tell you what she didn't want me to read there.)

In this book, a fictionalised Marco Polo describes fifty-five imaginary cities to Kublai Khan, the Mongol emperor and grandson of Genghis Khan. Or maybe he describes only one city, a real one, which is Venice, the city of his birth and death. It hardly matters, such is the book's beauty.

The suggestion that we all dream of the same city, though it may

appear differently to each of us, making its reality sometimes tanta-
lisingly unclear, is the loveliest idea in *Invisible Cities*. And the book
must have a particular resonance – simultaneously stirring and
comforting – for anyone who imagined a different place or world as
a child, but who may have never conceived that others might do the
same. (When an interviewer once asked Calvino if he had ever been
bored, he replied: 'Yes, in my childhood. But it must be pointed
out that childhood boredom is a special kind of boredom. It is a
boredom full of dreams, a sort of projection into another place, into
another reality.')

Calvino, of course, is only one of many writers and scholars who
have adopted the city as a metaphorical or allegorical frame. We
might think first of Plato's ideal city in *The Republic*, or the fifty-
four cities (one fewer than Calvino described) that fill the island
Thomas More described in *Utopia*. But above all, perhaps, Calvino's
imagery reminds me of Saint Augustine's distinction between the
earthly city and the divine one. Indeed, Calvino's cities and words
reinforced – or Kirun did, through her gift of his book – my faith in
the idea that behind all real cities lies one that is archetypal, though
our vision of it must be no less flawed and clouded than we are.
They remind me, as well, of the notion that all religions approach
the same truth, only from different starting points and by different routes – a hope to which Mom was strongly drawn throughout
the second half of her life, and one that it's easier for me to share, I
know, because its premise is so much like that of a map.

LONDON

When Mom retired, in 2001, the year I started my flight training, she didn't have enough savings to remain in her house, and my
brother and I did not yet earn enough to help her. So she moved in
with Sue, one of my aunts in our Berkshire family.

Five years later, in early November of 2006, Mom was hospitalised. She had suffered from hepatitis, which she got from a blood transfusion in the 1970s, and though her treatment, in the late 1990s, was considered successful, the medication caused neuropathy, which made it hard for her to balance and walk. These and other health problems seemed to build on each other in the subsequent years, and even her doctor was surprised by the speed of her decline. The doctor still thought she might be able to come home for Thanksgiving, so the Berkshire gang's traditional dinner was moved to Sue's house, to make it easier for Mom to attend if by then she had been discharged. She couldn't come home, however. She died eleven days before Christmas, aged only sixty-nine.

Now it's January 2007 and I'm back home – *Home?* I wonder – in London, where it rains, rather than snows, in this season. The boxes from Pittsfield arrived a few days ago. One of the more curious benefits of working for an airline is that you receive not only discounted flights, but discounted rates on freight. It's a benefit doled out by mass: 300 kilograms per year.

But I required only a fraction of that. When Dad and my stepmother decided to sell our old family home in Pittsfield and move to North Carolina, I threw most of my childhood belongings away, and I stored what little remained in the attic of Mom's new little house. When Mom retired and moved in with Sue, I'd culled again, keeping only my diaries, a few fragments of my rock and coin collections, and a handful of drawings and school papers.

After Mom died, my brother and I had to decide which of her own possessions we wished to keep. Among the items I chose were some books she'd written a little in, a few CDs and her high school yearbook (on her page was written 'Prefect of Our Lady's Sodality is one position which Chris has proudly possessed', along with the less mysterious: 'Gayety and cheerfulness follow her wherever she goes').

These and a few other objects, together with the last items from my childhood, flew across the ocean for free last week but I was obliged to collect them from the cargo warehouse at Heathrow. I drove to an unfamiliar part of the airport, signed the paperwork, and was pointed to the plastic-shrouded collection of boxes that on the customs form I'd attested were nearly without value. I fitted them easily in my small car and I drove them home along the North Circular, the northern arc of one of London's ring roads.

Now, I sit on the floor and sort. I take Mom's passport from the clear ziplock bag she carefully kept it in and examine the stamps from her two visits to London.

On her final trip here, her mobility was too impaired for her to use public transport – I'd never noticed before how many stairs a typical journey on the Underground includes – and so one day I drove her on a short tour right through central London. That was the first time I'd driven through the middle of town on a busy afternoon; Mom was thrilled, and surely as surprised as I was that my first such journey would be with her riding shotgun. We stopped in front of Buckingham Palace and I switched on my car's hazard lights while I helped her out to take a photo. Then other cars began to stop around us, and other motorists to step out to take photos, until a shocked policeman ran over to hurry us all along.

I look next at the stack of Mom's books that I've brought back from Pittsfield. Not many, a dozen or so. There's a weighty volume of Shakespeare, from her university days, I assume. The penmanship of the margin notations is familiar and meticulous, though I recall, too, a visiting relative from Belgium who couldn't decipher her formal and distinctively American handwriting. As I turn the pages it occurs to me that they have probably only been touched by Mom and by me; and that most of them, surely, have not seen light in half a century, since her untraceable hour in a Boston room.

Now the day I open them to is mine, and London's. I sigh and close the hardback volume. There's nothing to do with these feelings, I think, as I learn the new lightness of even such a sturdy object, and the weight of a past I can't see.

I set the book down and pick up another, a volume of poetry by Wendell Berry. Mom loved Berry's writing, and when I was in my twenties she gave me several of his books. Berry would later write about his long and fierce opposition to the idea that city life is '*the* experience, the *modern* experience, and that the life of the rural towns, the farms, the wilderness places is not only irrelevant to our time, but archaic as well'. I enjoy many of his poems for all the same reasons I love the Berkshire countryside, but growing up surrounded by it, I dreamed of steel and glass beyond the hills.

I set the volume of Berry's work back onto the pile and turn to my old school papers that Mom had kept. As a kid I was indifferent to poems and I have no memory of ever writing one. But apparently, I realise, I did, in clumsy, compressed handwriting on a sheet of greyish school writing paper with thin, widely spaced blue lines:

The night is dark and spooky gray.
The horses are saying Nay Nay Nay.
Bats are biting civilians necks
Ships take the chance of going a wreck.
People are snoring extremely loud
No ones gathering in great big crowds
Thieves are crawling in the quiet night
Birds are not in their usual flight.

I smile, maybe for the first time since Mom died. I lay the apostrophe-free page down on the floor. At least, I think, Mom must have liked the poem, to have kept it safe for so long. At least, I think again – as perhaps she remarked, too – it ended on flight.

DELHI

When I first began to enjoy the view from aeroplane windows, as a passenger and then as a pilot, I was struck by the apparent seamlessness of the world below. Now I look down at the line of light that runs across the dark land ahead of us, the one that divides Pakistan and India, and it's as if I'm turning the globe in my bedroom again, the one on which, after dark, every border glowed.

We're not far from Lahore and the local time below us is around midnight. Inder, Kirun's father, was raised here. The convulsions of Partition – when, in 1947, British India was split into Pakistan and India – drove him and his family to Delhi. I've sat with Inder in Kirun's home in Massachusetts, as the winter winds swirled up from the frozen river below her house to shake the windowpanes, and told him about the city lights I see when I fly above Pakistan: of Karachi, more a generalised glow than a defined cityscape, and greened by that port city's seemingly permanent marine haze; of Lahore, inland, its glow whiter and clearer; and of Islamabad, the lights of the capital pooled like snowmelt at the feet of the mountains that rise beyond it.

I've told him, too, about how the border between Pakistan and India, the line that his family crossed nearly as soon as it was drawn, is illuminated like no other I've ever seen. The scale of the suffering associated with Partition, which is often described as the largest mass migration in history, is incomprehensible. In merely visual terms, as well, the glowing border is hard to take in: from a distance the path of its band of light can resemble the slopes of hills, apparently shortened by the angle at which you approach them, or because they are rising towards you, or dropping away, and its curious zigs and zags only begin to make sense when moonlight reveals all three dimensions of the borderlands.

Now, as this line draws nearer, it's time to prepare for our descent to Delhi. We turn to our tablet computers and read the notes that accompany our charts of the various approaches to Indira Gandhi International Airport:

All ACFT entering Delhi TMA, except ACFT navigating under conditions of RNAV STARs, shall follow IAS as per following, unless otherwise instructed by ATC. . . .

The purpose of these notes is to convey – in a clear manner, as English is not the first language of so many of the world's airline pilots – how this airport differs from every other. The information is practical and succinct; it leaves no room for history or literature, of course, and so nowhere does Delhi's allude to Mir Taqi Mir (c. 1723–1810), the poet who wrote: 'The streets of Delhi were like painted pages / Every sight I saw looked like a picture.'

Turbojet ACFT use Continuous Descent Arrival (CDA) between 1630-0030.

Our technical guide to approaching Delhi from the sky does not refer to Amir Khusrau (1253–1325), the poet who is so associated with the city that *Dehlvī*, of Delhi, is often appended to his name, and who described Delhi as 'the twin of pure paradise, / a prototype of the heavenly throne on an earthly scroll'.

MNM taxi speed 15KT on the straight portion of TWYs and between 8-12KT during turning manoeuvres.

Nor does it mention the *Mahabharata*, the Sanskrit epic that by some reckonings is the longest poem ever written, and in which Indraprastha, believed by many to be Delhi's myth-laden antecedent, is described:

Krishna paused, 'Let Khandavaprastha be named Indraprastha after you, O Deva: for you must raise this city again, in greater glory than it ever knew in the past.' . . . At Viswakarman's touch, the dry pools were all full of clear water, on which the stars were reflected between white lotuses, vermilion and violet ones and flocks of water birds that slept with their heads tucked under their wings. Scented orchards and gardens flanked those streets. A deep moat, also full of the clearest water, ringed the impregnable outer walls. Those walls were like Garuda's wings, outspread.

Birds in vicinity of AD.

Delhi lies on the Yamuna River, the second-holiest river of Hinduism after the Ganges, of which it is a tributary. The scholar Upinder Singh wrote of the relationship between the two rivers: 'The goddess Yamuna is depicted along with Ganga in the sculpture of many ancient Indian temples, often flanking their entrance. Ganga, white as the moon, stands on a *matsya* (fish) or *makara* (crocodile). Yamuna is the dark goddess. She stands on a *kachchhapa* (tortoise).'

It seems apt to me that Yamuna is the dark goddess, because I associate Delhi strongly with night. Indeed, I so often arrive here then that I find it impossible to imagine the city, from above, at least, at any other time of day. The particular sense of descending towards a vast but slumbering city is made eerier still by Delhi's fog, above all in January, when the mist and the smoke build until they lie on the ground like a sheet of rough cloth through which, as we make our approach, the light cast up by so many millions is nearly obscured.

Delhi Control, good morning, I transmit. The first Indian controller of our journey answers to her city's name, as she does again and again, night after night. Like the notes on our charts, the language we both must use is succinct and internationally standardised,

and her reply does not include the characterisation of Delhi by Sarojini Naidu (the poet and activist whom Mahatma Gandhi dubbed
Bharat Kokila, the Nightingale of India) as the 'Imperial City!
dowered with sovereign grace. . . . Before whose shrine the spells of
Death are vain'.

Nor does the controller welcome us to the skies near the city
that Jawaharlal Nehru, India's first prime minister, described as 'a
gem with many facets, some bright and some darkened by age . . .
the grave of many empires and the nursery of a republic. What a
tremendous story is hers!'

Instead she says: *Namaskar*, Hello. Start your descent now.

Minutes later we switch to the next Indian controller, and then
another and another. Delhi Tower, I say, we're at ten miles. We
extend our flaps and the landing gear, slow to our final approach
speed, and descend into the thickest and lowest tranche of mist.
The tower controller issues our landing clearance. We acknowledge
it and touch down.

The late hour, and the fog that obscures even the looming outline
of the terminal building until the last moment, add to the sense
that, notwithstanding the whirring of our engines and the glow of
the cockpit's array of computer screens, we might have landed in
any of Delhi's ages. Then we park and walk out into the terminal,
where the brightly lit shops are open, accustomed, of course, to the
late-night arrivals, and I think, amid the announcements, the backlit banking advertisements I roll my flight bag past, and the lurch
of the starting luggage conveyor belts, that this is undoubtedly the
present, and it's much the same as everywhere.

Except that here I want, as always, to look around for Kirun.
It's not because she – having posted long letters to me during her
occasional periods of residence in this capital her father came to
call home – may be one of the more direct connections between
Pittsfield and Delhi. Rather, it's that she has written about arriving
in this airport, in a poem that I like to imagine was composed in

part to guide a friend, a pilot who knew little about either poetry or
Delhi, to the threshold of both.

ARRIVING, NEW DELHI

Smoke. Ocher smolders. Blue
sparks. Below the airplane's
steady arcs, the neon lights are

embers. Over the city's central rings
a flash, the tipping silver
wings. Over discotheques, the temple
dancers' ankle bells. Boys
selling oranges, cool feet
in public fountains. Great cows lounge
on garbage heaps. The steep dome
of the Friday Mosque. Burger and marble
Moghul palaces. Then,

tires slamming down on pitch.
Heat, a furnace in the ears.
Doors open and the blood pounds out
its local language along every limb.
Smell ashes. Men. Jasmine
climbing on a fence. A taxi driver
turbaned in a tongue of flame
says, Sister, I can take you into the city.
Sister, Shall I take you home?

The first time I flew to Delhi, I read Kirun's poem not long before
I walked out through those same airport doors at around 3 a.m., in

winter. The city was colder than London that night, and to me, in the monochrome near-darkness through which our bus rattled and plunged, the dust on the streets was like snow.

For that first visit, Kirun had suggested I visit some of the city's famous sites – Lodhi Gardens, India Gate, Khan Market – as well as places she had known as a child, and a café where she had sometimes come to work on her laptop during one summer in university, when she was employed by a magazine in the city. For some years after my initial trip I continued to fly to Delhi occasionally, and each visit was a chance to explore further the city that she would sketch for me from afar. I'd send her photos of the childhood spots she'd sent me to, and I'd tell her about important changes to the city that she had not yet seen, including – such are my passions, we'd laugh – the speedy and steadily expanding new metro. Then, suddenly, the flight schedules changed, and I stopped flying to Delhi.

Several years later, the schedules have changed again, and tonight I'm glad to be back. In the intervening years I've learned – from Kirun and from her father – a little more about Delhi and its long tradition of poetry, and about why this metropolis might be described as the 'city of poets' and the 'city of verse'. And so, a few weeks ago, I asked Kirun to choose another poem she associated with the city: one that I might read not as my feet slow to a halt on an airport moving walkway and I scroll down quickly on the screen of my phone, but after I've slept, caffeinated and found my way into town. I printed out the poem she emailed me and then I folded it, carefully, so as not to read any of it. I've kept it in my suitcase, in the little mesh pouch on the inside of the lid. My plan is to read it today, somewhere in Delhi.

It's 3:30 a.m. by the time we reach our hotel near the airport, which, it takes me a moment to calculate, is 10 p.m. in the UK – India Standard Time's 5½-hour time difference from Coordinated Universal Time being both engagingly unusual and a good reason for pilots to triple-check their calculations before making arrival announcements to passengers – and 5 p.m. for Kirun, in Massachusetts. I go to my room and draw the curtains. I'll try for the equivalent of a full night's sleep, and then head into town around midday.

In *City Improbable*, the writer and politician Khushwant Singh described Delhi as possessing 'a longer history and more historical monuments than any other metropolis'. Such a conclusion isn't easy to verify, but what is certain is that the Delhi region has been continually inhabited for thousands of years; and that among today's megacities, Delhi's past must be one of the deepest. Long before it became the capital of the world's most populous democracy – soon to become the world's most populous country – Delhi was described by Ibn Battuta, in the fourteenth century, as a 'vast and magnificent city, uniting beauty with strength'; it was later conquered by a descendant of Genghis Khan; and it gave birth, as well, to a history-shaping rebellion against British imperialism.

The film *Dead Poets Society*, about an iconoclastic English teacher at a straitlaced New England school, came out when I was fifteen. At one point the teacher, played by Robin Williams, ridicules a method for the calculation of poetic greatness (that I admit then seemed perfectly sensible to me), by which a poem's artistry and the importance of its subject are plotted on the x and y axes of a graph, to outline an area equivalent to its net worth.

This surely isn't the lesson I was meant to take from that scene, but I'll adopt and even double down on that approach as I try to measure the measureless wonder of great cities. A similar process, adding the z axis, might calculate the volume of a city's glory from three metrics: the city's age, its current population and the degree to which it has influenced or ruled other peoples and places. Such an assessment would leave Delhi with few rivals other than Beijing; perhaps, I suspect, with none.

Nevertheless, if Delhi is one of the greatest cities in history, I didn't learn anything about it in school, aside from the status of New Delhi as India's capital. I never learned, for example, how favourably

Delhi's prominence as an imperial metropolis might be compared to that of Constantinople, or the ubiquity of its cacophonic past to that of Athens, 'with its monumental, crumbling history' scattered throughout 'its ramshackle, seething present'. Nor that others have described it as the 'Indian Rome', a phrasing that may have it the wrong way round; after all, as the English historian Percival Spear wrote, 'Delhi can point to a history as chequered and more ancient than the "eternal" city of Rome; it was a famous capital before the days of Alexander, and has survived all the vicissitudes of time and fortune.'

As Rome has its seven hills, so Delhi is said to encompass seven previous versions of itself. Lists of the seven vary in terms of the city names themselves, not to mention their English spellings, but by a typical reckoning they are Lal Kot, Siri, Tughlaqabad, Jahanpanah, Firozabad, Dinpanah and, seventh and most famously, Shahjahanabad, built by Shah Jahan, the Mughal emperor who also built the Taj Mahal, a mausoleum for a beloved wife. (The Delhi he built in the seventeenth century is roughly aligned with what is now called Old Delhi, though such is the depth of the city's history that as late as 1902 Shah Jahan's city might still be referred to as 'Modern Delhi'.) Nor does such an accounting include Indraprastha, the fabled ancestor of all subsequent incarnations, or New Delhi, the twentieth-century capital.

This geographic and chronological intersecting and overlaying explains 'The City of Cities', Delhi's simultaneously transcendent and literal epithet. Indeed, the number of cities that time has transfigured into what today we call Delhi may also be given as ten, eleven, fifteen, or seventeen – a richness that, if nothing else, affirms both the technique (New New Delhi, Old New Delhi, New Old Delhi . . .) a Delhi-based friend relies on to help keep them straight, as well as the forthright summary offered by the writer and commentator Patwant Singh: 'No capital in the world has been built on the site of as many legendary cities of old, as Delhi.'

New Delhi, the present capital, was the imposition of a foreign empire – its first stone was laid by George V and its second by Mary, his queen-empress, and the city was largely designed by the London-born Edwin Lutyens, who as a child 'dreamt of construct-ing monumental buildings' and who then, as an adult, as if in a fable's twist, was given so much responsibility for doing so – yet there was nothing arbitrary about the selection of the site. Delhi remained 'a name to conjure with', according to the viceroy at the time of the city's foundation. While another official put it more directly: New Delhi 'must like Rome be built for eternity'.

Indeed, Delhi's name features in everyday idioms and expres-sions much as Rome's does – think of 'All roads lead to Rome', or 'When in Rome . . .' – but to an even greater degree, perhaps. *Dilli dilwalon ki*, Delhi belongs to the big-hearted: Be bold. *Kaun jaaye, par Dilli ki galiyan chhod kar*, But who can bear to leave, leaving behind the alleys of Delhi: You're stuck with what you love (a phras-ing adapted from a poem by the Delhi master Mohammad Ibrahim Zauq, who in 1837 was named 'King of Poets', or poet laureate, by the Mughal emperor). *Aas-paas barse, Dilli pani tarse*, It pours all around, while Delhi lies parched: Deprivation is surrounded by abundance. You can marry a fish, but don't marry a Delhi boy, a woman in Hyderabad once told me in English, with a laugh, in ref-erence to the perceived arrogance of the capital's scions.

Perhaps best known of all is the Hindi phrase *Dilli abhi door hai*, Delhi is still far. Its story is often told as follows: Ghiyāth al-Dīn Tughluq became the Sultan of Delhi in 1320 (and in 1321 founded its third city). A few years later, returning after a military expe-dition, and suspicious of the challenge the Sufi saint Muhammad Nizamuddin Auliya might pose to his authority, Tughluq ordered Nizamuddin to leave the city before he arrived. One of Nizamud-din's students, the poet Amir Khusrau, expressed his distress to his master. Unworried, Nizamuddin responded in Persian, *Hunuz Dilli door ast*, Delhi is still far. Sure enough, Tughluq never made it: he fell and died when the pavilion erected for an en-route celebration collapsed in a storm, and Nizamuddin's words eventually entered common discourse.

Delhi is still far; a lot can still happen, or you have struggle ahead of you yet. Until you don't: Kirun's father, Inder, once told me that he can still hear the song he heard as a teenager when he first reached India after Partition, its words from a loudspeaker – *Ab toh Dilli dur nahi*, Delhi is not far anymore – a riff on an idiom six centuries old.

∾

When I was a kid and dreamed of my imaginary city, I did so almost entirely in terms of the obvious details I found most compelling: skyscrapers, glittering lights, sweeping roads, a busy harbour, an airport (or three). It never occurred to me that poets and poetry might form part of a city's magnificence. One hurdle was that when I imagined my city, I often did so from above, from the perspective of a mapmaker or an arriving pilot. Poetry, unlike skyscrapers or metro networks, wasn't something I could envision on the cityscape below; I couldn't have pointed to a spot and thought, *I like these stanzas, here*, as if they were so many new lines of rail.

Then, as a young adult, and thanks to Kirun, Delhi became the world's sole city of poetry to me. Nonetheless, it's also true that I have never subsequently heard of another contemporary city so frequently praised in terms of its poetic greatness.

Delhi's poets 'dominated the city's cultural and intellectual landscape', notes the writer and scholar Rakhshanda Jalil; while Khushwant Singh wrote that 'Dilliwalas' – Delhiites – 'were known for their courteous speech and interest in poetry. . . . They were proud of their poets.' At various times, it was common for young poets from surrounding cities to seek a tutor, and their literary fortunes, in the metropolis. These fortunes could be considerable. Compensation could include six gold pieces per couplet, or an entire village, or the poet's weight in precious metals or gems might be distributed as alms.

Delhi's Mughal emperors not only nurtured poets, they often wrote poetry themselves. Poetry, however, wasn't confined to the elites; Saif Mahmood, the author of *Beloved Delhi: A Mughal City and Her Greatest Poets*, writes that 'Urdu poetry was mostly a spoken-word occupation and one did not have to be literate to be a poet or a lover of Urdu poetry', and he quotes the scholar Shamsur Rahman Faruqi: poetry in Delhi was not a matter of literature, 'it was life itself'. Mahmood notes that even today Delhi's classical Urdu poets 'remain the most quoted poets of the language ever'.

Akhil Katyal, a queer writer based in Delhi, once joked in a newspaper interview that it was easier to come out to his family as a gay man than as a poet. He has spoken, too, about the inspiration he took from the city's poetic past as well as the freedom he finds in its present: born in Lucknow, he came to Delhi as a young man and found it 'a place where you could escape, you could live your life on your own terms'; it was Delhi that 'allowed me to step out of my own constraint'. Delhi, he says, can be 'ruthless to some', but despite the challenges the city is his muse, and its inhabitants his inspiration: 'The different people you encounter in Delhi can only lead to poetry.'

I wasn't in town to attend a poetry workshop that Katyal offered, in which participants used a map of Delhi to help them locate the memories they wished to turn into verse (a creative process summarised in a blog post by the question, 'Does the city make the poet, or the poet, the city?'). But later we corresponded. In one email, he wrote of how the work of Delhi's most famous poet, Mirza Asadullah Khan Ghalib, 'casts a long shadow in South Asian films, music and popular culture'. Indeed, it was Ghalib who wrote the poem that Kirun sent to me, the one that's waiting in the pocket of my jeans on the chair here in my hotel room, to be opened today, somewhere in her city, and that of Ghalib.

In the email to which Kirun attached the poem she chose for me, she explained that Ghalib's bond with Delhi could hardly be closer. He was born in what is now Agra in 1797, first visited Delhi when he was seven, and in his early teenage years moved to the city of which he would eventually write: 'The world is the body, Delhi its soul.' I love that Ghalib suggested that letters be sent to him using only his name, followed by that of his city: 'Asadullah Khan Ghalib, Delhi', a bond that's exemplified by the title of a 2016 article about his legacy: 'Ghalib is Delhi and Delhi is Ghalib.'

Ghalib anticipated and lived through the sunset of the Mughal court, along with its ancient, poetry-laden traditions, which together constituted so much of the artistic life of the metropolis he loved. In 1854 – not long before the Indian Rebellion of 1857, the destruction of much of the city, and the rise of the British Raj – he wrote: 'Inside the Fort a few princes get together and recite their verses. Once in a while I attend these gatherings. Contemporary society is about to vanish. Who knows when the poets would meet next or meet again at all.'

Ghalib died in Delhi in 1869. His tomb stands near the mausoleum of Nizamuddin, the Sufi saint who declared that Delhi was still far; while in Old Delhi, at Ghalib's former *haveli*, or townhouse (though that English word hardly does justice to the cultural and architectural legacy of such grand, centuries-old havelis as his), signs describe him as 'arguably the best Indian poet'; list his favourite foods, including roasted mutton and sohan halwa, a traditional and still popular Delhi sweet; and note his hobbies, such as kite flying, chess and Ganjifa, an ancient game that's often played with round cards. Many of Ghalib's couplets, as well, hang on the walls: 'I wondered if any wilderness would be more desolate than this! / And then I remembered another of the kind – the home I'd left behind.'

In my hotel room I open the curtains and see that the sky is already getting light. I'm not going to be able to sleep, it seems. No matter; I'll only sleep better tonight. I shower, put on my jeans, a white T-shirt and a blue flannel shirt. I pack my bag with water, granola bars and a hat. I check the pocket of my jeans twice for the folded-up poem. I walk out of the hotel, past a uniformed attendant who adopts an expression of mingled pain and pity when I decline his offer of a taxi, and into the street.

On certain winter days Delhi's fog does not burn off at all and one night's banks of mist roll into those of the next. This morning, though, only a little mist remains, and while it's cold enough, it's not quite freezing. As I walk, the sun – even on ostensibly cloudless days the smoke and the haze here can be such that it's disturbingly easy to look directly at our star, whether it's near the horizon and blood-red as it is now, or higher and white as the moon – hangs above the crowds of commuters streaming towards me.

I reach Delhi Aerocity, the agreeably named metro station. I buy my ticket and descend to the platform in time to watch a gleaming train slow to a gentle stop. I board and find a window seat. Soon we're racing over Delhi Ridge, a forested highland between the airport and the heart of the city. Along with the Yamuna River, it's one of the capital region's most prominent topographical features. Having played a critical part in various battles for Delhi, it was later seeded with trees by British administrators. Today it's a much-needed green patch for the city, and a spot popular with lovers. I take my phone from my pocket and read up a little on the family, said to be descendants of an ancient royal line, who from the mid-1980s occupied a decaying medieval hunting lodge on the ridge that was all but overgrown by the forest. Then I think of Kirun and of a story she once told me about her father, and Ghalib, and a taxi driver.

She was a child, half asleep, and half listening to her father chatting with the driver as they wended through roundabouts and traffic jams. The street they were bound for in Old Delhi led the driver to mention the poets who had once lived in that vicinity. Seeing that he had a receptive audience in her father, the two began exchanging trivia and before long a volley of Urdu couplets filled the cab. Kirun dozed until a sharp elbow from her father caused her to tune in again – He's mixing, her father hissed. In the middle of quoting Ghalib, this fool is quoting Mir. Not so, the taxi wallah protested from the front seat as they careened through a yellow light, that couplet is pukka Ghalib (the real McCoy, Kirun explained to me). Her father was irate, and didn't return to good humour until they reached home and he could verify his claims with a book. Indeed, Kirun told me, her father had been involved in many Ghalib-related disputes over the years. If Ghalib is one of Delhi's most quoted poets, she added, he's also one of the most misquoted.

I listen to the Hindi announcements of the stations ahead and record a few of them to play for Mark once I'm home. As we approach New Delhi station, the last stop on the airport line, I try to repeat to myself, 'Nayi Dilli'. I disembark and walk to the Yellow Line platform, where I browse the names on the system map as I wait: Tikri Border, New Ashok Nagar and Civil Lines; Delhi Gate, Kashmere Gate and Welcome; the legendary Indraprastha and the confident Model Town. And as I ponder this world formed of place-names, and of routes that run as true as nerves, I ask myself how many streets I could draw and label by heart – surely no more than thirty? fifty? – on the clumsy maps I might make of Pittsfield or London, the cities I imagine I know best.

The Yellow Line carries me north towards the station and the road called Chandni Chowk. The Delhi-born poet Agha Shahid Ali wrote of the jasmine flowers scattered on this famous Old Delhi thoroughfare – its name means Moonlight Square – and of the goods from such cities as Isfahan, Kabul and Agra for sale along it.

Today the centre of Chandni Chowk is fenced off for construction, and yellow boards push the traffic – rickshaws, Japanese SUVs, ox-drawn carts – closer to and often onto the pavements that are crowded, even at this early hour, with beggars, shoeshine boys, hawkers and one professional letter-writer, seated on a cloth with a typewriter before him, which one nimble kid after another steps neatly over or around.

Distracted by waves of place lag, and by the signs – DELHI WEDDING, IMPERIAL PHOTO STORES, PROTEIN WORLD, VERMA JI PHOTOSTAT PRINTOUT – that flip past me like shuffling cards, I trip on a fragment of pavement, as a horn honks too close to me and the handlebar of a passing cycle catches my sleeve. I duck under an electro-shrub of thick, tangled wires strung mere centimetres above my head and take shelter in the alcove of a shop.

I sip from my bottle of water. I reach in my pocket for my phone to make a video for Mark, asleep on the far side of the world as Delhi rises on this one, and I find Kirun's poem. Reassured by its presence, and by the idea of hers, I step back into Chandni Chowk and let its currents carry me on towards the Red Fort.

The Red Fort is both the old heart of Mughal Delhi and a symbol of the modern Indian nation. Constructed by Shah Jahan in the middle of the seventeenth century, the writer William Dalrymple has described its importance to Delhi as like that of the Acropolis to Athens, or of the Colosseum to Rome. In 1943, Subhas Chandra Bose, a prominent Indian nationalist also known by the honorific 'Netaji', used the slogan 'Onward to Delhi' as he looked forward to a 'victory parade inside the ancient Red Fortress of India's metropolis'. On 16 August 1947, Nehru raised India's flag above it, and said: 'We have gathered here on a historic occasion at this ancient fort to win back what was ours.' Every year since then, the fort has been the focus of Independence Day celebrations.

I reach the eastern end of Chandni Chowk and wait to cross Netaji Subhash Marg, the wide and crowded avenue that crosses in front of the fort. I first stood at this junction with a friend who's also a pilot, and who had landed a 747 in Delhi only a few hours after I did. Traffic lights in Delhi are often not obeyed, and we waited here for ten or fifteen minutes, simply unable to cross. We discussed hailing an auto-rickshaw just to take us across the street, or even giving up, and we imagined the story we'd tell our friends, some night soon in a London pub, of how we got within metres of the Mughal Empire's seat, but no closer. Eventually, however, a family took pity and ushered us carefully over, one busy lane at a time.

This time the crossing is easier, and soon I'm approaching the barbican of the Lahore Gate, the fort's main entrance, where a sign tells me exactly where I am, and roughly when, too: FORT OF SEVENTH CITY OF DELHI.

I enter and walk through a grand arcade that holds a bazaar where Mughal princesses once shopped, and which today is filled with Indians and foreigners strolling past vendors of jewellery, clothing, handbags and tourist trinkets. Beyond, the fort opens up into what feels like the enclosed campus of an ancient university, characterised by a mix of Mughal structures – royal baths, gardens, pavilions, halls, a mosque, a Palace of Colors and a Drum House (beyond which only princes could proceed on horseback) – in different stages of restoration, together with British additions and various modern buildings.

Away from the main pedestrian routes I come across a bungalow that seems to have been all but abandoned in a stand of trees surrounded by untended fields, and so convincing is this image of a more rural life that I briefly forget that I'm in the central fortress of perhaps the greatest of Earth's cities. Wheeling above me are huge, storm-like clouds of large, dark birds. I've never seen so many birds above a metropolis, and I must remember to ask Kirun or her father about them.

I come to an arch bridge, its walkway flanked by arrow-slitted and partly fractured walls, which leads to the southern gate of

Salimgarh, another fort. Salimgarh once stood on an island in the Yamuna River, and Shah Jahan is said to have resided there during the Red Fort's construction. Now, rather than water, it's the anticlockwise lanes of Delhi's inner ring road – with their signs indicating the direction of the Kashmere Gate – that run between the two. A further pedestrian bridge – dust-red, and with Mughal-style embellishments along its railings – leads over the railway line that bisects Salimgarh as it runs from Delhi Junction, the city's first station, east to Ghaziabad.

Halfway across, I stop. There are trees everywhere, and suddenly, there's nothing to hear but the birds, and a few distant horns, until a train pulls up right below me, and I watch as hundreds of people, of all ages, jump down from the carriages onto the adjacent track, and start to walk the last of their journey to the station three-quarters of a mile or so further on.

Dozens of children wave and call up to me, and a warning I know Kirun loves – 'One train may hide another', from the title of a poem by Kenneth Koch – flashes in my mind and I panic that one of the kids, distracted, will get hit. So I walk on, but I'll remember their waves on another trip to Delhi, to another Mughal monument – the tomb of the sixteenth-century Emperor Humayun, which the poet Octavio Paz described as that 'high flame of rose' – when a group of smartly dressed schoolchildren run up and ask me where I am from, my profession, my salary and my name. Half an hour later, here in one of the many cities where my presence is so transient as to feel to me almost ghost-like, I'll hear voices shouting 'Mark! Mark!' and I'll look up to see them all smiling and waving down from the terrace on the tomb's monumental plinth.

Once I'm in the confines of the fort of Salimgarh proper, I walk over hilly lawns, past a disused prison, wells, the remains of artillery batteries, lonely lampposts and a few stray dogs, asleep where they've found shade. There are no other tourists, and only a few soldiers sit talking by a shuttered exhibition hall. A place where every-one else is a soldier must, I think, be a place I'm not meant to be, but they take no notice of me as I pass.

It's said that Ghalib would come here to fly kites with the emperor. Now, if I had a kite, where would I go? I walk up into the rustling, unmown portions of the dry lawn, towards one of the fort's highest points, from where I can look over Salimgarh's ramparts to the Yamuna River, and out to the span known as the Old Iron Bridge – the continuation, it takes me a moment to realise, of the railway line I stood above a few minutes ago. Along the river runs a road, lined with billboards, shops and informal settlements, and filled with motorbikes and auto-rickshaws and vehicles of every sort. The river's condition is not good, I'm told, but from here I cannot see that – only that there are many people moving near it, and many birds above.

I turn away from the river and walk towards a reddish stone bench whose seat has lost one of its corners. As I sit I remember how thirsty I am. I'm also chilly, a sensation that still manages to surprise me in Delhi. I fasten the top button of my shirt. A cicada-like medley of horns lifts from the road and drifts over the lawn as a flock of birds rises and another train clatters across the bridge. I drink half of a bottle of water, pause, then drink the rest. I take out my phone and read what Kirun wrote about Ghalib and the poem she's chosen:

The poem I'm sending you is one of his ghazals. It's a fairly popular one. Ghazals, as I'm sure you know,

– I did not –

are made up of couplets. Each couplet must function autonomously – it's not intended to be part of a narrative whole, as the stanzas of Western poems often are. Instead, it's linked formally and by a general mood.

I think of Kirun, of what time it is in Massachusetts, and of her father, who knows this great capital and its words so well. He is already ninety, but I don't know that he will pass on less than a year from now, and so I think, as I so often do, that when he next returns to Delhi I must do all I can to arrange a work trip that coincides with his days here. I reach into my pocket and take out the poem that his daughter sent, the pages now thigh-shaped and a little damp, even though, by Delhi's lights, this is a cold day.

I listen to the city that is not mine and I remember when I first told Kirun about the imaginary one that is. And though we've never been in Delhi together, it's easier than ever to believe that she's here with me now by this citadel above the holy river, or that we are together somewhere in Pittsfield. We're two friends on a broken bench beneath a tree; we're talking about a poem or our fathers; we speak over the noise from traffic on the nearby road, while above us a cloud of circling birds almost forms a spire. I unfold the pages and start to read.

CHAPTER 7

CITY OF RIVERS

Malacca, London,
Seoul and Calgary

NOT LONG AFTER my fortieth birthday I open, for the first time in years, a scrapbook Mom made for me. There are photos of humpbacks, taken from the deck of a whale-watching boat we boarded in downtown Boston, and a copy of a survey that she subsequently helped me write and distribute to everyone on our street, in which I asked our neighbours to 'please check the box which is your favourite vote': 'I would like to save whales' or 'I would not like to save whales'. (She also helped me send the unanimous responses somewhere, to the White House, I think; I remember a reply, a form letter, held by a magnet on the fridge.) There are report cards, and photos taken from atop the World Trade Center in New York sharing a page with ones of us in Pittsfield, which she's captioned 'City and Country!'

Midway through the scrapbook is a map of an imaginary city. I was in seventh grade, maybe, when I made it, and the city it depicts is a country mouse's wide-eyed dream: there are monorail stations, various churches, each marked by a blue cross, and an aeroplane that waits where the runways of the 'Intergalactal Airport' intersect. In the western quarter of the city is something I went to some trouble to conceal, with white correction fluid that's now as finely cracked as a cloud in an oil painting.

Beyond the churches, the highly developed transportation infrastructure, and my mistake, lie the banks of the city's river. In fact, the river appears to be the dominant feature of the metropolis, and I'm sorry that on this quiet afternoon, as I run my index finger slowly back and forth over the blue ink almost three decades after I drew it, I can't remember as little as its name, or which way it flows.

Seventeen years after we first met, Mark and I are in a park, walking down an arrowhead of land that ends at a point we can already see. Lacking a canoe, we've nowhere left to go. There are no leaves on the trees, and not much ice on the river, and we ask each other, looking out at the narrowing grey and brown land, how we might tell that this is March and not November.

To our left is the east branch of the Housatonic River. This Mohican name, said to mean 'river beyond the mountain', was recorded by the Dutch as Westenhook, and as Ausotunnoog in the time of Major John Talcott, who was the first Englishman to see its Berkshire reaches, and who was reported to have massacred twenty-five Native Americans on its banks in the summer of 1676.

When I first encountered the phrase 'People of the Waters that Are Never Still' in reference to the Mohicans, I assumed that the waters were those of the Housatonic. Later, I spoke with Heather Bruegl, the director of cultural affairs for the Stockbridge-Munsee Band of Mohican Indians, who told me that the phrase is a translation of *Muhheconneok*, from which the name Mohican was itself derived; and that the waters in question are those of *Mahicannituck*, the River That Flows Both Ways, also known as the (tidal) Hudson.

The Housatonic, in the east of the Mohican homelands, roughly parallels the Hudson's path through the western portions. And while the Housatonic, Bruegl explained to me, is traditionally her tribe's second river, it's nevertheless of great significance: a means of transportation through the area where Pittsfield arose; a source of fertility to the lands it passes, and of water and food to uncountable generations; and a living, breathing being.

When I spoke to Bruegl, she was around 800 miles west of Pittsfield, on her tribe's present-day lands in Wisconsin. She described the journeys her forebears were forced to make from the Berkshires in the aftermath of the American Revolution – first to central New York State, then to Indiana, and finally to a series of locations in Wisconsin – as a trail of tears. A few months before we spoke she had come to the Berkshires to visit Mohican sites, address a conservation group and spend time on the Housatonic. Nature, she told me, will speak if you open up to it, and today, she added, it's especially important for young people to return to their ancestral home and come to know its waters.

To our right is the river's west branch. Directly ahead of us now, as Mark and I come to a halt, the path runs off the embankment and down into a pile of mud that is only half a metre high, though its scale seems off, somehow, as its peaks zig and zag with all the detail of an alpine ridge. Beyond it the two branches of Pittsfield's river meet.

I think of Pittsfield as a watery city. There are two decent-sized lakes where the Berkshire gang picnicked, swam and skated. My middle school was a stone's throw from a river, and I crossed another each day on the way to high school. And there were maybe a half dozen spots in the woods where I played with my brother, or with Rich – the friend who moved away when I was in the toughest years of middle school – in or near what I thought of as separate rivers. We'd park our bikes and splash along on foot, and linger beneath the creepy damp undersides of small bridges until we scared ourselves, or we'd sit on muddy, sunlit banks and stare at beavers that took no notice of us as they paddled past, and look out for the bears that I never saw swimming, though others sometimes did. It was only as an adult that I realised that the nine or ten rivers or streams

I knew in Pittsfield were branches of the same river, or sometimes even the same branch.

I don't remember this park from my childhood, though it's less than a mile from my old house. It was restored in the early 2000s as part of a legal settlement related to the pollution in the river that resulted from General Electric's vast but now dismantled industrial operation in Pittsfield. At its peak in 1943, more than 13,600 people worked in those factories, a figure then equivalent to more than a quarter of the city's population. When I was a kid many thousands still did, including the parents of many of my classmates. I don't remember a time when I didn't know what neighbors meant when they mentioned GE, or, as older folks sometimes phrased it, 'the' GE.

The city's complicated relationship with its industry – generation after generation of excellent middle-class jobs, then the layoffs that hammered Pittsfield in the age of globalisation, and the environmental effects that lingered long after the paychecks stopped – may be of wider interest only because Pittsfield's story, in American terms, is archetypal: the city was home to Fourth of July festivities that for years were televised nationally as *Your Hometown America Parade*, and Lou Gehrig buried a home run in the same river of which Oliver Wendell Holmes Sr is said to have proclaimed 'There's no tonic like the Housatonic'. But none of this protected the river from pollution, nor the city it runs through from the devastating economic changes that arrived here from far beyond the Housatonic's headwaters.

The two branches of the river sparkle even on this grey afternoon. The water looks clean, but then it did when I was a kid, too, long before the cleanup began near the factories and slowly progressed south to the point where we're standing. I try but fail to see how the clear waters from the two branches might blend in front of us, as the words of a Carly Simon song – about dreamers, the city we call the New Jerusalem, and a river we should allow to run – rise in my mind.

I want Pittsfield's land and air and waters to be as clean, forever, as they now appear to be. And I want Pittsfield to be strong and well. I want everyone in Pittsfield to be secure, and for the size and stability of the city's middle class to be an object of admiration and study among economists and politicians from far away. I want new factories for Pittsfield, world-leading ones, and university-like facilities to house researchers and green technologies like those cited in the pages of the science magazines Dad loved to read.

What little can you do for your home? I think of when I first began to write not only in my diary but also for print, and how happy I was to publish an article about Pittsfield and the resurgence of its downtown in a London newspaper widely read in the world's boardrooms, and, in the course of my research, to have reconnected with former colleagues of my parents. Since then I've tried to work Pittsfield into any article I can.

But what, I ask myself again, can you really do for your home? A kid I remember well from the halls of our high school grew up to co-found a major Internet retailer – his father, a retired GE engineer, lent a hand in its early days – and not long ago he accomplished what I routinely fantasise I'd do if I won the lottery: he created hundreds of jobs in the very heart of Pittsfield, in a former clock factory and paper mill that stands along the west branch of the Housatonic.

The wind picks up and I pull my hat down over my ears. We're getting cold, Mark and I agree; it's time to find coffee. I heard it's meant to snow today, I tell Mark, but not much; the winters in Pittsfield – thanks in part, I know, to cars like the one we drove here, and planes like the ones I dreamed of flying, and industry like that which deserted my hometown – are not like they were. I place my hands in my pockets to warm them and then, before we start back, I take a last look south as the first flakes appear above us, swirl over the joined current, and vanish where they fall.

MALACCA

I find and board what I hope is the right bus at Kuala Lumpur's airport station. It's not full and it's easy to find a window seat. We join the evening traffic and inch our way out of Malaysia's capital, along a spotless highway lined with such breathtaking lushness that I can't help but speculate how often it must be cut back to prevent the jungle from reabsorbing the paving. The downpour we landed in finally stops and I look down at the elaborate drainage channels that edge the highway, and try to remember a day in Kuala Lumpur on which it didn't rain.

The traffic slows. I study the place-names on the signs and look up a few on my phone. I put on my headphones, sleep a bit, play a few games and listen to music. As we accelerate towards the State of Malacca and its eponymous capital I doze again, then wake to a sign over the road that reads:

MELAKA BERWIBAWA

– Excellent Malacca – and

SELAMAT DATANG KE MELAKA

– Welcome to Malacca.

We pull into a bus station in this city of around half a million inhabitants. It's dark, I'm tired, and I briefly wish I had never left KL, where I'd be having dinner with my colleagues now. I find a room, make my way upstairs and set down the bag I zipped up in London yesterday. Then I head out for a stroll.

On one of the picturesque pedestrian bridges over the river a couple ask for a photo not of them, but of me with them, and one degree of separation between Pittsfield and their home city in China vanishes. I stop at a street stall to have some chicken strips and a beer. As I chat with the cook I'm surprised to learn that his street stall is not what everything in Malacca appears to be in my first hours here: a fixture. He decided, he tells me, to try out this business only a few days ago. He bought a small grill, some chicken – that's the plan. He's doing well, in the sense that it's tasty and business seems brisk. He asks why I'm in Malacca and cannot believe I'm a pilot or that I landed in Kuala Lumpur only this afternoon; as I finish my small dinner and return along the river to my rented room, I can't quite believe it myself.

Hier Leyt Begraven Hendrik Schenkenbergh, in sijn leven Opper-Coopman en Tweede Persoon der Stad en Fortresse Malacca, overleden den 29ᵉⁿ Juny 1671

Here lies buried Hendrik Schenkenbergh. During his life Chief Trader and Second in Command of the City and Fortress of Malacca, died June 29th, 1671.

Refreshed by a deep sleep but winded by my walk up from the riverbank, I pause in the bright tropical light to read the antiquated Dutch on the gravestone, then look up to where the roof of the church of Saint Paul would be. This church, briefly home to the remains of Saint Francis Xavier, has a better excuse than most for lacking one: it was built in 1521, and a sign identifies it as the oldest church in Southeast Asia.

The origins of Malacca, as well as its later fortune and prominence, are inseparable from its location. Lying to the south of the mountains of the Malay peninsula, and untroubled by typhoons, it's also a fine spot to wait out the monsoon's seasonal reversal, on which, for centuries, so much of Asia's commerce turned. Most auspiciously, perhaps, the Strait of Malacca – named for this settlement – forms part of the shortest sea route between Africa, Europe, the Middle

East and the subcontinent on the one hand, and all of East Asia on the other.

Tomé Pires, a Portuguese apothecary who arrived in Malacca in 1512, described the strait as a 'gullet', marvelled that 'no trading port as large as Malacca is known', and added – with spices and the interlocking fortunes of far-flung cities in mind – 'Whoever is Lord of Malacca, has his hand on the throat of Venice.' Today, perhaps one-third of the world's maritime trade passes through the strait, including much of the oil that must travel from the Gulf to China and the other booming economies of East Asia; the strait and the city have even given their name to the largest category of ship that can pass through the shallow waters: Malaccamax. (Qualifying ships typically have a draught of less than twenty-three metres.)

While it's easy to imagine that there has always been a settlement at the spot where the Malacca River runs into the sea, the history of the city is often dated to the arrival, around the dawn of the fifteenth century, of a Sumatran prince named Parameswara. When he first landed, a small community of Orang Selat, Straits people, lived along the river's estuary. Parameswara made his home to the south of it, and a wooden bridge was raised between the banks.

Thus was born the Malacca Sultanate, which grew in power throughout the fifteenth century, as did its commercial and political ties to Ming-era China, perhaps best exemplified by the visits of Zheng He, the Chinese admiral whose vast fleets sailed as far as East Africa. It's said that more than eighty languages were spoken here during this period, Malacca's golden age, and that its harbour could hold more than 2,000 ships.

To me, on only my first full day here, and exhausted by my efforts to identify even a fraction of the languages I hear around me, Malacca still seems to be a city of worldly visitors. It is also a city of artefacts: one museum has examples of the fourteenth-century Malay currency that took the form of small but three-dimensional tin animals, such as crocodiles, crabs and fish; and in a traditional

Malaccan house I spot a dusty, jammed typewriter, its paper rest marked with BRITISH EMPIRE as ordinarily as the logo of a multinational corporation might be affixed to a business-person's laptop today. Malacca is a city of flowers, too – hanging in baskets, growing wild, painted into the tiles on the benches and depicted in the glass panels of streetlamps – and of varied names, such as the Malay (written with Roman letters, or in the Arabic-derived Jawi script), Chinese, Dutch, or English ones inscribed on its grave markers.

But I already know that what I will remember best about Malacca is its river. When I ask a Malacca-born man at a café about the river's importance today, he replies: We don't rely on it anymore, it's somewhat for tourists.

And so on my second day in the city I'm where I should be, on a dock on the Sungai Melaka, the Malacca River, waiting for sunset – jet lag usually troubles me much less in a city after dark, when the sun isn't moving around the sky, insisting on something like the true hour – and for the boat that will take a group of us upstream into the heart of the city and back.

I take a photo of the river to send to Seeta, an English friend whose Indian grandfather worked in Malacca as a court interpreter under British and then Japanese officials. Seeta's mother was born in Malacca's hospital, and recalls a 1940s childhood made memorable by air-raid sirens, and by the snakes and hens that ran under their stilt-raised wooden house not far from the riverbank.

Then, as a prayer call echoes out across the city, I try to reconcile the river before me with the paintings and old photos that I've come across earlier today in a museum here. An unsigned modern painting (based on notes taken in the early 1400s by Ma Huan, a translator who travelled with Zheng He, and who described the tigers of Malacca as creatures who might turn into men and walk the city's streets) depicts the river bisecting a settlement that looks little more than a village. The structure that Ma Huan called a palace rises from the south-east bank, within a rectangular compound shielded by a wall of vertical tree trunks. A guard stands by its only visible entrance, while, nearby, a wooden bridge leads to the north-west bank.

Today I also came across a photograph, taken of the riverside in 1901. In it, there are utility poles and a few streetlights on the south-east bank, and an awning that partly covers the steps that lead down to the water. A bicycle is propped on a stone embankment and three small boats with leaning sails float nearby. Another photograph, from the 1960s, also in black and white, captures a mix of boats on the river, some still with masts but now also some without. The age of motors has reached the shore, too: the bicycle has been replaced by six parked cars, behind which a solitary adult figure in light-coloured clothing is walking away from the camera, apparently unaware of the photographer. Whoever it was must be elderly now; or perhaps they are no longer alive.

The muezzin finishes and I look out over a young Dutch couple, several headscarf-clad Malaysian women and a dozen or so Chinese travellers waiting near me on the dock. There's an older couple, too; they are English and it's not impossible that I flew them from London to Kuala Lumpur a few nights ago. Something about them catches my attention. I know nothing about them, of course – not their exact ages, nor their hardships nor the state of their health – but they seem to me to be profoundly lucky: they're together and laughing, and able to make a long journey to a fascinating city on the far side of their world.

It's time: we climb into the small boat and motor off.

Moments later we pass under the first of the bridges dressed in multicoloured lights programmed to mimic water, as if light itself were streaming off like so much tropical rain; while the panels and recesses on their undersides, where in many cities you might expect to see nests, spiderwebs and graffiti, are lit in bright, pastel hues.

More light, and noise, too, pours onto the river from the cycle rickshaws available for hire along its banks. A music-blaring, Hello

Kitty–themed model – by far the hardest to look either at or away from – is encased in heart-shaped rings of pulsing, purple-white lights and plush, beribboned incarnations of the famous Japanese character. A cross between a slot machine, a jukebox, a penny-farthing and a one-man band, it's more light, sound and fury than vehicle, and the effect, at least on a jet-lagged introvert, is nearly hallucinatory.

Our little boat steams on beneath the riverside buzz of cafés, vendors, crowds of tourists and rickshaw drivers touting for customers. So garish is the light reflected by the water that I could forget that we are not inside, on a stream built to wind through the dazzling artifice of a Las Vegas casino, and it's hard not to feel a little sorry for the trees, whose nights must be far from restful. Some are lit by colourful splotches fired into their boughs from below; others are covered in dense white lights, not only their trunks but their branches, with further vines of white lights trailing from these, as if in a forest on another planet, in which trees spend their days soaking up light and their nights emitting it.

Along some of the river's reaches, the buildings cluster close to the bank, but the nearly medieval aura they might conjure is dispersed by the choppy surface of this narrow and much-trafficked river, which catches, repeats and twists the image of the bright red, green, blue, or yellow electric tube lights laid along its embankments. Further inland, right before our boat turns back, the bankside structures appear more residential. Even here, however, the railings are drenched in multicoloured lines of lights of the kind that are usually white in Pittsfield, and deployed only at Christmastime, to suggest icicles.

Perhaps, I think, it's the narrowness of the river here that helps it concentrate the light. In London, when you cross the Thames after dark, there are patches of smouldering reflections here and there, but the impression I have most often is of a realm that would still prove deadly to most of us – and one, at night at least, that contradicts the hopefulness embodied by the bright city, and its ancient promise of safety in numbers.

Our boat returns to its dock. I'm sad to disembark and unsure of where to go. I'm a little lonely, is the short of it. I don't know how to say thank you to the guide in Malay. I've made no connection or conversation with anyone else on the boat. There's no nod or flash of eye contact as we part, and I try to imagine the rooms to which we will each go home, in England or Holland or China, and the different surfaces on which we'll each lay out our suitcases in order to remove the clothing we wore tonight and throw it on a pile to be washed; and I'm struck by how, in this historically worldly city, ours was certainly not the first riverside gathering of travellers from these same lands.

I find my way back to a restaurant I noticed from the boat and sit at a wobbly table, mere centimetres from the embankment's vertical edge. The tubes of yellow lighting along the river here, which I now realise are part of a recent, tourist-focused restoration, twist on the water's dishevelled surface, and ripple like an old-fashioned flashback from a film, until a boat passes and its wake fractures the reflections completely. I send a zoomed-in photo of the river's surface to Mark. It's midday where he is and he has no idea what my camera was pointing at; I'll have to remind myself, as well, when the image next catches my eye, as I sit on the couch at home and scroll through my photos: I was in Malacca, and this was the light on its river at night.

LONDON

Mark and I are nearing the end of our fifth date. We had dinner at Pizza Express near Tower Bridge and now we're walking on the path along the south side of the Thames. We pass the capital's new City Hall, which I bank over most days in the last great turn before touchdown at Heathrow, and then we walk under the spot where a magician will soon suspend himself in a glass box that will survive, like a broadcaster's logo, in many of my memories of this time and this stretch of the river.

I don't look up at the planes as we walk. Not when I can hear that one is directly over us, and not even when I can tell from the sound that it's a 747, as we laugh about something on our way to get strawberries from a market, and head downstream to find a bench.

SEOUL

I'm reminded I'm not in Pittsfield by the sign: THOSE WEARING HANBOK – traditional Korean dress – CAN ENTER GYEONGBOK-GUNG PALACE WITHOUT A TICKET.

A few years ago a friend asked me: What's the largest city you've never been to? I didn't know, and I was surprised that I'd never been curious about this myself. The answer at the time, I later discovered, was Seoul.

On this, my first day in Seoul, I got up very early and took a twenty-minute train ride from the station near my hotel to what seemed from my map the right place to start: Seoul Station. Then I walked north, stopping to have coffee and to wander through Seoul's ultramodern City Hall, which curves like a glass wave above the original stone City Hall and a patch of green that's crowded today with workers preparing for a concert. Soon after, I reached the ticket booths of Gyeongbokgung – the Palace Greatly Blessed by Heaven – and now I join the crowds strolling through the gates, past red-robed guards holding gleaming, tasseled polearms.

The palace complex was first built at the end of the fourteenth century by King Taejo, the founder of the Joseon Dynasty, who chose the site of Seoul thanks in part to its position in a valley between four mountains, which was considered auspicious according to tra-ditional notions of geomancy. At its peak the walled complex –

itself almost a city – included around 500 buildings and around 7,500 rooms. 한글, Hangul, the writing system used by Koreans, was created in the Hall of Worthies in the fifteenth century. The script, which is the most fascinating I've encountered and much more easily learned, I'm told, than the thousands of characters used in Chinese and Japanese, is an achievement celebrated each year on Hangul Day, which falls on 9 October here in South Korea, where it's a public holiday, and on 15 January in North Korea.

My plan for the rest of the day is to walk to the Han River. The Han is strikingly wide where it passes through the city, stretching, in some reaches, more than two-thirds of a mile from one shore to the other. Its overall roughly east-west course meanders through the centre of the capital, tracing a path that, to a jet-lagged travel-ler, might echo that of the far narrower Thames in London, and, indeed, some bends seem so analogous that when I first looked at the Han's bridges on a map I half expected to see Waterloo Bridge instead of the Dongho, and Blackfriars where the Seongsu stands.

En route to the banks of the Han I wait to cross a large boule-vard. It's tree lined and partly pedestrianised; I can see an ice-cream shop and picnic tables, and hear running water. I start to walk down its median and come to water cascading through pools, and to steps leading down to a waterway that emerges midstream, as it were, from Seoul's concrete carapace.

This is the Cheonggyecheon, whose west-to-east flow was under-stood, in geomantic terms, to balance the east-to-west course of the Han. For many centuries Seoul's children played in it, while their mothers collected water or washed clothes nearby; at other times it served as a sewer. After the Second World War, urbanisation and industrialisation brought modern levels of pollution to the stream, and shantytowns to its banks. In the 1950s the stream was cov-ered over and in the 1970s, as in so many cities whose clear runs of waterways proved irresistible to transportation planners, an elevated highway was constructed along it. The name of the stream was kept alive, in part, by 'Cheonggyecheon 8th Street', one of South Korea's most popular protest songs in the 1990s. In the early 2000s, the roadway was torn down and the stream was unearthed and restored.

Today, the Cheonggyecheon runs below the level of the surrounding city, so you must descend via ramps, stairs, or elevators to reach the paths along it. Once there you can follow a naturalistic but highly planned corridor, lined with greenery, public art and signs that feature a flame and a number to indicate how many calories you may have burned. There are umbrellas, too, big enough to share, and to suggest that showers in this city, however unimaginable on this crisp autumn morning, can be not only intense, but brief enough to wait out in the company of strangers.

The times I walk the furthest are my first days in new cities, and Seoul is true to form. After meandering from the station to the palace, I now stroll for several more miles along this stream. The sound of flowing water must be soothing to the jet-lagged, I think – the restored stream is regularly described as a 'miracle' or an 'oasis', and leading architects such as Tadao Ando have given it high marks – but it's not accurate to describe its power here as that of nature, for the modern stream would hardly run on its own. It's not quite the engineered reversal of the Chicago River, but nevertheless, for the sake of an artificial urban amenity, much of the water has been pumped up from the river to which, via a tributary, it will shortly return.

Indeed, many have pointed out that the Cheonggyecheon isn't exactly a restored ecosystem: one critic suggested it might be better described as, in effect, a horizontal fountain, while the pastor and environmental activist Byung-sung Choi described it as a 'gigantic concrete fish tank'. Perhaps, then, it's only in contrast with the march of the surrounding megalopolis that nature appears to be thriving here. Shallow reaches and miniature marshes line its path; stands of native willows, poplars and Amur silvergrass rise along it; temperatures near the stream, studies report, can be at least a couple of degrees cooler than on roads several blocks away. The number of fish and bird species has increased since the stream was restored; particularly auspicious sightings include 일반 잉어, *ilban ing-eo*, common carp, considered lucky by Koreans, and 원앙, *wonang*, mandarin duck, said to mate for life and therefore, re-created in wooden pairs, a traditional wedding gift. The water is perfectly clear, and as shoals of silvery fins scatter from my shadow I recall summer days spent casting lines from a Pittsfield causeway with Dad and my brother; and I think, as well, of the signs that today line the Housatonic River's Berkshire reaches to warn you not to eat what you catch, with a capitalised admonition that appears in English and Spanish alongside four cutlery-flanked plates with a duck, a fish, a turtle and a frog on them, each beneath the diagonal slash that means: Don't.

If this Seoul stream suggests how cities might advantageously blend the natural and the artificial, it also offers opportunities to compare old with new. Again and again I stop to stare at the occasional decrepit T-shaped columns, which remain as monuments to a former age of urban planning, and to all the bottlenecked journeys that must have been made along the highway they once held high. I also love the historical markers that identify intriguing piles of rubble as the relics of more ancient infrastructure: 'This is the site of the Hyogyeonggyo. It was also called Yeongpunggyo. Or it was called Maenggyo or Sogyeongdari (meaning a bridge for the blind) because many blind persons lived all around here. It is not known when the bridge was first built.' Most entrancing of all is a map of 1820s Seoul mounted on tiles above the river. In this reproduction of the woodblock *Suseon jeondo*, the Comprehensive Map of the Capital, it's easy to appreciate the roundness of the city, and the fable-worthy perfection of the wall and the rings of mountains that enclose it.

Seoul is a city in which gas masks are stored behind clear panels on the platforms of subway stations. (The closet in my hotel room is also equipped with several, along with emergency flashlights and escape ropes.) So it's not surprising that along the Cheonggyecheon, as well, public safety is of prime concern. Placards warn of confined spaces where a flood might trap you, and escape ladders rise at regular intervals from the walkways, while swing-out panels in the grey stone walls under the bridges – by signs that warn BEFORE THE FLOODGATE OPENS DURING RAINFALL, EVACUATE THIS AREA IMMEDIATELY – remind me of every fairy tale with a castle and a secret door.

At points it's possible to cross to the far bank via stepping stones set not quite at random in the streambed. It's a more playful design than merely adding more pedestrian bridges, and I can't be alone in remembering what it felt like, as a kid, to hop between slick rocks that sometimes rolled away underfoot. Stepping between the river stones of central Seoul, too, is more easily done at speed, a fact that several children are learning today, and at least one pilot is recalling. And this is how I spend my first day in one of the planet's largest metropolises: so pleased by this manicured tributary, one whose flow is impelled by the turning of unseen pumps, that I never reach the real river.

CALGARY

It's only September, I remind myself, but the chilly and overcast weather makes it impossible to forget that this city lies deep in North America's interior, and that among Canada's large cities, it's by far the highest. At 1,099 metres, the elevation of Calgary's airport is barely higher than the peak of Mount Greylock, my reference mountain in the Berkshires, where the views encompass five states, and the trees grow stunted and bonsai'd by the wind; and so the easiest way for me to appreciate the magnitude of the elevation here is to imagine Calgary, if not as a city in the sky, then as one whose towers are perched on the summit of a snowy Mount Greylock, and whose suburbs and provinces are cantilevered out over its fast-falling slopes.

Through the thick windows of my high hotel room I can see but not hear that it has started to rain. I want to go for a run but cold, damp weather like this makes it hard to commit. I'll feel chilly only for the first minute, I say to myself, and maybe again when I stop at the edge of a road, as pedestrians do so faithfully here, until the lights indicate it's safe to cross. Soon after, I'll reach the riverfront and there will be no more lights or cars.

Whenever I read that 'being present' is the key to equilibrium and happiness, I'm reminded that I have no idea how mindfulness is meant to relate to the act of imagining, that is, to the ability to be somewhere other than where I physically am. When I was young and struggling with being gay, and with my speech impediment, and with whatever else loomed large then, it felt almost lifesaving to be able to travel to my imaginary city, or to imagine myself in a real one that was sufficiently distant to feel safe. Even now, in a reasonably content adulthood, I find that the ability to be elsewhere easily is often a joy, or at least a means of ensuring that dishwashing, dental procedures and delays – in traffic, on public transit, or in falling asleep – pass more agreeably.

It can also make exercise easier, at least on days like today, when I'm not in the mood for it. I know I should try to run outside, rather than on a treadmill in the hotel's climate-controlled gym. Outside, I'll be present enough to see something of the city and the world; present enough for honest Canadian rain to pelt me, and for me to nod to and be encouraged by other runners as it does. In contrast, in the hotel's gym, I won't get wet. I won't be cold for even a second. I'll likely speak to no one; I'll put in my headphones and run fast to my favourite music and think of anything or anyplace I like. And perhaps, I say to myself, this hotel has those newer treadmills on which you can run a virtual course through a forest or up a mountain trail or – my favourite – along the waterfront esplanade of a pleasant but unidentified city, one I run through only virtually, but again and again, in the often windowless gyms of hotels on six continents.

I put on my shorts and sit on the floor as I tie my trainers. The wind must be picking up, I think, as I watch the raindrops silently smack the panes. Inside or outside? I berate myself for my indecision, and half scowl at the idea of mindfulness, too. Still, on this occasion, the scolding (but potentially mindful) Puritan in me wins out. I leave my knotted white headphones on the desk by the room-service menu I may use to reward myself later, and head down to the lobby. An elderly couple are standing by the doorway, struggling with their wet umbrellas as they stare at me and my running shorts as if I'm a fool. I want to tell them that, yes, I agree, it's stupid, but I've promised myself a hot chocolate after, and a bowl of pasta after that. I nod as I pass them and run out into Calgary's cold drizzle, where I shiver – but only for a moment, the scold dutifully records – and start down to the riverfront.

The source of the Bow River is Bow Lake, which lies beneath Bow Glacier in Banff National Park. At Calgary it's joined by the Elbow River – Bow, Elbow, the names are hard to keep straight, and indeed, the city's tap water is an aptly even blend – and together they continue towards the often frozen and featureless expanses of Hudson Bay, which many flights from Europe crisscross on their great circle tracks to places as legendarily hot as Phoenix. Most of the Bow River's volume consists of snowmelt from the Rockies, and in some seasons its milkiness makes it easy to recall that particles of glacier-pulverised mountains are floating past. At other times the water appears clear, or emerald, as it does a little on even this grey day.

It's only early autumn, by my Pittsfield-bound reckoning, but in this high and interior Canadian city the yellow leaves are already piling on the edges of the paths. I run over the Jaipur Bridge – IN RECOGNITION OF THE FRIENDSHIP AND GOODWILL BETWEEN THE CITY OF JAIPUR, INDIA, AND THE CITY OF CALGARY, CANADA – and then cross back and head south-east down the riverfront trail.

I've walked or run on the waterfronts of many cities but Calgary's is particularly fine: the river burbles as it curves around small islands; there are nature trails – well-tended and well-signed – and pedestrian bridges and art installations; and in this microcosm of the country, people are friendly and it's not crowded. If I was wearing a camera, and it was a brighter day, I could be creating my own digital course for a high-end treadmill, though – and even as I wave back to a waving runner – I appreciate that it's difficult to conceive of a less mindful thought.

I cross under a bridge, past concrete abutments adorned with a public art project for which Calgarians were photographed wearing papier-mâché masks, including a blue-eyebrowed, red-lipped mask worn, I'll later learn, by a participant named Don, who explained that he chose that mask because its character seemed so neighbourly. I stop under another bridge for a quick break, by gauges that track the river's inconstant depth: seasonal variations, impending floods of the sort that have occasionally imperilled the city, and some measure of the Bow Glacier's accelerated melting in response to climate change. Then I head on, pausing only to jog in place before each of the informational signs I pass.

THERE HAVE ALWAYS BEEN SOME CALGARIANS WHO HAVE SEEN THE BEAUTY AND PUBLIC VALUE OF THE RIVER VALLEYS, says one.

WE ARE STILL MAKING CHOICES THAT DETERMINE THE KIND OF CITY WE WILL CREATE, reads another.

I'm wet now, a mixture of rain and sweat, and when my runner's high kicks in, it does so as a mad love for Calgary: *This, here and now, is the ultimate city*, I think, as my old imaginary one flickers to life as it once so often did, and alters itself even as I picture it, to accommodate and reflect the pleasing new facts of all that's real around me.

I see a freight train, rolling not much faster than I'm running, and I want to wave to its driver, in kinship, perhaps, with my next-door neighbour from Pittsfield, who worked as a conductor on the trains that run from Albany down to New York, and with all those who spend their working days looking out through the front windows of large vehicles. I run on, and then pause when I reach the meeting point of the Bow and the Elbow Rivers, where Fort Calgary – founded in 1875 by the newly formed North-West Mounted Police, the predecessors of the Mounties – stands. Rivers meet; a fort rises; a future city finds its name.

The rain lets up as I read an information board: IF EVERYTHING PLANNED HAD ACTUALLY BEEN BUILT, CALGARY WOULD HAVE BEEN THE SAME SIZE AS CHICAGO. I jog across the Elbow on a stylish pedestrian bridge – curving steel railings, wooden benches, sleek grey cylinders with lights mounted within – and look down a street that runs parallel to this greenway. Only a few cars stand outside its houses. Most people, I suppose, are at work. They drive away in the morning and come back in the evening. As a pilot it can be hard to recall this rhythm, or to remember that nearly all of Calgary's inhabitants will be at home tonight, brushing their teeth and climbing into their beds while I'm in the glowing cockpit of a jet parked at their airport, sipping tea as I carefully plan the trans-Arctic route that will carry me away.

I continue running, past a bear-proof rubbish bin covered with photos of flowers, and then a little further along the river before I decide, finally, that it's time to turn back. Not long after, I pause to retie the soaked laces of my left trainer beneath a bronze statue of a Mountie and his horse. Running around its grey concrete plinth are dark metal letters in a sloping script: *What was it like to stand in the middle of a wide open prairie and imagine a city?*

So I stand, close my eyes, and try this for myself: not only a prairie, but this one; not just any rivers, but these two; until – I'm in a T-shirt, it's raining again, this is Calgary in late September – I start to shiver, and I open my eyes and run on.

CHAPTER 8

CITY OF AIR

Copenhagen, Nairobi,
Petrópolis and Kuwait

WHEN I WAS A KID and I imagined my city, I never considered how it might smell. I never thought about the winds that might reach it in one season or the next – winds that might have been first named and mythologised thousands of years previously, and that more recently had been harnessed by the city's mills and ships, and that still ease or slow the migrations of the birds that touch down on the lakes in the city's parks, and on the restored canals that recall a former age of its industry.

Not once did I consider all the breaths that would be taken, or the millions of chests that must rise and fall at every moment of the lives that formed the metropolis. The problem, when you only imagine a place, and especially when you do so alone, is that there's no one to point out such obvious omissions; there are no helpful friends or stern inspectors to tap you on the shoulder and warn you: Your city has no air.

PITTSFIELD

I'm sixteen and as excited as I've ever been in my life. I've come to my hometown's municipal airport many times to watch the planes with my parents, but I've never before come for a flying lesson.

The instructor says he has some paperwork to complete before we head out to his aircraft. He's filling the boxes of a form, at a speed that suggests he's done this many times. He asks me how much I weigh. Then he looks to a gauge, which I realise indicates the temperature of the outside air, rather than the air of this room in a low, ordinary building next to the apron where Pittsfield's planes rest.

The air here isn't usually a problem, he says as he works, we're not that high up. It's nothing like you might find out west. And anyway, today isn't hot. But if you calculate your takeoff performance every time, he adds, as he opens a spiral-bound manual and runs his finger across a finely lined graph, if you do it no matter where you are in the world, you'll never get caught out.

COPENHAGEN

After takeoff from London we flew over the North Sea and the Jutland peninsula and across the island of Sjælland towards the Øresund, the busy strait on which Copenhagen lies. On the strait's far side we crossed briefly into Swedish airspace and now we start a series of turns back towards Denmark and its capital.

I'm twenty-nine. I've only recently qualified as an Airbus pilot and this flight is one of my first to Copenhagen. The westerly winds are fierce – about thirty knots on the ground – and so, looking down at the galaxy of whitecaps ripped from the sound's dark surface, I anticipate a bumpy final approach.

Surprisingly, however, the last minutes of this flight are rail-smooth. After we land my experienced colleague explains that both the strong winds and their evenness aren't unusual in the skies around Copenhagen, where there are no significant hills, either to slow fast-flowing rivers of air in the lower atmosphere or to introduce turbulence to them. I thank him for these facts about this city and its air, and I add them to the notes that I've been advised that a pilot, especially one early in their career, should make about the meteorological vagaries of every city they come to know.

NAIROBI

Dusk fell while we were over Sudan, near the place where the Blue and White Niles meet and Khartoum rises. Now, between the clear stars and the unseen highlands of Ethiopia, we're completing the preparations for our approach to Nairobi.

African cities such as Johannesburg, Windhoek, Kampala, Lusaka and Gaborone, as well as Addis Ababa, which is not far to the north-east of our present position, and Nairobi itself, dead ahead, have something in common: all sit at high elevations (Gaborone's airport, at around 1,000 metres, is the lowest of these seven; Addis Ababa is the highest, at around 2,300 metres). Temperature falls with altitude, and one result of their loftiness is that they all have a far more temperate climate than would otherwise be expected for inland cities on our hottest continent. Nevertheless, they are much warmer than the standard scientific model of the atmosphere postulates, and so pilots describe them – along with cities that share similar positions or elevations, such as Mexico City, Tehran and Denver, especially in summer – as 'hot and high'.

That standard model of the atmosphere is of enormous importance to pilots, because it allows us to calculate how divergences from it – most dramatically, those associated with hot and high cities – affect flight. Higher or hotter air is thinner, which means engines have less of it to breathe. In thinner air we must also fly faster to obtain the same amount of lift from the wings. On an approach to a hot and high city, thanks to our higher speed, our turns are wider, and we might require half as many miles again to slow to our landing speed. Finally, after we land, we require more of the runway to slow down, and in doing so we impart much more heat to the brakes.

Tonight, the air of Nairobi – whose airport sits at an official elevation of 1,625 metres, or just over one mile – offers a textbook example of hot and high conditions. The temperature at the airport is in the mid-20s. (Mom, who was no fan of New England's cold winters in her later years, nor its humid summers, once asked my well-travelled dad, in half-exasperation, if there was anywhere on Earth where the air is so mild that she could forget about its temperature entirely, throughout the year. A city near the equator, but one high enough to be temperate, like Nairobi or Quito, Dad amiably suggested, identifying 'hot and high' conditions without ever using the aviation term.) In fact, however, though the temperature in Nairobi tonight seems perfectly agreeable, its divergence from the standard atmospheric model – according to which we'd expect a city at this elevation to have a temperature of only around 4 degrees – is extreme.

We receive our final descent clearance and proceed south-west, past the city, before turning north-east to align with the runway. As we fly near the ridgeline-mounted navigation beacon known as Ngong we deploy the speedbrakes, the panels on the wing that produce a distinctive, low *hmmmm* as they extend into the fast-flowing air, and we lower the landing gear earlier than usual. Despite these efforts to slow ourselves, everything that happens now – the final descent, the lights of the city's outer settlements streaming past – does so more quickly than usual, and at higher altitudes, which only intensifies the sensation that we're approaching a metropolis at rest still some way up in the sky.

We pass over the runway threshold, close the thrust levers and guide 250 tonnes of 747 past a lifeless windsock. As soon as the wheels touch we set the engines to their maximum reverse setting – it's all we can do to ease the burden on the brakes – and after their long hours of forward propulsion the engines gather up what tonnes of Nairobi's attenuated air they can and hurl them out ahead of us. We turn off the glittering runway onto a darker and deserted taxiway, and as we roll through this African night it seems that in all Nairobi, if not on all the earth, ours might be the only vehicle in motion. We park and I carefully shut down the four engines – one at a time, from right to left. Their roars fall away sequentially, in long, metallic sighs, and I watch the digits spin down on the gauges, until each fan is still.

PETRÓPOLIS

To reach the cool and fragrant air of the city of Petrópolis you must leave the Atlantic Ocean and Rio de Janeiro behind and take the highway that leads north to the interior.

Rio is known from every postcard as a city of mountains. The nearby city of Petrópolis is hardly known at all outside Brazil, but every Rio-bound pilot to whom you describe the city's location will know exactly where you mean, because the mountains around Petrópolis are higher than those of Rio and so, on aviation charts, they are shaded in more alarming patterns of colours. The poet Elizabeth Bishop, long after the last of her visits to her boyfriend in Pittsfield, lived in Petrópolis with a woman named Lota, and remarked on the 'clouds floating in & out of one's bedroom' – a pilot's dream of a city's air, perhaps – and when Bishop described the mountains around Petrópolis as 'highly impractical', it's as if she was thinking first of the aviators who must carefully weave around these hills on their way down to Rio.

Reversing this journey on land, the road that leads up from the heat of Rio seems to know that no direct approach is possible, and so it makes wide arcs within the folds of the hills in order to climb to the city whose motto is *Altiora semper petens*, Always seeking what is higher. From a rattling bus I look across the steep valleys, these V-shaped volumes of Brazilian sky, to catch sight of further stretches of the road we're on, and I can't conceive of any arrangement of curves and climbs that could possibly get us from here to there.

Finally we enter the city, through a gateway on which is written CIDADE IMPERIAL and PETRÓPOLIS. This is the Imperial City and the City of Peter, of Pedro II (1825–1891), the last of Brazil's emperors, who fell in love with the city's cool, clear air and made a kind of summer capital here. Deposed after fifty-eight years, his line ended and a republic founded, the fate of Pedro II is nevertheless one that every emperor after Constantine must dream of: he is buried in a city that bears his name.

Like many pilots, I was drawn to the city by an alternative, aeronautical, royalty. Alberto Santos-Dumont, whom many Brazilians consider to be the true father of the airplane and who, in the age of pocket watches, worked with Louis Cartier to design the first wristwatch, so that he could check the time without lifting a hand from his aeroplane's controls, lived here. After his death his heart, in the tradition of French kings, was removed from his body. Encased in a small golden sphere held by a winged figure, it stands in a glass box on a pedestal in a museum in Rio. Many of his other belongings are in his small home here in Petrópolis.

On this, my first trip to the city, my two colleagues and I are happy to explore the house of the great aviator, but I'll fall in love with something else here: the Palácio de Cristal, the Crystal Palace, a greenhouse-like structure set in a small, lush park.

The Palácio, which opened in 1884, is made of simple cast iron and long, vertical panes of glass. Each of its main walls is three panes high. There's not much else to the Palácio, though some of its panes are fronted by curlicues and each of the floor's brown tiles is decorated with sand-coloured fleurs-de-lis, and the corners of the structure are fattened with column-like adornments that echo the trunks of the trees outside.

The inspiration for the Palácio was London's Crystal Palace; its parts were made in France and then shipped to the Brazilian highlands, where in 1884 a grand ball celebrated its assembly. On Easter Sunday of 1888, around one hundred enslaved persons of Petrópolis were manumitted in the Palácio, in an imperial ceremony that foreshadowed the abolition of slavery throughout the country.

The building also served as an agricultural exhibition hall, a skating rink and as a venue for the elegant dances of the city's summer society. Today, the Palácio's chandeliers – high in this stilled and delicately boxed portion of the city's air, and so many years after the music and voices of the Brazilian court were last reflected by so many walls of glass – are bleached and bone-like in the thick tropical light, while a plaque outside describes the structure as *um marco que honra os mais elevados aspectos da alma petropolitana*, a landmark that honours the highest aspects of the Petropolitan soul.

The otherwise sparse design of the Palácio has an unexpected detail, one that reminds the visitor that the balls once held here did not take place in the black-and-white realm suggested by old photographs: while most of its windowpanes are of ordinary, clear glass, a few are blue.

In the Palácio, on this spring day, these panes seem to redouble the sky's colour as it falls through them, forming richly marine-hued parallelograms that fall at oblique angles on the carefully laid patterns of the tiled floor. As I walk slowly through the Palácio it feels right to step over or around these – because the colour appears to be precious, perhaps, or because the eye naturally registers all such low-laid blueness as water.

The Palácio is one of the most peaceful places I've been. This calming effect is hard to explain, since, aside from its chandeliers and a low, empty stage, it contains nothing. Perhaps it's only that its simple iron outline acts on the city's air like the frame of a photograph, sustaining a moment that might have been lost, though otherwise it is like any other.

Whatever the reason, as I walk away from the Palácio I look back and I know I won't ever forget it: this quiet place where blue shapes fall from the sky, touch down and migrate with the grace of shadows; a volume that suspends and steadies us, as if it were filled not with air, but with clear water; a palace of glass that's open to all, though nearly everyone in Peter's city is busy somewhere else.

KUWAIT

An hour or so before dawn we leave the snowiest of Turkey's moonlit mountains behind, cross the Iraqi border and sail south along a great river. Fringes of light follow the turns of the Tigris as precisely as the greenery seen along it on daylight flights. Beyond, there's only the ink-darkness of the desert.

Further south, and as we near the meeting-place of the Tigris and Euphrates – for we are overflying Mesopotamia, meaning the land between the rivers – pinpricks of blood-bright light appear in the distance. As we draw closer it becomes clear that these are, in fact, flames, quivering at a considerable height above the surrounding sand. These flares, which burn off the natural gas released from oil wells and produce toxins that harm nearby communities, are one of the eeriest sights from the cockpit at night, as well as – especially since the gas is not burned for any productive purpose – one of the most haunting reminders I encounter of the challenges of the climate crisis.

In some regions the patterns these flares make on the earth appear random. Elsewhere the flames seem to run across the land in discernible lines, as if they were beacons, or as if each had, in turn, lit the next. En route to Kuwait, the appearance of these flares often coincides with the first hints of daybreak. From cruising altitude, we see the sky start to lighten only slowly, and solely along the smouldering rim of the sky and the world, where the most distant flares, from as far away as the deserts of Iran, appear to reach up towards the horizon itself, and even to be held against it, until the stars are swept away by a sudden conflagration of sideways-rushing brightness: the day has caught.

Typically, when a cloudless dawn reaches an aerial observer above a settled part of the world, the illuminated evidence of our electrified civilisation fades largely away, and the downward view is slowly transformed by the familiar colours and features of our sunlit planet. But in the skies above and around the city of Kuwait, the day often breaks differently. Here much more of the growing light is caught not by the land below, but by the air, which takes on a progressively more golden hue. As the new day gathers strength, this straw-coloured light intensifies until it fills our windscreens, which, in the most extreme of these conditions, appear as dusty panes of amber.

In the novel *The Shadow of the Sun*, the Kuwaiti writer Taleb Alrefai addresses the situation of guest workers in Kuwait through the character of Helmi, an economic migrant who has recently arrived from Egypt, where his wife and young son remain. Helmi, on his first walk through Kuwait City, is struck by the 'sun unlike the one I knew', and by a sky 'stained a rusty saffron'. While in the short stories of Craig Loomis, a writer and academic at the American University of Kuwait, the sky is like 'weak tea', 'butterscotch', a 'dirty vanilla' with the 'sun still a red idea beyond the sand and dust'.

Anyone who regularly comes to this city from the sky will know exactly what they mean. It's easy to imagine that the goldenness resting on this part of our planet is how heat itself might look if we could see it directly, or that we're looking down on the desert through the heights of a great mirage. This air-dust-light can sometimes be so thick that it entirely obscures the earth's surface, and, as I move through it on the approach to Kuwait, I often have a sense I have nowhere else: that I saw the world around the city more clearly before the sun came up.

The engines fall back to their idle setting and now, as we start our descent, the goldenness is on all sides of us. Not quite a cloud, it's something more than clear air; it's enough, indeed, to give the sensation that the wings are slicing at hundreds of miles an hour through something tangible, through some substance that would be visible, but only barely, if a glass of it were held up before a white wall.

We descend further and are transferred to air controllers based in Kuwait, who now direct what remains of our journey to their city. Following their instructions, we turn and soar out over the open waters of the Gulf. From below, through such air, there's none of the metallic flashing, the turning-school-of-fish quality that might sparkle and dazzle you on a different morning, or over another sea. There's only the haze, and a shadow that might be the island called Failaka. We turn over it, turn again, and approach the mainland to the south of the city. Looking down, I'm grateful for our instruments, and I'm struck once more by how the surface of a desert and the depths of a thick-enough slab of tawny air are all but indistinguishable; and by the sense, far stronger than any science fiction film could evoke, that we are deep in the future and in the final minutes of our approach to the greatest metropolis of a desert planet.

Indeed, on many mornings the ambient, obscuring glow blends

so evenly into the colour of the land that both can seem as expressionless as the snow you'd see on a television tuned to an empty and unnumbered channel. Then the first straight lines take form in the haze, along with the wide highways, and the roofs of the low-slung villas along the shore, and the city snaps into place, in the air and the hour that could hold no other.

~

We park and the door of the plane opens onto one of the hottest cities on Earth.

The writer and traveller Zahra Freeth, who was born in 1925 and spent much of her childhood in Kuwait, once accompanied an official mission to investigate the eradication of locusts from the desert. She wrote that 'the breeze from the moving car kept us cool enough; if we stopped, however, the metal sides of the jeep soon became too hot to touch'. Today, many car parks in Kuwait, as in other desert cities, feature canopies that throw shade onto the resting cars beneath. The city's airport also features overhanging covers for small jets, which I saw here before I saw them anywhere else.

My colleagues and I collect our bags and go through immigration. When we finally emerge from the terminal, it's into a covered, shaded area, where it's common to see fashionably dressed women pull in to drop off or pick up passengers, reminding me, as Kuwait's cathedral, with its lively crowds and image of Our Lady of Arabia does, too, that not all Gulf cities are alike. Immediately beyond this covered area lies the glare of the unshielded world.

Like me, you may have first seen the Gulf on a bedroom or classroom globe, or on maps on news broadcasts during the wars, and you may appreciate that this geopolitically important body of water runs roughly north-south, and that Kuwait City is somewhere at the northern end of it. Yet at the north-western corner of the Gulf, unseen – at least at the scale at which I first learned of it – is a bay.

Kuwait lies along the southern shore of that bay. So, when you stand on the city's waterfront, near Seif Palace, for example, and face out over the waves, you are, in fact, looking north-west, and the open waters of the Gulf lie where a foreigner, taking off their sunglasses to rub their eyes after a long journey, would least expect them to be: behind their right shoulder.

There are many examples of trading cities that grew up at the water's edge. Kuwait's existence, however, may be equally a function of the ocean of sand that surrounds it wherever water does not. On the city's desert side, immediately outside its wall, was once a kind of inland port, where the camels of the Bedouin and of traders from the interior were moored like vessels. Its other shore was what the Australian author and adventurer Alan Villiers, who chronicled the maritime traditions of the 'good city' of Kuwait in *Sons of Sindbad*, described as 'one of the most interesting waterfronts in the world', and the home of some of Earth's most skilful shipwrights and sailors.

Children here once had their hands marked with ink before the break in their classes, so that their teacher might check, when they returned, that they had not been to swim. Indeed, in such a severe climate, Kuwait at first grew all but linearly along its shore, leading a missionary doctor to remark on the old city's 'peculiar length and narrowness'. So slender was the city's form that on the first day of the festival of Eid, residents of the eastern city visited those who lived in the west, and on the second day westerners visited easterners, as if Kuwait was born in only this one dimension, and only later spread outwards into two and finally upwards into a richly skyscrapered three – as someone who began their study of cities with this one might imagine they all start, before slowly unfolding in space and time.

A Kuwaiti sheikh once told Villiers, who had arrived in Kuwait by boat, that when he decided to leave the city, he must do so by camel. It's a story that foretokens the description of the Janus-like city of Despina, in Calvino's *Invisible Cities*, as reachable by only these two means of transport; it also illustrates how inexorably, in the age before oil brought Kuwait unimaginable wealth, this entrepôt would arise at the junction of desert and maritime trading routes, and grow to become for a time the Gulf's largest port town. Its souk, or market, was known across northern Arabia, while 'the lustre of its pearls', Villiers records, 'is famous in Paris and New York; its merchants are respected from Syria to Singapore, from Cairo to Calicut'.

For me, Kuwait's air, and all that it has shaped and carried, is the most arresting characteristic of the city. Kuwait inverts the usual sense I have of the land and water around a city as real, while the air above it, even to a pilot who must so frequently consider it directly, is insubstantial.

We load our bags onto the crew bus and step inside. I sit at the front, for the best view. The width and congestion of the highway into the city evoke Los Angeles, and on some cooler mornings here my gaze may follow a car with its windows down, its driver's left arm resting on the outside of the door as his fingers tap along to music or in frustration at the bottleneck, and I smell the sea and then the golden, gauzy air is much like that of a California morning.

Then the names on the signs over the highway – the strong *k*'s and mellifluous *s*'s of Khaitan and Kaifan, Al-Siddeeq and Sharq – remind me of where I am, and there's the sense, as well, that a warmth almost otherworldly to me is rising, that the tawny heights we crossed through above the city are awakening, and it grows clear to me how far I am from home.

We pull into the hotel's forecourt. I take my keycard, head upstairs, close the blackout blinds and crawl into the cool bed.

⁓

When I open the blinds a few hours later, it's so bright that it's hard to look out. I press my palm against the glass of the window, and find that it's already as warm as the hood of a running car. I turn over my phone and discover it's midday.

In the old days in Kuwait, it was common, in the times of heat, to sleep on the roofs of houses, as it still is in much of the world nearby, in places that lack air-conditioning. At the end of the nineteenth century, a Kuwaiti leader was killed exactly where his assassins knew to find him: fast asleep on his roof. On the old seafront, meanwhile, sailors who had no home on the land would sleep comfortably outside in the summer, and the beach, Villiers wrote, was filled with 'youthful unmarried men', sleeping and snoring 'in the shadow of the ships they serve so faithfully'.

My hotel room, like virtually all interiors in the city today, is furiously air-conditioned. Yet clever manipulations of Kuwait's air are far older than the modern city.

Bedouin tents were traditionally pitched in relation to the wind, while internal divisions in the tent regulated the airflow; and an excavated palace on Failaka Island, thought to be from the seventh century, shows evidence of a wind catcher – a structure that naturally cools the building to which it's attached – as well as of a system of canals that may have been designed to cool the palace's interior further, an arrangement that has been described as one of the oldest known examples of air-conditioning. Kuwait's traditional houses also featured wind catchers, as well as roofs that were easily accessible and parapet-lined, and open-air courtyards with awnings, water features and greenery. Porous pottery allowed any air moving over its wet surfaces to cool the water within, and elaborate fans, traditionally crafted from palm fronds, were rigged within homes and mosques; while one of the city's museums displays models of early but otherwise ordinary desktop electric fans, showcasing how astounding it must once have been to flip a switch and set the city's air into refreshing motion.

Sometimes I convince myself, on short summer trips to sweltering Gulf cities, that it's simpler not to go out until after dark; and then I might go to the hotel gym or watch *Cheers* reruns on my laptop until I realise that it's too late to go out at all. Today, though, I decide I'll have a short walk down to the seafront, before returning to wash under my room's pizza-sized showerhead, from which cool, expensively desalinated Gulf water will flow, and then I'll meet my colleagues for dinner.

I stir and drink my second cup of instant coffee. I put on light-coloured trousers and a shirt, apply a little sunscreen, grab my sun-glasses and my blue Red Sox hat, and head downstairs.

As the lobby's revolving door spins me out onto the forecourt, I'm hit with a sensation that makes sense only if I imagine that I'm sur-rounded not by skyscrapers and highways, and the desert and Gulf beyond, but by four walls of smooth Finnish timber. Like a sauna, however, the experience, at least initially, is far from unpleasant, especially if I move slowly or occasionally allow myself to come to a stop. And it's marvelous – in the literal sense, it's something to mar-vel at – to suddenly feel the air all around, and moving over you, first here, then there, and then suddenly everywhere, as if it were the water of a pool you've jumped into fully clothed.

Stepping outside in Kuwait in summer, as in New England in winter, I often gasp as I take my first breath. Indeed, whenever I read about the calming effects of meditation, and of its focus on the physical sensation of one's breath, I think of Kuwait, and of how in summer such an awareness is always with me; indeed, it can be a struggle to focus on much else.

I blink and see this corner of Kuwait again – the palm-lined fore-court, the taxis – and I start to move. Even aside from the heat, this isn't the easiest city to walk in. Pavements sometimes end abruptly in walls that hide ongoing construction, or in the lots of open sand that are unsubtle reminders that this is a city of the desert; the mark-ings of zebra crossings seem to count for little; and drivers take scant notice of pedestrians, of which there are, in any case, few, especially in daylight in summer.

I cross to the shady side of the street and tell myself: *You're okay! This heat isn't so bad. Take it slow, you've nowhere to be.* Then I'm surprised – though I shouldn't be, as this always happens, ten or fifteen minutes after I first enter the open air of Kuwait in summer – when the heat hits me anew. My body seems to realise, suddenly, that what it feels is not just some transient error in its temperature-sensing, which it would have been a waste of perspiration to take seriously. And I start to sweat profusely, as if somewhere in my brain a panel of red lights is flashing, and a supervisor is frantically trying to make up for the minutes their underling chose not to believe the preposterous reports, and once again I have the feeling I associate with fast walks on the most bitter winter nights in Pittsfield: the paradoxical sense of being in a place I know well – a city, no less – even as I understand that, left unsupplied and unprotected, my survival here would be measured only in hours. And in this age of climate change, such moments offer a dramatic and anxiety-provoking preview of the unwalkable future days that not only Kuwait may face, days that all the air-conditioning in the world, depending on how its power is generated, may only worsen.

Sometimes, in Kuwait, this state has found me stranded on an island amid six lanes filled with outsize, sunlight-scattering, racing vehicles, my trainers covered in dust and my hat soaked through. I worry that I look as out of place as I am; I worry, as I wipe the sweat from my eyes, that I look as grumpy as I feel. At such a moment, I may remind myself how I admired Kuwait's name on my childhood globe, and drew routes to it from my imaginary city. Then, if I find I still wish to complain, I may say to myself: *Did you wish, after all, to know this place only in your imagination? Because all around you now are not only the facts but also the sensations of a place that you dreamed of flying to and walking through.*

I pass the outdoor seating area of the South Asian restaurant I'll dine at with my colleagues this evening. The aromas are delicious, and I briefly think of stopping for lunch here, rather than continuing to my favourite café. Science explains that we smell more clearly in warmer weather, in part because the heat liberates into the air more molecules of whatever substances we are near. Yet I sometimes find it hard to remember that extreme heat itself is not a smell, so obvious is it in my nose; and often when I walk past restaurants, the smoky stalls of food sellers, or even the spice merchants in the city's old souk, I have the feeling that the heat at least partly masks the smells of the city.

The essences of Kuwait's air have long been remarked on, however. Eleanor Calverley, an American who became Kuwait's first female doctor when she opened a dispensary in the city in 1912, 'came to expect that on some evening in February, when the wind was blowing from the direction of the desert, we should stand on our upstairs veranda and sniff the scent of perfume. Then we would know that the flowers were blooming again, as the result of the rains of winter'. For me the strongest smell in the city is that of the Gulf, which comes and goes depending on the direction of the wind. Its absence, then, must reveal the smell of the desert.

After my very late breakfast I continue towards the seafront, where families rest on the sand, and men play football – shirts versus skins like anywhere else – and the music from the open windows of the cars in the traffic jam on the coast road spills up into the air.

I follow the sea west, towards the hustle of the city's fish market. The smell of it – a gentle one, thankfully – ripples over the guest workers seated on benches and chatting on their mobiles in seamless arrangements of Hindi and English; over the expensive cars racing to the mall; and over me, as I catch a whiff of a far-off Boston – baked but recognisable – and recall my waterfront office in a renovated warehouse there, and my short walk to it from the subway station, and the sandpaper wind from across the harbour on January mornings, as here in Kuwait I dip inside the fish market and inhale – there's no doubt where I am – and move slowly down the rows of shining scales and bright, stilled eyes on the ice.

⌒

Another summer, and another overnight flight to Kuwait. We land immediately after dawn and soon we're in town. The first thing I do once I reach my room is place my jacket, trousers, shirt and shoes in a bag outside the door. Our hotel here offers free dry-cleaning of our uniforms, and polishing of our shoes until they're more lustrous than they were when new; in fact, the hotel, and by extension its city, is so well known for this that when I see a colleague at Heathrow who's looking particularly smart I might say: Kuwait, eh?

After my sleep I go to the gym, text home, and write a little. Outside, my phone confirms, the temperature is 38 degrees.

I don't leave the hotel until after dark, when my colleagues and I walk to dinner. When I finally step outside, the air temperature is somehow even more surprising without the glare of the sun, and there's a graininess to all the lights I see through the heat, a texture that makes distant streetlamps and skyscrapers look much like a photograph of them might, from the days before smartphones could take such nighttime shots clearly.

We walk slowly to the souk and enter its caverns of cheek-by-jowl shops. One of my fellow crew members – I've never met any of them before, a common situation in a large airline – is a semiprofessional cook with a long shopping list full of Indian spices, and the rest of us tag along as she expertly selects from bins filled with a dusty rainbow of colours. She says these are fresher than in Britain and cheaper, too. Like many Gulf cities, Kuwait has an enormous expatriate population, and surely this partly explains both the quality and the volume of the South Asian ingredients on offer. Then we go to the edge of the bazaar, where stalls and tables await us in an open-air food court. We order plates of lamb and rice, and talk about our families, the paths of our careers, our most memorable recent flights, and the cities we're flying to next.

After dinner, as we walk together back to the hotel, the heat feels bath-like, physically supportive, as if we might lean into it and find that it holds us up a little, again like water. I even find a kind of giddiness in this air that is so warm but not uncomfortable, and in our easy laughter and the nearly continuous hum of our conversations, which from a distance must sound like those of old friends.

∽

In the company of another crew I touch down in Kuwait on a late-winter day. When we get to the hotel I'm careful to set an alarm. After I wake, I pack a bag – lots of water, cereal bars, my camera – and head out into the cool air.

The explorer and writer Freya Stark described Kuwait's environs as lying within 'an immense and happy loneliness'. When you come to Kuwait from a cooler or lusher place – that is, from almost anywhere else on Earth – it's easy to imagine that the enormous and climate-controlled artifice of the modern metropolis has been erected within a vast natural desolation.

Yet more than 400 bird species either nest in Kuwait or pass through it on their migrations (roughly as many as the Royal Society for the Protection of Birds expects you might identify in the much larger, wetter and greener UK, a country where birdsong is so venerated that it's routinely broadcast on national radio). Kuwait's rich birdlife includes kingfishers, geese, harriers, warblers, herons, plovers, storks, cormorants (both pygmy and great), vultures (Egyptian and lappet-faced, among others) and at least nine species of eagle. The city's coastal location provides the habitats and food sources – mudflats, tidal zones, fish-rich reefs and shallow waters – that birds are grateful to find, not least along a great desert's edge. In addition, one of the planet's flyways, or major avian migration routes, passes directly above the city, and others pass near it. On maps the branches of these flyways, which airliner routes so strongly resemble, sprawl far out from Kuwait; one reaches from southern Africa to Russia's tundra.

I was wrong to have been surprised, then, to find, in a collection of contemporary Kuwaiti poetry, so vibrant an avian presence. In a poem titled 'The Black Sparrow', for example, Najma Edrees writes: 'Fold the wing on the wing / You who flies between the wounds.' While in 'Escaping from the Coma Cage', Ghanima Zaid Al Harb finds a haunting metaphor in the migrations that might incorporate the skies of her home city: 'Birds behind the sea / carrying these promises. . . . In that bereaved night / I crossed the borders, / And awoke.'

Today, instead of sleeping, walking and café-going, my usual three activities in any city, I've arranged to spend the day birdwatching with Mike Pope, an IT program manager and a keen birder. By midday we're in his SUV, heading out of the city centre to the first of the half dozen stops we'll make together. He knows the roads well, and as he describes his favourite places in the desert I'm reminded that Kuwait, despite the impression I've long had from afar, is not a city-state in the manner of Singapore, for example. To be sure, it isn't a large country, but its land area is nevertheless not too far off that of Massachusetts or Wales. There are many places to go beyond the city, and much emptiness from which to look back at it.

In summer, Mike tells me, we'd need to have left much earlier, if we went out at all. It's too hot then after midmorning, he says, and anyway, the air burns so riotously that photography of birds becomes difficult, if not impossible. 'The line of the horizon loses continuity and breaks up into segments and islands floating in mid-air,' wrote Barclay Raunkiær, a Danish explorer, about his journey from Kuwait in early 1912. Or as Freya Stark put it on an excursion out of the city, 'Water seemed to lie before us, but it was only mirage, the water of dust.'

Sometimes rain permits real lakes, rather than mirages, to take brief form in the desert, and birds will descend to crowd them. But this winter, nothing, Mike says, in reference to the rains. The winds have been so strange, he explains: if you look at the weather map, it looks like the systems come down to Kuwait and then they split, like there's a vacuum over the place. The storms build up over Basra and then they just dissipate, he adds, as he makes a sweeping, horizontal gesture with one hand.

We reach the first of the day's stops. When I landed in Kuwait early this morning there was already a decent breeze from the north, and now it's grown stronger. Near the shore and in sight of Kuwait's distant skyscrapers, vast flocks of birds form their own metropolis amid the grasses bent horizontal in the airflow. Later, when I listen to my recordings from the day, there's little of Mike's voice or mine, and not much birdsong, either. What I mostly bring home is the sound of the wind.

We watch a flock of greater flamingos. They come every year, Mike says, and are most abundant in these winter months. There's a single lesser flamingo, a separate species, recognisable by its dark maroon bill, that appears almost annually among the flock of pink-and-white greater ones. It must be the same individual that comes each year, Mike suggests. It cannot interbreed with its new tribe, and has left or lost its own.

There are white wagtails, which, like me, have recently flown to Kuwait from a chillier realm. There are both common terns and scarcer Arctic terns. Call them comic terns if you can't tell the difference, Mike advises with a smile. He describes the migration of Arctic terns between the Arctic and the Antarctic, two of the coldest corners of the earth, and their stopover here in one of the hottest.

An osprey grabs a fish from the waves and tears off across the sky. It swivels the fish lengthwise, holding it like a torpedo, surely to reduce the air resistance presented by its lunch. Air isn't the fluid that the fish was built to sail through, but its water-sculpted shape now speeds its last journey. A western reef heron chases after the osprey, trying to force it to drop its prey. The osprey lands behind a chain-link fence, only metres from the Gulf, where the gleaming, parenthetical body of the fish repeatedly inverts on the sand, at intervals that grow until it is still.

The sun whitens and the wind warms and strengthens. Whenever Mike parks at a new spot, depending on the direction of the car I either struggle to hold the car door back when I open it, or I must push it out with all my strength. This, too, a New Englander might struggle to remember, is winter. All along the shore the birds have hunkered down in defiance of the wind. Twice, Mike says, has he seen a great sandstorm, known as a haboob, hit the city. Once, the sky turned a deep yellow as the wall of sand approached. Right before the storm hit, all the birds landed.

For Helmi, the recently arrived Egyptian migrant in Taleb Alrefai's novel, sandstorms are among Kuwait's most striking features: 'A nasty sort of fine dust blew in from every direction, and there was no barrier or cover capable of resisting its passage. . . . I would sometimes feel it underneath my eyelids, on my scalp, and between my teeth.' Violet Dickson, a writer and botanist who came to the city in 1929 with her husband, H. R. P. Dickson, a colonial administrator – their home is now a pleasant, informal museum and cultural centre on the city's waterfront – described a sandstorm that fell upon her as she camped outside the city: 'I thought it was a bush fire. It was exactly like flames coming along.' The Bedouin she was camped with rapidly pulled the poles from their tents to collapse them, and then crawled underneath until the storm finished, an hour and a half later. The sand was scarlet, 'and today the Bedu talk about that as "the red year," because of that strange red storm'.

Dust storms prevalent from MAR to JUL inclusive, reads the plainly stated warning on our airport charts. Sandstorms may reduce visibility to almost zero, and during the 1930s and 1940s, when aeroplanes were a growing presence in Kuwait, crashes in such conditions were all too common. One aircraft, which was carrying the crown jewels of Iraq, was lost in a sandstorm over the sea, where I had not realised they could blow.

Another sandstorm, in February 1934, rolled over the patch of sand that then served as the airport immediately beyond Kuwait's city walls, where camels were still tethered, near the city gate at which guards would ask their riders for news from the desert. The storm ripped to pieces the fabric-covered wing of an aircraft parked there. The damage took six weeks to repair, before another storm did it all over again. The incensed captain of the damaged plane – and who could have foreseen how energy exports, not least to fuel the worldwide growth of aviation, would soon transform so many Gulf settlements? – suggested that Imperial Airways permanently cease its services to Kuwait. I am glad, of course, it did not.

Mike drives on, stops, and once again I force the door open in the wind. We see a desert wheatear and an Asian desert warbler together, a symbiotic pairing Mike says he sees often. A plastic bag sails past while a Daurian shrike, which Mike teaches me to identify by the eye-stripe that doesn't reach the bill, perches on a branch. The shrike's eyes are steady, but every other part of its body is as alive as a surfer's to balance in the gale.

Four greater spotted eagles bank overhead, and dozens of grey herons suddenly take flight, so dizzyingly that their crisp shadows seem to shatter into more herons on the sand below. Then a vast flock of common black-headed gulls lifts, too, against the shimmering background of the nearby city's silvery towers. Count them in tens, Mike advises, about the birds, if you dare to try at all.

⤦

When I boarded a 747 last night to prepare for another flight to Kuwait, I knew that within a few months I'd be retraining on a new type of aircraft, the Boeing 787. This change would mean a number of farewells, not only to the 747 but to some of the traditional routes that the 747 flies. I didn't know when I might go again to Kuwait. It even occurred to me that I might never return.

Now, six hours after takeoff from London, I set down my mug of tea, dial in the altitude the Kuwaiti controller has issued to us, and press the altitude selector button to initiate our descent. Beyond and below the cup holder's coffee-stained rim I see the chimneys of a large power plant at a place called Subiya. They rise around 200 metres into the sky, and their plumes function like a wind-sock, forewarning pilots of the direction and strength of the wind we'll encounter later and lower. We route out over the Gulf, where I look down on the tankers, apparently motionless and arranged with the orderliness of planets, as we make a series of clockwise curves towards the path of our final approach.

The wind rose of Kuwait – the graphic summary of the direction and the strength of the city's winds – shows enormous pulses out to the north-west, smaller ones to the south-east, and not much else. Its rare neatness will surprise no one who has landed (for Kuwait's runways run north-west to south-east) or sailed here, though it belies what might be my favourite description of any city's air. It's from Kuwait's Directorate General of Civil Aviation, and it grows to seem all the more tortured when you realise it applies only to one portion of Kuwait's long summer: 'In some periods, the winds are north westerly till noon then they change as a result of sea breeze to north easterly then to northerly only till afternoon then south easterly till sunset then southerly till midnight then westerly till sunrise.'

Before the age of oil, the sailing ships driven by Kuwait's winds were key to both the city's fame and its self-conception. There are few accounts of pre-modern Kuwait that don't mention the prowess of the city's sailors. In the 1860s, William Gifford Palgrave (the English explorer, diplomat, sometime Jesuit and friend of Alfred, Lord Tennyson) recorded that throughout the Gulf, 'the mariners of Koweyt hold the first rank in daring, in skill and in solid trust-worthiness of character'. 'As soon as a boy can swim,' H. R. P.

Dickson recorded, 'he is given a small boat . . . in this he paddles about the harbour, or puts up a little sail, should a gentle breeze be blowing.'

Indeed, in the iconography of Kuwait, depictions of wind-powered ships duel endlessly with those of birds. In my favourite park in the city, where the scrupulously irrigated greenery can seem to lower the temperature of the air by at least 5 degrees, there is a sculpture, *Freedom*, composed entirely of metal birds, in a flock shaped like Kuwait; while a nearby sculpture is called *Raising Our Sails*. A boom – a type of dhow, or sailing vessel – appears above the falcon on Kuwait's state emblem. Kuwaiti banknotes and stamps often feature ships when they don't feature falcons.

On occasion the city's two principal avatars have converged: traditional Kuwaiti vessels sometimes featured wind vanes crafted in the shape of birds, complete with real feathers; more recently, some of the airliners based in Kuwait, already emblazoned with a stylised bird, were given the names – *Al-Boom, Al-Jalboot, Al-Sanbook* – of the types of sailing vessels once common in Kuwait's famous and far-ranging fleet.

On this trip we have, unusually, forty-eight hours in the city. On the first day I do little but sleep. The following day I get up before dawn and go to stand by the hotel window. As usual I'm on a high floor. The window's outer surface is covered with pale, henna-like patterns of dust that have arrived in the night. Through them I can see the red lights atop the darkened towers. Beyond, the waters of the Gulf are only a notch or two off black, and the colour of the sky is the same, except where a swathe of gold is bisected by a red line near where the sun will appear.

After breakfast I wander down to the seafront south of the Kuwait Towers complex, and onto a long wooden pier that takes me out over the sparkling waves, past fishermen who nod to me as I approach. Where there are no fishermen I skip my hand along the railing. The further I go over the Gulf, the windier it gets, until at the pier's end I'm shaking with cold, and I pull up and tighten the hood on my thin sweatshirt and shove my hands in its pockets.

By midday it's warmer, and I'm walking along another portion of the shoreline promenade, where I hear the buzz of Jet Skis racing over the bay, and the joyful whoops from their drivers. I stop at a restaurant nestled in the shadow of a bridge, above the outlet channel of a bustling marina. I order a plate of fries and a lassi, a South Asian drink made with chilled, spiced yogurt, and look down on the small pleasure boats heading into the bay, with names such as *Al-Omani, Saba Blue*, and – somehow – the *Milwaukee*, each topped by a sunglassed skipper looking as relaxed as any Florida retiree.

On previous visits I've enjoyed my hours in a maritime museum here. I love its map exhibits, in particular a finely drawn 1825 chart titled 'Trigonometrical Plan of the Harbour of Grane or Quade', as Kuwait was once known; the models of old sailing vessels, from which Kuwait's former flag – blood-red, with the city's name in white Arabic script – is rigged in the dead air of the glass display cases; and documents like the one certifying a Kuwaiti ship's lanterns, by the Inspector of Lights in the city of Karachi.

I love, as well, the bilingual exhibits on knots whose names (the 'cow hitch with toggle', the 'barrel sling') must be among the very last terms a student of either Arabic or English would ever learn, and which remind me of how knots on long ropes were once cast overboard by sailors, a means of measuring speed that led to the unit still used by ships and aircraft today. And I love the museum's guest book, in which some visitors have felt moved enough to not only sign their names but to make little drawings of boats. 'Good & surprised to watch many ships!!' writes Peter, a traveller from South Korea. 'You don't make a great future without a great past,' adds a visitor named Aya.

Kuwaitis – beyond the trading routes their country sat astride, and the pearls beneath its sea – had a better reason than most to set sail. There are no rivers or natural streams here. No lakes. From vessels out on the Gulf, the city's famed pearl divers might swim down to fill leather skins from undersea freshwater springs that issued directly into the saline depths, but nowhere in the city itself did a spring reach the earth's surface. So, once the few wells – which were, in any case, found only beyond the city walls – could no longer supply the growing city, drinking water was brought by sea from the Shatt al-Arab, where the Tigris and the Euphrates lose themselves in one another en route to the shallow Gulf, on the specialised teak dhows known as water booms. In 1947, not long before the construction of Kuwait's first desalination plant, perhaps forty such vessels were engaged in bringing fresh water to their home port, where the water vendors brought it through the streets, in tin cans hung on the ends of a carrying pole called a *kandar*, or in goat skins piled on the backs of donkeys.

Nor were there trees in pre-modern Kuwait ('if groups of stunted tamarisk be ruled out', wrote Raunkiær). Yet, remarkably, many ships were built here, and these carried the reputation of the city's sailors and shipwrights into the world, from 'Sri Lanka to the Zambesi'. The wood for Kuwait's ships seasoned well in Kuwait's dry air but it came from distant and wetter places – typically the Malabar coast of south-west India, where Kuwaiti merchants established trading houses in the nineteenth century. The logs arrived in Kuwait on ships that were themselves made from logs like them: a cycle of timber centred far from where strong trees could survive, far even from fresh water, as if Kuwait was born only to offer so vivid an example of the gravities a skilful city may grow to exert.

And so the city's waterfront was once a continuous shipyard. On hot summer nights, residents falling asleep on their roofs might hear sailors hard at work and singing, as Violet Dickson put it, 'rhythmical songs which helped them to heave together to raise a heavy mast, or turn a capstan to drag a boat ashore'. In the Kuwait of old it was believed that if a childless woman jumped over a ship's newly laid keel, she would become pregnant, but at the cost – 'a life for a life', in the words of the dhow captain Ali bin Nasr al-Nejdi – of the skipper's life, or perhaps that of one of the ship's carpenters. So a ship under construction would be watched over by as many as twenty guards, bearing lanterns throughout the night.

Here at the marina café I finish my sandwich, text Mark and decide, with this water-borne history in mind, that on this, perhaps my last ever day in Kuwait, I'd like to visit one final maritime museum. In a city where English-language maps are often incomplete, it takes me a while to find it. I walk for about twenty minutes, backtrack a bit, then detour through an empty lot, of which there are more than you might expect in such a wealthy metropolis. Blinking in the sand that the wind throws up from its unfinished surface, I experience a discomfiture that occasionally intensifies and darkens my waves of place lag: that anyone who sees me, a foreigner, alone as sunset nears and without a car and to all appearances lost, might ask who I am and where I am possibly going. Sometimes, I wonder myself.

So I'm relieved when I spot three ships, arranged as ordinarily as tourist buses in a parking lot, right outside what must be the museum. Once inside, the sole, sleepy staff member greets me, points to the sign that explains that admission is free, and motions me past the welcome desk.

On display are maritime tools, and each is new to me: the *migsharah*, 'used to clean a ship hull below the water-line'; the *maibar*, a 'long and thick needle used for sewing the sail'; the *tarat manather*, 'used for decorating the ship'. Other presentations feature musical instruments that were once played by sea chanters on Kuwait's vessels as they sailed forth: the *yahlah* and the *hawan*, percussion instruments; and the *sernay*, a wind instrument. The exhibits are tastefully lit, while the deserted rooms are barely lit at all, and as I move slowly through them my steps are the only sound I hear.

When I've seen all there is to see I thank the guard and leave. As I walk out into the Arabian dusk, I'm surprised by the sight of the three marooned ships in the car park, about which I'd somehow forgotten. I've nowhere else to go in the city now, aside from back to my hotel, so I remain near the ships for longer than I otherwise might. I look up at the masts that have no sails, and shield my eyes from the sand that arrives on the dry wind that the hulls deflect; I stand where water should.

Among the stout wooden supports that keep the ships upright, I find a placard that explains that the keel of one of the vessels, the transport boom *Harbi* – around 33 metres long, and with a cargo capacity of around 200 tonnes – was laid almost exactly where she now rests. And as I stare up at the *Harbi* on this lonely evening of my last trip to Kuwait, I understand that all might nevertheless be as it should be: in one telling of her story, this proud, wind-born vessel lies beached in this gritty lot, estranged from the waves of the Gulf and the present age of her city; in another, she has completed her work and come home.

CHAPTER 9

CITY OF BLUE

Cape Town

> Jumping up and down in his ecstasy he beams
> into the empty blue, eastward, over the parapet
> toward the city   .   .
>
> — *Paterson*, William Carlos Williams

CHILDREN, WITH THEIR KNACK for asking the best questions, often ask why the sky is blue, since air is colourless. Parents who struggle to answer this question can take comfort in knowing that it also troubled Aristotle, Descartes and Newton (who was so interested in colours that he stuck thick needles between his eyeballs and his sockets, in order to trigger trauma-induced blooms of them). By the nineteenth century the origin of the sky's color was one of the more engaging and popular questions in science, crisscrossing disciplines and catching the attention of philosophers, poets and artists, too.

A short explanation: when sunlight encounters the molecules that make up the air, some of the light bounces off, or scatters. Shorter-wavelength colours, like blue, are scattered much more effectively. The remaining sunlight that reaches our eyes is slightly yellowed by the loss of some of its blue, while the sky, filled with that scattered blueness, takes on the hue to which sapphires have so often been compared.

When the sun is low in the sky, its light must pass through much more air to reach our eyes. This means even more of its blue is scattered, along with other colours, leaving the predominantly red hues we associate with sunrise. (That is to say, when we look up at the blue of the daytime sky, we see the colour that has been scattered; when we look towards the dawn, we see the colours that have not.)

The greater ability of red light to travel through air is one reason the colour is so well suited to traffic lights, for example, and to the steady beacons mounted on tall buildings for the purpose of warning off aircraft at night.

Often, through the wide windows of the cockpit, when the western sky is black, but red has started to burn in the east, a stunning spectrum of blues slowly asserts itself across all the sky in between: from a pale, almost grey shade through cobalt to a deep midnight blue still shot through with stars. Sometimes these blues flow continuously from one into another, and alter nearly imperceptibly as our gaze moves across the sky. On other mornings, especially ones experienced from within the icy clarity of higher altitudes, the blues seem to be arranged in distinct stripes spread across the sky; or perhaps that's only the brain attempting to segment what is, in nature, infinitely varied.

Later, in the brightness of day, it can be hard to remember that the stars have not been washed out by the sun. (In space you could be in direct sunlight and still see a night-like arrangement of stars shining out of a black sky.) Rather, in the daytime, the stars are obscured by the brightness of the blues that the particular components and proportions of our atmosphere scatter from the sun's light. Indeed, billions of years ago, and before the development of life itself altered it, the composition of the atmosphere was different, and so was the sky's colour – perhaps pale white or yellow, writes Götz Hoeppe, in *Why the Sky Is Blue*.

Finally, in the evening, at what is called the blue hour, the fading light steadily disassembles the high day's vivid blues until their final disintegration reveals the stars again, along with, on a moonlit night, some of the most subtle blues of all. Even when I was a little kid I loved dark blue, and according to one of Mom's favourite stories about me I used to often shout: I don't want the sun to shine. I want the moon to shine! Only as an adult did I learn that the midnight blue of a moonlit sky has the same origin as the brilliant cerulean of a sunny day – for the moon's light, of course, is only the sun's. It's a truth that reminds me that not every planet is blessed with blue skies, and that a love of the colour might arise naturally, and at any hour, in those who dream of crossing them.

I'm on my way to the hospital in Pittsfield to visit Sue, one of the few members of my parents' generation in the Berkshire gang who are still with us. Now, Sue is critically ill, and it'll be a few more days until it's clear that she'll pull through.

Until I was three, my family lived in the house next to hers, and there are more childhood photos of me with her daughter than with any kid other than my brother. (Her daughter was also the first person I kissed, when I was six; she and I still laugh whenever we remember my suggestion that we first hide ourselves in a closet.) Decades later, and after Dad and my stepmother had moved away, Mom sold the house she could no longer afford, and accepted Sue's invitation to move in, and so whenever my brother and I came to Pittsfield in those years, we also stayed at Sue's, and opened presents on Christmas morning in a living room I'd often played in as a child. *Family friend*, indeed, does not really do her justice.

I drive past my parents' first house and then Sue's. The temperature is around -10 degrees and even the south-facing yards are covered in grey snow. I can see the snow-smoothed forms of a portion of Sue's garden as I slow the car, and I can't make sense of the fact that she is not here, but in the hospital I'm driving to. Sue loves baking, and made several of my birthday cakes when I was growing up, including a spherical cake-planet with an accompanying cake-spaceship. She forgave me long ago for the mornings she drove me to nursery school, when I nagged her from the back seat: Why are you getting divorced? Why are you getting divorced? Why are you getting divorced? Not long after, when I was seven, maybe, I excitedly told her daughter the truth about Santa Claus, and it took Sue a little longer to forgive me for that.

Like me, Sue loves snow, and the excuse it offers to lock ourselves in tight with our loved ones for a few days. Like me, she loves Pittsfield. She believes in the city and in the sense of place and community she finds here, and she adds more to it than anyone I know. She's a very keen gardener and for many years helped run a garden tour in Pittsfield, and thanks entirely to her I began to think of my hometown as a city of beloved gardens. She knows that blue is my favourite colour, and when she told me about Vita Sackville-West's White Garden at Sissinghurst Castle, in Kent, I asked her if in her view, an all-blue garden would be possible, and, if so, wouldn't that be preferable, and she rolled her eyes as we laughed. One of her favourite Pittsfield stories – it's one of my mine, too – involves not the city's well-tended gardens, but the moose that ran through the laundry line in a friend's yard, and stomped and bellowed away down the minivan-clogged avenue as underwear streamed from its antlers.

A moment after I pass Sue's house I turn down my old street and near my parents' second Pittsfield house, the one in which I spent nearly all my childhood. I drive past it at least a couple of times a year on purpose. A few other times each year I pass it inadvertently, when I offhandedly take the most convenient route somewhere and then am surprised when it appears before me, already full-sized.

Its current owners, I notice today, have painted the ceiling of the small front porch. It's now a robin's-egg blue, and I remember how hard I once tried to convince Mom how much better it would be for her, for me, for all of us, for the world, in fact, if she chose a blue car from among those she was considering. In the end she picked a light blue Oldsmobile.

My childhood bedroom was at the back of the house, and so from the road I can't see the windows that face from it out onto the yard behind. The head of my bed rested by the northernmost of the two east-facing windows, and every night, before sleep, from the age of sixteen or so, I'd put on my headphones, cue up a favourite song, kneel on the bed, and lean far out the window and light a cigarette.

As I leaned out back then, listened to music, and smoked, I worried about setting the little tree below me on fire – especially as I myself had planted it, when I was a little kid – but I worried even more that a dropped cigarette would be visible as it fell past the kitchen window directly below, by which Dad was often seated. Depending on the wind, I sometimes had to lean much further out, to also make sure no smoke drifted back into the house. (In those years I was certain my parents knew I was gay but that they didn't know I smoked; in fact, the opposite was true.)

I'd lean out like this on even the bitterest winter nights. In fact it was on the clearest and coldest nights that I liked these minutes best. The songs, and the many stars I could see, seemed to put whatever problems I was having into some perspective, as did the lights of the occasional high-flying jet, and I loved the sharpness of the contrast the winter night's air made with the heat of the smoke. I'd shiver, half of me in bed and the other half out over the snow, and if the moon was right I'd watch its icy light filter through my visible exhalations, and then it grew easier to imagine not only these few homes, but many thousands more of them, each locked and warm, and this restful hour in the long life of the metropolis they formed beneath the midnight blue.

CAPE TOWN

SUMMER, IN THE SOUTHERN HEMISPHERE

With an hour or so to go until landing in Cape Town, the chime in the cockpit bunk sounds. Soothed by the *whoosh* of the nearly supersonic air that the nose of the 747 parts, and by the complete absence of light in the bunk – its lack of windows and its precisely sealed door form the most perfect darkness I ever sleep in – it takes me a moment to remember where I am. I stand, get dressed, fasten my tie and walk from the bunk out into the cockpit.

Flights from London to Cape Town usually follow one of two clusters of routes: an eastern one that crosses the North African coast over Algeria and then remains over land for the balance of the roughly eleven-hour journey to the skies of Cape Town, encompassing practically the entire north-south extent of the world's second-largest continent; and a western and typically less stormy and turbulent set, which also crosses the Sahara, but then leaves the West African coast near one or another of the metropolises – Accra, Lagos – that are themselves destinations for me on other flights, on other nights, to continue out over the Gulf of Guinea and the open waters of the South Atlantic, making landfall again over Africa perhaps only minutes before touchdown.

Tonight we're on a western route. Once seated back at the controls, and with a mug of coffee steaming in the cup holder, I check our progress and the fuel, flight time and miles that remain. I put on my headset, and through it I hear only silence on our short-range radios. As I peer ahead, and then below and to the right, I find it hard to believe that the jewelled, miniaturised brilliance of the lights of Bordeaux, Barcelona and Algiers, which we saw so clearly as we looked down last night, might form part of this same world. Now I see no lights of villages or great cities, nor those of any aircraft or ships; there's only the canopy of stars above the horizon-to-horizon disk of raven-dark waters.

On this route, in this season, dawn typically comes when we're out to the west of Namibia's desolate Skeleton Coast, a crimson-hued but often fog-shrouded coastal desert that, especially if I fly directly over it on a clear morning, is to me indistinguishable from a landscape imaged by a Mars orbiter. Its ominous name is said to follow from the prevalence of the bones of seals and beached whales, and the difficulties – above all the lack of fresh water and food – that the coast presented to sailors. Even today the shore is strewn with the ribs of vessels that met their end along it; and the sands shifted by winds, currents and heavy storms may steadily obscure the remains of one wreck, or unearth those of another.

Sunrises at high altitude are invariably stunning, but this morning, as always, my eyes are drawn not to the reds and the yellows that have begun to gather along the horizon, but to the spectrum of blues that slowly fills the sky above us. George Gershwin's famous rhapsody (it doesn't hurt that for years it was used to advertise an airline); the Tom Waits song that describes how colour might build in a room that lightens at dawn ('everything is turning blue now'); the folder of favourite photos titled 'Blue' on my laptop – blue is the only colour that has ever really moved me.

Swimming, not running, is my favourite exercise – I run more often only because it's easier to find places to do so, especially when jet lag rouses me at unsociable hours – and I suspect this preference has much to do with the opportunity swimming offers to immerse myself most fully in blueness. If I'm walking with Mark (who is colour-blind, but does okay with blues) through a city, and I express admiration for almost anything – a building, some interesting graffiti, a car – he'll turn to me and ask, deadpan, What do you like about it? And then I'll realise that whatever I've remarked on is mostly or entirely blue. On the rare occasions I wear something of another colour, friends may ask me: What have you done with Mark? (Ruling out virtually all non-blue items, I argue, makes shopping not only more pleasant but also simpler.)

I don't believe that my choice of career was driven by a desire to saturate my life with blueness. If it had been, however, then I wouldn't have been misled. Pilots are routinely exposed to what seems like every possible shade of blue. For long hours on a clear day, the mirroring realms of the ocean and the heavens may be the only things we perceive beyond the cockpit, and often they're indistinguishable, an effect that recalls a favourite line from Virginia Woolf's *To the Lighthouse*: 'So fine was the morning except for a streak of wind here and there that the sea and sky looked all one fabric, as if sails were stuck high up in the sky, or the clouds had dropped down into the sea.'

A 2015 poll reports that blue is the most popular colour in China, Indonesia, Thailand, Britain, the United States and five other countries. However, even in Britain, the most blue-impassioned of these, two-thirds of respondents preferred another colour. In contrast, I have yet to meet a pilot whose favourite colour is not blue. I'm struck by how often pilots close their emails with 'blue skies', followed by their name. I've come across the same words as a prayerful good-bye when pilots pass on.

One explanation, aside from how comprehensively blue dominates the view from our office, is that the colour shares with aviation a knack for beguiling both the scientific and the romantic sides of our nature. The Swiss scientist Horace Bénédict de Saussure, for example, was responsible for developing the cyanometer, a wheel that runs from white to nearly black, with about fifty shades of blue in between, in order to record the sky's colour at different times and in different places. Yet Saussure paired this precision with a love for what he described as blue's 'grandeur and its dazzling purity'.

Indeed, the links between Romanticism and the colour blue – we might think of the blue flower, a Romantic motif that stood for the truth and beauty that seem to always recede from our longing – are strong. Goethe, who made detailed, quasi-scientific investigations of colour, wrote that blue offers 'a kind of contradiction between excitement and repose', and that 'as we readily follow an agreeable object that flies from us, so we love to contemplate blue, not because it advances to us, but because it draws us after it'. There's a calmness to the blues that I'm most drawn to, and a depth and a vastness that are indistinguishable from those same qualities in the sky and the sea; and so it must be that blue embodies or intensifies the hope I long ago placed in journeys.

High above the South Atlantic, I sip my coffee as the stars fade. For the first time we contact a South African controller using a short-range radio. The air traffic control centres that deal with planes that are far from their origins or destinations are nothing like those we might picture from the movies; rather than a weather-thrashed, glass-walled box perched atop an airport's control tower, they're typically low, windowless and neutrally lit. From within such a centre, a woman with a South African accent calls to us as we cross the bluing sky off her country's west coast. She gives us a unique code to transmit as we come within range of her radar. You are identified, she says, the clarity of her voice the most obvious sign yet that our long oceanic journey is nearing its end. You are under radar control.

In the brightening sky ahead of us a flaw appears. At first, it's like nothing more than a dark crack in the far wall of a swimming pool, but slowly it grows. Other lines appear, in front of it and behind, too, recalling Melville's 'overlapping spurs of mountains bathed in their hill-side blue', from the passage in *Moby-Dick* in which he argues that not even such transcendent landscapes can compete with the elemental appeal of water. The blues of hills and ocean, and of sky, as well, now fill the windscreen as we near the ranges that dominate the landscape around the maritime metropolis known as the Mother City. In the cockpit we conduct our approach briefing and I make an announcement to the passengers about the weather they can expect on the ground: patches of morning mist under otherwise clear skies; a temperature of 18 degrees.

Hans Neuberger, a meteorologist, once compared the prevalence of deep blue skies in British and in southern European schools of landscape painting, revealing that they were much more common in the latter. Humidity makes even clear skies a little paler, and air in the Mediterranean basin, as so many holidaymakers know and appreciate, is generally drier than in northern Europe. In addition, the bluest skies are usually found at 90 degrees from the sun, a position that's more likely to be above the horizon at lower latitudes. (Imagine holding up a plate with both hands so that the sunlight hits it straight-on and then, in your mind's eye, expand its rim until this makes an arc across the sky. The sky's deepest blues should lie along that arc, and in my experience usually do.)

Cape Town, then – often free of clouds; at a latitude that, were the city in the Northern Hemisphere, we would describe as quintessentially Mediterranean; and blessed with less polluted skies, compared to other major cities, thanks in part to the dry, cleansing wind known as the Cape Doctor – is perhaps the first place you'd visit if you were on a science-guided quest for the urban world's most magnificent blues.

Nevertheless, I've sometimes worried that my irrationally deep love for the colour has left me minded to see a preponderance of blues in Cape Town that those who live there do not, or are less moved by. So, not long ago, I wrote to various family members, friends, pilots and correspondents who either live in Cape Town or grew up there.

No one was surprised to be asked about their city's most memorable colour (and no one suggested it might be anything other than blue). One Capetonian described her love of the skies and seas near her city, and mentioned, too, the 'spectacular blue' of the *Agapanthus africanus*, the African lily, a flower native to South Africa. (It was February when we corresponded, and she lamented that the blooms nearest her home were finishing.) Another Capetonian described his love for the 'incredible array of blues from deep indigo out in the Atlantic to the lightest turquoise in the shallows . . . blue water as far as the eye can see, with the blue haze of Table Mountain punctuating the far horizon'. He even remarked, as I never had until after I read his words, on the 'array of blue in the clouds and showers' that the violence of winter's cold fronts brings to the Cape, seemingly straight from the gusty southern latitudes known as the Roaring Forties.

Several expatriates told me that blue is what they miss most about their hometown. A Cape Town native who now lives in Helsinki, far in all senses from his first blues, and who counts himself lucky if he returns once a year, told me that the colour he misses the most begins to return as he crosses 'over the Namibian border, an hour or so before landing in Cape Town . . . there seems to be an air corridor that will place you right above the coast, with the deep blue of the sea on the right . . . this is when I get that "welcome home" feeling for the first time'. He also noted that the 'rock of Table Mountain and the Hottentots Holland range often seems more blue than grey . . . it's perhaps most stark on a really hot and clear day where the sky, the sea and the mountains all reflect off one another in some kind of self-reinforcing blueness'.

The engines throttle back, the nose lowers and our 747 begins its descent.

I'll make around two dozen trips here during my years on the 747; for many passengers, of course, this will be their only visit to the city, and I hope those on the right side are looking out to see Table Mountain rise like a stone step between the half-worlds of blue. Our long overwater hours end as we cross the coast near Blouberg (meaning Blue Mountain, it's home to a high density of archaeological sites and Stone Age burials of the Indigenous San and Khoe peoples, according to the archaeologist Jayson Orton, and it's also the scene of an 1806 battle that advanced the transition from Dutch to British colonial rule), where later today hundreds of kitesurfers will skid over some of their city's most reliably mighty waves.

The controller at the airport gives us a heading to fly, from which we'll intercept the radio signal that will guide us to Cape Town's sole long runway. On as bright a morning as this, however, we hardly need such electronic handholding. Table Bay, along which the core of the city rests, is now on our right, and False Bay, which lies to the south of the airport, is straight ahead. Every city on our navigation screens is marked by a circle of the colour described by our technical manuals as cyan, but some of them stand for bluer cities than others, I've learned, and on the morning after our 747 climbed through the uppermost sheet of London's layering greys, we lower the wheels, complete the landing checklist and touch down in the bluest city I know.

∽

WINTER

The conversation on the bus has died down as the rest of the crew and I submit to a familiar weariness, one that's more a reaction to the rush-hour traffic that's brought our bus to a halt than to the long flight – perhaps my fifteenth from London to Cape Town – that we completed only an hour or so ago.

Cape Town, in terms of its proximity to other major airports, remains one of the most remote places I've ever flown to. Imagine the city's line of latitude as it encircles the globe: more than 99 percent of humanity lives north of it. At virtually every turn, something – as little as a road sign bearing the city's telltale name, or as jarring as the appearance of Antarctica on the departures board at the airport – reminds me that I'm at one of the most picturesque ends of terra cognita. And this, despite the fact that for centuries, until the opening of the Suez Canal, the growing settlement, like a pulley steering lines of commerce and power between Europe and Asia around Africa, was central to the forces of imperialism that did so much to shape the modern world.

Cape Town's fabled blue sky, like the summit of Table Mountain right ahead of us, is hidden this morning by heavy clouds and waves of intensifying showers. And it's only in the worst weather in this usually bright metropolis that it occurs to me that despite its stirring geographic location, the days here might mostly feel like the days of a thousand other cities: that dreariness might collect even here, in the troughs of ordinary hours.

I first fell in love with the name of Cape Town when I was a child; then, in university, a professor of African history kindled my deeper interest. She taught us about the Indigenous pastoralist and hunter-gatherer peoples who have called the region home, and about the city's complex and often deeply troubled story, from the European invasion and settlement in the seventeenth century and the unfolding tragedy of those from afar and near who were enslaved here, both in law and in practice, to the city's role in the ending of apartheid in the early 1990s.

Today the city remains divided largely along racial lines, and by vertiginous economic disparities that are visible well before you land. Such disparities aren't unique to Cape Town, of course. (Indeed, their wide prevalence is not only a warning about one of the gravest potential downsides of urbanisation, but also the starkest reminder to me of the limitations of my repetitive but often brief, shallow, or insulated interactions with so many of the cities I fly to.) If Cape Town's inequities are among the most conspicuous to me, that is because – thanks to the enormous appeal of the city's climate, physical geography, history, diversity and cultural life to travellers from across the world – I so frequently fly here as a pilot and see them.

In a 2017 paper, Bradley Rink, a human geographer at the University of the Western Cape, described George Bernard Shaw's flight over Cape Town in 1932, which was organised to promote tourism to the city. (The pilot, Shaw reported, 'was annoyed by my cap, which, he told me, threatened to blow into the propeller'.) Shaw and his wife, Rink notes, 'were amongst the first tourists to enjoy Cape Town from the air for no other purpose than to enjoy the aerial perspective'. Rink's paper also wrestles, as do I, with what it means to travel a great distance in order to explore your preferred aspects of a place that's far more deprived than your own, and to do so with an ease that is denied to most of its own residents: 'From the blue skies above,' Rink writes, 'the spectacle of the touristic city is illuminated, while the rest of the urban landscape is cast in its shadows.'

More recently, climate-change-induced droughts, accompanied by newly ominous blue skies, have made Cape Town a harbinger of what many cities will face, even as the city remains especially reliant – once again, as do I – on the tourism and commerce that carbon-emitting planes carry. Yet if the Mother City's social and economic challenges reflect those of the whole world, and if its environmental circumstances frame questions that I've had no more luck than anyone else in easily resolving, the city also embodies a particularly compelling kind of hope to me, and perhaps in this regard, as well, Cape Town has lessons to offer. As urbanisation continues (and city life, after all, is said to be more environmentally sustainable than the alternatives) the success of Cape Town's short-term drought response will be instructive to communities around the world, while in the longer term, Cape Town has an opportunity to build on its reputation as one of Africa's greenest cities. And as an outsider, I wonder if it's right to look to this widely beloved city for other kinds of lessons. In a conversation over email, Rink pointed out to me that Cape Town is a place 'where layers of history, racial identities, religions and languages have resulted in a complex and rich cultural landscape'. Indeed – from the limited perspective of a brief but frequent visitor – it is one of the most worldly, multicultural and gay-friendly metropolises I've ever encountered.

When I was younger, of course, I knew none of this. I only knew that I was mesmerised – a cape, a town – by the city's straightforward name. It embodies, I later learned, both the city's location and its early purpose: a settlement to provide fresh food, water and rest to some ships and sailors, and to sustain the power to deny them to others; and a stronghold – a fortress was constructed soon after the city's foundation – not only to exert control over the Indigenous Khoe pastoralists and their land, livestock, water and nearby seas, but also to further the administration of places far beyond them. Better than anywhere else I know, the city's name alone can evoke both its geography and something of the violent complexity of its story, especially when you come across it in triplicate, in English, Xhosa and Afrikaans – CITY OF CAPE TOWN; ISIXEKO SASEKAPA; STAD KAAPSTAD – on a sign on which is also painted the city's emblem: a set of concentric yellow, red, blue and green rings, as if from the interior of a tree that grows nowhere else.

~

SPRING

I lurch sideways in my seat as our small white rental car leans into yet another curve on the vertiginous road. I open my eyes and in the side mirror see a sunglasses-clad motorist in a convertible close behind us, while behind him, in the distance, stands a wall of rock as sheer as those into which Wile E. Coyote might crash after the Road Runner has disappeared into a tunnel painted on it.

We're slowing him down, I guess; so be it. I look over at Mark, who I don't think is aware that I'm awake. His eyes are wide and bright; I suspect he is enjoying not only the fact that we are in Cape Town but that he's the one driving. He's a new driver – he learned only in his late thirties, which is unremarkable in much of the world, but nearly inconceivable to an American of my generation.

I was in the cockpit on the flight from London last night, so I flew while Mark slept. In aviation lingo, he is a Klingon, a cling-on, a passenger accompanying a relative or friend who is a member of the crew. Cape Town's popularity, especially during the Northern Hemisphere's winter, makes it a prime route for Klingons, but also an occasionally stressful one, as their heavily discounted tickets do not guarantee a spare seat in either direction.

At the last minute, and despite our expectations, he did get a seat, and he dashed to security to make the plane whose cockpit I was already sitting in, carefully programming our route to the opposite side of our world. We want to make the most of our handful of days here, so instead of going to sleep for four or five hours, as I'd have done if I were on my own, we left the hotel only a few minutes after checking in, and have come out for a drive on this scenic road to the south of the city centre. And for the first time on any trip we've taken together, Mark is doing the driving. My eyes close again until the next curve, when, through the windscreen and one half-open eye, I see a sheet of cobalt blue, which might be the sky if we're going up this road, or the open Atlantic, if down.

It's hard to believe that the temperature of the shining waters far below us is anything less than tropical, but in fact the Atlantic here is notoriously chilly. On another work trip I went to the beach with a friend who's both a pilot and a kitesurfer. He left most of his gear at the hotel but brought his wetsuit anyway, in order to swim, while I – recalling Dad's belief in the restorative powers of frigid water and his apparent immunity to all colds and flus – joked that my New England upbringing would help protect me. I swam for fifteen or twenty minutes and convinced myself that I felt not only fine, but especially invigorated. Then, when I tried to stand up and walk out of the sea, I fell over, my legs almost entirely numb.

Cape Town's geographic situation, too, takes some getting used to, even with the help of the rental car agency's map half-opened between us on the seat. At the scale at which I first saw the city – on a globe, surely – it appears to be at the tip of Africa. In fact, the city is not at Africa's southernmost point, which lies more than a hundred miles to the south-east. Also disorienting is that *Cape* might seem to refer not only to the entire southern cone of the African continent (the three modern South African provinces with *Cape* in their names encompass an area three times larger than Great Britain) but also to the much smaller outshoot near Cape Town, which is in fact called the Cape Peninsula (confusingly, to me, as it pairs two similar words whose difference I can't always remember), and which runs south from the city and narrows towards the rocky headland that is, finally, signposted as the Cape of Good Hope, and as Africa's 'most south-western point', though still more dramatic are the craggy heights of nearby Cape Point – indeed, it's the most breathtaking promontory I have ever seen – beyond which lie some of the earth's most mountainous and treacherous seas, and then Antarctica.

The city's geography is simplified, however, by Table Mountain. I don't know of a more fabled urban massif, or a more photogenic one: it appears in all of the best photographs of Cape Town and in much of the city's iconography, and you can't turn many corners here without being reminded of its stately presence. A few affluent neighbourhoods rise a little way up it, but otherwise the mountain divides the metropolis and diverts its routes as neatly as a stone parts a stream. A Berkshire partisan might note that Table Mountain is only 22 metres taller than Mount Greylock; but while Greylock rises from a rolling landscape that's already around 300 metres up, Table Mountain – indeed, its Khoe name is *Hoerikwaggo*, the mountain in the sea – is as instructive an image of the concept of sea level as any geography textbook's illustration, rising, it seems, right from the blue ocean itself.

Its summit, which can be accessed by popular hikes or the effortless cable car, is a different, cooler realm, one that's often an unwelcome or even dangerous shock to travellers dressed only for a sun-drenched holiday. Above all, the summit is notable for the winds that produce a tablecloth of white mist as they sweep over it, cooling enough as they rise for the water vapour they contain to briefly condense – a phenomenon you can also observe on aeroplane wings, typically right after takeoff, when the temperature and humidity are right. Indeed, the winds on the summit can be gusty enough to stop the cable cars for hours at a time, which once forced a worried pilot to find a mountaintop phone box and warn his boss that he might not be down in time to fly 330 travelers to London. (In the end he made it.)

Beyond the city centre and the mountain, a mix of suburbs – displaying extreme variation in terms of density, racial makeup, microclimate, wealth and geographic beauty – fan out from the north-east clockwise to the south. To the south-east lie the airport, and the townships of the Cape Flats, the swathe of land north of False Bay (so named as its shark-filled waters once fooled westbound sailors into thinking they'd rounded the entire Cape, and were therefore closing in on the respite offered by the city known as the Tavern of the Seas). Perhaps 1.7 million Capetonians, or more than one-third of the metropolitan area's population, including many from the mixed-race community known as Cape Coloureds, live in the Flats – under the brutality of apartheid, the residents of inner neighbourhoods such as District Six were forcibly removed here, in order to reserve the heart of Cape Town for whites – in dense tracts of often (though by no means exclusively) informal housing that are visible on all but the foggiest mornings from the window seats of arriving and departing planes. Some international travellers will only ever see the Flats from above; others will visit them during their stay in Cape Town, often as part of group tours guided by residents.

To the west and south of the city's historic core, beachfront neighbourhoods such as Camps Bay – which Cape Town resident Yoliswa Dwane, in a 2012 interview with the *New York Times*, described as still unwelcoming to Black people: 'You don't get the perception that this is an integrated country' – are dotted with high-end cafés, restaurants and some of Africa's most expensive houses, which cling precariously to the vertiginous terrain. Journeying south along this coastline you come to Chapman's Peak Drive, a road cut into the mountainside a century ago by convict labour, which offers those able to pay its toll a city-adjacent version of the giddiest heights of California's Pacific Coast Highway.

This morning, though, Mark and I, so recently arrived, are sticking closer to town. We're following the most obvious tourist trails, crowded with tiny, sparkling-clean rental cars like ours, up and over the roads of this incomparably three-dimensional cityscape.

Later we'll joke that the agency should have crumpled the map up into a ball before they gave it to us, in order to better match the character of the land it's meant to guide us over, and that it's only the gentle descents of the hang gliders that remind us which way is up, and which blue is which. We'll stop for sandwiches, and then drive on to pullouts crowded with cyclists, walk to the edge, and look down to where the land cracks the heaving blue into brows of exploding white, all of it, from such heights, as if in slow motion, and as silent as the sky.

EARLY SUMMER

I'm on a tourist boat tied up in the harbour, awaiting the briefest, most sanitised taste of what it must have once been like to sail away from this seafaring city.

Here, as nearly everywhere in Cape Town, the mountain looms. The further away an object is, the bluer it may appear – in part because the sky is blue, and there's more of it between us and whatever it is we're looking at. This effect offers a clue as to why there are many ranges known as 'Blue Mountains', in one language or another, across the world, and it explains why Leonardo da Vinci advised artists that objects meant to be five times further away should be painted 'five times bluer'. From aeroplanes, of course, practically everything we see between takeoff and landing is slightly blued by the tremendous distances we look through; and in Cape Town – so dominated by its seas that, as Jan Morris has noted, even in the 1840s, nearly two centuries after the future city's establishment, 'only one surfaced road' ran out of it into the interior – it seems right for a pilot to seek out this perspective once from a ship, and to watch Table Mountain alter as it must have in the eyes of centuries of sailors.

The engine roars and we pull away from the dock.

This is my twentieth trip to Cape Town. When Mark accompanied me here, on perhaps my fifth trip, we took a boat to Robben Island and we talked about his home city of Southampton, where the Union-Castle liners started their weekly circuit ('every Thursday at 4 p.m.') south to the Mother City.

The train that met these ships to take their passengers north-east – towards Johannesburg, its gold mines and the nation's administrative capital of Pretoria – came to be called the Blue Train, as the Birmingham-built carriages introduced in 1937 were painted a saturated Atlantic hue. The Blue Train still runs from Cape Town to Pretoria, a roughly thirty-hour journey. The Union-Castle service between Southampton and Cape Town, meanwhile, ended in 1977. It was finished off, in part, by the Boeing 747, the plane on which I often cross over the lights of Mark's hometown only minutes after liftoff from Heathrow.

To reach Robben Island on that long-ago trip, Mark and I went down to the harbour, past the stacks of shipping containers – many of which, once they're taken out of use, are repurposed elsewhere in the city as shelters and as small venues for shops and hairdressers – and took one of the boats that run out to it. The island had already been a notorious prison for centuries before Nelson Mandela's incarceration there began in 1964. In his autobiography he describes the view from the windows of an unheated military plane: 'Soon, we could see the little matchbox houses of the Cape Flats, the gleaming towers of downtown, and the horizontal top of Table Mountain. Then, out in Table Bay, in the dark blue waters of the Atlantic, we could make out the misty outline of Robben Island.' Mandela would be confined there for eighteen years, until 1982, and then in other prisons until 1990.

Soon to join the Robben Island ferry fleet is the catamaran *Krotoa* – blue, of course, like the other Robben Island ferries, and christened in honor of a seventeenth-century Khoe woman, the first to be named in the European records of Cape Town, to which we must turn, cautiously, for the fragments that remain of her story. Krotoa laboured from a young age in the household of Jan van Riebeeck, the city's founder, who renamed her Eva (and left no records of her wages, if any); became an interpreter and negotiator; and had three children with her husband, a Danish doctor. In the late 1660s her husband died in Madagascar, on a slaving expedition; in the following years, Krotoa's children were taken from her and she was repeatedly banished to Robben Island, where she died in 1674. Described in our age as a 'peacebroker' and a 'matriarch of resistance', her name has been proposed for Cape Town's airport.

Today, Mark is not with me, and the vessel I'm on is not bound for Southampton, nor even Robben Island, but only to the spot a few miles out where it will turn around to allow us to take photos back towards Cape Town.

The land's heat is swept away by the sea breeze as we pass moored trawlers – the *Beatrice Marine*, the *Isabella Marine* – whose scrubbed white superstructures rise from sky-blue hulls. I can see, as well, the futuristic curves of the stadium, built for the 2010 World Cup, between kayakers paddling over kelp beds and Signal Hill, from which a naval gun has been fired at noon for more than two centuries. The purpose was to help those on ships set the clocks that were necessary to determine longitude on their perilous journeys to come (for the same reason there used to be a time ball, as well – think Times Square on New Year's Eve – whose drop sailors could easily observe from their anchorages in Table Bay), and even when I'm far from Cape Town I can almost hear these guns, which each midday use their Twitter account to discharge a single, all-capitalised word: BANG!

As we move into deeper water, the boat's motion transitions from two dimensions to a vigorous three; the stern's six-coloured South African flag, with its long blue trapezium running immediately above the waves, snaps in the intensifying breeze; and I'm reminded that while many cities have risen on coastlines, no other large city I've been to offers as proximate a sense of the primal ocean. At one point in the nineteenth century Lloyd's of London, the venerable insurer, refused to cover vessels that wintered at Cape Town, and today around a fifth of the more than 2,300 shipwrecks along South Africa's long coast are said to lie in Table Bay. Our little tourist boat glides above a graveyard.

From its loudspeakers a saxophone starts to play, and the jazz of Kenny G mixes with excited talk in German, perhaps about dolphins, from the other side of the boat. The music changes and I realise the water has, too: there are large swells but they don't break into obvious seams, let alone into whitecaps. Instead the silvery-blue surface takes on an almost blurry texture, as if it's a simulation in a game, one that switches to a lower resolution once you move a certain distance beyond the more detailed domain of the shore.

Years from now an oceanographer will explain to me that at the beach we rarely encounter the ocean's deepest blues, which lie much further out; indeed, he will note, most people who are lucky enough to see these exquisite colours will do so only from an aeroplane. But here, only a few miles off Cape Town, the blue looks as regal as any I've seen from above.

To generations of scientists, the cause of water's blueness was as great a mystery as that of the sky's. At times it was thought that water appears blue only because it reflects the blueness above. Others suspected that the sky was blue precisely because of the water that air naturally contains, but – as Peter Pesic records in his book *Sky in a Bottle* – in the nineteenth century Michael Faraday calculated that all the water in the sky, if condensed out, would amount to a layer of only a few inches over the earth, which, as each filling of a bathtub demonstrates, is not enough to render water blue. 'I leave you to judge how utterly insufficient this would be to produce the blue skies seen in this country, much less those of Italy and other parts of the world,' Faraday wrote.

The explanation for the sea's colour is the complement to that for the sky's. Compared to air, water absorbs much more of the light that falls upon it. Nevertheless, water, like air, absorbs shorter-wavelength colours such as blue less easily. Blue, having not been absorbed, can therefore penetrate water more deeply, and is also more likely – again, having not been absorbed – to be scattered back up to our eyes. All of which, as Robert Pincus, an atmospheric scientist, wrote to me, is 'an elaborate way of saying that water is a blue liquid, or has a bluish cast'.

The ocean's blue isn't uniform across the world, in part because it's affected by suspended particles, the water's depth, the nature of the seabed and life-forms, particularly phytoplankton. Indeed, the colour of the sea is so varied that scientists rely on satellites to monitor and study it, and I like to imagine that a rigorous comparison of the waters off the world's great coastal cities would confirm what seems as clear as the day to me, as the saxophone plays on and our seal-chased vessel turns: that the blue of Cape Town's waters, like that of its skies, has no equal.

~

LATE SPRING

I'm walking through a park in the centre of Cape Town that's known as the Company's Garden – the garden of the Dutch East India Company, that is, where food was once grown in order to victual passing ships – but however cool and green it is, I'm going to have to leave because the pedestal-mounted sundial I've just encountered has reminded me that it's time to find a coffee.

So monumental is the scenery around Cape Town that it can be easy to forget the city that remains at its centre. Then, when I next come into its heart to walk beneath its massif-shadowed skyscrapers, I'm likely to experience, as I do today, flickers of a worryingly Ozymandian sensation: that all that man has built here – and by extension, everywhere – is fragile and contingent, at least in comparison with this mountain and this ocean, and with the timescales on which their existence, rather than ours, is measured. And yet the moment in which I think this – in this metropolis that stands, I'm unable to forget, on the very edge of my permanently Pittsfield-centred world – must be as ordinary as any other here, as all around me the Capetonians who fill these streets, and know them best, continue to be immersed in the everyday: small groups of young men with loosened ties laugh and talk shop, a businesswoman steps into a taxicab, a worker has opened a telecom cabinet and does something skilful with its colourful, spaghetti-like contents.

My quest for coffee takes me north-east until, at the corner of Burg Street and Longmarket Street, I see a café named Heaven, attached to a Gothic-style church that could be the sturdy centrepiece of an English village. Built in the late nineteenth century, and presided over today by Alan Storey, a minister who was the last conscientious objector to be put on trial by the apartheid regime, the Central Methodist Mission offers a permanently cool retreat from the sun and the crowds, and it's my favourite building in what might be the city I love best. In addition to its own services, it hosts a gay-affirming congregation on Sunday evenings, and a few years from now, it will be the site of a months-long occupation by refugees from other parts of Africa.

Outside the church are various blue signs cut in the shape of Gothic windows: CENTRAL METHODIST MISSION IS A CITY

CHURCH, says one. YOU ARE BORN IN LOVE – BY LOVE – FOR LOVE, says another, a phrasing that reminds me of the religious beliefs of my parents when they were young, which were strong enough to govern the entire first halves of their lives; and of how aspects of their faith, though Dad's ended and Mom's changed, might have shaped my life, and even the hope I've placed in cities, far more than they could have expected.

Michel Pastoureau, in his book *Blue: The History of a Color*, wrote that 'blue was essentially absent from Christian worship during the thousand years preceding the creation of blue stained glass in the twelfth century', in particular the creation of a hue – Chartres blue – that ages more gracefully than other colours used in stained glass. Later, of course, blue would become deeply associated with images of the Virgin Mary, especially the precious pigment ground from lapis lazuli and known as ultramarine, which lay outside Michelangelo's budget and broke Vermeer's. Its name, as Pesic notes, is a reference not to the sea's colour but to the pigment's origin, as it came 'from beyond the seas', typically from Afghanistan.

Here in the Central Methodist Mission the loveliest windows are filled with patterns of translucent white glass, bordered and divided by blues that run from the soft, near-greyness of an early morning sky through the colour of glass cleaner to a deep, nearly oceanic hue. As I look up, I question how far I'd get if I was tasked with giving each shade a telltale name; I half smile as I think of the cabin crew member who, as we flew high over the open Atlantic last year, presented me and my colleague with a set of light brown swatches from a high-end British paint retailer, so we could more accurately specify the strength and milkiness of tea we wanted; and then I squint, to try out the possibility that one of the small blue windows of this church is missing, and that what I believe to be one more pane held by the stonework is, in reality, the sky of the city beyond.

～

WINTER

On a grey morning I'm nearing the Kasteel de Goede Hoop, the Castle of Good Hope, as it was named by its Dutch founders in 1666. The pentagonal fortress helped its occupants to hold and project power over African communities as well as over oceans near and far, and – as South Africa's oldest building – it remains a potent symbol of the role that force has played in the story of the nation's oldest city. Indeed, the castle was once the hub of an elaborate communications network – signal fires, flags and cannon shots – designed to identify friendly ships as they approached the city, to advertise that the city was still safe under Dutch control, or to summon help to safeguard it. Even today the castle is administered by the country's Department of Defence.

The background to the frieze above the gate, and the arched ceiling under which I pass to enter the castle, are a limpid blue. I have the castle nearly to myself today, it seems, and I walk slowly over its pathways and stairs of blue slate, quarried on Robben Island and set off here by the dusty yellow walls. Further on, I come across a grey utility box on which there is a small heraldic shield – that of a command of the South African Army once headquartered here, I believe – which incorporates a springbok, two swords and an image of Table Mountain set against a navy sky. As an evocation of the city, it's no less clear than the University of Cape Town's coat of arms, which features an anchor, a heaving blue ocean on a black background (an arrangement described as 'party per fess wavy, Sable and Azure' in the mind-blowingly byzantine terminology of heraldry), and the propitious motto that the university shares with the Province of the Western Cape: *Spes Bona*, Good Hope.

Before the Cape Town-based writer Nobhongo Gxolo first visited the castle, she burned *impepho*, a herb said to facilitate contact with ancestors, and offered a prayer. In a 2016 article, she wrote: 'The murder and torture contained in dark chambers has diffused into the walls and left a stain. You feel it.' Many travellers visit Cape Town's castle to try to contemplate this history, and also to see the art collection that is tied to an important date in the story of the country's liberation. The collection was first put on public display in the castle in 1952, as part of a festival organised by the apartheid government to commemorate the 300th anniversary of the arrival of Jan van Riebeeck on 6 April 1652. The festival led to boycotts and protests, with the African National Congress and the South African Indian Congress calling instead for 'A National Day of Pledge and Prayer'. Two and a half months after the tercentenary, on 26 June 1952, the Defiance Campaign was launched against apartheid, with Nelson Mandela as one of its founders.

As an artistic and cultural phenomenon, blue's ancient history is spottier than that of most colours. For example, no blue was used in Greek ceramics; indeed, William Gladstone, the British politician and classicist, once believed that the ancient Greeks – despite the stunning colours of their home skies and waters – were blue-blind, incapable of seeing the colour, in part because they so rarely described the sea as such ('wine-dark' being the most famous Homeric phrasing). Romans, meanwhile, associated the colour with eccentricity and woad-dabbed locals.

Here in Cape Town's castle, many of the European-style paintings feature seascapes in which a ship, or many ships, sitting at terrifying angles to the waves as their Dutch or British ensigns snare in the gale, proceed towards a settlement at the foot of Table Mountain. In some, the future metropolis appears to be little more than a fortified village; in others the very castle in which the painting now hangs is visible. The sky in these paintings is rarely entirely blue; more commonly, the heavens are dominated by mountainous cloudscapes billowing across a background azure. The ominous sea, meanwhile, especially in the earlier paintings, is often grey, black, or green.

Later, I'll have a chance to speak with Nomusa Makhubu, a practising artist and a professor at the Michaelis School of Fine Art at the University of Cape Town. Born near Johannesburg, Makhubu grew up in an area dominated by metal industries whose pollution discoloured the air. She describes to me the joy she now takes in Cape Town's blue skies, particularly on hikes around Constantia Nek, an east-west pass that runs to the south of Table Mountain. She knows the hills of the Berkshires, too – her work once brought her to Williamstown, not far to the north of Pittsfield.

Cape Town may be a beautiful place, but it is also a very unequal one, she tells me, as she shows me examples of blueness in art that engages with the history and ongoing struggles of her city and country. One of her former students, Buhlebezwe Siwani, is an internationally successful artist who works in a variety of media, including video, paper and sculpture. In her 2015 photograph *iGagasi* (its title means 'wave' in Xhosa) a woman standing in the ocean beneath blue-grey hills and an indigo sky holds a blue-and-white rope – associated in Xhosa traditions with healing – and leans back into the wave that meets her. We like to think of blue as tranquil, Makhubu tells me, but it's suggestive, too, of the dispossession and displacement that arrived by sea.

She also shares an image of *Police Raid*, a 1977 work by George Pemba, who grew up in the Eastern Cape and chronicled life in its townships, and who is remembered as one of South Africa's greatest artists. The painting depicts four township residents and the two police officers who have just entered their home, where illicit alcohol – the only source of income for some township residents – has apparently been brewed. One officer struggles with a woman over a bottle; another's truncheon is raised. The headscarves of the two women and the back of a tipped-over chair are blue; so are the bottles of alcohol, the beard of one of the residents and the faces of the police officers. Makhubu also draws my attention to the blue mountains and skies of the world beyond this room, and to how – in contrast with the open perspectives and often unpeopled landscapes in the European-style tradition of painting in South Africa – their beauty can only be glimpsed through the small window and the door the police have left open.

Here in Cape Town's castle I wander away from the halls of paintings and come to an exhibit that focuses on the ceramics that arrived on the same trade routes that the city was founded to further and to guard. Much of what's on display follows the traditional blue-on-white arrangement that we associate with earthenware from the Dutch city of Delft (which shares its name with a township that lies directly east of Cape Town's airport). Most bewildering, perhaps, to a pilot already confounded by place lag, are the Chinese export works from the first half of the eighteenth century. On these, Cape Town's mountains, skies and seas have been drawn by Chinese artisans who worked 7,000 miles away from a city they would never see, and who surely couldn't have imagined the circumstances in which I'd pause to look upon their work in the twenty-first century, nor those by which, in a few months, I'll descend through the skies of the Pearl River Delta en route to Hong Kong.

∽

EARLY SUMMER

I'm covered in sweat after the hike up through the streets of Bo-Kaap, and the well-shaded swing, suspended from a tree and swaying gently in the breeze, is tempting, but even as I walk towards it I realise I'm not certain I'm allowed to use a swing that hangs in a cemetery.

Bo-Kaap, the inner Cape Town neighbourhood spread out

below me, is the historic heart of the Cape Malay ethnic group –
descendants of those, especially Muslims, who were brought to Cape
Town (often as enslaved persons or prisoners from the Dutch-ruled
territories that are now part of Malaysia and Indonesia) and who
formed the nucleus of a community that under the apartheid regime
would be classified as Coloured. Even today, as waves of gentrifica-
tion sweep over Bo-Kaap, Malay-derived words may still be heard
on its cobblestone streets. I had always thought that the *Bo* in the
name of this undeniably striking location was a corruption of *beau*,
and therefore, perhaps, a legacy of France's brief military presence
in Cape Town in the early 1780s; whereas in fact *bo* is Afrikaans for
'above'. Bo-Kaap, in any case – positioned on the slopes of Signal
Hill, with views across to Table Mountain, down to the city centre
below, and out to the sea beyond – is beautiful largely because it is
above.

Butterflies scatter as I walk through the long grass and approach
the swing. Muslims won their religious freedom in the Cape in
1804, and the first land for the Tana Baru Cemetery – its name
means 'New Ground' in Malay – was granted in 1805, in part to
promote Muslim support for the Dutch administration in the event
of a British attack. (A prescient fear, as one took place the following
year.)

Many of the leading lights of Cape Town's Muslim community
rest here. Some were exiled from Dutch colonial possessions for
alleged crimes related to political activism; others, like the Indone-
sian prince known as Tuan Guru, for conspiracy with the English,
with whom Dutch commercial and imperial ambitions in the Far
East were often in conflict. After his release from imprisonment on
Robben Island, Tuan Guru founded South Africa's first mosque, on
Dorp Street, which he said would last for as long as the world.

Here also is the tomb of Tuan Said Aloewie, whom a sign describes
as the first official imam in the Cape. Originally from Mocha, on
the Red Sea coast of Yemen, he was arrested either there or in Indo-

nesia, and 'banished to the Cape to be kept in chains' for the rest of his life. However, after eleven years as a prisoner on Robben Island he was released. He remained in Cape Town and became a policeman, a role that allowed him to tend to the faith of enslaved persons.

Bo-Kaap, so emblematic of Cape Town's diverse and globe-encircling roots, is also its most colourful neighbourhood. Whenever I ask Capetonians about the blues of their city, the houses of Bo-Kaap are typically mentioned next after the sea and the sky. There are other colours among these homes, including yellows, purples, pinks and reds (one popular but disputed account suggests that as it was a requirement for tenanted houses to be kept white, the colours were a jubilant reaction by freed persons newly able to buy property). It's the blues, however, and especially from close up, that echo and even intensify the colours of the city's sky and waters.

One home strikes me above all. Its blue is a deep marine, set off by the white of its door, windows, shutters and iron fence, all blazing in the blinding sun, and by the bright hues – yellow, red – of its neighbours. This blue is so appealing that I walked past the house several times today, enjoying the sensation of its gravity, until I started to worry that I might look suspicious, and only then did I continue on up to this graveyard.

I'm still unsure whether to use the swing, a simple plank of wood hanging on an inverted Y of rust-coloured rope. So I try to stand still, for once, in this city where I sometimes walk from breakfast until dinnertime.

I look down at my dusty shoes. Then I look straight up. Mom would love this sky, I think, as I try to photograph it, but the camera seems to not be able to focus without an object, and perhaps the colour, too, is beyond its powers. Mom never knew that one day I would fly long-haul routes, but wherever she is, that's surely not a problem: if she can look out for me, then she'll know where to do so.

When my stillness fails I walk towards the tree and try again in the shade of its branches. In the neighbourhood below, a garage door opens and a security alarm momentarily sounds. The breeze picks up. I hear it work through the tall grass between the graves, and for a moment I close my eyes, so refreshing are its tides of coolness after my climb in the afternoon sun.

The *blip blip* of a locking car brings me back. I open my eyes to see a couple below me walking towards their home, their hands full of plastic shopping bags. There are worse places to park your car after a day's work or a visit to the shops, and there are worse hills to spend eternity on, I think, as I take my phone from my pocket, confirm the departure time of tonight's flight, check the distance from this cemetery to my hotel, and understand that it's time to start down.

CHAPTER 10

CITY OF SNOW

London, Istanbul, Uppsala,
New York and Sapporo

I'M IN MY ROOM, on a late summer afternoon when I'm fifteen or so. The window above my desk is open, and as I listen to my brother and his friends play in our yard and the yard next door – my brother yelled up to me a few minutes ago; I should go down in a minute – I turn my globe in order to follow Pittsfield's latitude, roughly 42½ degrees north, all around it. I don't yet know what Pittsfielders share with folks whose homes also lie along this line: the stars that fill our skies, the length of our days and our twilights and our nights, the very speed at which we turn.

I only know it's a fun way to map a journey. Pittsfield's parallel, if I follow it east, crosses the Atlantic, Andorra, the centre of the Caspian Sea and the southern reaches of Mongolia. Before it arcs out over the open Pacific it passes not too far from the Japanese city of Sapporo. Sapporo is a good name. It sounds a little like Siberia, and indeed at this scale, and from this distance, the city isn't far from it. So Sapporo's winters must be long, I think, and maybe even snowier than those of Pittsfield.

PITTSFIELD

*Approximate depth of the snowdrifts in March 1888, after more than
one metre of snow fell during a three-day blizzard, stranding travellers
from California in their snowbound railway carriage here: five metres*

I'm nine, maybe; my brother is eleven. Our parents have gone
out. Maybe to the home of another family in the Berkshire gang;
or possibly, though this would be rare, to a restaurant. It's early evening and dark outside, so it must be autumn or winter.

My brother and I are sitting on the couch in the living room on
either side of Russell, our babysitter. He lives on the next street and
is fifteen or sixteen. He's tall and wearing an athletic team jersey in
the purple-and-white colours of Pittsfield High. This corner of the
room is always golden after nightfall, thanks to the thick shade of
the lamp on the glass table.

Russell has heated and fed to us whatever my parents left on the
stove. Mom asked him to read to us before bedtime, from one of
the later books of *The Chronicles of Narnia*. So far, I love *The Lion,
the Witch and the Wardrobe* best, mostly because of the winter that
Lucy finds Narnia locked in when she passes through the wardrobe.
Indeed, I love snow so much that at first I didn't understand that
this permanent winter is a means of punishing the world (though
the absence of Christmas is a clue). And when spring came to Narnia at last, I confessed to Mom that I was a little disappointed.

On the sofa in the living room, Russell opens the book to where
Mom left off. He reads a few lines then stops, looks up and sighs.

Reading aloud is not his thing. Or maybe the problem is fantasy novels. Whatever the reason, the words themselves seem to embarrass him. He reads a few more, then turns to me and then to my brother and says: You guys don't actually like this shit, do you?

Our mom likes it, my brother says, truthfully, but I'm already gone; I'm in Narnia, briefly, where I wait for my brother to join me; then, when I understand from the continuation of his conversation with Russell that he is still in our living room, I find myself walking in the snow that falls on the city that only I can see.

LONDON

Number of additional men employed to clear snow from Kensington in March 1891, after a blizzard so crippling to the metropolis that a magistrate, investigating the pub landlord who supplied rum to an on-duty constable, chose to absolve them both: 6,963

En route to Heathrow, I steer through the murk and rain towards the road known as the Westway. In these years in which I fly short-haul routes, I often drive to the airport, as neither the train nor the Tube can get me there in time for the earliest flights to the continent.

London is like the world, and unlike Pittsfield, at least in one straightforward sense: the more I know of it, the bigger it seems, I think, as a sign for White City reminds me of home, which – five hours behind – lies in the depths of a snowy and far colder night. As I pass the sign I think, too, of the old house, and the light mounted below the overhanging roof of the garage, and the four little panes around it that were always broken, and I wonder whether the people who live there now leave it on overnight, to add to my hometown's other lights, which scooped up and balled together might equal the brightness of only a few hundred metres of central London.

And I try to picture the moonlit, snowbound fields on the edges of Pittsfield, and the subzero stillness of the dark forests beyond.

It's my impression that introverts like snow more than extroverts do, perhaps for the silence it brings to the world, or merely for the genuine excuse it offers to stay in. I imagine I first came to love snow only because heavy overnight storms saved me from having to go to school, and from confronting the challenges that lived there. (Indeed, sometimes I suspect I grew into such an introvert in part for similar reasons.)

Mom, however, is an extrovert, and from her I've come to appreciate that – whatever one's personality – snow can make daily life much more difficult as you get older. Ever since I left Massachusetts for England she gives me blow-by-blow accounts of every snowstorm, and regular updates on the depth in the yard, but only because she knows how happy these reports make me, especially as Christmas nears. Now, however, winter has become too long for her – the difficult driving, the shovelling, the slippery paths, the plans with friends cancelled, the medical appointments postponed – and I know that these days she spends my favourite season waiting for spring.

ISTANBUL

Consecutive days of snow in early 1621, the winter in which the city's inhabitants could cross easily between Europe and Asia on the ice that spanned the Bosphorus: 16

High off the Atlantic coast of France, en route from Bilbao to London, Mike – the captain – and I turn our thoughts east to the skies of Istanbul.

After touchdown at Heathrow, we'll take a different aircraft on to that city, and in the quiet cruise segment of this flight we order the fuel for the next. Normally a fuel decision for Istanbul is easy, but tonight's forecast warns of 'SN' – aviation shorthand for snow – preceded by a '+' that means 'heavy', a pairing more typically associated with Minneapolis or Moscow.

After a careful read of the weather at Istanbul's standard alternate airfields – Heraklion, on the Greek island of Crete; Varna on Bulgaria's Black Sea coast; and Ankara, the inland, mountainous Turkish capital – Mike decides to increase the fuel order enough to allow us to hold for an hour above Istanbul and still reach any of those cities if we need to afterwards.

Our departure for Istanbul is remarkable only for the slightly higher power setting and longer stretch of runway we need to get airborne at a heavier-than-usual weight, and soon we're at our cruising altitude, enjoying dinner as we cross Europe under its starry winter sky.

In these early years of my career I love flying to Istanbul for a number of reasons, aside from the fascinations that the metropolis once said to be the 'Queen of Cities' and 'sovereign over all others' holds for even the most world-weary traveller. There's the fact that it is once again the largest European city (a title it previously held for more than eight continuous centuries), and the glory suggested by the number of its former names (Byzantion or Byzantium, Constantinople and at least half a dozen others, including the most stirring, Nova Roma, New Rome). It's also one of the most distant cities I fly to as a pilot of the short-haul Airbus A320, and so, in the same simple terms in which I thought as a child, flights to Istanbul are by definition among my most momentous.

Every twenty minutes or so we download a weather update, and the news isn't good. The heavy snow has arrived earlier than forecast, and it's accompanied by strong winds, in an ominous pairing that meets the official definition of a blizzard. We calculate the landing distance, crosswind and visibility limitations that apply to a landing in such conditions, and recalculate as the weather wors-

ens. Not long after we start our descent we're instructed to level off
and to take up a holding pattern, and the controller tells us what
pilots never wish to hear: delay undetermined.

The snow has now also hit Heraklion, however hard it is to imagine a blizzard sweeping over a sea-level city on a Greek island. But
Varna and Ankara are both still wide open.

We contact colleagues in Istanbul and in London, and all advise
us to divert to Ankara. Mike speaks to the cabin crew to advise
them of his decision. Meanwhile I initiate a climb and steer the
Airbus onto its newly programmed route to the ancient settlement
that Kemal Atatürk, in the 1920s, transformed into Turkey's capital.
Barely fifteen minutes later, we start our second descent of the flight
and soon after we touch down in Ankara, where despite the higher
elevation, and the steep mountains that rise from the side of the
airfield, only a cold rain is falling.

We park and shut off the engines. A moment later a soaked but
cheerful member of the ground staff knocks on the cabin's forward
door. He was at home when London rang and we have, it seems,
interrupted an Ankaran family's quiet evening.

A group of Japanese passengers, en route from Tokyo to Istanbul via Heathrow, believe they've reached their final destination
and have stood and already gathered their belongings. In my limited Japanese I cobble together something that I hope conveys: I'm
sorry, this is not yet Istanbul. Then I stand on the stairs and look
north-west, out into the darkness beyond the refuelling truck and
the apron lighting, as the rain, as icy as any in Pittsfield in November, blows over my regulation black shoes.

Soon, some news: Istanbul's airport has reopened. Having confirmed our flying-hour limits, we depart again and retrace our route.
Thick flakes gust over the windscreen as we descend over the Sea
of Marmara, and when we emerge from the clouds and above the
approach lights, we recognise that snow has already begun to accu-
mulate since the runway's most recent ploughing. The covering is

not deep, though, and the crosswind is within our limits. We touch down in near-silence; the noise of engines seems louder when a runway is close enough to reflect it, but a blanket of snow can quiet even turbofans, I learn tonight.

It takes us almost an hour to reach the gate, so slippery are the taxiways. At last we park, complete our paperwork and say farewell to our tired passengers. We pass through immigration and board a bus that slides back and forth across the nearly deserted airport highway – tonight I wish for a driver more accustomed to snow, one from Pittsfield, perhaps, rather than modern Byzantium – but soon we're safe at our hotel in a skyscraper on the seafront.

I hang up my uniform, plug in my phone and put on my pajamas, but I know it'll be some time before I can sleep. I sit by the window and put on some music. London, Bilbao, Ankara and Istanbul: it must be true that Mike and I are the first people to stand in all four of these cities on the same day, I think, as I look past the last flakes of the storm swirling against the smoky glass, out to the dark waters that lead to the Bosphorus and the lights of its waiting ships.

PITTSFIELD

Depth of the snow that fell in the blizzard of early March 1916, during which horse-drawn ploughs were deployed, and the 'trolley car schedules suffered to a marked extent': sixty-one centimetres

The snow in the parking lot of Canoe Meadows Wildlife Sanctuary is already too deep to park in, so I stop my rental car on a nearby side street. Rich, my childhood friend, lived on this street until he moved away to Connecticut, and as I step out from the warm car into the whirl of flakes I glance at a large house a few doors down; when it was under construction Rich and I would sneak out on sleepovers and, in the moonlight, climb down into the site and up the little mountains of gravel that workers had stored in what must now be a basement laundry area or rec room.

I unfasten my cross-country skis from the top of the car. There's barely any call for skis in Boston, where I live and work now, and so my old skis live in the basement at Mom's house in Pittsfield, to be brought up only when I'm in town in winter. They're not the sort that require waxing, but as I drop them on the snowy road and parenthetical white sighs fly out from their fibreglass edges, I recall Dad's wooden skis, and his multicoloured collection of waxes, in containers that resembled deodorant sticks, for different temperatures and types of snow: new, fine, old, wet, granular. I remember, too, a photo of my parents skiing in Burlington, Vermont, before they moved to Pittsfield. Mom is in a yellow jacket and she looks as if she is laughing at the fact that she is standing – and meant to propel herself, too – on a pair of wooden planks. (She has a slightly more terrified version of the same expression in another photo I love, from Pittsfield, decades later, in which she's poised on a friend's all-terrain vehicle in the woods, having just been told how to make it go.)

Another car pulls up and parks behind me. A man gets out and unloads his skis. He waves and says: Big storm, eh?

He's not wrong. Perhaps twenty-five centimetres have already fallen and another twenty are on their way. But you must be used to that, right? he adds, gesturing, I realise, to the Minnesota number plate on the rental car I picked up in Boston. He looks like he skis all the time and perhaps, I think, Minnesota carries a kind of cred among such folks that I was not aware of.

I'm about to explain that the car is a rental, and that I'm from Pittsfield – indeed, I'm from a few blocks away. But – I skid – if I'm from here, why am I in a rental car? So instead I only nod: Yeah, big storm. And my shoulders relax a little as I pull this new identity on like another insulating layer – I'm straight; from a suburb of Minneapolis; a skillful skier, yes, even a Minnesota state champion back in the day – and click my light-grey boots into the bindings of my skis.

I ski a few dozen metres down Holmes Road and enter Canoe Meadows. It's hard to see ahead, so thick is the snow, but I know well enough where I'm going. This preserve embodied wilderness to me when I was a child, but in fact its boundaries enclose only a few hundred acres.

Gravity rather than skill propels me down the hill and into the woods at its base. I pass a frozen pond and think of the time Dad and I went to watch one of my brother's speed skating competitions on Pontoosuc Lake, and of how, when I asked Dad how the skaters could know it was safe – I must have had the incident on our backyard goldfish pond in mind – he pointed to the gigantic Zamboni ice resurfacer that was progressing as steadily as a tank across the blinding-white lake, and said that it was probably safe for my brother and his competitors, too.

The snow cakes my hat, my gloves, even as my exertion melts whatever hits the exposed parts of my face. My skier's high hits, and it's better than any runner's one: this is winter at its best, Pittsfield at its best. Maybe I don't live here now but today I'm home. A few metres ahead of me the snow that's weighing down a branch – if my brother was with me, even now in our twenties, one of us might shake it onto the other's exposed neck with a laugh – at last exceeds its angle of repose, tumbles into the air and sifts down to the floor of the forest as the bough rises up to gather more.

I may look the part of a Minnesotan skier, but now I've made a full circuit of my favourite trail and I'm tired. Nearby is a bird hide that offers a bench and a viewpoint onto the surrounding wetlands. I click off my skis, lean them against the railing and take a few steps down the boardwalk and into the hide. The marsh beyond its unglazed windows is frozen and snow-covered, a field of grey-blue as blank and open as any other.

I look back out of the blind, where the prints left by my ski boots are already nearly obscured. There's hardly any wind, and no birds; there's only the rustling of so many crystals touching down, and the accelerated pulse of so much blood in my ears.

I'm still breathing deeply from my exercise but within minutes of sitting down I grow cold. I look out at the ice-locked marsh and shiver. This is how it would begin, I think: this reflexive motion as everything starts to stop.

I stand and stomp my boots. It feels wrong to wear them indoors, if that's the right word for the interior of a building with no door, no glass and no heat. I step out and click my skis back on. Before I start I look back, to where powder has drifted half a metre or so in through the doorless frame, and I pause to imagine how some future partner and I might try to make it work: how we'd want to seal the windows as best we could, and look for stones to break free from the ice on the edge of the marsh, then pick a corner and arrange them in a hearth.

UPPSALA

Date of the snowstorm known as Yrväderstisdagen, Wild-Blizzard Tuesday, which killed around 100 Swedes, and swept over the region of Uppsala with particular force: 29 January 1850

I step off the train that has taken me north from Stockholm to Uppsala, Sweden's fourth-largest city. It's not late, maybe 9 p.m., but at this time of year it's been dark for hours.

Many decades ago one of my uncles moved from Belgium to Stockholm (where he went on to work in the city's transport department, which suggests a genetic component to my interest in cities, transport and maps). And so, since I've started flying, I've come here as often as I can, swapping my MAD, Madrid, or my TXL,

Berlin's Tegel Airport, for a colleague's ARN, Arlanda, Stockholm's largest airport.

Arlanda is easy to love, and not only because of the opportunity it offers to see family. The syllables that form its name are so liquid that it's hard to believe their arrangement is artificial, incorporating an ancient place-name and the verb *landa*, to land. And, as one of my cousins proved, you can get married here, in either a VIP lounge or the airport chapel. (Mark, perhaps fearing I might insist on this, quickly agreed to a 747-shaped cake instead.) The airport also has a policy that it will never close due to snowfall, and snow clearance and de-icing procedures are predictably refined in this wintry land.

Arlanda lies roughly equidistant between Stockholm, to its south, and Uppsala, to the north. Most times, after touchdown at Arlanda, I change out of my uniform in the washroom nearest the cockpit, give my luggage to a colleague whom I've asked to take it to our crew hotel in Uppsala, and make my way to the sleek airport train that runs down to Stockholm. I remember my first work trip here: after disembarking at Stockholm's Central Station, I took the metro for several stops, walked down a tree-lined avenue, asked for directions, found my way to a narrower street, wandered in search of a house number, crossed the street, backtracked a bit and at last reached an apartment block no different from the dozens of others I'd passed, except that my surname was printed by one of the buzzers. Even now, I can't quite believe that someone who's such a dead ringer for Dad is waiting upstairs to offer me hugs, a tasty hot dinner (always fish), and all the comedic Swedish lessons (*Var är mitt flygplan?* Where is my airplane?) I could wish for.

After this evening's visit with my uncle and his family I returned as usual to Uppsala, but I'm not quite ready for sleep. Stepping over snowbanks and through the pools of white that spread beneath each streetlamp, I leave the station and head away from the hotel, towards Fyrisån, the Fyris River.

Uppsala, with around 230,000 inhabitants, may be a small city, but its prominence was assured long ago. Anders Celsius, who came up with the temperature scale in use by most everyone outside the United States, and by pilots everywhere – it's hard to believe that the scale was originally arranged in the opposite sense, so that water froze at 100 degrees, and boiled at zero – was a professor at the university here, which is the oldest in Scandinavia. Carl Linnaeus, who developed the system of Latin-based taxonomy for species, was a professor here, too. (He appeared, as the ennobled and knighted Carl von Linné, on the 100-krona, or -crown, banknote my uncle showed me on a visit to Pittsfield when I was little; the same denomination will later bear an image of Greta Garbo.) Uppsala also houses the headquarters of the Svenska Kyrkan, the Church of Sweden, and has been the country's religious capital for more than eight centuries, while Gustav I (1496–1560), father of the Vasa line and of Swedish independence, is interred in the city's cathedral.

I reach the path that runs beside the river and button up my coat. On an icy night like this it seems right for me to tip my hat not only to Professor Celsius, but also to another of Uppsala's former residents, Olaus Magnus. Born in 1490, he became a canon here, and was later named as the last Catholic archbishop of Uppsala – though he occupied his seat from afar, and in name only, as Sweden was by then a Lutheran kingdom, to which he would never return.

Olaus Magnus attended the Council of Trent, where another archbishop enquired about his homeland in the north. He later described these conversations as the genesis of his twenty-two-volume history and description of Scandinavia, *Historia de Gentibus Septentrionalibus, A Description of the Northern Peoples* (its Latin title is an opportunity to recall the pleasing etymology of *septentriones*, north, which recalls the seven oxen, i.e. the stars in the northern sky that form the Plough, and help direct our eyes to Polaris), a work that shaped European notions of the region for centuries to come.

From his Roman exile Olaus Magnus wrote of snowflakes: 'It seems more a matter for amazement than enquiry why and how so many shapes and forms, which elude the skill of any artist you choose to name, are so suddenly stamped upon such soft, tiny objects.' Many of the woodblock prints in his great work depict a world that's striking in its familiarity from my own childhood: icicles hang from the eaves of houses, a rare stretch of open water smokes in the bitter air, a group of boys throws snowballs at another group hiding behind a snow fort. Other images approach the mythical: a man on horseback departs an inn built only on ice; the Oriens, the east wind, brings fresh snow; a ski-clad hunter glides beneath the looming stone statues that line a pilgrim's route to Norway. And in one memorable depiction of Uppsala on a winter's night, a full moon shines in the dark sky above the frozen Fyris, while traders – of barrels, a flagon, a bow, a knife, an axe – engage in a busy commerce on the ice.

Lovers of winter and historians of science, meanwhile, may take a particular interest in another of the prints. Its upper left corner depicts two frosted windowpanes; the lower left corner reveals a sky filled with snow that flies like a storm of half notes blown free from their stave. The right half of the print is crowded with small drawings. Some have the shape of arrows, hands, or crowns, or resemble flowers or hats; others are like the spikes of the hair of the little prince in Saint-Exupéry's masterpiece, or astronomical bodies plucked from the sky around the boy's beloved planet. Nevertheless, on its own, only one of these drawings – a six-pointed star – might be identifiable to me, on this nearly half-millennium-old page that contains the first known sketches of the shapes of snow crystals.

NEW YORK

Highest speed of the wind at Kennedy Airport during the storm of 8 March 2005, in which the snow was seen to be 'strangely immune to gravity – blowing up and sideways as well as down': 48 miles per hour

It's early March, and late, in New York, for a winter storm as severe as this.

The cabin of this stationary Boeing 777 is dark, aside from a few scattered reading lights above some of the handful of other occupied seats. It's quiet, too, except for the background *sh-sh-sh* of the air-conditioning and the idling engines. Everyone is asleep, or as tired as me, surely, after the long flight, and now this delay to our disembarkation.

This morning I'd gotten home to London after a multiday work trip – to Edinburgh, then Basel, and finally a there-and-back to Brussels, in Dad's native Belgium – when I got the news that he had suffered a stroke. The doctors at the hospital in North Carolina, where Dad and my stepmother live, tell us he will not survive; they can only wait for our family to gather and then they must remove him from life support. A colleague at my airline rushed to get me a seat on this plane, the last to New York tonight. Now I can't get off it, because it can't park, because of the snow that's blocking our gate. I fear I'm about to miss my connecting flight to Raleigh; soon I'll learn it's already cancelled, like most every departure from Kennedy tonight, and from the warm cabin of the jet I'll look out at the snow and sense a new kind of numbness: as a result of this blizzard, Dad will live a few hours longer.

I'm seated by a window on the right side of the plane. Frost has formed in the gap between the panes while the storm blows to and fro beyond it. From this jet that shakes a little in the Queens wind I think of the warm and spring-like afternoon we left behind in London, which now seems from another life and world.

We wait and we wait. I think of the snowy woods in Narnia and an impassable road to Pittsfield. I think of a winter storm that reaches my imaginary city as I arrive in it, too.

From the cabin I look out at the apron, and something – perhaps the bright geometric solids that form as the snow passes under the conical gaze of the tall light posts – returns me to a night in the mid-1980s, when Dad and I parked at the ski area in Pittsfield, waiting as we often did to pick up my brother and some of his friends. It's maybe 9 p.m., and from the dark interior of the car the floodlit trails are almost too bright to look at. Dad has the engine running and the heater is whirring. When my brother and his buddies arrive, several doors will open and cold air and laughter and jokes will rush in. But, before they do, Dad is explaining what he has recently read about HIV in his science magazines – did I, aged eleven or twelve, outright ask what it was? – in a measured manner. He usually speaks this way, of course, but frozen in my seat I'm certain his careful tone is a means of avoiding a topic that I, as well, want to avoid, and when I finally come out to him, seven or eight years later, it's this night I'll think of first, these minutes we shared in front of this mountain of ice and light, when he tells me that he did not know.

SAPPORO

As the principle of classification, importance was laid on the structure of the crystal, not on its apparent form. For undertaking the general classification of snow crystals, the land of Hokkaido was very favourable, because the variety of crystals observed in this district was very great.

– Ukichirō Nakaya, *Snow Crystals: Natural and Artificial*

The warning posted in the jet bridge says THE ROAD IS SLIPPERY and so my first steps in Sapporo, Japan's fifth-largest city, in the south-west corner of Hokkaido, Japan's second-largest island, are careful ones.

Other signs capture the wintry nobility of this airport and of Japan's northernmost metropolis: the cyan hue of the seven-pointed star on the backlit logo of the Hokkaido Airports Company represents the island's snow and ice; directions are posted in Russian to an airport railway station that's closer to Vladivostok than Tokyo; and placards in the terminal museum reference THE DAWN OF A NEW AGE: BIRTH OF THE AEROPOLIS OF THE NORTH.

Aeropolis of the North is a fair description of the airfield of a city where it snows like nobody's business. In Sapporo snow typically falls on more than one of every three days, including most days from December to March, and nearly every day in January. This isn't the snowiest city on Earth (that is likely Aomori, on Japan's main island of Honshu, where the average annual snowfall is around eight metres). But on rankings of the planet's snowiest cities, Sapporo is usually the largest: with two million residents, it's four times the size of Quebec City, for example, where the average annual snowfall is in any case only around two-thirds of Sapporo's nearly five metres.

It's no surprise, then, that Sapporo has hosted the Winter Olympics (in 1972); that its most important annual event is a snow festival, which each winter welcomes millions of visitors and features more than one hundred snow and ice sculptures, some more than 15 metres tall; or that one of history's most important snow scientists, Ukichirō Nakaya, is so strongly associated with the city.

Nakaya was born on 4 July 1900, in Ishikawa, the same prefecture on the west coast of Japan in which I spent a summer homestay as a high school student. He studied physics in Tokyo and London before taking up an academic post in Sapporo in 1930, where he remained for the rest of his career. He described snowflakes as 'letters sent from the sky' – in the sense of correspondence, rather than the units of an alphabet – and attributed his great interest in them not only to the frequency with which they fell on Sapporo, but also to the beauty they brought to the city.

Snowflakes, as the exquisite variety of their structures suggests, are more than mere frozen droplets of water. Rather, a snow crystal is vapour that has become solid without passing through a liquid phase. Or, we might say, snow is vapour that has condensed directly into a crystalline form, a kind of frost that forms not on a blade of grass during a clear late-autumn night, but on a nucleus, a particle of dust swirling high in wintry clouds. Given the challenges of conducting research within icy cloudscapes, the best way to study the conditions that lead to snow is to replicate them in a laboratory, which Nakaya was the first to do. He grew his snow crystals not on frozen motes of sky dust, but on filaments of rabbit hair.

While snowflakes had been carefully observed by Johannes Kepler, Robert Hooke and René Descartes, it was Nakaya who developed the scientific system of snowflake classification, work that he chronicled in his seminal book, *Snow Crystals: Natural and Artificial*. Filled with hundreds of the loveliest photographs of snowflakes I've ever seen, it's a work not only of science but of art. Nakaya also investigated the problem of de-icing in aviation, and the possibility of artificially dispersing fog from airfields (later, his daughter Fujiko Nakaya would become famous for her success in a related endeavour, the creation of fog sculptures). He founded the Institute of Low Temperature Science at Hokkaido University, whose website chronicles such Narnian milestones as the opening of the Section of Snow Disaster Science (1963), the Frost Heaving Section (1964) and the Section of Snowfall Mechanism (1981).

Nakaya died in Tokyo in 1962. Kenneth Libbrecht, a physicist at the California Institute of Technology and the author of several books about snow crystals, described Nakaya's legacy to me in straightforward terms: Nakaya was the first 'to consider the detailed science underlying how ice grows from water vapor'. Today Nakaya's name graces both a museum of snow and ice near his hometown and a group of Antarctic islands, while a six-sided monument to his work stands in Sapporo: a site of pilgrimage, like the city itself, for anyone who loves snow.

From a window in the airport terminal I look out at the slowly windmilling fans of the engines of the parked jets. Winter's cogs are turning, too: much heavier snow has begun to fall, and I consider the disruption it might cause to the flights of departing passengers. On the apron and the runways of Sapporo, though, I see only the ordinary bustle of a large airport, and those who work here must surely be among the world's most skilful in winter flight operations.

I make my way through the airport to the train station, its crowds a reminder to me of what I all too easily forget: that Tokyo, which I fly to so often, may be the largest city on Earth, but it is not the only large city in Japan. I step onto the train and its doors close. Soon we're accelerating across white fields and through stands of snow-drooped firs and stately white birches, and along other tracks that are featureless aside from the dark parallels of their cleaned rails.

In Japanese class in university, I was pleased to learn – perhaps in a conversation exercise, or from a short story in a textbook – that 雪, *yuki,* snow, forms part of many given names. A friend of a friend is named Miyuki, for example. She was born in Shimane, a warm region in the south-west of Japan's main island, but nevertheless it snowed there on the day she was born, an event that her name commemorates. 'Miyuki' can be written in characters that mean 'deep snow' or 'beautiful snow', among other possibilities, but her mother made the unusual choice to write it in phonetic script, because that way it might suggest more than one kind of snow.

Miyuki now lives in Sapporo – her mother jokes that she didn't choose her name to ordain this – where I wrote to her to ask what it's like to live in one of the earth's snowiest cities.

'We love winter's beauty. People here are super sensitive to nature. We love snow scenery,' she replies. She describes a winter festival near her city in which candles are set in the snowscape ('a mystical forest where lights and reflections naturally melt into each other', reads the festival's website), while further from town, an ice village, including a music store, a bakery, a church and even an outdoor hot spring bath, is carved and assembled on a frozen lake. She talks about the bears that wander into Sapporo (as they sometimes do into downtown Pittsfield) and the annual arrival of 雪虫, *yukimushi*, snow bugs: 'We say, when you see yukimushi flying around in late autumn, you have the first snow very soon.' She tells me about 越冬キャベツ, *ettō kyabetsu*, wintering cabbage, that's harvested but stored in the fields, under the blanket of snow that allows its sweetness to build and its taste to improve.

The angle of the flakes streaming past the window slowly tilts from near-horizontal back to vertical as the train slows. As I turn to look directly out, I recall, as a child and late at night, pulling aside the blind in my bedroom to see if a promised storm had begun to transform the world into one in which no school could open. Then my brother and I could have pancakes and spend the day playing in the snowy yard, once we'd shovelled our pavement, and maybe made some cash by shovelling for neighbors, too.

At an intermediate stop, I notice railway staff in yellow hard hats and high-visibility vests pushing snow over the platform with lime-green shovels of a sort I've never seen in New England. Instead of a stick-like handle, these feature a crossbar attached to a capacious scoop that you push in the manner of a lawnmower, rather than lifting the snow to move it, which must be gentler – I note in middle age – on your lower back, and on your heart, too, I think, as I recall every Berkshire story that involved a heavy, wet snowfall, a dutiful older shoveller and a cardiac emergency. Later I'll learn that these shovels are called *Mama-san Danpu*, Mrs Mom Dumps, because armed with one of these, as one description puts it, 'Mama-san can carry snow like a dump truck.'

The train starts to move again as the snow ebbs to flurries. I listen carefully to all the train announcements, even if I needn't worry, as they're in English, too: 'The stop after Shin-Sapporo' – New Sapporo – 'is the Sapporo Terminal.'

✳

Needle crystals of snow have hitherto been regarded as one of the rarest types. This type seems to be very rare in Europe and America. . . . However, it is more frequently observed in Hokkaido. In Sapporo we could see this type an average of four or five times during one winter.

It's dusk by the time I've dropped off my luggage and got warmly dressed for my first long walk in Sapporo. I head south on a street that runs between the city's main station and the rectangle of Odori Park. In this new city and after a long journey, I cross the slushy streets carefully, untrusting of my intuitive sense of which way to look for oncoming cars.

The sky is overcast and it hasn't stopped snowing since I landed, but it's little more than flurries now and it's not particularly cold, just below freezing, maybe. It feels a little like Boston the night after a blizzard, when traffic is finally starting up again and some pavements are clear enough to make a stroll a reasonable prospect. I pull my hat further down, turn up my collar and try hard not to think of either Pittsfield or Boston as I remind myself: what's all around me now is a place that's new to me; it's not a familiar one, briefly transformed by the all-transforming snow.

Japanese onomatopoeia is so dizzyingly rich that I found it intimidating when I began to study the language. The challenge of the terms is ameliorated – at least in part – because they usually involve repetition, much like 'woof woof' does in English (except that in Japanese, dogs go ワンワン, *wan wan*). Perhaps nothing else illustrates the importance of snow in Japanese culture as well as the number of snow-related onomatopoeic expressions. Snow might be said to fall しんしん, *shin shin*, silently; or はらはら, *hara hara*, as if twirling in a gentle wind (although a Japanese friend reports she would use this more for a tumbling blossom); or, as tonight, ふわり

ふわり, *fuwari fuwari*, as if it were floating in an erratic but generally circular way – dancing, we might say – onto the city below.

I stop at a small café to get warm. I order a drink and lay the banknotes in the little plastic tray, as I often forget you're meant to do in Japan, rather than handing them directly to the cashier. Then I find an empty table, where I remove my hat and unbutton my heavy coat and think of Pittsfield, and of the years when the price of oil rose so high that our woodstove became our primary source of heat. I became obsessed with stacking wood, outside and also in our basement, where we placed the logs to season further, under pipes covered in dusty, cracked asbestos that my brother and I would sometimes punch, again and again and as hard as we could, as we shouted: Let's make it snow in July!

When I was first allowed to make a fire in the woodstove on my own I was happier than I'd be years later when I got my driver's licence. (Perhaps this permission came too soon, however: one time I made the fire so hot that the handle on the door of the woodstove began to char; another time, when the wood wouldn't catch, I went to the garage with a mug, filled it with petrol from the can next to the lawnmower and poured it over the kindling.)

But even more than sitting by the fire I'd got going, one way or another, I loved to go out to the woodpile in the backyard and then return, staggering under an armful of logs, to a house glowing between the clear stars and a landscape that in winter would never grow truly dark. Later I understood that what I love even more than the cold is the experience of becoming warm – which requires winter, of course, and which, for me, is inseparable from the act of coming home, whether from a brief excursion in the bitter yard or from a difficult day at school. Such early and essentially physical memories perhaps explain why, as a traveller, I find encounters with foreign incarnations of cosiness – with a warmth that suggests a home that nevertheless cannot be mine – simultaneously welcoming and bewildering.

I look around the café and remind myself again of where I am. I finish my mug of coffee and head out again. I reach the park and turn east towards the Sapporo TV Tower. So many cities – Toronto and Tokyo most famously, perhaps – have placed observation decks on their communication towers; a view-bestowing virtue made of what was a sudden technological necessity. After I enter Odori Park I pass the darkened, partly melted remains of the city's recent Snow Festival, one that this year – in a haunting warning about the severity of the climate crisis, and a reminder of both the global and the highly localised challenges it poses to all who work in travel and tourism – required tens of thousands of tonnes of snow to be trucked in from the countryside.

I look up, to where the tower's metal bars disappear in the snow that falls now, as it does in a famous children's song, こんこ or こん こん, *konko* or *konkon*, without stopping. I'm not sure I'll see much from the observation deck. Still, I'm here, so I buy my ticket. The tower, a sign tells me, has been 'chosen as a Night View Inheritance of Japan', a project established 'by cooperating members of the Night View Inspectors Group', and I briefly envision a life in which I, as a retired pilot, become a junior member of a committee with such a name, and am charged with keeping the minutes of our long meetings about the proper criteria for the judging of night views: height of tower, brightness of city, clarity of air.

I step into a glass-walled lift in which the only other person is an attendant who bows to me and presses the button for English automated announcements – 'We hope you enjoy the magnificent views' – and we start to rise, past flights of yellow emergency stairs and the Erector Set framework of this red tower that barely slows the gusting snow.

When I get out I could be in a control tower – the dim lighting, the soft voices, the objects that glow in the mist beyond thick, muffling windows – except that Heathrow doesn't have Terebi-Tōsan, Television Dad, or Old Man Television (*terebi* is an English loan word, from 'television'), a red, tower-shaped mascot who wears a green sash. On this midweek winter night in the quiet aftermath of the snow festival there are more incarnations of Old Man Television than fellow humans with me on the observation deck, and it all starts to get a little weird, especially after I see a sign that warns me to beware of Terebi-Tōsan imposters.

I turn to the windows, to where a combination of night, cloud and intensifying snow is settling onto a neatly gridded city. The flat roofs of the buildings are as smoothly white as fields, as if the city might disappear entirely if you were to look directly down on it. A Ferris wheel in the distance breaks the spell and I think of one of the cycles that animate the earth's hydrosphere: the molecules of water that evaporate into the air, rise, and then, perhaps two miles up, form crystals that spend an hour or so tumbling back to our planet's surface, where they might sit out the winter in a snowbank at the edge of a park in the city of Sapporo, waiting for spring and the rush to the sea.

❄

Table 4. General classification of snow crystals.

. . .

III P   Plane crystal
  1. Regular crystal developed in one plane
  2. Crystal with irregular number of branches
  3. Crystal with twelve branches
  4. Malformed crystal
  5. Spacial assemblage of plane branches

It's a cold, bright morning and I'm heading out for a walk.

It's not only Mom who found Pittsfield's winters harder and harder; my stepmother broke her arm in a bad fall on a patch of ice, not long before she and my father moved south. As I step along carefully I think of Miyuki, and of how in our correspondence she is frank about the dangers that Sapporo's winters pose: 'I choose good shoes every winter, and buy a new pair before the soles are damaged.' Winter gets 'harder when you get older', Miyuki affirms, and each Sapporo spring is more welcome to her than the last: 'When we find spring signs, like butterbur, we tell family and friends and share a small happiness.'

The streets of Sapporo, unlike those of Pittsfield, feature bins of public grit, so if you find the going つるつる, *tsuru tsuru*, slippery, you can put sand down yourself. THIS SAND IS FOR THE ICE. PLEASE USE IT FREELY, says the sign on the bin. There are roadside versions, too, at which thoughtful motorists can pull up to grit an icy spot. Occasionally I come to a portion of pavement or a driveway fitted with internal heating, recognisable not only by the absence of snow but by its perfectly dry surface. I'm struck, too, by the sight of trucks carrying neatly piled loads of snow out of town, past trees fitted with Japan's traditional, cone-like contrivances known as 雪吊り, *yukitsuri*, snow suspenders – a central wooden pole, with lines running down and out from it – which allow Sapporo's trees to bear the burdens of each winter storm.

Not even Sapporo, though, has found a way to eliminate the calf-deep pools of slushy water that form where its pavements meet a street near a snow-blocked drain, and often I must take a running leap, climb over the adjacent snowbank, or walk on until I find a higher or drier place to cross. Nevertheless, my shoes are wet by the time I leave the business-oriented heart of the city and move into an area where small shops jostle with tidy residences. Here, where snow seems to be piled rather than trucked out, and mountains of it, some the size of wedding marquees, line car parks, I remember the taller-than-me snowbanks in our Pittsfield yard, and some of the happiest sights and sounds of my childhood: the plough's strange pre-dawn yellow lights that appeared on our driveway before dawn, and then danced and reversed on my bedroom's ceiling as the huge blade rasped and whispered, *No school for you today.*

The name of the island on which Sapporo stands, Hokkaido, was bestowed on it in the nineteenth century. It means the 'northern sea way' (a remarkably similar etymology to that commonly given for the name of Norway, whose landscape Hokkaido's much resembles), and it echoes the name of the Tōkaidō, the Eastern Sea Way, the ancient road between Kyoto and Tokyo that gave its name to what's now one of the world's busiest high-speed rail lines. Sapporo itself, meanwhile, a name most familiar to Westerners thanks to the eponymous beer, means something like 'long, dry river' in the language of the Ainu, the Indigenous population of the island.

That river, along which Ainu settlements preceded the city's foundation, is now known as the Toyohira. I'd like to see if its surface might be frozen, and so I check my map and set off towards the river's northwest bank.

In the middle and late nineteenth century, Hokkaido was seen by many in Japan as a frontier land, rich in resources but otherwise a blank canvas, much as the American West was perceived by generations of Americans of European descent. Indeed, the Japanese government was well aware of the scale of the ongoing settlement of the American West and the concomitant displacement of Indigenous communities, and went to some trouble to bring dozens of Americans to assist in Hokkaido, including the Massachusetts-born Horace Capron, whom Washington had previously tasked with the negotiation of treaties with Native Americans in the American Southwest. Capron proposed an American-style homestead act for Hokkaido and is responsible for Sapporo's American-style street grid; today his statue stands in Odori Park.

Later I'll ask another friend in Japan, Yukako, about the Ainu. She'll kindly go to the library and check out a few books, as she – like many Japanese people, she'll tell me – is not especially familiar with Ainu culture. She'll report that their myths are similar, perhaps, to Greek ones, as their pantheon is full of gods who 'love, hate, and fight with each other or with humans'.

In one story, the gods are in the middle of a snowball fight, when one snowball falls to the earth. The World-Making God offers the realm of man to whichever god can hit the fallen snowball with an arrow. Many try, but only one – known as Aynurakkur, the father of the Ainu – succeeds. Another tale features a magical folding fan, which is distinguished by depictions of snow on one side and the sun on the other. One day, a cruel wind goddess sees a peaceful village and decides to destroy it. She begins to dance and the wind rises and blows the houses, crops and trees away. Then a semi-divine Ainu hero fans the goddess. As he does so, a blizzard tears her clothes and cuts her skin. Then, when the fan is turned, it burns her, and the destructive winds never return to the village.

One of the most famous works of Ainu literature is the epic poem 'Tobu Sori', 'The Flying Sled', by the Hokkaido-born poet Hideo Oguma. Dedicated to the Ainu people and set on Sakhalin – the now-Russian island that was part of the Ainu's traditional homeland – it opens the day after the winter's first snow: 'Back and forth across the sky / Birds flew in confusion.' The snow is met with gratitude by the Ainu, for whom winter is 'the new master who has banished the loneliness of fall'. The poem chronicles, as well, how 'the bears who symbolised the Ainu way of life, / Were disappearing. / That was their greatest sadness'; the growing presence of the bureaucratic state; and the moonless night on which an avalanche is born on the slope above a settlement in a northern corner of Ainu country.

As I learn that assimilation policies known as Japanisation resulted in cultural losses among the Ainu that are painfully reminiscent of those suffered by many Native American communities, I realise that I've no sense at all of winter's significance in the culture of the Mohicans, who inhabited the lands on which my hometown would be built. Later, I'll be astonished to discover the similarities – most conspicuously the importance of snow, stars and varying degrees of arctolatry, or bear worship – between Mohican and Ainu cultures, despite the many thousands of miles that separate them.

As the early brightness gives way to overcast skies, I continue towards the river, paralleling snowbanks that are chest high, though some are higher and those on the street corners higher still. The further I get from the centre of the city, the narrower the section of the pavements that has been cleared, so I must often step aside, into much deeper snow, to let people pass, as I've seen others do for me, and I bow, multiple times on each block, and remember how in the English countryside people raise a hand in acknowledgement when they give way to another motorist on narrow country lanes, though they may have had no choice about doing so, and how American drivers, passing each other on dusty, rural roads, far more than wide enough for two cars, may lift one index finger from the wheel in greeting all the same.

It starts to snow as I reach the Toyohira River. Signs indicate there's a path along it, but it's not been cleared, and everything from the edge of the busy road to the open and fast-running black water is locked in white. I should have rented skis, I think, as I turn away. Heading north, I come to what I think is a park, but it's hard to be sure until I see that the snow is level with what I can barely make out are the tops of picnic tables. I walk on, past vehicles and Narnian lampposts half-buried by snowbanks, and a telephone box with only its door clear, as if its threshold has a heat or a magic all its own.

※

Observation of Snow Crystals

. . . As the source of illumination, the light of the sky was used in the daytime, and at night an electric lamp was used. When the temperature

is below -10°C, no arrangement for absorbing heat rays from the lamp is necessary; thus the lamp light may be used without any adaptation. Photographing by transmitted light is advantageous in getting a clear picture of the boundary and internal structure of the crystal, or, in other words, the crystal pattern.

Seven miles into the snowiest urban walk I've ever taken, I turn left down the white path that leads into Moerenuma Park.

The park is the last creation of the twentieth-century Japanese American sculptor and artist Isamu Noguchi. Best known for his iconically modernist glass tables and for his take on Japanese paper lanterns ('arguably the most ubiquitous sculpture on the planet', said a curator at the Noguchi Museum in Queens), Noguchi's large sculptures and landscapes decorate many American cities, notably Detroit, where there's a fountain that I'd love to visit, not least because Noguchi, a fan of aviation, described it – as related in *Listening to Stone*, a biography by Hayden Herrera – as suggestive of aircraft and jet engines, with a structure that echoed 'the aeroplane wing in its relation to the fuselage'.

In 1933 Noguchi, who had spent part of his youth in Japan, in a house that looked to Mount Fuji, proposed a New York City project called Play Mountain, an unfenced playground for children who could climb up the hill that was its central feature and then slide or sledge back down. He described his proposal in terms of long-ago sorrows and the American metropolis in which, in adulthood, he dreamed of feeling at home: 'Play Mountain was my response based upon memory of my own unhappy childhood. . . . It may be that this is how I tried to join the city, New York. To belong.' He presented his proposal to Robert Moses, whose car-centric vision reshaped New York and influenced urban planners across America in the twentieth century. 'Moses just laughed his head off and more or less threw us out,' Noguchi recollected.

As a result, his Play Mountain would instead be built here in Sapporo, as one element of the park created to transform a patch of land – previously home to a waste facility and a mountain of rubbish – oxbowed by the Toyohira River. Noguchi, who fell in love with the site, made his final visit in October 1988, not long before his death in late December; he never saw the finished park.

The path I turn down now takes me to a bridge across the river and into the heart of its roughly 470 acres (equivalent to a little more than half the size of New York's Central Park). Noguchi's glass pyramid is my first stop, not least because it's near the park's entrance and it suggests the possibility of greenhoused warmth. When I enter, the Louvre-like pyramid – Noguchi was friends with I. M. Pei – is indeed warm, deserted and utterly silent. It feels like the office of a wealthy and publicity-shy foundation, or perhaps a new Scandinavian airport that has not yet opened to the public, though I've never seen an airport as handsome as this.

A few clean-lined wood benches frame the stone base of the glass walls. The sight of perhaps a yard's worth of snow pressing against the panes – and my memory of those widely shared photos, typically from snowbelt cities like Buffalo, in which someone has opened their front door the morning after a storm to find the wide world replaced by a featureless wall of snow – leads me to speculate on the forces that the sides of this glass pyramid were built to withstand, and the depth of snow that even I might agree is too much.

It's so cosy inside the pyramid that I grow curious about how hot it must get in summer. A few minutes later I read that it's equipped with an ingenious and climate-friendly solution: each winter around 1,700 tonnes of snow are bulldozed into a containment area, then, throughout the spring and summer, air is piped over and through them in order to cool the pyramid.

I wander up a staircase and into a tranquil exhibition of Noguchi's signature paper lanterns. Their glow, suspended before the wall of glass that gives onto a colourless land, is as yellow as a low moon. There's a restaurant in the pyramid, named ランファン・キ・レーヴ, *ranfan ki rêvu*, as a Japanese person might transliterate the French *l'enfant qui rêve*, the dreaming child.

'The child's world would be a beginning world, fresh and clear,' Noguchi once wrote.

I leave the pyramid, pull my hat and gloves from the pocket of my winter coat, and follow a snowy path towards the foot of Play Mountain. On this grey day it's indistinguishable from the clouds, except where its symmetrical slopes cross the sky as faintly as two pencil-drawn lines. I turn away and walk towards Mount Moere, another artificial peak. At around 62 metres, it's twice as high as Play Mountain, and I can't believe it's only thanks to middle age that its slopes look completely terrifying – a feeling that's intensified, rather than assuaged, by the presence of orange retaining nets at the base of the hill. While small distant figures in bright snow-wear accelerate down their miniature Fuji, I trudge through the snow to read a board on which the rules are posted.

PLEASE DO NOT CREATE JUMPS OR SNOWMEN ON THE COURSE THAT IS MEANT FOR SLEDS.

ENJOY THE SNOW IN KEEPING WITH YOUR PHYSICAL STRENGTH.

And if you choose to bring a snowman to life elsewhere in the park,

PLEASE REMAIN CLOSE TO YOUR CREATION, AND MAKE SURE TO CLEAR IT AWAY BY THE END OF THE DAY.

As I leave the park and button up for the long walk back to town, I'm tempted by a café whose signs advertise hot drinks for 300 yen, along with TOILET OK! and FREE SLED! Snow shovels stand neatly near a table that has been carefully cleared of snow, and outside, as well, there's a metre-high ice-cream cone, its swirls of plastic vanilla barely distinct from its snowbound surroundings.

I step inside. The café is tiny, but I'm the only one here. A record player is spinning – 'Danger Zone', by Kenny Loggins – and the shelves are packed with LPs: Earth, Wind & Fire, ABBA, The Carpenters, and some classical music, too. Every surface, aside from the counter at which I take a seat, is occupied by some small object – a ceramic squash; a knitted house with a red roof, lace trim and a Christmas tree (not for the first time, I recall the almost certainly apocryphal tale of the Tokyo department store's Christmas display in which Santa was nailed to a cross); several small painted clowns; boxes of high-end Scotch; an Arabia-evoking teapot – and I have the sensation, familiar to many tall foreigners in Japan, that any unconsidered movement will result in the sound of something breaking.

I lose myself in staring at a poster on the far wall, for the film *Roman Holiday*, until the sound of shuffling recalls me to Sapporo. From the far end of the café where it opens into a home, an older woman emerges to greet me. She asks what I would like. I don't see a sign for hot chocolate. In Japanese it is ホットチョコレート, *hottochokorēto*, but having struggled to make myself understood when I asked for one earlier in the day, I don't want to try again. I opt, instead, for what I know I can easily order: コーヒー, *kō-hee*, coffee. She smiles and my tongue unties and we talk a little in my clumsy Japanese. Her husband comes in. His English is better than hers, and far better than my Japanese.

He asks where I'm from. I say that I came to Sapporo from Tokyo, and also that I'm from near New York, which Pittsfield is, when you're 6,000 miles away. I realise he thinks I mean I live in Tokyo, that I'm an expat there and that I'm here for a short break, and I don't correct him, because it might be challenging to do so in either language, or because part of me is enjoying imagining a life in which Mark and I have lived in Tokyo for decades: we've made our life there, let's say, in a corner of the city we've come to know and love better than any other, and although we can't quite envision growing old there, we also can't imagine that we'll ever wish to leave.

I ask if they like Tokyo. They both laugh, as if they would rather not say, or as if the world's largest city casts such a long shadow on the rest of Japan that they don't believe their answer could matter. Tokyo, the woman clarifies after a moment, it's crowded in comparison. We prefer it here. She gestures at a horizontal volume of air that must stand for Hokkaido, and for the spaciousness that contrasts with the essence of their capital on the island down south.

I laugh a little, too, mostly out of relief at understanding. As I warm my hands around my mug, I notice the woman is looking at my wedding band, as if she's about to pose a question, and I prepare myself to answer. There's only silence, however, which I break by asking her if it will snow in Sapporo tonight. 降りますよ, *furimasu-yo*, she says, suddenly more serious; the *yo* suffix an emphatic affirmation: it certainly will fall.

The man talks about Sapporo and New York. He says their climates are similar; he makes gestures that I think equate to lines of latitude. Can I remember how to say 'hometown' in Japanese? I could look it up, and then show them Pittsfield.

I'd love to share much more with them: maybe that when I first studied Japanese, the Japanese-born teachers I encountered in New England often compared the landscape and weather of Massachusetts to that of Hokkaido. Or I could find Pittsfield on a map on my phone and maybe mention Melville – *Moby-Dick* being well known in Japan – and the Japanese-timbered masts of the *Pequod*. With the classical recordings on their shelves in mind, I could tell them about Tanglewood, the music festival in the town next to Pittsfield, where I worked in the music shop and beer stands for a number of high school and university summers. Tanglewood, too, is well known in Japan, thanks in part to Seiji Ozawa, the music director of the Boston Symphony Orchestra for many years; I could maybe share how a high school friend and I once snuck into an after-hours Tanglewood party and ended up in a conga line a few places behind the man we'd been instructed to address always as 'Maestro'. On this snowy day I could even use my phone to show them the Norman Rockwell print that Kathleen, one of my Berkshire aunts, kept above her Pittsfield mantelpiece, the one that depicts winter in the nearby town of Stockbridge, and that looked all the better in the light of her Christmas tree.

But I can't say any of this in Japanese, and my phone is almost out of power, so I pour another plastic pot of milk into my coffee and swirl away as I look up at their faces and nod along to words that I can't always follow. The man is talking, I think, about the sort of heating elements that I found built into pavements and driveways; they're 便利, *benri*, convenient, he says, but expensive, and there's the cost of the electricity to operate them, too.

Our conversation dwindles. I've certainly already used every word I know in Japanese several times, and as I'm still the only customer I worry I'm keeping them from whatever they were doing. I finish my cup of coffee and decline their offer of another. They can't believe I walked here from the centre of the city, let alone that I plan to walk back. The woman looks particularly concerned by the prospect and she points across the street to indicate that I must take the bus from the stop there; but that first I must wait here in the warmth, while she fetches some paper and writes down the times.

I take the slip of paper from her and thank them both as best I can. I stand, check for my gloves, hat, scarf and backpack, and then walk out into the cold and cross the road. The half-empty bus arrives on time. I climb aboard and fold myself into a seat, and as the bus rolls south towards central Sapporo and snow starts to fall, I close my eyes in order to doze, or to imagine a city where:

the temperature rarely climbs above -4 degrees in the winter, and the nights are much colder, which means that even accounting for the 'heat island' effects of the city, its parks are filled with dry, powdery snow for months on end

small, humped bridges are laid over cuts in the kerbs where slush tends to pool in early spring, allowing pedestrians, cyclists, wheelchair users and those with strollers to cross with ease, safety and dryness   there is a hotline you call to request one, or you use an app to submit a geo-tagged photo of a deep icy puddle and an hour or so later a truck will come by to fit the temporary bridgelet

Tokyo's Narita Airport was once known as New Tokyo International Airport   in English it was easy to parse this not as the new international airport of Tokyo, but as the international airport of New Tokyo, suggestive of a vision of a future metropolis

New London   New York   New Rome

the new Aeropolis

The weather channel says the storm will start around midnight. It will begin as rain downtown and on the islands

but after dusk it will change to snow, everywhere in the metropolitan region

two brothers are on two different planes that must taxi slowly

in designated winter-weather emergencies only two runways are ever used at a time, while two others are being cleared, before they swap around and the process repeats

their parents wait in the arrivals hall, under skylights that first whiten under the storm, and then darken

up to thirty centimetres will fall downtown and on the inner islands.
Forty-five centimetres are expected at the airport

more than half a metre in the foothill suburbs

all schools are closed.

CHAPTER 11

CITY OF CIRCLES

*London, Raleigh, Erbil,
Tokyo and Pittsfield*

KATHLEEN – THE BERKSHIRE AUNT to whom I complained about the worst Thanksgiving I ever had, when I was three – stands, walks to the lectern of this church near downtown Pittsfield and unfolds her pages.

She, Mark, I and the rest of the Berkshire family are here for the memorial service for Sheila, another of my aunts, who passed away two months ago. Sheila's obituary in the *Berkshire Eagle* describes her precisely as I remember her – a 'quick-witted, wry woman with a fiery spirit' – and I wonder if it's too much to hope that her young granddaughter, seated in front of Mark and me, is old enough to retain her own memories of her.

Sheila was born in eastern Massachusetts in 1940. She became a nun and worked in education in some of Boston's most deprived neighbourhoods. After thirteen years she left her order and married a former priest, Gene. They met my parents in Boston and eventually moved to Pittsfield, around the time my parents also left Boston, for Vermont. It was Sheila and Gene who told Dad about a job opening in Pittsfield; they are the reason I was born here. In the Berkshires, Sheila worked in public housing and education, and as a poet and playwright (when I was little I occasionally showed her some short pieces I wrote, which she marked up with many encouragements and corrections). For some years Sheila and her family lived not in Pittsfield but in nearby Williamstown, on a partly wooded farmstead that, among the Berkshire gang's homes, was the most suited to expansive Easter egg hunts.

As Kathleen speaks I remember the day, twelve years ago, when Sheila's daughter gave a eulogy at Mom's memorial service, which was held in this same church. Among our Berkshire family now there aren't many left of my parents' generation, while the kids' table at our holiday gatherings is once again filled with young children.

Kathleen speaks softly as she concludes her eulogy with these words: Sheila was a good friend.

She folds her pages carefully and returns to her seat. We end the service with several hymns and then we all make our way to the church hall, where jugs of coffee, pots of milk, bottles of soda, and plates of cake and homemade cookies are laid out on the large central table. I hug Sheila's daughters and tell them how much I miss their mom. We talk about Mark's first trip to the Berkshires with me, for his first Thanksgiving, the year the Berkshire gang gathered in Sheila's little house on a hill above the eastern shore of Pontoosuc Lake. We didn't always play board games at these gatherings, but that year we played Pictionary, and Mark and Sheila were a team. At one point after the Thanksgiving dinner, I recall, Sheila stood and gestured to the grey surface of the windswept lake beyond the window and described the colourful tents of the fishermen, which she said would appear in numbers as soon as the ice thickened.

In addition to twenty-five or so members of the three generations of the Berkshire gang, a few dozen of Sheila's other friends and relatives have come to say good-bye. I don't recognise most of them, but many remember me from when I was a kid. Several have heard I'm a pilot, and ask me how I like my work, and where I've flown recently. A few ask how my parents are, but most know that they have been gone for years, and they share with me how and when they knew them.

Half an hour or so into the reception a man approaches Mark and me. He says that he's not sure if I'll remember him. I don't, not even when he gives me his name. I introduce him to Mark. He shakes Mark's hand vigorously and smiles and then, I'm startled to see, he begins to cry.

He explains: he was involved in the youth group that I sometimes attended, the one that met upstairs in this same church three decades ago. It was he who read out and then answered the question I'd written on a card – the one I fearfully realised he knew was mine – about whether it was possible to not be gay.

I've never stopped thinking about that day, he tells us, shaking his head as he wipes the tears from his cheeks. It's good to see you again, he says. It's good to see you.

LONDON

I'm twenty-two and it's the first morning of my life in England. As the bus leaves Heathrow I see signs for the M25, the 'London Orbital'. I have no idea what an orbital is. I've never heard the word used as a noun, rather than as an adjective.

The bus pulls onto the motorway, heading roughly north at first, and I get it: we're moving clockwise around the unseen capital.

I know we're not far at all from the original – Royal – Berkshire, which is at once both comforting and alienating. I don't yet know how differently its name is pronounced here, or that I'll soon form a lasting friendship with someone from Slough, one of its large towns; I only know that I want to go sometime soon, and that it'll be fun to report on it to the gang back home.

The engine of the bus revs, the driver changes lanes. Gantries bearing signs for the roads that lead to other cities – Birmingham, Oxford – fly past. Ahead, a sign for THE NORTH tells me that I'm on an island small enough for such terms, and it reminds me, too, of where I've touched down on it.

For now the bus and the road turn away from Berkshire and the North, as best I can tell. We remain, all the blue signs indicate, in orbit.

I look around at the other passengers, all of them strangers, most of them dozing. The realm that the M25 encloses – Greater London and then some – is a mystery to me, aside from what little I saw of it from the window of the plane this morning. I don't know that 'inside the M25' is a shorthand for metropolitan sensibilities and influences, much as 'inside the Beltway' encapsulates the perspective from Washington. It'll be some time yet before I first cross London's North or South Circulars, which form another, more inner ring road, the one that years later, as a new short-haul pilot who lacks the seniority to avoid the earliest report times at Heathrow, I'll spend many pre-dawn hours driving around.

So recently arrived, I also don't know how close we are to some of the still-standing coal tax posts that once formed a complete ring around London, asserting the capital's power – to tax, at least, and to build yet more bridges in the metropolis that had risen at the lowest elevation where the Thames might still be spanned. I'm here only for graduate school, now, so I don't know that in a few years it will be on a bus from the same airport, following this same arc of road, that I decide it's at last time to become a pilot.

Nor do I know that – accustomed as I am to American cities – few intercity rail lines and not one expressway cross through the heart of London; instead, like imperfect radii or broken spokes, they end in the crowded halls of stations whose locations themselves trace an inner ring, or in the ordinary roads that the motorways fracture into when they get too close to town. And I've certainly no idea that along a route called the A1 – partly Roman in origin, the country's longest road crosses the London Orbital at a clean angle and makes its way south-east towards the city's most ancient districts – stands a town hall in which, a decade and a half from now, my husband and I will exchange rings.

I gaze again at the cars below my window – more and more of them with each minute; of course, I realise, it's morning, and this is rush hour – then I look ahead again, past the driver's head, through the front window and out along the lanes, to where I try to see their markings curve.

RALEIGH

Dark pines sweep under the wing's leading edge and emerge, only slightly larger and better defined, behind it. Further descent, and scattered lights: an office park, a busy road, the perimeter fence and racing concrete.

Dad and my stepmother no longer live in the old house in Pittsfield, the one I grew up in. After my stepmother's fall on the ice in Pittsfield, she and Dad decided to find a warmer place. Raleigh, North Carolina – for its weather and its friendliness, the high standards of medical care and the cultural life invigorated by the many universities in the region – was their choice. They moved to a town right outside Raleigh not long after I first moved to England.

Before they left Pittsfield, I returned to my old house for one last visit. I transferred some of my childhood belongings to the attic of Mom's small home, a few blocks away, and then I threw the rest – model airplanes, school notebooks and textbooks, sketched maps and cities, the globe that no longer lit – away.

On the afternoon of my last day in the house I stood alone in my bedroom for a few minutes. Then I took my luggage down to the kitchen and gave Dad and my stepmom my key. Behind the house, under the window that I used to smoke from, grew the fir tree I planted when I was five or six years old. I offered it a good-bye and a silent apology – for all the hot ashes I'd caused to drift onto it over the years, and for leaving it now – as I gave its needles a brush with my hand.

Dad and my stepmom took me to Pittsfield's nearly deserted bus station. I took the bus down the turnpike to Boston and returned to England, to morning at Heathrow, to a bus along another road I was getting to know well, and finally to a student house that was, I realised with gratitude when I walked through its front door, full of new friends.

Now, some months later, I've landed on my first visit to Raleigh.

The plane parks and the seat-belt signs are turned off. I look out at a tarmac like any other, stand and put on my backpack.

Dad – looking older, I'm startled to see – and my stepmother are waiting for me at the gate. I try to take in everything about this new airport as we walk to the parking deck. I'm surprised, and maybe even a little hurt, by their familiarity with the parking-ticket procedures, and by how easily they make what sound like in-jokes about the heat.

Dad knows that I've been nervous about coming here. He knows the divorce wasn't easy for me and that the sale of the old house was some kind of punctuation mark on that and on much else.

He knows, too, something of my love for cities, even if I never told him about my imaginary one. And he's certainly familiar with my love for maps and motion across them. He hands me the keys. I get into the driver's seat of his minivan, the one – blue-green, with a miniature Belgian flag sticker – we all call the Minivanhoenacker, humouring, we hope, any ancestors gazing down from the heaving tables of their Flanders afterlife. Dad sits next to me up front. My stepmother sits behind us, in the Minivanhoenacker's middle row. I pull out of the airport car park, following Dad's instructions and the first signs for Raleigh.

As we drive Dad and I talk transportation. I listen carefully as he lists the many destinations you can reach from Raleigh's airport – even London, non-stop – and as he describes how closely the railway line that carries Amtrak's New York–to–Miami service passes to their new home. He tells me the unfamiliar numbers – 147, 40, 64 – of the roads that are among the most important to them here, and points out how, on another day, we might follow one of them to Durham, where we can visit a botanical garden and a chapel that he and my stepmother expect I'll love, and then go for lunch in a restaurant they describe as one of their favourites.

As Dad guides me on towards their new house, I imagine a city where no one slips on the ice; the pavements are immaculately cleared and salted and sanded before anyone could.

I imagine a city in which it's easy for anyone to start over.

I imagine a city with roads that never jam.

We come to the first signs for Raleigh's Inner Beltline and Outer Beltline. Dad, anticipating how much I'll enjoy these signs, doesn't wait for me to ask. From the middle of the middle row my stepmother smiles as Dad explains that these terms refer not to separate roads, but to the inner and outer sets of lanes on the same ring road.

So the Inner Beltline runs clockwise around the city, Dad says, while the Outer Beltline runs anticlockwise. The confusion that results from this is a common joke among residents, Dad adds, and it's downright bewildering to tourists and newcomers, especially to foreigners who come from places that drive on the left, for whom the meaning of the signs would be reversed.

Several years from now, after Dad's gone, I'll learn that this convention has been discarded and that the signs for Raleigh's inner and outer beltlines have all come down. For now, though, Dad and I agree that while the terminology may at first be perplexing, its precision must appeal to the purist, so neatly does it work around the uncertainty of directional signs – north, south, east, west – on roads that never stop turning.

ERBIL

Our 747's path roughly parallels that of the Tigris, which alternates between black and blinding as the sun catches on first one and then another of the sweeping curves it makes through the desert and the tawny sprawl of Baghdad.

The first incarnation of Baghdad, constructed in the 760s, was the Round City. Its circular plan – which in 762 was drawn on the land first in ash and then in fire, in the form of burning oil and cotton seeds, to allow the Abbasid caliph al-Mansur to better imagine the form of his new capital – featured four gates, from which four grand avenues led towards the centre of the city, where a mosque and a palace were surrounded by buildings such as the Arsenal, the Treasury and the Bureau of Correspondence.

Only half a century after its construction, Baghdad was one of the largest cities on Earth, and set, as it was, astride busy trade routes and the banks of the Tigris, it grew to be perhaps the world's busiest port: not only 'a waterfront for the world', as al-Mansur had hoped, but – in the words of the ninth-century geographer al-Yaqubi – the 'crossroads of the universe'.

Nothing remains of the Round City. Nonetheless, when I fly over Baghdad I sometimes think of anthropologists in South America, circling their light propeller-driven aircraft low over the forests in which they're finally able to discern the outlines of lost settlements, and I'm tempted to imagine that the Round City left a similar sort of pattern within the sprawl of modern Baghdad, one that only in the early days of aviation would have again become apparent.

I first saw Baghdad more than ten years ago, on my first regular trip on the 747 after the completion of my training on that aircraft. On our late-night journey from Bahrain to London, and not long after we reached cruising altitude, I noted on our charts that we were nearing an airfield identified by the code ORBI. Given Baghdad's rounded past, it was tempting to relate this coding to the Latin root that means 'circle' or 'disk', but it's only a coincidence, of course: 'O' is used to denote much of the Middle East and parts of South Asia, 'R' stands for Iraq (while an 'I' in this position would indicate Iran), and 'BI' is presumably for Baghdad International.

Now, years later, on this clear and bright winter morning, not long after we fly over Baghdad, I look down and see another city, one that's new to me even after so many years of long-haul flying. It lies on what looks like a flattish plain, to the south of a choppier sea of low, brown hills. Beyond these, further north, several parallel ridges rise into snowcapped peaks.

This city – I calculate on our charts, as it's unmarked by any airport-indicating circle on our navigation screens – must be Erbil. Its elevation, I'll later note, is similar to that of Pittsfield, while the raised feature at its centre is something that Pittsfield never had: a citadel.

The tell, or settlement mound, that supports Erbil's nearly round stronghold is encircled by at least four additional dark concentric rings – roads, surely, though from our high altitude they are as distinct as walls – that enclose a cityscape whose densely set structures, from this high up, appear to form a surface of braille. It's the rings, however, not the citadel or buildings within them, that are most compelling, reminding me, as they do, of elaborately stacked place settings, and of Lois, the friend of my parents who was living with us during the summer in which my parents told me and my brother about their planned divorce, and who, when she was far away from Pittsfield, was my most faithful correspondent, occasionally replying to my letters in an oval fashion, starting her writing at the top-left corner of the page she'd laid lengthwise and turned again and again until she ran out of room or words in the middle.

LONDON

I adjust my surgical-blue face mask and pilot the wheels of my bag towards the opening doors of a nearly empty train bound for Paddington. I'm off to Heathrow, to board an airliner that will carry many tonnes of cargo to Miami, and less than a dozen passengers, though every seat in several entirely empty sections of the cabin will be carefully arranged with still-wrapped blankets and headsets.

For several months after the pandemic began, I flew nowhere.

In this period several friends became ill with COVID-19, and an elderly relative died from it. Some of my colleagues retired early. A number of others, including many of those who had come to aviation most recently, were furloughed or lost their jobs, along with so many who work in travel and tourism all around the world. Eventually, I began to fly perhaps half a normal schedule, including some flights with entirely empty passenger cabins but bellies full of cargo: pets, bags of letters, enough gold and pallets of banknotes to remind me that the world's financial system isn't yet entirely virtual, tens of tonnes of Scottish salmon, and medical supplies whose technical descriptions my colleagues and I would read out to each other from the cargo manifest with heightened interest and a new kind of pride: 'diagnostic probes', 'reagents' and 'perishable cargo – antibody'. Meanwhile the fleet of 747s I once flew was retired, and as a result other types of aircraft, such as the 787, began to fly to cities I believed I would never return to as a pilot. I've flown several times to San Francisco, for example, and had a chance to hand out a few flyers, and to look again for Henry.

Here on this Underground train I sit next to a smudged plastic partition and balance my bags between my knees. When I'm settled I look to the windows opposite, and then to the poem printed above them, by Leanne O'Sullivan. With its loveliest lines in mind – 'with the noise of the city growing too / loud and the day burning out so quickly', and 'Just once let's imagine a word for the memory / that lives beyond the body, that circles / and sets all things alight' – I wonder if it's only a coincidence that I've found it here on one of the Circle Line's trains, or if, alternatively, it was selected precisely for them.

I close my eyes and try to imagine a new city, alone on its island. When I fail, I imagine a city with multiple circle lines. They're not concentric, let's say, nor do they meet only at their edges, like gears. Rather, they intersect like the sets drawn on a Venn diagram, each encompassing a partially overlapping portion of the city's historic core. Maybe the shape of the portion in which they overlap – it's not actually as perfect as the heart of a Venn diagram; it's uneven, asymmetrical – could have inspired the transit system's logo, I think, as I open my eyes and read the poem again.

TOKYO

I've said good-bye to Steven, an old friend of Mark's who I was happy to discover would be in Tokyo on the same June days as me. He has a meeting now, one important enough to have brought him here from the other side of the Pacific. I have no meetings. In fact, I have a couple of days before I fly back. So I don't force myself to do something I think I should, like go to a new museum or for a long run; I can do these things tomorrow.

Instead I walk into the station, buy two cans of sweetened iced coffee from a vending machine, and pause where I must choose between two flights of crowded steps, a decision that's made more difficult because it hardly matters. I pick the right-hand staircase and walk up to an island platform where a bright-green and shining-silver train stands waiting in the late-morning rain. I step into a carriage immediately before the music stops and the doors slide shut.

I'm facing towards the centre of the city. The station that this train is about to leave, however, is itself nearly a city. Around three and a half million people, equivalent to more than a third of London, pass through each day. The joke is to say that you will meet someone here, at 新宿, Shinjuku, New Post Station, named for one of many such places of rest on Japan's ancient network of highways, without specifying at which of its more than 200 exits. The humour lies in assuming that you'll somehow find each other at the busiest train station on Earth.

I first passed through Tokyo on my way to my high school home-stay with a Japanese family in Kanazawa. Later, at university, I spent a summer working in Nagatachō, a district in the heart of the city, commuting on rush-hour trains and going out after work with colleagues, when I often had the sense that I was trying on both adulthood and the world's largest metropolis. Subsequently, when I worked in Boston after graduate school, and thanks to the smatter-ing of Japanese I'd acquired in those previous visits and in university classes, I was often sent to Japan for extended work trips.

On one of those trips, I left the office at lunch and went to a record shop. I bought an album of solo piano by an artist whom I'd never heard of, though the clerk indicated that he loved his music and that he hoped I might, too. I went back to the office, and then out for a long, late dinner with colleagues, and finally back to my hotel, not far from this vast station.

I didn't go straight to bed, as I wanted to study for the entrance exams for the pilot course I hoped to enrol on. One test involved looking at a calculation that popped up on the screen (2,356 + 789 = 3,045, say) and clicking 'correct' or 'incorrect' as quickly as pos-sible. I put my new music on and began to practise a spreadsheet version of the task I'd made on my computer. When I grew bored I stood and walked to the rain-covered window. Then, for the first time since childhood, I started to cry a little.

I didn't – and still don't – know why; I wasn't sad. Perhaps it was the beauty of the piano. Or perhaps I was reminded – by my recently concluded business dinner, which, even though I'd shared it with kind people, had left me tired; by the sight of my suit, care-fully arranged on its hanger, and to all appearances much better prepared than me to face another day of work; or by the view from my hotel room of the silent, wet towers of the real Tokyo, as opposed to the one I'd imagined as a kid – not only that I'd definitely grown up, but also that there'd been no obvious moment to mark this transition, whenever it had happened. There'd only been hours and days in which I'd done some things, and not others; hours and days nearly like those that came before, and nearly like those that followed.

After I became a pilot I didn't return to Tokyo for many years, as short-haul pilots based in London never fly that far. When I dreamed of learning to fly the 747, Tokyo was the city I most looked forward to seeing again, and once I completed that retraining I came here as often as I could. Then the 747 stopped flying to Japan, and once again years passed, until I retrained on the 787, one of which I flew here yesterday. So the city is a little like a distant relative, maybe a great-aunt I see irregularly, and whenever I do, I can never tell whether the biggest changes are in her, or in me.

The train leaves Shinjuku smoothly, unswayed by the rain from the west that intensifies and gusts onto the left-hand windows of the carriage.

Tokyo stands on the Pacific coastline of Japan's main island of Honshū, to the east of the Japanese Alps and along the north-west reaches of Tokyo Bay. The population of Greater Tokyo, more than 37 million, is around twice that of the New York region, and three times that of metropolitan Paris.

The official name of the city is:

東京都,

pronounced

Tōkyō-to,

meaning the Tokyo Metropolis.

This formal name – I close my eyes and repeat it to myself – could not be improved by any I might imagine.

But I try anyway, until an announcement interrupts me with the name of the next station:

新大久保 Shin-Ōkubo, New Large Hollow.

Charles V, the Holy Roman Emperor, granted a coat of arms to Juan Sebastián Elcano – after Magellan's death, he led the remains of his expedition home to Spain, and to the honour of becoming the first people to circumnavigate the world – that features the words *Primus circumdedisti me*, You first encircled me. More stirring to me, however, as perhaps to anyone transfixed not only by globes, but by dreams of the largest cities on them, might be the name of the Yamanote Line, and its image at the heart of Tokyo's transport maps.

The Yamanote Line is an aboveground railway that loops around central Tokyo, encompassing thirty stations and a circumference of around twenty-one miles. The most straightforward measure of its greatness, and that of the city it orbits, is to note that, by a 2013 reckoning, six of the world's ten busiest train stations are on the Yamanote Line.

The next station, the planet's tenth busiest, is the rhythmically syllabled:

高田馬場 Takadanobaba, the Riding Grounds of Takada (a surname that means High Rice Field).

On leaving certain Yamanote Line stations a pre-recorded voice announces that you are on the *sotomawari*, the outside circle, a Japanese reminder to me of the pleasing terminology of the ring around distant Raleigh. The character for *soto*, outside, is 外. This character is combined with 人, person, to form the word pronounced *gaijin*, foreigner, a term that encapsulates the fascinating but occasionally frustrating cocktail of privileges and limitations associated with holding that position in this country.

In Japan, trains, like cars, drive on the left, so the sotomawari, the outside circle, is the clockwise one. If you are not on the sotomawari then you must be on the *uchimawari*, the anticlockwise-running train on the inside circle. 'Uchi' is a homophone for 'home'. In other words, if your Japanese is as limited as mine, you might naturally think of these as the 'foreign circle' and the 'home circle'.

Today I've chosen to travel clockwise around Tokyo; perhaps it seems slightly more correct to do so, as a Yamanote Line train – like a striding pedestrian atop the walls that still encircle York – takes around one hour to complete an orbit of its city.

The question of which way to travel around the Yamanote Line plays a role in Haruki Murakami's short story 'A Slow Boat to China'. In this tale, a young man takes a young woman to a disco in Shinjuku, where they dance while a Filipino band covers songs by Carlos Santana. After the disco they go for a walk with nowhere particular in mind. When they say good-bye at Shinjuku Station, and take the Yamanote Line in opposite directions, it's perhaps the archetypal Tokyo farewell. Then, as the young man rides away, he realises that he guided his date onto the wrong train. If she quickly understood the mistake, he considers, maybe she reversed, and will meet her strict curfew; or not, he thinks, for she's 'the type to keep riding the train the wrong way around'. (And perhaps – he seems to belatedly realise – she intended to part with him.)

A friend of mine, Mei, grew up in Tokyo. When I first asked her about the Yamanote Line she laughed and then, for the first time in our friendship, she started to sing: a camera-store jingle, roughly set to the tune I know from the 'Battle Hymn of the Republic', which begins with an exaltation of the train line – 'round, green, the Yamanote Line . . .' – that leads to the chain's flagship store, near Shinjuku Station. When Mei stopped singing, she explained to me that even for Tokyoites, the city and its dense transportation networks can be confusing. So the Yamanote Line, especially when stylised to a perfect ring, makes it easy to orient yourself on every map and in your internal Tokyo, too: you've always got your green circle.

The other thing about the Yamanote Line, according to Mei, is that in its journey around the heart of Tokyo, but not through it, the line transits a number of residential areas, and so a lot of her friends took it to school. After school, each kid knew which was the shortest way around to their home but they'd often try to convince a friend to ride the other way, to be together longer.

Now we're approaching:

目白 Mejiro, White Eyes,

at which it's not possible to transfer to any other transit lines. This is unusual: at almost every other Yamanote Line station, travelers can transfer to another train or metro line, or even to half a dozen or more.

The multitude of potential transfer points also explains why Yamanote Line trains may carry a little more of the melancholy already associated with the repetitions of commuting. In contrast to Mei's happy memories of riding the Yamanote Line with her friends in childhood, another Japanese friend, Yukako, recalls how the line sometimes evokes sadness in her as an adult. When she and her friends gather for dinner or a night out, they typically arrive alone, directly from work. When it's time to leave, many of them will get on the Yamanote Line to travel to the various stations at which they'll transfer to whichever other line will take them home.

On such nights they'll board the train together and travel along an arc of their city, but in an ever-shrinking group. So the line for me has a bit of a sentimental side, Yukako explains, and then she adds: The Yamanote Line reminds me of farewell.

The next station, the third busiest in the world, is:

池袋 Ikebukuro, Bag-Shaped Pond.

When I first came to Japan for work, before I became a pilot, I was surprised by how easily I learned to doze on the trains and subways, as many Tokyoites do, and as I now do on this grey-skied late morning, as the train parts the rain and rolls through

大塚 Ōtsuka, Large Tomb-Mound,

and

巣鴨 Sugamo, Duck's Nest,

and also

駒込 Komagome, Crowd of Horses,

where I wake, rub my eyes and stare at the characters that form this name on the digital display. I can't make sense of either of them.

Japanese is the hardest language I've ever studied, and yet its complexity to me, particularly that of its writing system, can obscure its more matter-of-fact qualities. For example, I might see a Tokyo metro station name such as 御茶ノ水, Ochanomizu, and it looks and sounds as foreign to me as anything I've ever come across in my life. The two nouns it contains, however, are among the first a student of Japanese will learn: *ocha*, tea, and *mizu*, water. So the name of the district is like Teawater (which, I find it hard to remember, isn't also the name of a neighbourhood in London).

Many of the names of Yamanote Line stations are no more complicated. A number contain the character 田, or more intricate characters of which 田 forms part. It means what it vaguely resembles: 'rice field', and it's the second character in the names of both of Tokyo's two major airports, Haneda and Narita, and the first character in the name of the next station my train comes to, the northernmost on the line,

田端 Tabata, Edge of the Rice Field.

A Japanese writer, Saisei Murō, lived in Tabata, a few hundred metres from the tracks of the Yamanote Line. He was born in 1889, in Kanazawa, the city in which I spent my first summer in Japan, and from his writing it can seem that, from the vast and anonymous metropolis in which he settled, he's often thinking of his more peaceful and greener first home. Takako Lento, a literary translator who once lived in Tokyo, has translated many of Murō's poems but none in which the Yamanote Line appears. A year or so from now, I'll write to her to ask if she might translate 'Earthen Banks' for me, from Murō's book *Those Who Came from Stars*:

. . .

Once in a while between them the Yamanote Line train travels
Windows brightly lit
White clothes flickering
Rounded knees of a woman passenger
The single signal is shivering in blue . . .

'The Yamanote Line is special,' she'll agree in an email. It 'draws a circle as if to connect and embrace the most important areas and spots of Tokyo . . . it seems we somehow end up traveling on the line no matter where we go.' She'll also explain the name of the line. While a literal translation is 'the hand of the mountain', a more accurate one is 'in the direction of the heights'. The name originally referred to 'the plateaued areas of Edo' – as Tokyo was known until 1868 – where temples and the residences of warriors stood, 'as opposed to the downtown areas where commoners lived. Hence the name itself still has a classy ring'.

Each week more people – around 28 million – use the Yamanote Line than ride on the entire London Underground system. During rush hour around fifty trains are orbiting the city. At peak hours a train leaves each station, in one direction or the other, about every minute, so when I look out the window, I'm as likely to see a train curving past in the other direction as I am Tokyo, while at other times the train I'm on parallels one on another line, and for a moment our speeds are identical, until we separate through the city in a sideways falling.

Now we arrive at:

西日暮里 Nishi-Nippori, West All-Day-Long Village,

whose name is said to refer to how long you might remain without growing tired of the place. It's written with 日, the first Japanese character I ever learned; it means 'sun', and 'day', and appears most memorably in 日本, Japan.

When I first became familiar with the Yamanote Line I joked to Dad that if the line were any busier, then the railway company would need only one continuous train running in each direction. Yamanote Line trains aren't, of course, long enough to encircle the city, but they are nevertheless enormous: around 220 metres long, while the distance from this station to the next is around 500 metres, that is to say not much more than two trains' worth of track, forming the circle's shortest segment, and so it's not long until we're pulling into:

日暮里 Nippori, All-Day-Long Village.

A truth of topology is that there are on our planet always two antipodal, or opposite, points that have – despite a distance that could not be greater – the same temperature and air pressure. It's a conclusion derived from the premise that if a function varies continuously, as meteorological phenomena like temperature or air pressure must, then you cannot move from one point to another without passing through every value between them.

With this in mind I like to imagine a set of stories premised on the idea of Yamanote doppelgängers: once each day in the metropolis – at noon, let's say – two people who are riding the line on separate trains are struck, at the moment they're exactly opposite one another across the circle the line forms, by thoughts of intersecting plans for the afternoon that neither would have made on their own; by memories of events that occurred simultaneously in their separate pasts; or by an image of someone they have not yet met. The first names of the two individuals in each such pairing could form the title of each tale; or perhaps there could be a month's worth of stories, each of the thirty titled for a station, starting, perhaps, with one of the more expressively named ones, such as

鶯谷 Uguisudani, the Valley of Bush Warblers.

Uguisu – Japanese nightingales, or bush warblers – have a strong presence in Japanese literature. They were once popular as pets, and their melodic call is said to mimic a phrase of the Buddha. They gave their name to a type of floorboard fashioned to make a sound like that of the bird in order to warn of an intruder's approach, and for centuries their droppings have been used in the manufacture of face creams. The colour used on Yamanote Line carriages, and in the line's branding, is 'Yellow Green Number 6' or 'Uguisu colour'. Confusingly, the birds are of a more olive-like shade, but they are nevertheless considered an omen of spring, the season of bright new green, while one of the better places for a traveller in Tokyo to find birdsong and a tree-shaded bench is the leafy park close to the next station,

上野 Ueno, Upper Plains,

which lies near the easternmost point on the line. A nearby station, Keisei Ueno, is a busy gateway to Narita Airport, and as a result

Ueno is the first Tokyo neighbourhood that many foreigners walk through. Some trains from Narita itself also arrive here; Narita is the city where I've so often stayed as a pilot, one of the many hundreds of crew members who do so each night, and who, as we seek a meal so ill-timed as to be indefinable – breakfast? dinner? – in the narrow lanes, form a separate, inconstant and global night city within the ordinary Japanese one that lies mostly sleeping around us.

The train continues to

御徒町 Okachimachi, Foot Soldiers' Town,

where an unmounted rank of shōgun-guarding samurai were once barracked. I fiddle with the ring on my finger. Mark once accompanied me on a trip to Tokyo, and I'm keen to make him a brief video, but my camera has trouble capturing anything of the city itself rather than the raindrop-splashed window, and as its focus shudders between the two we reach:

秋葉原 Akihabara, Field of Autumn Leaves.

I look at the display on the inside of the carriage and admire the smooth, idealised curve of the digital version of the line that leads on to the next stations.

I close my eyes. Next week Mark and I will be together, on a trip to Pittsfield. We'll be walking together in a cool, deserted forest, yet still well within my first city's limits, and from there, I know, Tokyo will seem hardly more real to me than the city I took comfort in imagining, when I was young in my hometown and felt alone or ashamed.

I open my eyes as the train crosses a river and soon we arrive at:

神田 Kanda, Sacred Rice Field.

The Kanda River runs east to the Sumida River; I stayed in an apartment above the Sumida the summer I worked in Tokyo, and in the sultriest evenings I would walk along its banks, or stop to smoke and watch the many barges that motored past, and when one of the crew members waved to the obvious foreigner on the riverbank I would nod and wave back. Each vessel bore the character 丸 on its hull; a Japanese friend later explained that it means 'circle' and it's also – confusingly, he admitted, as even he saw no connection – the suffix for boat names. (According to one theory, boats were once seen as like castles, which are encircled by their defences; another theory invokes Hakudo Maru, a celestial being who taught humans to make ships, and whose name is now appended to vessels in order to secure his protection.)

One way for the numerically minded to mark their progress around the Yamanote Line and the city is to remember that the stations are numbered. The next station,

東京 Tōkyō, Eastern Capital,

is Station One.

The numbers, which fall as you move clockwise, reset here. In the direction I'm travelling the next must be Station Thirty, or

有楽町 Yūrakuchō, Pleasure Town.

To be followed by Station Twenty-Nine, better known by its straightforward name,

新橋 Shinbashi, New Bridge.

The first segment of what would become the Yamanote Line opened in 1885. Initially, its tracks were as convenient a thoroughfare for pedestrians as they were for trains. (One day in 1913, the writer Naoya Shiga was returning home and decided to walk along the tracks. What happened next is related in the first sentences of his short story 'At Kinosaki': 'I was struck and thrown to the ground by a trolley car of the Yamanote line. To recuperate from my injury, I went by myself to a hot springs inn at Kinosaki in Tajima.')

The loop line was finally completed in 1925. Its shape isn't really that of a circle, however frequently and memorably it's characterised as one on maps. From above the line is more like an arrowhead, or an inverted raindrop, wider in the north and narrowing further now, as we route south towards

浜松町 Hamamatsuchō, Seacoast Pine Town,

which stands near two well-known public gardens, and the waters of Tokyo Bay from which they were reclaimed. It's interesting to note that the last character of its name, 町, which bears the rice field character within it, on the left, is the same as the last character in the name of the following station, but it is pronounced *chō* in this case and *machi* in the next.

Many Japanese characters have multiple readings. The characters themselves and some pronunciations are Chinese in origin, but they're also used for indigenous Japanese words. They're generally deployed semantically, though their meanings may be multiple, and occasionally they're deployed purely phonetically. Japanese also uses syllabaries, which are alphabets of a sort, in which each 'letter' encodes a syllable; you'll often see these in a small font above the Chinese characters for place-names signed in train stations, a potentially helpful guide for everyone, given the great variation in the pronunciation of Chinese characters, and especially for those foreigners and children who are still learning to read the names of even well-known places.

It's difficult to find a satisfying English analogy for how the Japanese language uses Chinese characters. The rise of emojis helps. As does mathematics; take '+', the plus sign, for example. It has an obvious meaning, but one that isn't as precise as we might think. And crucially, for the purposes of this analogy, we know to pronounce it differently depending on where we find it. We might read it as 'plus' when we read out '7 + 8', for example, but as 'and' if we see a sign for a stylishly branded architectural firm, say 'Jones + Associates'. In chemistry class, meanwhile, a teacher might write '+ve' on the chalkboard and students quickly learn to pronounce it as 'positive'.

Since Japanese has borrowed not only characters from China, but some of their pronunciations as well, we might imagine – though, once again, every analogy is imperfect – that the Normans had bequeathed the English not only a significant French vocabulary, but also an entirely distinct system of writing, one that was subsequently adopted and adapted to write many English words, too. Or we might imagine that in English we use a set of characters that were first standardised – where else? – in ancient Rome, and that one of these symbols is ▯. If we then saw, for example, 'that ▯ is old', we would know to read ▯ as 'book' (setting aside, in this example, that term's Germanic roots); but if we saw 'She is studying to be a ▯ ian', we would read out a version of ▯'s Latin pronunciation, i.e. 'librarian', and we would do this so naturally that the depth of the history embodied by our words and our script might not always occur to us.

The train rolls on and pulls into

田町 Tamachi, Rice Field Town.

A few moments ago we passed near an outlet of Mister Donut, a popular chain that I visit more than I probably should, and I consider reversing direction as I recall the unlimited doughnuts Dad promised me were mine as soon as I could bike up and down our street on my own, and how, seated proudly with him at the counter of the Dunkin' Donuts nearest his office, I made short work of one Boston Kreme, then another, and then, as he started to look a little worried, a third.

I catch sight of several faces on an anticlockwise train, and I forget doughnuts as we sail past a station that is not yet open,

高輪ゲートウェイ, Takanawa Gētowei, Tall Loop Gateway,

which is not only the newest station on the line, but also the only one whose name incorporates an English loan word: 'gateway'. The name of this neighbourhood, Takanawa, at a historic entrance to Tokyo, includes the character for 'ring' or 'circle'. It's a coincidence – the name predates the construction of the Yamanote Line station – but an entrancing one, especially as the character is also used as a counter term (think 'loaves' of bread, or 'sheets' of paper) for wheels.

Lois, the family friend who used to send me letters written in an oval, liked to stamp her letters and envelopes with the image of a ladybird. Each station on the Yamanote Line, like almost all in Japan, has a seal that collectors can ask to have stamped on a page in a special book. The seal of the next station, the ninth busiest in the world,

品川 Shinagawa, Goods River,

displays a woodblock print by the nineteenth-century artist Utagawa Hiroshige, who's best known for his depiction of the fifty-three stations of the Tōkaidō, the ancient thoroughfare between Edo – now Tokyo – and Kyoto. This busy railway station is named for the first way station along Japan's most storied road.

Next is

大崎 Ōsaki, Big Cape,

the southernmost station on the line.

True circle lines are difficult to run. Any delay is likely to ripple backwards through the loop, and there's nowhere convenient for a train to empty, change drivers and be cleaned, repaired, or respaced. When I first moved to London I found the Circle Line unreliable. Now it's much less so, but – not coincidentally – trains now leave the circle. This means you cannot circumnavigate London continuously, a surprising fate for one of the world's first circle lines, I think, as we pull into

五反田 Gotanda, Five Tan Rice Field.

The 'tan' here refers to a Japanese unit of area. One tan is about 1,000 square metres.

Moscow has its Koltsevaya Line – whose name is translated as Circle Line, and whose shade of brown on maps is said to reflect the ring left on a plan by Stalin's coffee cup – and its mostly surface-running Moskovskoe Tsentralnoe Koltso, Moscow Central Circle, too (while a third line, the aptly named Bolshaya Koltsevaya Line, or Big Circle Line, is under construction; it will be the world's longest circle line, a title it may hold until the completion of Paris's Line 15). Beijing has two circle lines – one follows the path of a demolished Ming wall – and Berlin has its Ringbahn, the inspiration for the Yamanote Line. Nonetheless, no circle lines that I've seen elsewhere come close to rivalling the majesty of Tokyo's: it's older than most, as well as far busier, and because its tracks not only run aboveground, but are elevated along so much of their route, you can observe the city as you circumnavigate it, or you can simply watch, as I do today, how the rain that blew onto one side of the carriage at the start of my journey now blows onto the other as we approach

目黒 Meguro, Black Eyes.

I doze, until a rare lurch of the train wakes me in time to see the outskirts of

恵比寿 Ebisu, Blessings for Long Life (and the name of the God of Fishermen and Good Fortune).

I close my eyes again for a few moments, then a few moments more, until the announcement of our imminent arrival at the second-busiest train station in the world,

渋谷 Shibuya, the Bitter Valley (or more pleasingly, the Elegant or Refined Valley),

which is also the favourite station of my friend Mei. She likes the buzzing station itself, as well as the shopping on offer in the neighbourhoods nearby, including

原宿 Harajuku, Field Post Station,

which is famous for Tokyo's oldest surviving wooden station building – though it's due to be shortly replaced – and for its private platform, to be used only by the Imperial Family, to access the nearby Meiji Jingū, one of the capital's most prominent shrines. While the next station,

代々木 Yoyogi, the Many-Generations Tree,

is the highest on the line, and the one whose name I like best. The second character, 々, indicates merely that the first character is to be repeated, and that the tree has therefore stood for more than one generation.

I'm nearly back to where I began, but as I prepare to disembark I know to avoid the automatic ticket barriers, which don't always manage to price journeys to nowhere. Instead, I'll need to go to a counter and try in my ham-fisted Japanese to explain to an agent what I've done. They'll tap some keys to perform a brief operation on my fare card and wave me through. Sometimes they smile, but they never seem surprised; I'm certainly not the first to make, as the announcement of the next stop,

新宿 Shinjuku, New Post Station,

proves, a full circle.

Throughout Japan, whenever the doors of a train open, what's known as a 発車メロディ, *hassha merodii*, departure melody, may start to play. It's a railway version of musical chairs: when the music stops it means the doors are about to close. The idea is to urge commuters onwards without stressing them unduly.

Most Yamanote Line stations have their own tune – or two, as many stations have separate melodies for clockwise and anti-clockwise trains – which may derive from a popular song, or refer to the musical heritage of the neighbourhood around each station, or to cultural figures such as manga characters. The melodies have such cosmopolitan names as 'Cielo Estrellado', starry sky, in Spanish; 'Dance On', in English; and '春', *haru*, spring; while the one that begins to play as the doors open here in Shinjuku, encouraging me off the train at last and others onto it, is known by the English name 'Twilight'.

The station songs that form this transport art, this circle of music that plays all around the city, are both catchy and popular. You can buy Yamanote Line ringtones that play the songs of individual stations, and alarm clocks that do the same – though I hardly need one of these, it seems, when I find myself humming a departure melody as I get up to shower or make coffee, several mornings after I have left the train, the busy station and the metropolis where I last heard it, and flown back home around the world.

PITTSFIELD

Cindy texts me and Mark to ask: blueberry pie or strawberry rhubarb pie? Or both?

Both kinds of pie are organic, Cindy adds in a subsequent message, explaining that she and her husband, Dan, grow the blueberries, strawberries and rhubarb in their backyard and make the pies from scratch. It's no trouble, she writes, one of each kind is in the freezer, ready to go. There's vanilla ice cream, so we can have our pie à la mode.

Blueberry? Or strawberry rhubarb? I think of the little strawberry patch we marked out when I was a kid, in the backyard of the house I grew up in, the home that now belongs to Cindy and Dan. We grew squash, as well, and corn that I don't believe resulted in even one meal, though cornstalks seemed to grow easily all around the city in late summer. We had tall sunflowers with faces so large that they tipped under their own weight. Maybe carrots, but definitely no rhubarb – though a neighbour up the street grew it in her garden, and one day she showed me which parts were safe to eat, the sort of lesson from an elder that we must have evolved to remember well.

Blueberry, Mark and I agree. We'll bring sandwiches from a café in downtown Pittsfield, I say. Come between 12:30 p.m. and 1 p.m., Cindy tells us. The weather looks good. We'll sit in the yard.

My stepmother has often told me that she knows a little about the family who bought our old house, and that she was certain it'd be no trouble if I ever wished to visit. I liked the idea of going back to the house, but maybe not as much as I thought, because for years I never pursued it.

Recently, though, it's occurred to me that I'd like to see the rooms of my old home again. My stepmother knows the names of the current owners, but not their emails or telephone numbers, so I wasn't sure how to get in touch, until I realised that, of course, I had their home address. For the first time in decades, I wrote my old house number and street name on an envelope.

Cindy emailed me a week later, when I was in Dallas, I think, or Los Angeles. Come anytime, she said. Anytime except Sunday mornings, when we're at Mass. Whenever you are next here. Dan and I would love to have you. Our kids have left home; it's only us now. We have two chickens in your old yard: Poppy and Ivy.

Mark and I pick up the sandwiches we promised and head towards my old neighbourhood. Keen not to be late, we're running early, so we park on the next street and roll down the windows.

Birds chirp, a lawnmower buzzes and a group of kids, aged maybe ten or twelve, are shouting as they bike past. After a quarter of an hour I restart the car and drive to my old house. We park on the street and gather the sandwiches, as well as a bottle in a shiny gift bag, the only one on the rack in the shop that wasn't decorated with a particular occasion in mind.

We start for the side door, which my family used almost exclusively, but Mark suggests that perhaps we should go to the front. We're guests, after all, I realise. Before we can alter our course I see Cindy, her husband, and my old neighbour waiting at the side of the house to greet us.

The side porch is unchanged, as is my neighbour, bewilderingly; she looks a full two decades younger than her age. After a warm but awkward round of introductions – I once knew the neighbour very well, but I've never met Cindy and her husband; they all know each other; none of them know Mark – Cindy and Dan motion us into their kitchen.

I step in, stoop to remove my shoes, and then look up and around. The fridge is in the wrong place; the oven is different, the countertops, too. Only the dark wood of the window frames, and the oval shape of the openings on the radiator grate, reassure me that I've been here before.

We had it done, Cindy tells me as she gestures around the kitchen.

I say, truthfully, that it looks great. The kitchen looks more alive now, busier, more lived-in. It's woodier, there's less white. In my memory our counters were empty, though surely they couldn't have been. Now there are more stacks of papers, more ornaments and kitchen implements. In my memory, too, the kitchen's south wall is blank, but now Shaker-style drawings of trees hang on it.

Cindy asks if maybe the kitchen was once two rooms. Yes, I say, bewildered by a confidence that I realise only my brother and I could possess now. There used to be a little office, with a built-in gun cabinet and a desk where Dad kept his accordion file of bills, and a printing calculator that whirred and clicked as he worked. In the 1980s, when many nearby families were enlarging their kitchens and adding microwaves, my parents had an argument about doing so in our home – about the cost, I think – until Dad finally agreed and they had the wall knocked through.

We walk through the swing door into the dining room and here, it seems, is where the memories have gathered, as if for one of the many Christmases, Thanksgivings and birthdays the Berkshire gang celebrated here. The china cabinet built into the corner, with glassware above and spirits below, is unaltered, and I tell Cindy and her husband about other parties, the ones my brother and his friends threw when our parents were away, and how they would drink from Mom and Dad's stores and then carefully add water to the bottles, to leave the levels of their contents unchanged.

The low cabinet – was there really a time when Dad would occasionally smoke cigars he stored in there? – along the window is gone. So is the old table, and so are the five chairs that were left after my brother and I sawed up and threw away the remains of the one I broke. Gone, as well, are the bookcases that held the encyclopaedias and atlases that I spent so much time with. Sometimes when I was ordered not to leave the table until I finished my vegetables – mushrooms were the most challenging, as they still are – I'd wait until my parents returned to the kitchen. Then I'd throw the vegetables onto the top of these bookcases, to be retrieved later, or, once, to be forgotten, until my parents found them, shrunken and mummified within their dried-up halos of sauce. Mom and Dad tried to be angry but they were laughing, too.

For sure this is the same room.

As we step out of it, it's difficult to look up from the door handles, which I couldn't have described an hour ago but which are now, once again, so comfortingly familiar. They are, I suppose, what you'd see right in front of you if you were a fraction of my height. The wallpaper in the hall – greyish white, with a horizontal, textured pattern – is unchanged. We were allowed to scribble on the walls before that paper was put up – a kid wouldn't forget a day like that – but I can't remember what we wrote.

Cindy invites me to open a door onto the little front hall, the same door on which Mom would hang a creepy embroidered Santa who stared out with shiny, wet-coal eyes and spooked me each December morning if I forgot to put the lights on before I came downstairs. I look into the front hall, down to where letters from my pen pals – including Lily, in Hong Kong, whose home island I've so often flown near, and Emma, in Sydney, whom I visited on my first trip to Australia as a pilot – would land. Among the ordinary floor tiles are a few that display a simple outline of a castle. Like every door handle in the house it's so familiar, but this detail is one more I'd never have been able to recall unprompted. Another Shaker tree, formed of light green leaves and skilfully decorated with spotted orange and dark green circles, almost fills the south wall. Cindy explains that she painted it herself, and I tell her that Mom, a frequent visitor to the former Shaker village conserved on the western edge of Pittsfield, would have loved it.

We turn left, into the living room. The woodstove I so carefully kept fed is gone but the hearth remains, and holds an elaborate autumn arrangement. A pumpkin stands at either side, and a scented candle is burning in a glass jar on the bricks. On the mantelpiece are photographs, gourds and a pendulum clock. I look at the French doors that lead out from the living room's far side. I tell Cindy that the room beyond them was my bedroom when we had guests, and for a few years after Dad remarried, too; and how, before this, Mom sometimes met with speech therapy clients there. These were often older men who had suffered strokes, and whose speech problems, I understood, were many times worse than my own; during their sessions my brother and I were not allowed to watch television, or even to speak loudly in nearby rooms.

A quarter of an hour from now we'll all step outside the house and take a look in the garage, and I'll take a photo of the logo of the band KI44 that my brother and his buddies painted on one of its inside walls sometime in the 1980s. They did a good job, Mark will agree, and I'll text the image to my brother and his wife. My neighbour will laugh as she reminds me of the worrisome day she first saw my brother and me, after she and her family had bought the house next door and moved in: we had soaked a tennis ball in petrol, lit it and were using hockey sticks to pass it around the driveway. Then we'll be in the backyard, seated around a table, eating and laughing as the chickens peck the grass around the table and Cindy's elderly dog comes to rest his head on my foot. I'll notice that there's no woodpile, and that the little fir tree I planted when we moved in is gone, too – it got sick, Cindy reports – as is the crab apple from which Mom hung suet for the birds each winter. My gaze will trace the barely discernible depression in the grass that marks where, the spring after I fell through the ice, my parents filled in our little goldfish pond. Once in a while I'll look up from the table, to the back of the house, and for half a second or so the sight will not seem foreign to me. It will be, instead, as familiar as it once was; it will be as if my brother and I are playing in the leaves or the snow, and my parents are inside, preparing a meal, and soon to call out to us.

For now, though, we leave the living room and return to the hall. A chair lies across the stairway.

It's to stop the dog, Cindy says with a smile, it's not to stop you. Would you like to go upstairs? Mark looks to me, but I'm not sure. I start to turn away down the hall and then stop. Well, I ask, if you don't mind, is it possible to take a quick look in my old room?

Cindy laughs and says that she has no idea which room was mine, but that we're free to go anywhere we like. I start up the stairs, and touch the hard angles of the square spindles that become round and narrow as they rise to the railing they support along the hall above. I used to count these stairs as I climbed, I remember, and now I do so again.

The room nearest to the top of the stairs is the closet-sized sewing room, where Mom really did keep a sewing machine, until that age gave way to another and we got our first computer. I did a lot of my schoolwork here then and played on an early flight simulator, too. It would be 1985, maybe: I'm making an effort to listen to pop music so as to fit in better at school when other kids talk about bands. I've shut the door and tuned to a local station on the radio, and Dad comes in, to ask – only out of curiosity, I now realise, so out of character was this for me – What are you listening to? And I'll turn and shout I'M LISTENING TO THE RADIO! and he'll look at me in silent bewilderment and gently close the door. Or it's 1986, and I'm listening to a different radio, the shortwave one that Dad connected to a wire that he ran out high above the lawn to the garage. From across the ocean an English accent comes through the crackle. The voice of the BBC's World Service speaks from the city in which I have no idea I'll ever live, land a 747 hundreds of times, or marry the man who's here with me, leaning against this doorframe. The announcer is talking not about London but New York, about its glowing skyline and what he describes as the typically American display of fireworks in its harbour: the Statue of Liberty has turned 100.

The next room along the hall was mine. The rest of the house hasn't seemed small to me. As I look into my bedroom, though, it's so tiny that I can hardly believe it, or understand how it could hold all the memories that lift now like startled birds, and bank and part around where Mark and I stand in the narrow doorway. My brother and I are dressing up as vampires for Halloween; I'm ill on a hot August afternoon, and when I hear the shouts of other kids in the street I step from the clammy bed to the window, where the blind is pulled down over the summer brightness that breaks along its frayed edge; I'm alone – alone and assembling planes; it's a New Year's Eve in high school, Dad is out with my future stepmom, and so the university guy I'm sort-of seeing, the one with whom I first drove, at Pontoosuc Lake, has come over to hang out; I've made a map at my desk and I'm writing my imaginary city's latest name, the one it will keep; Lois is with us for a few months, she's living in my room and I'm sleeping downstairs, it's the summer in which my parents decide to get divorced, and now both her arms are lifting and she is walking towards me across this wooden floor because she sees on my face that I've just been told.

Mark and I step into the room, pause, and look around. I tell myself we shouldn't stay too long, we shouldn't impose. The room ticks and tocks; nothing, everything. Surely I should feel sad; but I don't especially, I'm surprised to realise. It's been thirty years since my parents last lived in this house together, and nearly a quarter of a century since I last stood here. Now Mark is with me, my brother is safe and at home with his own family, and my stepmother and I are close. The day is warm and dry. Cindy and Dan have prepared the table in the backyard.

Everything, nothing. I try to remember the glow of my light-up globe, and which hemisphere would face the room if you spun it gently and let it come to rest.

In my mind, I rearrange things: this bed is where my dresser was. That bookcase is where my bed was. The desk is near the same window that mine stood by. I think again of the maps I used to make on it, and I turn to Mark, who is so far from his own childhood home, on England's south coast, as I recall a gift I made for him early on, before I first brought him here: a subway map of a fictional city, on which every stop was a place we'd recently been to together.

Can a room know you? Can it forget you once it has? I notice a fuzzy 'P', for my city and high school, tacked on a bulletin board; a Red Sox mug; and a Star Wars poster, where I hung one of an airliner's glowing cockpit. This is a kid's room, but it's so clean, so ordered, and when I see the neatly arranged schoolbooks on the bookcase I get it: once again this is the room of someone who has left home.

I listen for Mom's or Dad's voice calling me down for dinner, or my brother's laugh as he busts in without knocking. I try to picture Snoopy, his nose patched by Mom where it scorched one night after he fell on my night-light, and all the planes that were motionless until I held them and moved them horizontally as if for takeoff, on the runway my imagination made of the top of the dresser. I look to the open window, where birdsong and a breeze come through, and try to recall the winter nights I loved better than any summer day, when ridges of frost would rise from the inner pane as gusts of snow broke over the storm window beyond. I lower my gaze to the metal handles set into the frames of the windows, and the equally familiar dials on the low radiators.

I blink and try to imagine my city. I reach for anything there: the blurred light of a fast train that resolves into a line of rounded windows as it slows; the freshly marked lanes beneath the grey cables that suspend the longest bridge above the harbour; the incomplete and half-dark frames of new towers.

I blink again and there's only the room, and the breeze through the open window, and the murmur of Cindy, Dan and my old neighbour conversing in the hall. A minute passes. And another.

I look to the window and out again over the blooms of the garden, to the garage, and beyond it, to the east, to where the weather heads next. I turn towards the door and look to Mark. When I take his hand he gives me half a smile, and asks if I'm ready to go.

Acknowledgements

In addition to those I thank in the individual chapter notes, I would like to express my gratitude as follows.

I wish to offer my deepest thanks to my editors, Dan Frank and Tom Pold of Knopf, and Clara Farmer of Chatto & Windus, for their constant encouragement, warm support and wise guidance throughout the long process that led to this book. Dan Frank passed away in May 2021; I know that I am only one of the many writers, readers and colleagues who owe Dan so much, and deeply miss him. Thank you, as well, to Victoria Murray-Browne, editor of this paperback edition, for all her guidance and warm-hearted encouragement, and to Charlotte Humphery and Amanda Waters, for all their careful work. Thank you to Karen Thompson and Sally Sargeant, for their seemingly endless attention to detail, and to Stephen Parker, Tyler Comrie, Anna Knighton and Peggy Samedi for their skilful work on this book's design and production. And thank you, of course, to my publicists, Jessie Spivey, Jasmine Marsh, Kealey Rigden and Rhiannon Morris, for all their help in bringing this book to the attention of readers.

I would also like to extend my warm gratitude to my agent, Caroline Michel of Peters Fraser and Dunlop, for reaching out to me so many years ago. I am so grateful for her help, and that of her colleague, Tim Binding, in guiding and shaping this book. Thank you also to their colleagues Rebecca Wearmouth, Kim Meridja, Rose Brown and Laurie Robertson. Thank you to the amazing Harriet Powney, for her occasionally ruthless suggestions, for her efforts to teach me that less is often more, and for coining (and so effectively wielding) the term 'a fact too far'. Thank you also to the sharp-eyed Hilary McClellen for her assistance with meticulously checking those facts I couldn't bear to cut, and for so gently bringing, for example, the differences between a rhea and an ostrich to my attention. And thank you to everyone in Pittsfield and the Berkshires who helped me – in particular Ann-Marie Harris of the Berkshire Athenaeum and Erin Hunt of the Berkshire County Historical Society, together with their colleagues.

Thank you to my fellow AP211ers – Jez, Bomber, Seb, Cat, Neil, DAVE!, Adrian, Adam, Kirsten, Chris, Balbir, Lindsay Boy, Lindsay Girl, Mo, Hailey, Carwyn and James – for friendships that have now lasted two decades across our ever-growing list of ranks and aircraft types. Thank you also to my colleagues Allister Bridger and Anthony Cane for their kindness and support with this latest of my writing projects. I'm deeply grateful to all my flight crew, cabin crew and ground-based colleagues for making my job so enjoyable, whether in London, on the flight deck, or in the streets of the cities that form our down-route world. It seems that every pilot, when they retire, says that the best thing, after all, was the people; I'm certain that when the time comes – and despite my deep love for both flying and cities – I will agree.

Thank you to Anjali, Lola and Silas; and to Sophie, for reminding me of how exciting it can be to write. Thank you to Drew Tagliabue and Peter Catapano for their sensitive and enormously useful advice at times when I was uncertain about this book's direction. Thank you also to Seeta Seetharaman, Helen Yanacopulos, Eleanor O'Keeffe, Jamie Cash, Thellea Leveque, Jim Ciullo, Jordan Tircuit, Meredith Howard, Wako Tawa, George Greenstein, Adrian Campbell-Smith, Julian Barratt, Zareer Dadachanji, Jason Vanhoenacker, Anika Vanhoenacker and Nancy Vanhoenacker; and, of course, to Rich and to Cindy and Dan.

A number of family members, friends and correspondents spent many hours reading drafts of the book over the last three or so years, often in their entirety, and it really is impossible to thank them adequately for the time they so kindly offered, and the great care they took. Thank you to

Steven Hillion, for all his keen intelligence and frank but warmly offered advice on city and book matters both small and large; to Alec MacGillis, an old friend and fellow Pittsfielder, for the time and attention he found for this text at what was already an extraordinarily busy time for him; and to Tom Zoellner, for his thoughtfulness as we discussed cities, both real and imagined, on our walks in Los Angeles. Thank you also to Desirae Randisi, for sharing my love of cities, and giving her thoughts on how to write about them; to Alain de Botton, for his generosity and for his brilliant and inspiring books; to Leo Mirani, for his help and for a friendship that started, appropriately, at Heathrow; and to Sebastien Stouffs, for his careful reading from the perspective of both a pilot and a friend. And thank you to Kirun Kapur, who gave so much as she helped to guide this book – from one draft to the next and then the next and the next – as she has helped to guide my writing from the beginning. I am so grateful for our friendship, and our journeys together.

I'd like to close by expressing my love and gratitude to my parents; to Jason, Lois and Nancy; and to Kathleen, Sue and everyone else in our Berkshire family, who have always been one of the greatest blessings of my life. And thank you, above all, to Mark: for so much joy, for giving me such encouragement and wise advice with the writing of these words, and for helping me home.

Notes

A NOTE TO READERS

I've changed the names of five individuals, either at their request or because I have not been able to contact them. For one of them, I've also changed another biographical detail. Otherwise, throughout the book, I've tried to describe my experiences as accurately as possible. On several occasions, however, I repeated a memorable walk, museum visit, etc., in order to take more careful notes, or to check those I had made; and on these first (or second or third) retracings of my steps I would sometimes notice something else.

A number of organisations offer both advice and community to LGBTQ+ young people and those who support them. PFLAG (pflag.org) and the Trevor Project (thetrevorproject.org) are great places to start, especially for those in the United States, while Stonewall (stonewall.org.uk) offers a number of UK-based resources. I also recommend the It Gets Better Project (itgetsbetter.org).

There's no simple answer to the question of how best to support the communities – urban and otherwise – that we encounter as travellers. Even seasoned travelers may find Lonely Planet's recent (2020) *The Sustainable Travel Handbook* a useful read before a trip. During and after a trip, local advice is, of course, best. The same book offers guidance on how to travel in a more environmentally friendly manner – a topic much on the mind of those who work in aviation and the wider travel and tourism industry – and addresses such issues as biofuels and carbon offsets.

With the exception of the London section of the final chapter (the one in which I'm wearing a mask) the last of the trips that this book is based on took place in February 2020 – and most took place long before that – after which the world of aviation was altered. Studying and guiding the long-term impact of the pandemic on cities will no doubt be a generation's work for urbanologists, architects, planners and leaders. For those interested in learning more about the effects of both the pandemic and the climate crisis on the urban world, I recommend Bloomberg's reliably insightful CityLab (bloomberg.com/citylab).

Except where otherwise specified, I have used the units of measurement that are customary in the United Kingdom.

Even with the help of others, I struggled, at various points, to decide how best to render foreign words in English, and when it might prove interesting or helpful to use, for example, Japanese text in addition to romanised versions of Japanese words. If the flexibility I've adopted seems excessive, allow me to fall back on the words of John Julius Norwich, who wrote, in the author's note at the start of *Four Princes: Henry VIII, Francis I, Charles V, Suleiman the Magnificent and the Obsessions That Forged Modern Europe*, 'Far too much, I believe, is sacrificed on the altar of consistency. . . . In every case I have been guided by what sounds right to my ear – and will, I hope, sound right to the reader.'

Travellers can learn more about Pittsfield at the city's websites (lovepittsfield.com and cityofpittsfield.org) or at the website – motto: 'Life is calling' – for visitors to Berkshire County (berkshires.org).

I hope that the chapter notes and the bibliography that follow will provide guidance on my sources, as well as suggestions for further reading.

I'm deeply grateful to all those who helped me check the facts and interpretations in this book; I alone, of course, am responsible for any errors that remain.

I'm always happy to hear from readers – in particular, I'd love to hear your recommendations for your favourite book about your favourite city – though it may sometimes take me a while to reply. I can be contacted via my website, markvanhoenacker.com.

PROLOGUE: CITY OF MEMORY

The illustration is based on an elm tree in Pittsfield.

Coleridge's 'like night, from land to land' is from 'The Rime of the Ancient Mariner'.

My decision to become a pilot is described in more detail in my first book, *Skyfaring: A Journey with a Pilot*.

The United Nations data I reference is from *World Urbanization Prospects: The 2018 Revision* and the report *The World's Cities in 2018* that was compiled from it. The first page of that report, headlined 'What is a City?', provides a good description of the difficulties in comparing the populations of cities and urban areas that are defined differently.

My father's autobiography was printed for family and the Berkshire gang. Someday I would like to help to bring it to a wider audience.

Giuseppe Garibaldi's words about Rome appear in several versions in both Italian and English, though the substance is the same.

CHAPTER 1: CITY OF BEGINNINGS

William Carlos Williams's 'a man in himself is a city . . .' is from the author's note to *Paterson*. An author's statement precedes the note and is nearly as compelling: 'I wanted something nearer home, something knowable,' writes Williams, about his choice of Paterson.

Kipling's 'To the City of Bombay' appears in more than one version; the one I've excerpted is from *Collected Verse of Rudyard Kipling.*

'Ye are the light of the world . . .': I'm not sure which translation of this famous passage I heard first. The text here is from the 1599 edition of the Geneva Bible; I understand that John Winthrop is thought to have relied on an edition of the Geneva Bible in composing his sermon. See, for example, Abram C. Van Engen's 'Origins and Last Farewells: Bible Wars, Textual Form, and the Making of American History', published in *The New England Quarterly.*

Joseph Smith's 'When this square is thus laid . . .' appears as I have it here in various sources, such as Volume 1 of *History of the Church of Jesus Christ of Latter-Day Saints.* The website of the Church Historian's Press (josephsmithpapers.org) begins this remarkable quote with 'Where' rather than 'When'.

The quote from Richard Francis Burton – 'Memphis, Benares, Jerusalem, Rome, Meccah' – appears on the first page of *The City of the Saints,* in a subsection, 'Why I Went to Great Salt Lake City', which begins: 'A tour through the domains of Uncle Samuel without visiting the wide regions of the Far West would be, to use a novel simile, like seeing Hamlet with the part of the Prince of Denmark, by desire, omitted.'

I struggled with which version to use of Brigham Young's legendary quote, especially since 'This is the place' is the best known. My understanding, from such sources as *The History of Emigration Canyon: Gateway to Salt Lake Valley,* by Cynthia Furse and Jeffrey Carlstrom (page 54), is that the first version of Young's words to be recorded is: 'It is enough. This is the right place. Drive on.'

Benedict Anderson's discussion of 'new' city names is in Chapter 11 of *Imagined Communities: Reflections on the Origin and Spread of Nationalism.* While I was editing this book in the autumn of 2020, I published a version of the 'worst Thanksgiving I ever had' story in an op-ed titled 'Thanksgiving in a Strange Land', in the *New York Times,* on 24 November 2020.

Ovid's statement about Rome and the world is included, for example, in Michèle Lowrie's 'Rome: City and Empire', published in *The Classical World*: 'The land of other peoples has been given within a fixed boundary: the expanse of the Roman city and of the world is the same.'

My trip to Rome with Mark, and our encounters with examples of 'SPQR' throughout the city, led me to Mary Beard's *SPQR: A History of Ancient Rome,* which I cannot recommend highly enough. The extensive quotes from Livy are from pages 8 to 11 of *The Early History of Rome: Books I–V of the Ab Urbe Condita,* translated by B. O. Foster.

The story of Pittsfield's baseball bylaw is best told by Alec MacGillis, in 'Hometown Home Run', published in the *Baltimore Sun* on 18 May 2004.

When it comes to the past of Pittsfield, I have been particularly reliant on the vast *The History of Pittsfield, (Berkshire County,) Massachusetts, from the Year 1734 to the Year 1800,* and its three subsequent volumes covering 1800–1876; 1876–1916; and 1916–1955. I understand from local historians that while these works are generally reliable, a critical eye is especially appropriate for passages regarding Native Americans. The million-volt lightning bolt is described on page 8 of *The History of Pittsfield* (1916–1955). The invention of night skiing at Bousquet Ski Area in Pittsfield is well documented, for example in the Berkshire County Historical Society's 2016 volume *Pittsfield,* which also notes that Clarence Bousquet 'invented and patented' a grip for the rope tow.

The Dutch mapmaker's description of the Berkshires region and Vermont appears on page 15 of *The History of Pittsfield* (1734–1800). The descriptions of Native Americans from my high school US history textbook are documented in 'PHS Text Doesn't Measure Up', a letter I published in the *Berkshire Eagle* on 16 October 1991.

The General Court of Massachusetts' 'Proprietors of the Settling-lots in the Township of Poontoosuck' is from page 91 of *The History of Pittsfield* (1734–1800); a version of the English translation of this Mohican name appears on page 16; and the description of William Pitt ('by his vigorous conduct . . .') is from page 132.

The description of the snow that fell on the morning of the city's inauguration – 'a benediction from above' – is from 'Our New City', an article on the front page of the *Berkshire County Eagle* on 8 January 1891. Judge Barker's speech is recorded in *Proceedings of Inauguration of City Government – January 5, 1891,* available in the Berkshire Athenaeum. 'We are at home . . .' is from page 5; 'The old order is about to pass . . .' is from page 9; 'Who shall say how beauty . . .' is from page 14; and 'Just how much the fact that Rome . . .' is from pages 14–15.

'Matronly dignity', 'masculine stability', and '1,000 candle power strong' are from 'The Inaugural Ball', an article I found in a notebook of original clippings concerning the inauguration, stored at the Berkshire Athenaeum. *Evening Journal* is handwritten above this particular clipping and is presumably the name of the publication. The article begins: 'Monday, January 5, 1891 was indeed a red letter day for Pittsfield.'

Livy's 'It is the privilege of antiquity . . .' is from page 4 of Foster's translation, mentioned above. The description of 'Mrs. Seth Janes' and her adventure with the wolf is from *The History of Pittsfield* (1734–1800), in the footnote on page 140. Pittsfield's 'Records of the Revolutionary Service' begin on page 477 of that same volume. Noadiah was Sarah Deming's son; the other Demings are Benjamin and John, whose relationship to Sarah I was unable to confirm.

Sarah Deming's marble obelisk stands in the East Part Cemetery on Williams Street (known before the Revolutionary War as Honasada Street). *The History of Pittsfield* (1734–1800) records (in the footnote on pages 86–87) that the burial ground was 'near the spot where she fixed her home in 1752', and that the inscription 'A mother of the Revolution and a mother in Israel' is on the monument's east face. Today, that inscription faces west.

For this chapter in particular, but also for the whole of my book, I'm extremely grateful to Ann-Marie Harris of the Berkshire Athenaeum's Local History and Genealogy Department, not only for so warmly welcoming me and showing me around, but for answering dozens of questions by email in the following months. It was a pleasure to once again spend many hours in the library that was so important to me and my family when I was a child; and to be reminded, too, how quickly one can reach Dunkin' Donuts for a snack and a break. Thanks also to Dave. I'm glad we've reconnected.

CHAPTER 2: CITY OF DREAMS

I told the story of my mom's letter to me at my flight school in 'The Unopened Letter', an article in the *New York Times* on December 26, 2015. Afterwards I was touched to receive a number of letters from readers, describing their own remarkable stories of correspondence that had been lost and then found.

The quote from Carl Jung is from pages 197–98 of *Memories, Dreams, Reflections*. Today, a bust of Jung stands in Mathew Street in Liverpool, above the inscribed words: 'Liverpool is the pool of life' and 'C.G. Jung 1927'.

The various quotes from my dad are either from his shield, the text on the back of it, or his autobiography. The app for locating fruit in Brasília is the aptly titled Fruit Map. Clarice Lispector's 'space calculated for clouds' appeared in 'Nos primeiros começos de Brasília', in *Jornal do Brasil* on 20 June 1970, which is referenced in 'Chronicles as Memorials: The Brasília of Clarice Lispector (and the Temporary Disappearance of the Invisible)', by Maria Caterina Pincherle.

In *The Modernist City: An Anthropological Critique of Brasília*, James Holston notes that the population density of the region of Brasília was less than one person per square kilometre (about two-fifths of a square mile) at the time of the city's construction. In 2018, Mongolia – one of the world's least densely populated countries – had a density of two people per square kilometre.

Kubitschek's 'integration through interiorisation' appears on page 18 of *The Modernist City*. Caroline S. Tauxe's description of Kubitschek is from 'Mystics, Modernists, and Constructions of Brasilia', page 48. Holston's quote, 'The most complete example ever constructed', is from page 31 of his book. Oscar Niemeyer's 'the cathedrals of Saint-Exupéry' is from page 109 of *The Memoirs of Oscar Niemeyer*.

My father's description of his aeroplane flight during his first days in Salvador is as follows:

> There were no street names in these poorer sections. Since I could not find any maps either, I went to the airfield and easily found a pilot to take me 2,500 feet above the neighbourhood to help me take pictures of the neighbourhood. . . . On the photographs, I could actually count individual houses. There were some 5,500 houses on the square mile with a population that I soon estimated at 23,000. New mud huts went up every week because a developer was selling building lots as fast as his draftsman could trace them. People came mainly from rural towns within a couple of dozen miles from the state capital and clustered by town as much as they could to have friends live close together.

Holston's 'the modernist idealisation of new . . .' is from my personal correspondence with him. Yuri Gagarin's 'disembarking on a different planet, not on Earth' is from Tauxe, page 56; a slightly different translation appears in 'Landmark Anniversary for Brasilia Leaves Architect "Sad"', an unsigned AFP story published in the *Independent* on 17 September 2011 (reflecting, too, how often the accent above the first *i* in *Brasília* is omitted in English).

The translated excerpt of Dom Bosco's dream appears on page 16 of Holston's book. For the complete text and an alternative translation, see Eugenio Ceria's 'The Biographical Memoirs of Saint John Bosco', available on the Don Bosco Salesian Portal (donboscosalesianportal.org).

The description of Brasília as a 'capital of hope' appears, for example, in 'O Capital da Esperança', a dissertation by Gustavo Lins Ribeiro, and in English, too, e.g. 'The Capital of Hope', published by Alex Shoumatoff in the *New Yorker* on 26 October 1980.

I would like to thank James Holston not only for his wonderful book, but for the

time he took in assisting me with my research both before and after my visit to Brasília, and for his permission to include portions of our personal correspondence. I'm
grateful to Eduardo for his lifelong kindness and love for my brother and me, and for
the stories he shares with us of our father. Thank you to Fernando for connecting me
with Vívian, to whom I wish, of course, to express my particular thanks for her open-
ness and generosity while spending several days showing a stranger around her city.
Vívian and Fernando also assisted with fact-checking, as did Andrea Brotto. Addi-
tionally I would like to thank Rebecca Eldredge, Jonathan Lackman, Dan McNichol,
Robin Tudor of Liverpool John Lennon Airport, Karen Cariani of WGBH and Paul
Grondahl; and James Gardner, whom I reached via the website (salesians.org.uk) of
the Salesians of Don Bosco (UK).

CHAPTER 3: CITY OF SIGNS

The name first given to Los Angeles is a matter of some contention; see, for example,
'City of Angels' First Name Still Bedevils Historians', an article by Bob Pool in the
Los Angeles Times on March 26, 2005. The version I've used is my favourite, from
page 7 of Remi Nadeau's *Los Angeles: From Mission to Modern City*.

I came across Miguel Costansó's quote 'furnished us points . . .' on page 22 of
David Kipen's remarkable *Dear Los Angeles;* the traveler who compared the city's air
to that of 'Old Egypt' is E. D. Holton, whose words from 1880 are recorded on pages
65–66 of Kipen's book. The quote from Eleanor Roosevelt is from her 'My Day'
column of 23 March 1946, which can be accessed through the Eleanor Roosevelt
Papers Project (erpapers.columbian.gwu.edu).

The quote from a New York newspaper about Los Angeles – how it can 'never be
a great business center because it is too far away from the ocean' – is from the New
York *Tribune*, as cited on page 83 of Nadeau's book. I have not been able to find the
original article or its date. Los Angeles annexed the port city of San Pedro in 1909.

I'm always struck by signs that refer to 'city' or 'the city', so you can imagine how
thrilled I was to learn, from Thomas F. Madden's evocatively titled *Istanbul: City of
Majesty at the Crossroads of the World*, that ' "Istanbul" is simply a Turkish hearing of
the Greek phrase στην Πόλη, meaning "in or to the City." '

The description of Boston as 'The Athens of America' is common; see, for example, *The Athens of America: Boston, 1825–1845*, by Thomas H. O'Connor. 'The Hub
of the Universe' apparently derives from an essay that erstwhile Pittsfield resident
Oliver Wendell Holmes Sr. published in the *Atlantic Monthly* in 1858, in which he
wrote that 'Boston State-House is the hub of the solar system' (see 'From "Bean-

town" to "The Hub," How Did Boston Earn Its Nicknames?', a report on WGBH by Edgar B. Herwick III on 30 August 2017); indeed, one wonders how Holmes's former neighbours in Pittsfield viewed Boston in that age.

Episode 16 of Season 1 of *Cheers* is titled 'The Boys in the Bar'. As Brett White writes in 'That Gay Episode: How Sam Malone Showed Acceptance Is Macho on "Cheers,"' a 28 March 2017, article in *Decider*, the show's writers were inspired by the story of Glenn Burke, whom the *New York Times* (in a 1 June 1995, obituary) described as 'the first major league baseball player to publicly acknowledge his homosexuality'.

Frasier Crane assists Berkshires-loving anxious fliers in Episode 19 – 'Airport V' – of Season 6 of *Cheers*.

The exact function of the Milliarium Aureum in Rome remains unclear to me. In Samuel Ball Platner's *A Topographical Dictionary of Ancient Rome* we read that 'on it were engraved the names of the principal cities of the empire and their distances from Rome, although these distances were reckoned from the gates in the Servian wall, not from milliarium itself'. In J. A. Cramer's *A Geographical and Historical Description of Ancient Italy*, in contrast, we read that the Milliarium was 'that point in the Forum from which the distances to the several gates of the city were alone reckoned'.

The slogan of Amboy, California – 'the ghost town that ain't dead yet' – appears on the town's website (visitamboy.com). I recommend a visit. The signs to distant cities in Daggett, California, stand in front of the El Rancho Mobile Home Park on Route 66. The botanist 'in camp at Los Angeles' is William H. Brewer; he's quoted on pages 440–41 of Kipen. Nadeau's 'like the land of milk and honey . . .' is from page 162 of *Los Angeles: From Mission to Modern City*.

Mulholland's famous line – 'If you don't get the water now, you'll never need it' – appears in several forms. I've used the version that Margaret Leslie Davis records in Chapter 3 of *Rivers in the Desert: William Mulholland and the Inventing of Los Angeles*, her fascinating study of Mulholland and Los Angeles; while in 'Just Subtract Water: The Los Angeles River and a Robert Moses with the Soul of a Jane Jacobs', an essay published in the *Los Angeles Review of Books* on 18 December 2015, Joseph Giovannini includes this version: 'If you don't get the water, you won't need it.' (He also notes the important role of the film *Chinatown* in telling the story of Los Angeles and its water wars.) Mulholland's even more famous 'There it is! Take it!' is recorded by Davis in Chapter 7 of her book.

The story of the distant NOW ENTERING LOS ANGELES CITY LIMITS sign, and David Kipen's 'You could trek . . . ', are on page xv of the preface to his book.

Nadeau's 'tributary province . . .' appears on page 180 of his book. Wallace Stegner's 'out over empty space' is from Ed Madrid's interview of him, published in the *Oregonian* on 18 April 1993. The bowling ball–and–trampoline analogy was first shared with me by Mr Gilbert, in physics class at Pittsfield High School, and is described in such interesting articles as 'General Relativity: Beyond the Bowling Ball and the Trampoline', published on the website of the Ontario Association of Physics Teachers (oapt.ca) on 23 November 2020.

The quote about the city of Tamara – 'rarely does the eye light . . .' – is from the chapter titled 'Cities & Signs 1' of Italo Calvino's *Invisible Cities*. The quotes from the *Manual on Uniform Traffic Control Devices* are from the 2009 edition (including Revisions 1 and 2), which is available on the Federal Highway Administration's website (mutcd.fhwa.dot.gov). 'To be effective . . .' is from Section 1A.02, para. 2; 'Arrows used . . .' is from Section 2D.08, para. 18; 'The lateral spacing . . .' is from Section 2E.15, para. 2; 'the background . . .' is from Section 2E.06, para. 1.

'Our great city of many cities' is from the homily offered at the Cathedral of Our Lady of the Angels, by Cardinal Roger M. Mahony, on 2 September 2002, and archived at the cathedral's website (olacathedral.org).

I would like to thank Bob Cullen, Jameelah Hayes and Tony Dorsey of the American Association of State Highway and Transportation Officials, Kristen Pennucci of the Massachusetts Department of Transportation, and Jon Brodsky of the Arizona Department of Transportation for their patience with my questions about control cities; and Liv O'Keeffe, formerly of the California Native Plant Society (cnps.org), and the photographer and botanist Stephen Ingram (ingramphoto.com) for their generous help in plant identification. Thank you to James D. Doyle for his explanations of the weather patterns of the Owens Valley. I'm also grateful to Toon Vanhoenacker, Peter Schrag, Andreas Zanker, Dieter Moeyaert and Ton Heuvelmans for their kind guidance.

CHAPTER 4: CITY OF PROSPECTS

I wasn't absolutely certain that the right to go out at lunch was granted only to juniors and seniors at Pittsfield High School back in the day, although half a dozen classmates remember this as I do. The song 'Shenandoah' is sometimes titled 'Oh, Shenandoah'. Mrs T's pierogies are to be found in the freezer section of supermarkets across the US (mrstspierogies.com).

The statistics on tall buildings, from the Council on Tall Buildings and Urban Habitat – the excellent motto on its website is 'Advancing Sustainable Vertical Urbanism' – are only ever a snapshot; as a result, it's fun to check in occasionally to see how their statistics (at ctbuh.org) are shifting. The predominance of non-Western cities on the more recent lists of the one hundred tallest buildings is striking. It's worth noting that the equation of stories with height I used is inexact, as any must be;

the relationship depends not only on differing floor-to-floor heights, but also on the nature of lobbies, screens for rooftop equipment, and crowns. For example, a modern and spacious office building of around 150 metres might have 35 floors, whereas a hotel of that height might have 45.

Statistics on the number of bridges in cities are potentially not only problematic – should an almost imperceptible structure that carries an ordinary road over a railway line be in the same category as the Brooklyn Bridge? – but hard to keep up to date. The most common total for Pittsburgh is 446, given, for example, in 'Pittsburgh: The City of Bridges', posted online by the Heinz History Center on 5 May 2017, while in terms of river crossings – the sense that might come to mind most naturally – 'Just How Many Bridges Are There in Pittsburgh?', published by WTAE-TV on 13 September 2006, states that in Pittsburgh 'more than 29 bridges cross the three rivers'. A rough total ('400 or so') for canal crossings *(ponti)* in Venice is given on the website of *Encyclopaedia Britannica*; the total number of bridges in New York City is commonly reported to exceed 2,000; a figure for Hamburg (2,300) appeared in '25 Record-Breaking Cities: Highest, Cheapest, Oldest and Most Crowded', in the *Telegraph* on 1 November 2017. The database of the Massachusetts Department of Transportation lists 64 bridges of every sort in Pittsfield.

I encountered the request to 'please pray for us and the Steel City of Pittsburgh for which this church is both a beacon and a protector' in Saint Mary of the Mount on Grandview Avenue.

The Mahanna Cobble Trail in Pittsfield is maintained by the Berkshire Natural Resources Council; I wrote about it in 'Leaf Peeping Is Not Canceled: 6 Drives and Hikes to Try This Fall', published in the *New York Times* on 2 October 2020. Melville dedicated his novel *Pierre; or, The Ambiguities* to 'Greylock's Most Excellent Majesty'. The pollution and the cleanup of the Housatonic River is well documented by the *Berkshire Eagle*; please also see the notes for Chapter 7. The café I love in downtown Pittsfield is Dottie's Coffee Lounge (dottiescoffeelounge.com); across the street is the Lantern (thelanternbarandgrill.com), which 'serves the best fries'. The world's best cider doughnuts are from Bartlett's Apple Orchard and Farm Market (bartlettsorchard.com) in Richmond.

In this chapter I found myself returning again and again to Pittsburgh's official website (pittsburghpa.gov), as well as to the sites of *Pittsburgh Magazine* (pittsburghmagazine.com) and the *Pittsburgh Post-Gazette* (post-gazette.com).

I would like to thank Andrew and Matthew Popalis for their kindness in sharing their memories of Shenandoah; Jenny Hansell and Mariah Auman of the Berkshire Natural Resources Council (bnrc.org), and Becky Cushing Gop of the Massachusetts Audubon Society (massaudubon.org), for their assistance with various Pittsfield elements of this chapter, and for their work in preserving what's best about the Berkshires; and Shawn Ursini of the Council on Tall Buildings and Urban Habitat, for his advice on how to try to relate the height of a skyscraper to its floor count. I'd like to express my warm gratitude to Jim Ciullo for his long friendship with my dad and his help with the paragraphs about my dad's office. I'm also grateful to Rob Koon, Jon Millburg, Margaret McKeown, and Ellen O'Connell for their assistance with this chapter.

CHAPTER 5: CITY OF GATES

The illustration is based on the triple arch of the Cinquantenaire Arcade in Brussels.

Calvino's 'What line separates . . .' is from 'Cities & Signs 3' in *Invisible Cities*. I described my love of such gate-names as Brandenburg and Kashmere in the final chapter of *Skyfaring*. The Pet Shop Boys song I refer to is 'King's Cross'. After I moved to London I assumed the song was written in the aftermath of the fire at the King's Cross St Pancras Underground station; however, I later learned that the song's release preceded the terrible fire by two months. The Finland Station is mentioned in 'West End Girls'.

The description of Aurangabad as the City of Gates is widespread; see, for example, the tourism section of the District Aurangabad website (aurangabad.gov.in). The idea that Frémont intended English speakers to use the Greek name Chrysopylae for the Golden Gate is fascinating to me; Erwin G. Gudde, in *California Place Names: The Origin and Etymology of Current Geographical Names*, notes that 'Frémont was apparently determined to fix the Greek name on the entrance.' My father's words are an excerpt from a short piece he wrote about his search for Henry.

The sections on Jeddah in this chapter were among the book's most difficult for me, partly because English sources on the city are few, and partly because, as I note in the text, many of the gates have been moved, rebuilt, or renamed. I was particularly reliant on three resources. The first was Angelo Pesce's *Jiddah: Portrait of an Arabian City*, which several historians have assured me is considered reliable. Thanks to its clear text and many remarkable images, I strongly recommend it to anyone with an interest in learning more about the history of the city. The second was various UNESCO documents, including *Historic Jeddah, the Gate to Makkah: Nomination Document for the Inscription on the World Heritage List*, Volume 1, which I'll refer to as 'UN' in subsequent notes. (It's no surprise that Jeddah was the first urban Saudi site to be nominated to that list.) The third was Ulrike Freitag's extremely helpful *A History of Jeddah: The Gate to Mecca in the Nineteenth and Twentieth Centuries*, which is also the most recent (2020) of the three.

The year of the first arrival of pilgrims by aeroplane is given as 1938 on page 131 of

Pesce; Freitag, however, notes that 'in 1936 Egypt Air offered to transport pilgrims to Jeddah' on page 227 of her book. Many of the examples of the varied spellings of Jeddah's name appear on page xiii of Pesce, as do the other quotations in the same paragraph, including that by al-Bakri. Pesce's 'at best a fishermen's hamlet' is on page 3; 'his followers to join him' is from page 61. The report on the poor state of Jeddah's walls was by Carsten Niebuhr, quoted by James Buchan in *Jeddah: Old and New*. I would love to learn more about the history of the term *corniche* in Arabia.

'Bride of the Red Sea' appears, for example, in the title of Chapter 6 of Loring M. Danforth's *Crossing the Kingdom: Portraits of Saudi Arabia;* 'Town of the Consuls' appears in Pesce, page 135; 'Town of Consulates' on page 73 of UN; and 'Gate to Makkah' throughout UN. Ibn Jubayr's description of arriving in Jeddah by sea is recorded by Ross E. Dunn in Chapter 6 of *The Adventures of Ibn Battuta*. I'm sorry I did not have room to include more about Ibn Battuta's stays in Jeddah; for example, a full version of the tale of the ring: Ibn Battuta gave a ring to a beggar in Mecca. After Ibn Battuta arrived in Jeddah, 'a blind beggar led by a boy' came to him, saluted and used his name, though 'I had no acquaintance with him, nor did he know me.' The blind beggar took Ibn Battuta's hand and felt for the missing ring. Ibn Battuta told him how he had given it away as he left Mecca. The beggar told him to 'go back and look for it, for there are names written on it which contain a great secret'. Mystified, Ibn Battuta concluded: 'God knows best who and what he was.' (From Chapter 7 of Volume 2 of *The Travels of Ibn Battuta, A.D. 1325–1354*.)

Al-Maqdisi's 'very hot' is on page 68 of UN. The words of Nicholas of Cusa are recorded on page 19 of *Philosophia Perennis: Historical Outlines of Western Spirituality in Ancient, Medieval and Early Modern Thought*, by Wilhelm Schmidt-Biggemann. Nasir Khusraw's 'one toward the east . . .' is noted on page 77 of UN. The account of the anonymous enslaved person who noted three gates is on page 31 of Pesce; it was recorded by Richard Hakluyt (see 'Imperialist Beginnings: Richard Hakluyt and the Construction of Africa', by Emily C. Bartels, in *Criticism*).

Laila al-Juhani's 'You know already that the things we love . . .' is from her novel *Barren Paradise* and appears on page 297 of *Beyond the Dunes: An Anthology of Modern Saudi Literature*. John Winthrop's 'as a citty upon a hill' is from page 39 of 'A Modell of Christian Charity, Written on Boarde the Arrabella, on the Attlantick Ocean, 1630', available through the website of the New-York Historical Society; I had understood that the sermon was given in the Holy Rood Church in Southampton, Mark's hometown, but Daniel T. Rodgers, on pages 18–19 of *As a City on a Hill: The Story of America's Most Famous Lay Sermon*, suggests that the story of these words is more complicated.

Henry Rooke's descriptions of Jeddah's coffeehouses – 'always full' with 'the common people . . .' – is from page 36 of Pesce. The magazine article framed on the café's wall is from pages 606–7 of the 12 June 1926, issue of *L'Illustration*. The eleventh-century visitor who noted that there is no 'vegetation at all' is Khusraw, recorded on page 8 of *Jeddah: Old and New;* the sixteenth-century traveller who wrote that 'the land does not produce one single thing' is Ludovico di Varthema, recorded on page 53 of *The Travels of Ludovico Di Varthema in Egypt, Syria, Arabia Deserta and Arabia Felix, in Persia, India, and Ethiopia, A.D. 1503 to 1508.*

My letter to the 'house near the tree' took three months to return to me; it was stamped with Arabic text, and, in English: 'Saudi Post – Makkah Region – Address Incomplete'. The lovely quote from Jan Morris – 'that in every row of houses . . .' – is from 'Day 17' of *Thinking Again: A Diary.*

I would like to thank Ulrike Freitag for her generosity and patience in answering my questions about Jeddah and its gates, and for sharing maps from her book in advance of its publication. I would also like to express my gratitude to Ibrahim, Ali and Samir for their kind assistance in Jeddah or from afar, as well as to Chris Denham of Network Rail, Jen Lesar, Peter Carroll and Dieter Moeyaert.

CHAPTER 6: CITY OF POETRY

R. Parthasarathy's translation of 'Twilight in Delhi' was published on page 8 of the April 2006 issue of *Poetry.*

I wished to write that the England brothers were Bavarian-born; while this was definitely true of Moses, I have not been able to confirm this of Louis. I own a postcard on which England Brothers is described as 'a "big" city department store in the heart of the Berkshires'; it was published by the Crown Specialty Advertising, Inc., of North Adams, Massachusetts, and is copyrighted 1972. The slogan 'It Wouldn't Be North Street Without England Brothers' is recorded, for example, in 'Escalator Rides, Robert the Talking Reindeer and Other Things That Made England Brothers Special', by Jennifer Huberdeau in the *Berkshire Eagle* on 25 January 2019. As for the question of whether to call it 'England's' or 'England Brothers', the former was written on the iconic blue boxes; the latter was spelled out on the store's North Street façade. Us Berkshire gang folks have strong but differing opinions on which we used more often.

Morris Schaff's 'A Word to Pittsfield On Her Change from Town to City Government' is recorded on page 64 of the Berkshire Athenaeum's *Proceedings of Inauguration of City Government – 5 January 1891,* where it is dated 30 December 1890; the poem is also included in the write-up of the 5 January festivities in the *Berkshire County Eagle* on 8 January 1891.

Melville's 'I have a sort of sea-feeling . . .' is well known in the Berkshires, and is recorded, for example, in 'Herman Melville at Home', published by Jill Lepore in the *New Yorker* on 22 July 2019. Melville's description of Cairo's Gate of Victors appears in Canto 11 of Part 2 of 'Clarel: A Poem and Pilgrimage in the Holy Land'; his 'the Parthenon uplifted on its rock first challenging the view on the approach to Athens' is from the poem 'The Apparition'; his 'Crowning a bluff' is from the poem 'Pontoosuc'. All are found in *Herman Melville: Complete Poems,* as is (in the 'Note on the Texts') the conclusion that Melville 'did not intend a final 'e' in the title of the uncollected poem "Pontoosuc" '.

The term 'Township of Pontoosuck' for Pittsfield appears, for example, on the 'Plan of 1752' between pages 88 and 89 of *The History of Pittsfield* (1734–1800).

There are several versions of Bob Seaver's words to Elizabeth Bishop. 'Go to hell, Elizabeth' appears in Brett C. Millier's biography, *Elizabeth Bishop: Life and the Memory of It.* Oliver Wendell Holmes Sr's 'Angel of Death . . .' is from 'Dedication of the Pittsfield Cemetery' in *The Complete Poetical Works of Oliver Wendell Holmes.* (When it comes to Holmes and his city poems, Pittsfield got off easy: consider 'Chicago sounds rough to the maker of verse; / One comfort we have – Cincinnati sounds worse'; from his 'Welcome to the Chicago Commercial Club'.)

Henry Wadsworth Longfellow's 'The Old Clock on the Stairs' is available through the website of the Poetry Foundation (poetryfoundation.org).

'Larger than a sail . . . ', from Anne Sexton's 'To a Friend Whose Work Has Come to Triumph', appears on page 53 of *Anne Sexton: The Complete Poems;* the definition of *hegira* is on page 481; 'the street is unfindable for an / entire lifetime', from her poem '45 Mercy Street', is on page 483. 'The dreams all made solid' is from the song 'Mercy Street' by Peter Gabriel. Calvino's 'Yes, in my childhood . . .' is from his interview with William Weaver and Damien Pettigrew, 'Italo Calvino, The Art of Fiction No. 130', in the fall 1992 issue of the *Paris Review.*

My mother gave me several Wendell Berry books; my most treasured is *Collected Poems of Wendell Berry, 1957–1982,* inside of which she wrote 'Wendell Berry is one of my favorite poets. Perhaps these poems will give you pleasure – With love, Mom – Christmas 1993.' His *'the* experience, the *modern* experience . . .' is from *What I Stand On: The Collected Essays of Wendell Berry, 1969–2017*; however, I first read it in 'In Wendell Berry's Essays, a Little Earnestness Goes a Long Way', by Dwight Garner, in the *New York Times* on 20 May 2019.

'All ACFT entering Delhi TMA . . .' and other references to the Airport Operational Information for Indira Gandhi International Airport may be found in the 'VIDP/Delhi' section of Part 3 of the eAIP documentation on the website of the Aeronautical Information Management office of the Airports Authority of India (aim -india.aai.aero); however, our on-board documentation features the all-capitalised abbreviations I've recorded here.

Mir Taqi Mir's 'The streets of Delhi . . .' appears at the start of the chapter 'Mir Taqi Mir' in *Beloved Delhi: A Mughal City and Her Greatest Poets*, by Saif Mahmood, a book I recommend to anyone in search of an introduction to Delhi's poetry traditions. (Elsewhere, I have seen 1723 as the year of Mir Taqi Mir's birth.) Amir Khusrau's 'the twin of pure paradise . . .' is from the introduction of *In the Bazaar of Love: The Selected Poetry of Amir Khusrau*. 'Krishna paused . . .' is from Chapter 55 of Book 1 of *The Mahabharata: A Modern Rendering*, by Ramesh Menon. Upinder Singh's 'The goddess Yamuna . . .' is from page 11 of *Ancient Delhi*.

Sarojini Naidu's 'Imperial City . . .' is from her poem 'Imperial Delhi', published in her collection *The Broken Wing: Songs of Love, Death & Destiny, 1915–1916*. Nehru's 'a gem with many facets . . .' is from his 6 December 1958 convocation address at the University of Delhi, as recorded in Volume 4 of *Jawaharlal Nehru: Selected Speeches*. Kirun Kapur's 'Arriving, New Delhi' is from page 94 of *Visiting Indira Gandhi's Palmist*.

The description of Delhi as a 'city of poets' is widespread; see, for example, 'Resurrecting the City of Poets' by Nikhil Kumar in the January 2019 edition of the *Book Review* (India). 'City of verse' appears in Maaz Bin Bilal's article in the *Hindu* on November 3, 2018, *'Beloved Delhi – A Mughal City and Her Greatest Poets* Review: The City of Verse'. Khushwant Singh's 'a longer history . . .' is from page xi of his *City Improbable: An Anthology of Writings on Delhi*. Ibn Battuta's 'a vast and magnificent city' is recorded in Chapter 9 – 'Delhi' – of Ross E. Dunn's *The Adventures of Ibn Battuta: A Muslim Traveler of the Fourteenth Century*.

The comparison of Delhi to Athens – 'with its monumental, crumbling history . . .' – is in Rukmini Bhaya Nair's 'City of Walls, City of Gates', included on page 281 of *City Improbable*. 'Indian Rome' is from Chapter 1 of Gordon Risley Hearn's *The Seven Cities of Delhi*. Percival Spear's 'Delhi can point to a history . . .' is from his *Delhi: A Historical Sketch*. The description of what we now call 'Old Delhi' as 'Modern Delhi' appears in the List of Illustrations and elsewhere in H. C. Fanshawe's *Delhi: Past and Present*, published in 1902.

'City of Cities' appears, for example, on the Archaeological Survey of India's sign outside Humayun's Tomb in Delhi. Patwant Singh's 'No capital in the world . . .' is from 'The Ninth Delhi', a lecture he delivered on 25 February 1971, as recorded in the *Journal of the Royal Society of Arts*. The characterisation of Edwin Lutyens having 'dreamt of constructing monumental buildings' is by Jagmohan, in his *Triumphs and Tragedies of Ninth Delhi*. Lord Hardinge's 'A name to conjure with' is widely recorded – for example, in 'Where Life Comes a Full Circle', an article by Ziya Us Salam published in the *Hindu* on 20 January 2016. 'Must like Rome be built for eternity' are the words of George Birdwood, recorded in Tristram Hunt's *Cities of Empire: The British Colonies and the Creation of the Urban World*.

The idioms and expressions that relate to Delhi are fascinating, but – even with the assistance of several Delhiites – they were a challenge for this foreigner to describe. I understand that my version here of 'Kaun jaaye . . . ', without Zauq's name, is an informal adaptation of the original. 'Either can be used idiomatically – and colloquially, you'd drop his name', reports a friend. There are several versions of the story behind 'Delhi is still far.' Neither I nor several correspondents have been able to locate the song that Inder described to me not long before his death, the one he remembered from 1947 and that incorporates the words 'Delhi is not far anymore' (though *Ab Dilli Dur Nahin* is the title of a 1957 film, and *Delhi Is Not Far* is that of a 2003 novel by Ruskin Bond). If any readers know more about this song, please do contact me.

'Dominated the city's cultural and intellectual landscape' is from Rakhshanda Jalil's foreword to Saif Mahmood's *Beloved Delhi*. Khushwant Singh's 'Dilliwalas were known . . .' is from page xiv of his *City Improbable*. The remarkable custom of the weighing of poets against precious metals or stones is described in Hadi Hasan's *Mughal Poetry: Its Cultural and Historical Value*. Saif Mahmood's 'Urdu poetry was mostly . . .' and 'remain the most quoted . . . ', as well as the words of Faruqi, appear in the introduction to Mahmood's *Beloved Delhi*.

Akhil Katyal's 'a place where . . .' and 'allowed me to . . .' are recorded in 'Akhil Katyal's City of Poems', his interview by Shivani Kaul, published in the *Hindu* on 2 March 2020. Katyal's 'ruthless to some' and 'the different people . . .' are from ' "Delhi Is Capable of Its Moments of Liberation": Akhil Katyal on Being a Queer Poet and His Undying Love for the Capital', published in the *Indian Express* on 15 April 2018. The description of his workshop – 'Does the city make . . .' – is from 'Recap: Poetry and the City with Akhil Katyal', published on the blog of Juggernaut (juggernaut.in) on 16 November 2018.

Ghalib's 'the world is the body, Delhi its soul' appears in several versions; this one is from 'Remembering Mirza Ghalib as He Turns 220: "The World Is the Body, Delhi Its Soul" ', by Gulam Jeelani, in the *Hindustan Times* on 27 December 2017. The article titled 'Ghalib is Delhi and Delhi Is Ghalib!' was published by Firoz Bakht Ahmed on Ummid.com on 15 February 2016. Ghalib's 'Inside the Fort . . .' is from Chapter 1 of Pavan K. Varma's captivating biography, *Ghalib: The Man, the Times*.

'Onward to Delhi . . .' forms part of a speech given by Subhas Chandra Bose on 25 August 1943, and is recorded, for example, in the appendix of Hugh Toye's *The Springing Tiger: A Study of the Indian National Army and of Netaji Subhas Chandra Bose*. (In a subsequent speech, on 21 May 1945, Bose said that 'the roads to Delhi are many, like the roads to Rome'.) Nehru's 'We have gathered here . . .' is from a speech recorded, for example, on page 59 of *The Aftermath of Partition in South Asia,* by Gyanesh Kudaisya and Tan Tai Yong.

Kenneth Koch's poem 'One Train May Hide Another' is published in *The Collected Poems of Kenneth Koch.* Octavio Paz's 'high flame of rose' is from 'The Mausoleum of Humayun', in *The Collected Poems of Octavio Paz 1957–1987.*

In this chapter I was particularly dependent on the assistance of others. I would like to offer my warmest thanks to Raghu Karnad and Akhil Katyal for their kindness and care with all my questions, week after week, about Delhi, its poets, and its proverbs, and to Sophia Psarra of University College London, for the time she took to discuss Calvino's *Invisible Cities* with me. I would also like to extend my gratitude to Saif Mahmood, R. Parthasarathy and Rana Safvi, as well as Angel Gonzales of *Poetry* magazine; Theresa Knickerbocker of Skidmore College; Anand Vivek Taneja; Linda Gray Sexton; and Erin Hunt and her colleagues at the Berkshire County Historical Society. Inder Kapur and Don MacGillis, the fathers of two dear friends, helped guide me to the poetry of Delhi and of Pittsfield. I miss them both.

CHAPTER 7: CITY OF RIVERS

Translations of 'Housatonic' vary; the *Dictionary of American-Indian Place and Proper Names in New England: With Many Interpretations, Etc,* offers, under the entry 'Housetunack': *'Housatonic* River, Berkshire. "Beyond the Mountain."' The term 'Westenhook' appears on the 'Map of the Boundary between Massachusetts & New York: Showing the Ancient Colonial and Provincial Grants and Settlements', available online from the Map Collections of the University of Texas at Arlington. 'People of the Waters That Are Never Still' appears on the website of the Stockbridge-Munsee Community Band of Mohican Indians (mohican.com).

Your Hometown America Parade was broadcast from Pittsfield from 1989 to 1994 (at least). Evidence is thin for Oliver Wendell Holmes Sr's widely quoted 'There's no tonic like the Housatonic'. In *The Poet Among the Hills: Oliver Wendell Holmes in Berkshire,* J. E. A. Smith reports, on page 98, only that Holmes 'approved the time-honored local pun that the best of all tonics is the Housatonic'. (Smith also records that Holmes, on a trip to Cambridge, England, compared the River Cam's width to that of the Housatonic in Canoe Meadows.)

The Carly Simon song I reference is 'Let the River Run'. My article about Pittsfield, 'The Brooklyn of the Berkshires', was published in the *Financial Times* on 11 September 2010. In the article's penultimate paragraph I noted that Pittsfield is sometimes described as the 'Brooklyn of the Berkshires' before, in the final paragraph, I expressed scepticism of the need for and the merit of such a comparison. However, that final paragraph was deleted at the last minute, either because an editor didn't like it or for reasons of length, and the article, as printed, seems to endorse the Brooklyn of the Berkshires epithet, which now appears in Pittsfield's Wikipedia entry, with my article linked as the source.

It is difficult to pin down the share of the world's trade that passes through the Strait of Malacca. One-third is a fairly typical answer and appears, for example, in 'Whose Sea Is It Anyway?', published in September 2015 in *1843,* the *Economist*'s sister publication.

'Malaccamax' is a category but not, I was interested to learn, a standardised or regulated limit. The strait's minimum depth is 25 metres; I understand from Paul Stott of Newcastle University that a minimum depth of one metre beneath the keel is desirable, but two metres is even better.

The words of Tomé Pires are recorded as follows: 'gullet', in 'When the World Came to Southeast Asia: Malacca and the Global Economy', by Michael G. Vann in *Maritime Asia;* 'no trading port . . .' on page lxxiv of *The Suma Oriental of Tomé Pires, Books 1–5*; and 'whoever is Lord . . .' on page lxxv of the same.

The tin-animal currency and paintings I describe in Malacca are in the History and Ethnography Museum, located in the Stadthuys building. The typewriter with BRITISH EMPIRE on its paper rest is in the Baba & Nyonya Heritage Museum. The photographs of the Malacca River are displayed at the Royal Malaysian Customs Department Museum.

Examples of the characterisations of Seoul's Cheonggyecheon appear as follows: as a 'miracle' in In-ho Park's 'Miracle of Cheonggyecheon Begins . . . Expecting 23 Trillion KRW Economic Impacts', published by *Herald POP* on 27 September 2005; as an 'oasis', for example, in Kyung-min Kang's '10-Year Anniversary of Cheonggyecheon Restoration . . . Becoming a "Cultural Oasis" of the City', published in the *Hankyung* on 29 September 2015; as 'a kind of artificial fountain in which running water is pumped up and sent flowing along the course', by Eunseon Park, quoted in 'Story of cities #50: The Reclaimed Stream Bringing Life to the Heart of Seoul', by Colin Marshall in the *Guardian* on 25 May 2016; as a 'gigantic concrete fish tank' by Byung-sung Choi, in Hyuk-cheol Kwon's ' "Concrete Fish Tank": Cheonggyecheon's Wrongful Restoration Will Be Repaired', published in the *Hankyoreh* on 27 February 2012. Tadao Ando's praise ('it was impressive to walk around the reformed Cheonggyecheon . . .') is recorded in Hyung-suk Noh's 'Tadao Ando, an 'Environmental Architect', Cherishes Cheonggyecheon?', published in the *Hankyoreh* on 15 November 2007.

The statue of the Mountie stands on the south-eastern side of the pedestrian bridge in Calgary described on Google Maps as the Elbow River Traverse.

I'm deeply grateful to a number of people for their assistance with this chapter, above all to Heather Bruegl, for her generosity and her time; I very much hope we'll have a chance to meet in the Berkshires or Wisconsin in the near future. Thank you also to Monique Tyndall, her successor as director of cultural affairs for the Stockbridge-Munsee Band of Mohican Indians. Warm thanks also to Junho S. Kang for his help with research and translation, and for responding so quickly to my queries. Thank you to Masaki Hayashi of the University of Calgary for his enthusiastic guidance and advice; I would love to take him up on his offer of a trip to Bow Lake on a future visit to the city. Thank you also to Douglas Jau, Lena Schipper, Grace Moon, Paul Stott, and the Korea Tourism Organization.

CHAPTER 8: CITY OF AIR

SKYbrary (skybrary.aero) has a comprehensive explanation of hot and high flying; climate change means that pilots will have even more reason to consider the operational effects of such conditions in the years to come. The quotes from Elizabeth Bishop – 'clouds floating . . .' and 'highly impractical' – appear, for example, in 'The Art of Losing', by Elizabeth Bishop and Alice Quinn, published in the *New Yorker* on 28 March 1994. Some of the former uses of the Palácio are described in Volume XIX of the *Imperial Museum Yearbook*, available on the website of the museum (museuimperial.museus.gov.br).

The quotes from Taleb Alrefai – 'sun unlike . . .' and 'stained a rusty saffron' – appear on page 108 of *The Shadow of the Sun*.

The quotes from the short stories of Craig Loomis are taken from the following pages of *The Salmiya Collection: Stories of the Life and Times of Modern Kuwait*: 'weak tea', page 74; 'butterscotch', page 156; a 'dirty vanilla', page 184; 'sun still a red idea beyond the sand and dust', page 198.

Zahra Freeth's 'the breeze from the moving car . . .' is on page 11 of *Kuwait Was My Home*.

Alan Villiers's *Sons of Sindbad*, about the nautical traditions of the Gulf, is one of the most extraordinary books I've read; I cannot recall ever being so quickly entranced by the sense of a window opening onto a world of which I had previously known nothing. His 'good city' of Kuwait is on page 359; 'one of the most interesting . . .' is on page 308.

Lewis Scudder's description of old Kuwait's 'peculiar length and narrowness' is recorded on page 85 of Farah Al-Nakib's *Kuwait Transformed: A History of Oil and Urban Life*.

The story of the sheikh advising Villiers to leave Kuwait by camel is on page 312 of *Sons of Sindbad*; 'the lustre of its pearls . . .' is on page 359; 'youthful unmarried men . . .' is on page 322. Eleanor Calverley's 'came to expect . . .' is on page 110 of her fascinating *My Arabian Days and Nights: A Medical Missionary in Old Kuwait*. Freya Stark's 'an immense and happy loneliness' is from page 123 of her *Baghdad Sketches: Journeys Through Iraq*; she is referring to the Gulf, whose loneliness must incorporate both the land she is standing on and the surroundings of the town that she could, at that moment, already see.

More than 400 species appear on the helpful list maintained on the website of Birds of Kuwait (kuwaitbirds.org). The question of how many bird species may be seen in the UK was enjoyable to pursue. The online bird identifier of the Royal Society for the Protection of Birds (rspb.org) lists 406. Anna Feeney of the Society told me that 272 species breed in the UK, but 627 species have been seen. 'The figures for birds in the U.K. are a bit tricky, purely, as you say, because of the migrants and birds that might just pass through very occasionally.' The figure of 627, 'for example, would include the black-browed albatross, even though there's only been one individual seen'.

Najma Edrees's poem 'The Black Sparrow' begins on page 113 of *The Echo of Kuwaiti Creativity: A Collection of Translated Kuwaiti Poetry*, and Ghanima Zaid Al Harb's 'Escaping from the Coma Cage' begins on page 102. Barclay Raunkiær's 'The line of the horizon . . .' appears on page 68 of his *Through Wahhabiland on Camelback*; Freya Stark's 'Water seemed to lie before us . . .' is from page 127 of *Baghdad Sketches*.

Alrefai's 'A nasty sort of fine dust . . .' is on page 109 of *The Shadow of the Sun*. Violet Dickson's 'I thought it was a bush fire . . .' and 'and today the Bedu talk . . .' are recorded in her interview by William Tracy in the November/December 1972 issue of *Aramco World*. 'Dust storms prevalent . . .' appears on the Airport Operational Information pages for Kuwait International Airport. The story of the Imperial Airways captain is recorded by Violet Dickson on pages 122–23 of her *Forty Years in Kuwait*. 'In some periods, the winds . . .' can be found on the website of the Kuwait Meteorological Department of the Directorate General of Civil Aviation (met.gov .kw).

William Gifford Palgrave's 'the mariners of Koweyt . . .' appears on page 386 of Volume 2 of his *Narrative of a Year's Journey Through Central and Eastern Arabia, 1862–1863*. H. R. P. Dickson's 'As soon as a boy can swim . . .' appears on page 38 of his *Kuwait and Her Neighbors*. The first maritime museum I mention is the Al Hashemi Marine Museum; the second is the Maritime Museum. The extraordinary story of pearl divers and undersea springs is told by Saif Marzooq al-Shamlan on pages 103–4 of his captivating *Pearling in the Arabian Gulf: A Kuwaiti Memoir*.

Raunkiær's 'if groups of stunted tamarisk be ruled out' is on page 51 of *Through*

Wahhabiland on Camelback. 'Sri Lanka to the Zambesi' are the words of Peter Clark, the translator of Saif Marzooq al-Shamlan, on page 12 of his introduction to *Pearling in the Arabian Gulf.* Violet Dickson's 'rhythmical songs . . .' appears on page 82 of *Forty Years in Kuwait.* Ali bin Nasr al-Nejdi's 'a life for a life' is recorded by Villiers on page 310 of *Sons of Sindbad.*

I would like to express my gratitude to Sophia Vasalou of the University of Birmingham for her research, her translation of the quotations from Taleb Alrefai's *The Shadow of the Sun* and her patient help with several other questions. Thank you to Andrea Brotto for her assistance with research and translation related to the Petrópolis section. Warm thanks also to Mike Pope for one of my most memorable downroute days, anywhere in the world; to Herbert S. Klein for his thoughts on Petrópolis; to Robin Evans and Doug Wood for their helpful thoughts on aircraft performance; and to Anna Feeney for her help with counting birds.

CHAPTER 9: CITY OF BLUE

The epigraph is from Book 2, Part 2, of *Paterson*, by William Carlos Williams.

Various portions of this chapter (in particular the explanations of the sky's and the sea's colour) were previously published in, or are closely adapted from, 'From Sea to Sky – A Pilot's Life in Shades of Blue', an article I published in the *Financial Times* on 20 September 2019.

Peter Pesic's book, *Sky in a Bottle*, offers a spellbinding account of the quest for the origin of the sky's colour; I was equally reliant on Götz Hoeppe's *Why the Sky Is Blue: Discovering the Color of Life* and Michel Pastoureau's *Blue: The History of a Color.*

Obstruction lighting for aircraft can also be a flashing white; my understanding is that red lights are considered most effective at night, and flashing white lights most effective during the day. Hoeppe's discussion of the color of the Earth's ancient sky begins on page 272 of his book.

The Tom Waits song I refer to is 'Ruby's Arms'. The Virginia Woolf quote about the pleasing equivalence of the sea and sky is from Part 3, Chapter 7 of *To the Lighthouse* (which is Chapter 8 of my e-book version, for some reason). The data on the most popular colour comes from YouGovAmerica's article 'Why Is Blue the World's Favorite Color?', published on 12 May 2015. I was unable to find data on the favourite colours of South Africans.

Much of what I learned about Saussure came from Pesic's *Sky in a Bottle*; the quote I include by Saussure is on page 60 of that book. The blue flower motif in Romanticism derives, as I understand it, from the 1802 novel *Heinrich von Ofterdingen*, by Novalis; I came to it through Penelope Fitzgerald's 1995 novel *The Blue Flower.* I first encountered Goethe's description of blue in '19th-Century Insight into the Psychology of Color and Emotion', by Maria Popova, published in the *Atlantic* on 17 August 2012.

The Herman Melville quote about 'overlapping spurs of mountains bathed in their hill-side blue' appears in the sixth paragraph of the first chapter of *Moby-Dick*. He mentions 'the valley of the Saco' – the river in north-eastern New England, presumably – but it's not too much of a stretch to imagine he was looking up at the Berkshire hills between the writing of these words.

There are various explanations for Cape Town's 'Mother City' epithet; perhaps the most straightforward is that it is widely described as the first city in South Africa. (I'm sure 'Tavern of the Seas' requires no explanation.)

Hans Neuberger's 1970 paper, 'Climate in Art', describes his survey of more than 12,000 paintings, and what they reveal about the climate of different places.

The reference to the archaeologist Jayson Orton is based on our correspondence via email, and 'An Unusual Pre-Colonial Burial from Bloubergstrand, Table Bay, South Africa', a paper he co-authored in *The South African Archaeological Bulletin*.

The calculation for the percentage of the world's population that lives north of Cape Town was initially laborious, and then easy. At first, I took the world's population and subtracted the entire populations of all the countries that Cape Town's latitude passes through, and then I added back in cities in those countries that were obviously to the north of Cape Town. Eventually, Susana B. Adamo from Columbia University's Center for International Earth Science Information Network directed me to an online tool (sedac.ciesin.columbia.edu/mapping/popest/pes-v3/) that provides the population of a user-selected geographic area. I found it fascinating to explore how unevenly settled the world is.

Bradley Rink's paper 'The Aeromobile Tourist Gaze: Understanding Tourism "From Above"' was published in *Tourism Geographies* in 2017. The quote from George Bernard Shaw appeared in the *Cape Times* on 25 January 1932.

Cape Town's reliance on long-haul tourism is clear to visitors; it's also documented by reports such as the World Travel & Tourism Council's 'City Travel & Tourism Impact 2019'.

The idea that city life is more environmentally friendly is perhaps counterintuitive, but it seems well supported. See, for example, Richard Florida's article 'Why Bigger Cities Are Greener', published on Bloomberg's website on 19 April 2012. Although, for an alternative perspective, see 'The Myth of the Sustainable City', published on *Scientific American*'s website on 21 August 2016.

Some of Cape Town's recent green-economy initiatives can be found at the website of GreenCape (greencape.co.za). The Economist Intelligence Unit's Green City Index ranked Cape Town as one of the leading African cities. From a traveller's perspective, the company Tourlane ranked Cape Town as the second-best African city (after Nairobi) for sustainable travel.

My awareness of the Southern Ocean has been hugely enriched by Joy McCann's *Wild Sea*. Mount Greylock's height is typically given as 3,491 feet (for example, on the official website of Mount Greylock State Reservation) but 3,489 feet is also sometimes seen.

Figures for the population of the Cape Flats are difficult to find. Documents for the Cape Flats Planning District, based on 2011 census data, give a population of around 583,000. The comparable figure for the Mitchells Plain/Khayelitsha Planning District, a region that many would consider part of the Cape Flats, is 1,113,000. These sum to 1,696,000. In 2011, the metropolitan area's population was 3,698,000, according to the United Nations' World Population Prospects (in 2021 it was 4,710,000).

Leonardo da Vinci's quote about rendering further objects bluer can be found in *Leonardo's Notebooks: Writing and Art of the Great Master*, edited by H. Anna Suh.

'Every Thursday at 4 p.m.' is widely associated with the Union-Castle liners; see, for example, *The Port of Southampton*, by Ian Collard. I described a little of the Union-Castle history in my first book, *Skyfaring*.

Nelson Mandela's description of Cape Town and Robben Island from above appears in Part 8, Chapter 59 of his *Long Walk to Freedom: The Autobiography of Nelson Mandela* (which I'm grateful to my stepmother for giving me, one Christmas long ago).

The description of Krotoa as a 'peacebroker' is by Nobhongo Gxolo in 'The History of Van Riebeek's Slave Krotoa Unearthed from the Masters' View', published on the website of the *Mail & Guardian* on 5 September 2016. The description of Krotoa as a 'matriarch of resistance' appears in the title of 'Special Role of Krotoa, Khoi Matriarch of Resistance', an article in the *Cape Times,* which appeared online on 30 August 2019. The proposal to rename Cape Town's airport for Krotoa is described in 'What's in a Name? Cape Town Airport Debate Gets Heated', published by the Associated Press on 5 June 2018.

The Twitter handle of the Signal Hill gun is @Signal_Hill_Gun. The quote from Jan Morris about the sole good road out from Cape Town appears on pages 32–33 of *Heaven's Command*, the first of the three volumes of her extraordinary *Pax Britannica Trilogy*. I found the figure for the number of shipwrecks in Table Bay, and the decision by Lloyd's not to insure ships that wintered in Cape Town, among the exhibits of the Iziko Maritime Centre in Cape Town.

I came across the quotation from Michael Faraday in Pesic's *Sky in a Bottle*. For information on the scientific investigations of the ocean's colour, see, for example, oceancolor.gsfc.nasa.gov.

After recalling David Feldman's book *Why Do Clocks Run Clockwise?*, which my mom gave me many years ago, I was determined to stare at the sundial in the Company's Garden long enough to perceive its shadow moving anticlockwise, as it must in the Southern Hemisphere, but my desire for coffee overcame me.

The quote from Pastoureau's *Blue: The History of a Color* appears on page 34 of that book, and the description of the absence of blue in Greek ceramics on page 25; the translation of ultramarine appears on page 25 of Pesic's *Sky in a Bottle*.

The seal of the Castle of Good Hope – on welcome signs, for example – uses the old Dutch *Casteel*, rather than the *Kasteel* of modern Afrikaans. My description of the castle as the hub of a communications network is based on exhibits within the castle museum.

Nobhongo Gxolo's description of her visit to the castle appears in her *Mail & Guardian* article noted above.

Buhlebezwe Siwani's extraordinary 2015 photograph *iGagasi* and her other work can be found at her website, buhlebezwesiwani.com.

The biographical information on Tuan Guru is taken from the website of the Auwal Mosque and from 'Tuan Guru: Prince, Prisoner, Pioneer', published by Gerrie Lubbe in *Religion in Southern Africa*. The biographical information for Tuan Said Aloewie is based on signs in the cemetery, from which 'banished to the Cape to be kept in chains' is also taken.

In addition to the news sources cited above, I frequently found myself browsing the websites of South African History Online (sahistory.org.za), *National Geographic*, *BBC Science Focus* magazine (sciencefocus.com) and the BBC. For a general history of one of the world's most fascinating nations, I recommend Leonard Thompson's acclaimed *A History of South Africa*.

I'm grateful to Bradley Rink and Nomusa Makhubu for all their guidance, helpfulness and patience with my many questions. I would also like to thank Buhlebezwe Siwani, Andrew Flowers, Suzanne Lang, Paul Beauchamp, Susana B. Adamo and Jayson Orton; and I would like to express my particular thanks to Robert Pincus for his detailed feedback on my explanations of the sky's and the sea's colour, both for my *Financial Times* article and again for the versions in this chapter.

CHAPTER 10: CITY OF SNOW

The section on Istanbul is adapted from 'Four Cities in a Day', an article I wrote for *The Monocle Escapist* in the summer of 2015.

The description of Istanbul as 'sovereign over all others' appears in Michael Krondl's *The Taste of Conquest: The Rise and Fall of the Three Great Cities of Spice*, a book about the spice trade; its description as the 'Queen of Cities' is from the preface to Thomas F. Madden's extraordinary book *Istanbul: City of Majesty at the Crossroads of the World*, in a list of some of the city's names: 'Byzantion, New Rome, Antoniniana, Constantinople, Queen of Cities, Miklagard, Tsargrad, Stamboul, Islambul, the Gate of Happiness, and perhaps most eloquently of all, "the City"'. In our correspondence, Dr Madden pointed out that Istanbul has been Europe's largest city for a millennium now – albeit not continuously.

The quote concerning how the 'trolley car schedules suffered to a marked extent' appeared on page 2 of the *Berkshire Evening Eagle* on 9 March 1916. Recent local write-ups sometimes give a total of 20 inches for the 1916 storm; but the following day, on page 2 of the same paper, the total is updated to 24 inches. Canoe Meadows Wildlife Sanctuary is one of my favourite places in the world; its upkeep relies on the dues-paying members of the Massachusetts Audubon Society (massaudubon.org).

The translation of *Yrväderstisdagen* has proved both frustrating and fascinating. Swedish relatives and correspondents have offered various suggestions, including: Whirlwind Tuesday, Crazy Weather Tuesday, Dizzy Weather Tuesday and Blizzard Tuesday. One cousin advised that the term would make most Swedes think of 'strong winds and horizontal snow', but that the term can also be used to describe a person as wild, or as a whirlwind. Olaus Magnus's quote 'it seems more a matter for amazement . . .' is from ' "Things to Be Marveled at Rather than Examined": Olaus Magnus and "A Description of the Northern Peoples"', by Barbara Sjoholm, in the *Antioch Review*.

Several sentences in this chapter are adapted from 'Enjoying Snow, While We Still Have It', an article I published in the *New York Times* on 26 January 2013. In it, I mentioned the non-profit Protect Our Winters (protectourwinters.org), which focuses on climate change issues from the perspective of those who love outdoor winter activities.

The quote about the snow in New York on the night before my father's death – 'strangely immune to gravity – blowing up and sideways as well as down' – and the maximum wind speed at Kennedy Airport are from 'In Wind, Snow, Cold and Frustration, a Dangerous Storm', an article published in the *New York Times* on 9 March 2005.

As happy as I am to share the quotations from Ukichirō Nakaya's *Snow Crystals: Natural and Artificial*, I'm sorry it's not possible to include any of the many photographs that make his book even more of a treasure. Indeed, I can't recommend it highly enough as a gift for the lover of snow. The quotes I use as epigraphs for the four subsections of the Sapporo section are found, respectively, on pages 306, 54, 80 and 7 of his book. Versions of his 'letters from the sky' quote appear in various sources, including 'Ukichiro Nakaya – 1900–1962', an obituary published by Akira Higashi in *Journal of Glaciology* in 1962. There are English versions that use 'hieroglyphs' rather than 'letters', but my understanding is that the commonly referenced Japanese version of his quote refers to letters in the sense of correspondence, rather than the units of a writing system.

To the best of my knowledge, the snowflake-like symbol of the Hokkaido Airports Company was originally a reference to a prefectural flag, and in turn to the North Star; today, the company's website suggests that its seven points also refer to seven of Hokkaido's airports. 'The Dawn of a New Age: Birth of the Aeropolis of the North' appears on a sign in the Airport History Museum.

Lists of the snowiest cities on Earth are problematic, both because the underlying statistics are not always up to date, and also because some such lists are dominated by places that are very snowy but not very large. Be that as it may, Aomori tops many lists, regardless of their methodology, and I haven't yet come across one on which Sapporo isn't the snowiest major city.

Images of Mama-san Danpu snow shovels are available at mama-dump.com, where the 'Mama-san can carry snow like a dump truck' quote also appeared. Snow suspenders for trees aren't only a Sapporo thing; they're found in many other parts of Japan, including Kanazawa, where I spent my summer homestay.

One of the stronger Massachusetts-Hokkaido bonds ('Sister States since 1990, Friends Since 1876', as the Hokkaido Association of Massachusetts puts it) was forged by William S. Clark. Born in 1826 in Ashfield, a small settlement about thirty miles east of Pittsfield that even today has fewer than 2,000 inhabitants, Clark spearheaded the development of what would become the University of Massachusetts. The Japanese government invited him to Sapporo in the late nineteenth century to found the future Hokkaido University, the same university at which Ukichirō Nakaya would later carry out his pioneering studies of snow.

The story known as 'The Divine Snowball Fight' is recorded by Umejirō Kudō in *Ainu Folk Tales*. The story of the magic fan is titled 'The Younger Sister of Kotankor-kamuy'; it was recorded by Tōru Asai in *Ainu Yukar: The Stories of Gods and the Ainu*. 'The Flying Sled', by Hideo Oguma, is translated by David G. Goodman in *Long, Long Autumn Nights: Selected Poems of Oguma Hideo, 1901–1940*. My three quotations are from pages 84, 86 and 96, respectively.

The words of the curator at the Noguchi Museum in Queens – 'arguably the most ubiquitous sculpture on the planet' – are quoted in 'Why Isamu Noguchi's Lanterns Are So Beloved', published on the website of *Architectural Digest* on 18 June 2017.

In this chapter I was greatly helped by Hayden Herrera's eloquently titled *Listening to Stone: The Art and Life of Isamu Noguchi*. Noguchi's 'airplane and jet propulsion' quote is recorded in Chapter 46 of that book; his 'the aeroplane wing in its relation to the fuselage' appears in footnote 5 of the same chapter; his 'Moses just laughed . . .' in Chapter 16; his 'The child's world . . .' in Chapter 41.

'Play Mountain was my response . . .' is from the online write-up of Episode 351 of the podcast *99% Invisible*, about Play Mountain. Liane Pei describes her parents' friendships with Noguchi and other artists in 'Christie's to Offer the Collection of Eileen and I.M. Pei', a press release published on the website of Christie's on 27 August 2019. I also relied on 'A Journey to Isamu Noguchi's Last Work', by Alexandra Lange, on curbed.com.

The story of Santa, the cross and the department store window is well known among foreigners in Japan. It was rated as 'Legend' (that is, 'essentially unprovable') in 'Santa Hung on a Cross in Japan?', published on snopes.com on 23 October 1999.

The Japanese elements of the *Pequod* are described in Chapter 16 of *Moby-Dick;* 'Her masts – cut somewhere on the coast of Japan, where her original ones were lost overboard in a gale – her masts stood stiffly up like the spines of the three old kings of Cologne.' The Norman Rockwell painting above Kathleen's mantelpiece is the widely beloved *Home for Christmas*.

In writing this chapter I turned repeatedly to the *Japan Times* (japantimes.co.jp) and the *South China Morning Post* (scmp.com), as well as to the websites of the Isamu Noguchi Foundation and Garden Museum (noguchi.org), Uppsala University (uu.se), Japan-guide.com, the Church of Sweden (svenskakyrkan.se), Swedavia Airports (swedavia.com), the British Museum (britishmuseum.org) and the Institute of Low Temperature Science at Hokkaido University (lowtem.hokudai.ac.jp).

I am very grateful to Yukako Okamoto and Lisa Hofmann-Kuroda for their great care and attention in assisting with the research and translation for the Sapporo section of this chapter. I'm also grateful to Miyuki Chiba for her kindness to a stranger; I hope that someday we will have the chance to meet. I'm grateful to Nathalie Ehrström for her research and translation assistance with the Uppsala section, and to Kenneth Libbrecht for his guidance and his wonderful books about snow. I would also like to thank Didrik Vanhoenacker, Ewa Söderpalm, Nadine Willems, Jenni Glaser, Morgan Giles, Peter Gibbs, Edouard Engels, Mei Shibata, Drew Tagliabue, George Greenstein, John Villasenor, Lennart Wern, Edward Lu and Kevin Carr.

CHAPTER 11: CITY OF CIRCLES

Sheila Barry's obituary was published in the *Berkshire Eagle* on 31 March 2018.

There is a lovely map of the coal posts around London available at the web-

site of the North Mymms History Project (northmymmshistory.uk). I was struck
by the description of Londinium's location – 'the lowest bridgeable point on the
Thames' – in the prelude to Robert Tombs's marvelous *The English and Their History*. Today's A1 is associated with the Roman-era Ermine Street and the Great North
Road, but not exactly; it does incorporate Upper Street in Islington.

The history of Baghdad on which I most relied is Justin Marozzi's *Baghdad: City
of Peace, City of Blood*, which is where I came across al-Yaqubi's description of the
city as 'crossroads of the universe'. Al-Mansur's hope that Baghdad would become
'a waterfront for the world' comes from Lincoln Paine's extraordinary *The Sea and
Civilization: A Maritime History of the World*; Paine also notes that a mere fifty years
after its foundation, Baghdad had grown to be the world's largest city outside China.
I have not been able to confirm the exact derivation of the 'BI' in the airport code
ORBI, though 'Baghdad International' seems a safe bet. It seems that the previous
code (ORBS) and name (Saddam International Airport) were changed to the current
ones after the start of the Iraq War in 2003.

Several sentences in this chapter's second London section are adapted from 'A
Pilot's Rapturous Return to Transatlantic Flight', an article I published in the *Financial Times* on 11 November 2021. Leanne O'Sullivan's lovely poem 'Note' is available on the website of Poems on the Underground (poemsontheunderground.org/
note) and is perhaps still in circulation on trains, too. It was published in her book *A
Quarter of an Hour*.

Capturing even a basic English sense of the names of the places that the Yamanote
Line connects proved a fascinating challenge: my Japanese language skills are limited;
the provenance of many names is disputed, while others make sense only within a
cultural context that is almost impossible to summarise neatly; and some characters
are used phonetically, without regard to their meaning, which makes literal translations problematic, to say the least.

As I've noted elsewhere, it's difficult to compare the populations of cities and
metropolitan areas whose boundaries may be defined so differently. However, *The
World's Cities in 2018*, a report by the United Nations, gives 37.5 million for the
population of Tokyo, and notes that by 2030 Delhi will overtake Tokyo as the world's
largest city.

It's possible that the first person to circumnavigate the world was not a European
member of Magellan's crew (Magellan himself was killed in the Philippines), but
rather the enslaved man known as Enrique, whom Magellan acquired in 1511 in
Malacca, and whom he brought west to Europe, and then took on the westbound
1519 expedition. Enrique left Magellan's crew in Southeast Asia – but still to the east
of Malacca – where records of his story end.

The list I referred to for the world's busiest train stations appeared in various publications in Japan in 2013 (for example, in *Japan Today* on 6 February 2013). The list was widely shared and as late as 2018 reputable sources, such as Bloomberg, were still relying on it. But even setting aside the effects of the pandemic on public transport, it must nevertheless now be out of date. Although I have not been able to find a more recent list, nor the complete data that would allow me to compile my own, it seems certain that an updated list would show more stations in China, where I often visit railway termini (in Beijing, for example) that seem to be as large and as busy as many of those in Tokyo.

The camera store near Shinjuku Station is Yodobashi Camera; its extraordinary earworm of a jingle can easily be found on YouTube.

'Earthen Banks' is from Saisei Murō's book *Those Who Came from Stars*. Takako Lento's complete translation of it follows here. (Murō also wrote a poem titled 'The Yamanote Line'.)

EARTHEN BANKS (土手)

At the far end of the Tabata station is an overpass.
Earthen banks on both sides of the overpass
Have now turned lush green with deep dense grasses
I make a point of taking a walk there in the morning
In the afternoon when I get bored with work
Even after dinner I take a walk there

Strange to see the opposite bank in the evening
Lie swollen and solid
The bank this side is also long and dark
Reminding me of a deep valley
Roofs of homes over the other side
Trees surrounding those roofs
Beautiful stars flickering among trees
Soft soothing winds stroke me
Like breath from the greenery

Once in a while between them the Yamanote Line train travels
Windows brightly lit
White clothes flickering
Rounded knees of a woman passenger
The single signal is shivering in blue

Even when I am so very tired
I feel refreshed when I come to these banks
No one walks there at night
Only the wind whispers . . .

When I first began to learn Japanese I was struck by how the role of Chinese charac-ters in the language seemed to have no direct parallel in English. Any analogy, then, is problematic, but the effort to make one is nonetheless fascinating. The comparison of the relationship between Latin and English to that between Chinese and Japanese is common; but then, English has its Greek-derived words, too (some of which, of course, passed through Latin on their journey to us).

The Yamanote Line departure melodies are available online (for example, at eki .weebly.com/yamanote-line.html).

In this chapter I was particularly reliant on the websites of the BBC and *Japan Times* (japantimes.co.jp), as well as on information I found at VisitBritain (visit britain.com), WRAL-TV (wral.com), Japan Visitor (japanvisitor.com) and Live Japan (livejapan.com).

Sachiko Kaku first brought Saisei Murō's work to my attention, and in the course of her generous correspondence she also provided me with several other insights into the history and stories associated with the Yamanote Line. I'm grateful to Takako Lento for her translations of Murō's work and the biographical research she prepared on his life, and I hope that her kindness to me will bring his writing to the attention of a wider English readership. My enormous thanks are due to Lisa Hofmann-Kuroda for her patience with fact-checking and with all my place-name translation questions, and to Mei Shibata and Yukako Okamoto for sharing their memories of the Yama-note Line. Thank you to Ilya Birman for his kind help with my description of Mos-cow's various circle lines. Deb Cairns, Wako Tawa, Kevin Carr and Jarrett Walker also provided invaluable assistance with this chapter.

Words are insufficient to express my gratitude to Cindy and Dan for their warmth and open-hearted hospitality. I am very glad to know them.

Bibliography

Addis, Ferdinand. *The Eternal City: A History of Rome*. Pegasus Books, 2018.

al-Hazimi Mansour, and Salma Khandra Jayyusi and Ezzat Khattab. *Beyond the Dunes: An Anthology of Modern Saudi Literature*. Palgrave Macmillan, 2006.

Al-Ḥijji, Yacoub Yusuf. *Kuwait and the Sea: A Brief Social and Economic History*. Arabian Publishing, 2010.

Al-Nakib, Farah. *Kuwait Transformed: A History of Oil and Urban Life*. Stanford University Press, 2016.

Al-Sanusi, Haifa. *The Echo of Kuwaiti Creativity: Collection of Kuwaiti Poetry*. Center for Research and Studies on Kuwait, 2006.

Al-Shamlan, Saif Marzooq. *Pearling in the Arabian Gulf: A Kuwaiti Memoir*. London Center for Arabic Studies, 2000.

Alharbi, Thamer Hamdan. 'The Development of Housing in Jeddah: Changes in Built Form from the Traditional to the Modern', PhD thesis, Newcastle University, 1989.

Ali, Agha Shahid. *The Half-Inch Himalayas*. Wesleyan University Press, 2011.

Allawi, Ali A. *Faisal I of Iraq*. Yale University Press, 2014.

Allison, Mary Bruins. *Doctor Mary in Arabia: Memoirs*. University of Texas Press, 2010.

Almino, João. *The Five Seasons of Love*. Host Publications, 2008.

Alrefai, Taleb. *Zill al-shams (The Shadow of the Sun)*. Dar Al-Shuruq, 2012.

Alshehri, Atef, and Mercedes Corbell. 'Al-Balad, The Historic Core of Jeddah: A Time Travelogue', *Once Upon Design: New Routes for Arabian Heritage*, exhibition catalogue, 2016, 17–28.

Anderson, Benedict. *Imagined Communities: Reflections on the Origin and Spread of Nationalism*. Verso, 2006.

Anderson, Robert Thomas. *Denmark: Success of a Developing Nation*. Schenkman Publishing, 1975.

Angst, Gabriel Freitas. *Brasília Travel Guide: English Edition*. Formigas Viajantes, 2020.

Annual Reports of the Officers of the Berkshire Athenaeum and Museum. Berkshire Athenaeum and Museum, 1903.

Anthony, John Duke, and John A. Hearty. 'Eastern Arabian States: Kuwait, Bahrain, Qatar, the United Arab Emirates, and Oman'. *The Government and Politics of the Middle East and North Africa,* edited by David E. Long and Bernard Reich. Westview, 2002, 129–63.

Arkeonews. https://arkeonews.net/bosphorus-was-frozen-people-crossed-by-walking/. Accessed September 20, 2021.

Asai, Tōru. 'The Younger Sister of Kotan-kor-kamuy'. *Ainu Yukar: The Stories of Gods and the Ainu*. Chikumashobo Ltd., 1987.

Baan, Iwan et al., editors. *Brasilia-Chandigarh: Living with Modernity*. Prestel Publishing, 2010.

Banham, Reyner. *Los Angeles: The Architecture of Four Ecologies*. University of California Press, 2009.

Bartels, Emily C. 'Imperialist Beginnings: Richard Hakluyt and the Construction of Africa'. *Criticism*, vol. 34, no. 4, 1992, 517–38.

BBC Science Focus Magazine. https://www.sciencefocus.com/space/what-colour-is-the-sky-on-an-exoplanet/. Accessed September 14, 2021.

Beal, Sophia. *The Art of Brasília: 2000–2019*. Springer International Publishing, 2020.

Beard, Mary. *S.P.Q.R.: A History of Ancient Rome*. Liveright, 2015.

Berkshire County Historical Society. *Pittsfield*. Arcadia, 2016.

Berkshire Natural Resources Council. https://www.bnrc.org/land-trusts-role-expanding-narrative-mohican-homelands/?blm_aid=24641. Accessed August 16, 2021.

Berry, Wendell. *Collected Poems, 1957–1982*. North Point Press, 1985.

———. *Wendell Berry: Essays 1969–1990*. Library of America, 2019.

The Bible, New King James Version. Thomas Nelson, 2005.

The Bible, 1599 Geneva Version. https://www.biblegateway.com/. Accessed May 1, 2021.

Bidwell House Museum. https://www.bidwellhousemuseum.org/blog/2020/06/16/the-last-skirmish-of-king-philips-war-1676-part-ii/. Accessed August 16, 2021.

Bloom, Harold, editor. *John Steinbeck's 'The Grapes of Wrath'*. Chelsea House, 2009.

Boltwood, Edward. *The History of Pittsfield, Massachusetts: From the Year 1876 to the Year 1916*. City of Pittsfield, 1916.

Bose, Subhas Chandra. *Famous Speeches and Letters of Subhas Chandra Bose*. Lion Press, 1946.

Boston Public Library. https://www.bpl.org/news/mckim-building-125th-anniversary/. Accessed June 5, 2021.

Boston: An Old City with New Opportunities. Boston Chamber of Commerce, Bureau of Commercial and Industrial Affairs, 1922.

Breese, Gerald. 'Delhi-New Delhi: Capital for Conquerors and Country'. *Ekistics,* vol. 39, no. 232, 1975, 181–84.

Bruchac, Margaret, and Peter Thomas. 'Locating 'Wissatinnewag' in John Pynchon's Letter of 1663'. *Historical Journal of Massachusetts,* vol. 34, no. 1, Winter 2006.

Buchan, James. *Jeddah, Old and New.* Stacey International, 1991.

Buhlebezwe Siwani. https://www.buhlebezwesiwani.com/igagasi-2015-1. Accessed August 31, 2021.

Bulkeley, Morgan. *Berkshire Stories.* Lindisfarne Books, 2004.

Burton, Isabel, and William Henry Wilkins. *The Romance of Isabel, Lady Burton: The Story of Her Life.* New York, 1897.

Burton, Richard Francis. *The City of the Saints: And Across the Rocky Mountains to California.* New York, 1862.

———. *Personal Narrative of a Pilgrimage to Mecca and Medina.* Leipzig, 1874.

Calgary River Valleys. http://calgaryrivervalleys.org/wp-content/uploads/2014/12/Get-to-Know-the-Bow-River-second-edition-2014.pdf. Accessed August 17, 2021.

California Historic Route 66 Association. https://www.route66ca.org/. Accessed June 5, 2021.

Calverley, Eleanor. *My Arabian Days and Nights.* Crowell, 1958.

Calvino, Italo. *Invisible Cities.* Houghton Mifflin Harcourt, 2013.

Carlstrom, Jeffrey, and Cynthia Furse. *The History of Emigration Canyon: Gateway to Salt Lake Valley.* Lulu, 2019.

Cathedral of Our Lady of the Angels. http://www.olacathedral.org/cathedral/about/homily1.html. Accessed June 6, 2021.

Ceria, Eugenio. *The Biographical Memoirs of Saint John Bosco.* Volume 16. Salesiana Publishers, 1995.

Cheonggyecheon Museum. https://museum.seoul.go.kr/eng/about/cheongGyeMuse.jsp. Accessed August 17, 2021.

Christie's. https://www.christies.com/about-us/press-archive/details?PressReleaseID=9465&lid=1. Accessed October 19, 2021.

City of Boston. https://www.boston.gov/departments/tourism-sports-and-entertainment/symbols-city-boston#:~:text=the%20motto%2C%20%E2%80%9CSICUT%20PATRIBUS%2C1822.%E2%80%9D. Accessed June 3, 2021.

City of Pittsburgh, Pennsylvania. https://pittsburghpa.gov/pittsburgh/flag-seal. Accessed May 26, 2021.

Cleveland, Harold Irwin. 'Fifty-Five Years in Business'. *Magazine of Business* 1906, 455–66.

Collard, Ian. *The Port of Southampton.* Amberley Publishing, 2019.

Corne, Lucy, et al. *Lonely Planet Cape Town & the Garden Route.* Lonely Planet Global Limited, 2018.

Cortesao, Armando, editor. *The Suma Oriental of Tomé Pires, Books 1–5.* Asian Educational Services, 2005.

'CPI Profile – Jeddah'. Ministry of Municipal and Rural Affairs and United Nations Human Settlements Programme, 2019.

Cramer, J. A. *A Geographical and Historical Description of Ancient Italy.* Clarendan, 1826.

Crowley, Thomas. *Fractured Forest, Quartzite City: A History of Delhi and Its Ridge.* Sage Publications, 2020.

Crus, Paulo J. S., editor. *Structures and Architecture – Bridging the Gap and Crossing Borders: Proceedings of the Fourth International Conference on Structures and Architecture.* CRC Press, 2019.

Curbed. https://archive.curbed.com/2016/12/1/13778884/noguchi-playground-moe renuma-japan. Accessed September 2, 2021.

Dalrymple, William. *City of Djinns: A Year in Delhi.* Penguin, 2003.

———. *The Last Mughal: The Fall of Delhi, 1857.* Bloomsbury, 2009.

Danforth, Loring M. *Crossing the Kingdom: Portraits of Saudi Arabia.* University of California Press, 2016.

Daoud, Hazim S. *Flora of Kuwait.* Volume 1. Taylor & Francis, 2013.

Davis, Margaret Leslie. *Rivers in the Desert: William Mulholland and the Inventing of Los Angeles.* Open Road Media, 2014.

Dayton Aviation Heritage. https://www.nps.gov/daav/learn/historyculture/index .htm. Accessed May 26, 2021.

Delbanco, Andrew. *Melville: His World and Work.* Knopf Doubleday, 2013.

Dickson, H .R. P. *The Arab of the Desert: A Glimpse into Badawin Life in Kuwait and Saudi Arabia.* Taylor & Francis, 2015.

———. *Kuwait and Her Neighbours.* Allen & Unwin, 1956.

Dickson, Violet. *Forty Years in Kuwait.* Allen & Unwin, 1978.

Dinesen, Isak. *Seven Gothic Tales.* Vintage International, 1991.

District Aurangabad. https://aurangabad.gov.in/history/. Accessed July 2, 2021.

'Djeddah – La Ville de la Grand'mere'. *L'Illustration,* June 12, 1926.

Douglas-Lithgow, Robert Alexander. *Dictionary of American-Indian Place and Proper Names in New England.* Salem Press, 1909.

Dowall, David E., and Paavo Monkkonen. 'Consequences of the "Plano Piloto": The

Urban Development and Land Markets of Brasília', *Urban Studies*, vol. 44, no. 10, 2007, 1871–87.

Drew, Bernard A., and Ronald Latham. *Literary Luminaries of the Berkshires: From Herman Melville to Patricia Highsmith.* Arcadia Publishing, 2015.

Dunn, Ross E. *The Adventures of Ibn Battuta: A Muslim Traveler of the Fourteenth Century.* University of California Press, 2012.

East Village. https://www.evexperience.com/blog/2019/9/19/behind-the-masks-katie -greens-bridge-installation. Accessed August 17, 2021.

Edwards, Brian et al., editors. *Courtyard Housing: Past, Present and Future.* Taylor & Francis, 2006.

1843. https://www.economist.com/1843/2015/09/30/whose-sea-is-it-anyway. Accessed October 18, 2021.

Eleanor Roosevelt Papers Project. https://www2.gwu.edu/~erpapers/myday/display doc.cfm?_y=1946&_f=md000294. Accessed June 3, 2021.

Emblidge, David. *Southern New England.* Stackpole Books, 2012.

Environmental Protection Agency. https://www.epa.gov/ge-housatonic/cleaning -housatonic. Accessed August 16, 2021.

Facey, William, and Gillian Grant. *Kuwait by the First Photographers.* I. B. Tauris, 1999.

Fanshawe, H. C. *Delhi: Past and Present.* John Murray, 1902.

Feldman, David. *Why Do Clocks Run Clockwise? An Imponderables Book.* Harper-Collins, 2005.

Fireman, Janet R., and Manuel P. Servin. 'Miguel Costansó: California's Forgotten Founder', *California Historical Society Quarterly*, vol. 49, no. 1, March 1970, 3–19.

Fitzgerald, Penelope. *The Blue Flower.* Flamingo, 1995.

Flood, Finbarr Barry, and Gulru Necipoglu. *A Companion to Islamic Art and Architecture.* Wiley, 2017.

Florida Department of Transportation. https://www.fdot.gov/docs/default-source /traffic/trafficservices/pdfs/Pres-control_city.pdf. Accessed June 5, 2021.

Foreign Affairs. https://www.foreignaffairs.com/reviews/capsule-review/2007-11-01 /last-mughal-fall-dynasty-delhi-1857-indian-summer-secret-history. Accessed August 9, 2021.

Forster, E. M. *Howards End.* Penguin, 2007.

Fort Calgary. https://www.fortcalgary.com/history. Accessed August 17, 2021.

Fortescue, John William. *Narrative of the Visit to India of Their Majesties, King George V. and Queen Mary: And of the Coronation Durbar Held at Delhi, 12th December, 1911.* Macmillan, 1912.

Fraser, Valerie. *Building the New World: Studies in the Modern Architecture of Latin America, 1930–1960*. Verso, 2000.

Frazier, Patrick. *The Mohicans of Stockbridge*. University of Nebraska Press, 1994.

Freeth, Zahra Dickson. *Kuwait Was My Home*. Allen & Unwin, 1956.

Freitag, Ulrike. *A History of Jeddah: The Gate to Mecca in the Nineteenth and Twentieth Centuries*. Cambridge University Press, 2020.

Frémont, John Charles. *Geographical Memoir Upon Upper California, in Illustration of His Map of Oregon and California*. Wendell and Benthuysen, 1848.

Gladding, Effie Price. *Across the Continent by the Lincoln Highway*. Good Press, 2019.

Globo. http://especiais.santosdumont.eptv.g1.globo.com/onde-tudo-terminou/amorte /NOT,0,0,1278057,Uma+historia+cheia+de+misterio.aspx. Accessed September 5, 2021.

Grondahl, Paul. *Mayor Corning: Albany Icon, Albany Enigma*. State University of New York Press, 2007.

Gudde, Erwin Gustav. *California Place Names: The Origin and Etymology of Current Geographical Names*. University of California Press, 1960.

Gupta, Narayani, editor. *The Delhi Omnibus*. Oxford University Press, 2002.

Gyeongbokgung Palace. http://www.royalpalace.go.kr:8080/html/eng_gbg/data /data_01.jsp. Accessed August 17, 2021.

Handbook of Rio de Janeiro. Rio de Janeiro, 1887.

Hasan, Hadi. *Mughal Poetry: Its Cultural and Historical Value*. Aakar Books, 2008.

Hearn, Gordon Risley. *The Seven Cities of Delhi*. W. Thacker & Company, 1906.

Heinly, Burt A., 'The Los Angeles Aqueduct: Causes of Low Cost and Rapidity of Construction'. *Architect and Engineer*, vol. XIX, no. 3, January 1910.

Heinz History Center. https://www.heinzhistorycenter.org/blog/western-pennsylva nia-history/pittsburgh-the-city-of-bridges. Accessed September 4, 2021.

Herrera, Hayden. *Listening to Stone: The Art and Life of Isamu Noguchi*. Farrar, Straus and Giroux, 2015.

Higashi, Akira. 'Ukichiro Nakaya – 1900–1962'. *Journal of Glaciology*, vol. 4, no. 33, 1962, 378–80.

'Historic Jeddah: Gate to Makkah'. Saudi Commission for Tourism and Antiquities, January 2013.

'History of Pittsfield'. City of Pittsfield, https://www.cityofpittsfield.org/residents /history_of_pittsfield/index.php. Accessed May 14, 2021.

Hitchman, Francis. *Richard F. Burton: His Early, Private and Public Life; with an Account of His Travels and Explorations*. London, 1887.

Hoeppe, Götz. *Why the Sky Is Blue: Discovering the Color of Life*. Translated by John Stewart. Princeton University Press, 2007.

Holmes, Oliver Wendell. *Poetical Works*. London, 1852.

Holston, James. *The Modernist City: An Anthropological Critique of Brasília*. University of Chicago Press, 1989.

Homer. *The Iliad*. Penguin Classics, 1991.

Honig, Edwin. 'Review: The City of Man'. *Poetry*, vol. 69, no. 5, February 1947, 277–84.

Honjo, Masahiko, editor. *Urbanization and Regional Development, Vol. 6*. United Nations Centre for Regional Development, 1981.

Hornsey Historical Society. https://hornseyhistorical.org.uk/brief-history-highgate/. Accessed July 2, 2021.

Housatonic Heritage https://housatonicheritage.org/heritage-programs/native-american-heritage-trail/. Accessed May 13, 2021.

House of Representatives. https://www.govtrack.us/congress/bills/110/hres1050. Accessed August 16, 2021.

House, Renée. *Patterns and Portraits: Women in the History of the Reformed Church in America*. Eerdmans, 1999.

Hunt, Tristram. *Cities of Empire: The British Colonies and the Creation of the Urban World*. Henry Holt and Company, 2014.

Ibn Battuta. *The Travels of Ibn Battuta, A.D. 1325–1354*. Volume 2. Taylor & Francis, 2017.

Ice. British Glaciological Society, International Glaciological Society, Issues 32–43, 1970.

Investigation of Congested Areas. US Government Printing Office, 1943.

'Islamic Culture'. *Hyperbad Quarterly Review*, Islamic Culture Board, 1971.

Jagmohan. *Triumphs and Tragedies of Ninth Delhi*. Allied Publishers, 2015.

Jain, Meenakshi. *The India They Saw, Vol. 2*. Ocean Books, 2011.

James, Harold, and Kevin O'Rourke. 'Italy and the First Age of Globalization, 1861–1940'. Quaderni di Storia Economica (Economic History Working Papers), 2011.

Janin, Hunt. *The Pursuit of Learning in the Islamic World, 610–2003*. McFarland Publishers, 2006.

Jawaharlal Nehru: Selected Speeches Volume 4, *1957–1963*. Publications Division, Ministry of Information & Broadcasting, 1996.

Jeddah 68/69: The First and Only Definitive Introduction to Jeddah, Saudi Arabia's Most Modern and Varied City. University Press of Arabia, 1968.

Johnson, David A., and Richard Watson. *New Delhi: The Last Imperial City*. Palgrave Macmillan, 2016.

Johnson, Rob. *Outnumbered, Outgunned, Undeterred: Twenty Battles Against All Odds*. Thames & Hudson, 2011.

Judy: The London Serio-Comic Journal. April 8, 1891.

Jung, C. G. *Memories, Dreams, Reflections*. Knopf Doubleday, 1963.

Jütte, Daniel. 'Entering a City: On a Lost Early Modern Practice'. *Urban History*, vol. 41, no. 2, 2014, 204–27.

Kang, Kyung-min. '10 Year Anniversary of Cheonggyecheon Restoration . . . Becoming a "Cultural Oasis" of the City'. *Hankyung* (Seoul), September 29, 2015, https://www.hankyung.com/society/article/2015092935361. Accessed September 2, 2021.

Kapur, Kirun. *Visiting Indira Gandhi's Palmist*. Elixir Press, 2015.

Karan, Pradyumna. *Japan in the 21st Century: Environment, Economy, and Society*. Press of Kentucky, 2010.

Kaul, H. K., editor. *Historic Delhi: An Anthology*. Oxford University Press, 1985.

KCRW. https://www.kcrw.com/music/articles/anne-sextons-original-poem-45-mercy -street-the-genesis-of-peter-gabriels-mercy-street. Accessed August 7, 2021.

Keane, John Fryer. *My Journey to Medinah: Describing a Pilgrimage to Medinah*. London, 1881.

Khusrau, Amir. *In the Bazaar of Love: The Selected Poetry of Amir Khusrau*. Translated by Paul E. Losensky and Sunil Sharma. Penguin, 2011.

Kim, Eyun Jennifer. 'The Historical Landscape: Evoking the Past in a Landscape for the Future in the Cheonggyecheon Reconstruction in South Korea'. *Humanities*, vol. 9, no. 3, 2020.

Kipen, David. *Dear Los Angeles: The City in Diaries and Letters, 1542 to 2018*. Random House, 2019.

Kipling, Rudyard. *Collected Verse of Rudyard Kipling*. Doubleday, Page & Company, 1916.

Koehler, Robert. *Hangeul: Korea's Unique Alphabet*. Seoul Selection, 2010.

Kramer, J. A. *A Geographical and Historical Description of Ancient Italy*. Oxford, 1826.

Krondl, Michael. *The Taste of Conquest: The Rise and Fall of the Three Great Cities of Spice*. Ballantine Books, 2008.

Kudō, Umejirō. 'The Divine Snowball Fight'. *Ainu Folk Tales*. Kudō Shoten, 1926.

Kumar, Nikhil. 'Resurrecting the City of Poets'. *Book Review* (India). January 2019, vol. 43, no. 1.

Kwon, Hyuk-cheol. ' "Concrete Fish Tank" Cheonggyecheon's Wrongful Restoration Will Be Repaired'. *Hankyoreh* (Seoul), February 27, 2012, https://www.hani.co.kr/arti/area/area_general/520891.html. Accessed September 2, 2021.

Landscape Performance Series. https://www.landscapeperformance.org/case-study -briefs/cheonggyecheon-stream-restoration. Accessed August 17, 2021.

Leavitt, David. *The Lost Language of Cranes*. Bloomsbury, 2014.

Le Corbusier. *The City of Tomorrow and Its Planning*. Dover Publications, 2013.

Libbrecht, Kenneth, and Rachel Wing. *The Snowflake: Winter's Frozen Artistry*. Voyageur Press, 2015.

Lilly, Lambert. *The History of New England, Illustrated by Tales, Sketches, and Anecdotes*. Boston, 1844.

Livy. *The Early History of Rome: Books I–V of the Ab Urbe Condita*. B. O. Foster, translator. Barnes & Noble, 2005.

Lloyd, Margaret Glynne. *William Carlos Williams's 'Paterson': A Critical Reappraisal*. Fairleigh Dickinson University Press, 1980.

Loh, Andrew. *Malacca Reminiscences*. Partridge Publishing, 2015.

Loomis, Craig. *The Salmiya Collection: Stories of the Life and Times of Modern Kuwait*. Syracuse University Press, 2013.

'The Los Angeles Aqueduct, 1913–1988: A 75th Anniversary Tribute'. *Southern California Quarterly*, vol. 70, no. 3, 1988, 329–54.

Lowrie, Michèle. 'Rome: City and Empire'. *The Classical World*. vol. 97, no. 1, 2003, 57–68.

Lubbe, Gerrie. 'Tuan Guru: Prince, Prisoner, Pioneer'. *Religion in Southern Africa*, 1986, vol. 7, no. 1, 25–35.

Madden, Thomas F. *Istanbul: City of Majesty at the Crossroads of the World*. Penguin, 2017.

Magnus, Olaus. *A Description of the Northern Peoples, 1555*. Edited by P. G. Foote. Taylor & Francis, 2018.

Mahmood, Saif. *Beloved Delhi: A Mughal City and Her Greatest Poets*. Speaking Tiger Books, 2018.

Mail & Guardian. https://mg.co.za/article/2016-09-05-00-the-history-of-vanriebeeks-slave-krotoa-unearthed-from-the-slave-masters-view/. Accessed October 19, 2021.

Mandela, Nelson. *Long Walk to Freedom: The Autobiography of Nelson Mandela*. Little, Brown, 2013.

Mann, Emily. 'In Defence of the City: The Gates of London and Temple Bar in the Seventeenth Century'. *Architectural History*, vol. 49, 2006, 75–99.

Manzo, Clemmy. *The Rough Guide to Brazil*. Apa Publications, 2014.

Marozzi, Justin. *Baghdad: City of Peace, City of Blood*. Penguin, 2014.

———. *Islamic Empires: The Cities That Shaped Civilization – From Mecca to Dubai*. Pegasus Books, 2020.

Mason, Michele M. *Dominant Narratives of Colonial Hokkaido and Imperial Japan: Envisioning the Periphery and the Modern Nation-State*. Palgrave Macmillan, 2012.

McCann, Joy. *Wild Sea: A History of the Southern Ocean*. University of Chicago Press, 2019.

Melville, Herman. *Herman Melville: Complete Poems*. Library of America, 2019.

———. *Redburn, White-Jacket, Moby-Dick*. Library of America, 1983.

Menon, Ramesh. *The Mahabharata: A Modern Rendering*. iUniverse, 2006.

Merewether, E. M. 'Inscriptions in St. Paul's Church, Malacca'. *Journal of the Straits Branch of the Royal Asiatic Society*. no. 34, 1900, 1–21.

Miller, Sam. *Delhi: Adventures in a Megacity*. St. Martin's Publishing, 2010.

Millier, Brett C. *Elizabeth Bishop: Life and the Memory of It*. University of California Press, 1995.

Ministério da Educação e Saúde. https://museuimperial.museus.gov.br/wp-content uploads/2020/09/1958-Vol.-19.pdf. Accessed September 5, 2021.

Molotch, Harvey, and Davide Ponzini. *The New Arab Urban: Gulf Cities of Wealth, Ambition, and Distress*. NYU Press, 2019.

More, Thomas. *Utopia*. Penguin Books, 2012.

Morris, Jan. *Heaven's Command*. Faber & Faber, 2010.

———. *Thinking Again: A Diary*. Liveright, 2021.

Mulholland, Catherine. *William Mulholland and the Rise of Los Angeles*. University of California Press, 2000.

MultiRio. http://www.multirio.rj.gov.br/index.php/assista/tv/14149-museu-aeroespa cial. Accessed September 5, 2021.

Murakami, Haruki. *The Elephant Vanishes: Stories*. Knopf Doubleday, 2010.

Murō, Saisei. 'Earthen Banks' and 'The Yamanote Line'. *Those Who Came from Stars*. Daitokaku, 1922. Privately translated by Takako Lento.

Nadeau, Remi A. *Los Angeles: From Mission to Modern City*. Longmans, Green, 1960.

Naidu, Sarojini. *The Broken Wing: Songs of Love, Death & Destiny, 1915–1916*. William Heinemann, 1917.

Nakaya, Ukichirō. *Snow Crystals: Natural and Artificial*. Harvard University Press, 1954.

Naravane, Vishwanath S. *Sarojini Naidu: An Introduction to Her Life, Work and Poetry*. Orient Longman, 1996.

National Catholic Register. https://www.ncregister.com/blog/why-don-bosco-is-the -patron-saint-of-magicians. Accessed June 1, 2021.

National Geologic Map Database, US Geological Survey, https://ngmdb.usgs.gov /topoview/viewer/#14/40.8210/-76.2015. Accessed May 17, 2021.

National Museum of Korea. https://www.museum.go.kr/site/eng/relic/represent /view?relicId=4325. Accessed July 2, 2021.

Nawani, Smarika. 'The Portuguese in Archipelago Southeast Asia (1511–1666)'. *Proceedings of the Indian History Congress*, vol. 74, 2013, 703–8.

Neaverson, Peter, and Marilyn Palmer. *Industry in the Landscape, 1700–1900*. Taylor & Francis, 2002.

Neimeyer, Oscar, and Izabel Murat Burbridge. *The Curves of Time: The Memoirs of Oscar Niemeyer*. Phaidon Press, 2000.

Netton, Ian Richard, editor. *Encyclopedia of Islamic Civilization and Religion*. Taylor & Francis, 2013.

Neuberger, Hans. 'Climate in Art'. *Weather*, vol. XXV, 1970, 46–66.

New-York Historical Society. https://digitalcollections.nyhistory.org/islandora/object /islandora%3A108209#page/1/mode/2up. Accessed September 4, 2021.

99% Invisible. https://99percentinvisible.org/episode/play-mountain/. Accessed August 31, 2021.

Noh, Hyung-suk. 'Tadao Ando, an "Environmental Architect", Cherishes Cheong-gyecheon?' *Hankyoreh* (Seoul), November 15, 2007, http://h21.hani.co.kr/arti/ society/shociety_general/21151.html. Accessed September 2, 2021.

Norwich, John Julius. *Four Princes: Henry VIII, Francis I, Charles V, Suleiman the Magnificent and the Obsessions That Forged Modern Europe*. John Murray, 2016.

Novalis. *Heinrich von Ofterdingen*. 1802.

O'Connor, Thomas H. *The Athens of America: Boston, 1825–1845*. University of Massachusetts Press, 2006.

Oguma, Hideo. *Long, Long Autumn Nights: Selected Poems of Oguma Hideo, 1901– 1940*. Translated by David G. Goodman. University of Michigan, 1989.

Orcutt, Samuel. *The Indians of the Housatonic and Naugatuck Valleys*. Hartford, Conn., 1882.

The Oregonian. https://www.oregonlive.com/oregonianextra/2007/07/wallace_steg ner_the_heart_of_t.html. Accessed June 5, 2021.

Orton, Jayson, et al. 'An Unusual Pre-Colonial Burial from Bloubergstrand, Table Bay, South Africa'. *South African Archaeological Bulletin*, 2015, vol. 70, no. 201, 106–12.

Osborne, Caroline, and Lone Mouritsen. *The Rough Guide to Copenhagen*. Rough Guides Limited, 2010.

O'Sullivan, Leanne. *A Quarter of an Hour*. Bloodaxe Books, 2018.

Ovenden, Mark. *Metro Maps of the World*. Captial Transport Publishing, 2003.

Ovenden, Mark, and Maxwell Roberts. *Airline Maps: A Century of Art and Design*. Particular Books, 2019.

Paine, Lincoln. *The Sea and Civilization: A Maritime History of the World*. Vintage, 2015.

Palgrave, William Gifford. *Narrative of a Year's Journey Through Central and Eastern Arabia: 1862–1863*. London, 1866.

Parini, Jay. *The Passages of H.M.: A Novel of Herman Melville*. Doubleday, 2011.

Parish and Ward Church of St. Botolph Without Bishopsgate, https://botolph.org .uk/who-was-st-botolph/. Accessed July 2, 2021.

Park, In-ho. 'Miracle of Cheonggyecheon Begins . . . Expecting 23 Trillion KRW Economic Impacts'. *Herald POP* (Seoul), September 27, 2005, https://news. naver.com/main/read.naver?mode=LSD&mid=sec&sid1=102&oid=112& aid=0000017095. Accessed September 2, 2021.

Parliamentary Papers. Volume 59, H.M. Stationery Office, United Kingdom, 1862.

Pastoureau, Michel. *Blue: The History of a Color*. Translated by Mark Cruse. Prince ton University Press, 2001.

Paz, Octavio. *The Collected Poems of Octavio Paz, 1957–1987*. New Directions, 1991.

Pesce, Angelo. *Jiddah: Portrait of an Arabian City*. Falcon Press, 1974.

Pesic, Peter. *Sky in a Bottle*. MIT Press, 2005.

Pet Shop Boys. https://www.petshopboys.co.uk/lyrics/kings-cross. Accessed July 2, 2021.

———. https://www.petshopboys.co.uk/lyrics/west-end-girls. Accessed May 25, 2021.

Peterson, Mark. *The City-State of Boston: The Rise and Fall of an Atlantic Power, 1630–1865*. Princeton University Press, 2020.

Philippopoulos-Mihalopoulos, Andreas, editor. *Law and the City*. Taylor & Francis, 2007.

Pincherle, Maria. 'Crônicas Como Memoriais: A Brasília de Clarice Lispector (e o temporário desaparecimento do invisível)'. *Revista da Anpoll*, vol. 51, 2020, 11–15.

Pittsburgh History & Landmarks Foundation, https://www.phlf.org/dragons/teach ers/docs/William_pitt_city_seal_project.pdf. Accessed May 26, 2021.

Pittsfield Cemetery. https://www.pittsfieldcemetery.com/about-us/. Accessed August 6, 2021.

Platner, Samuel Ball. *A Topographical Dictionary of Ancient Rome*. Cambridge University Press, 2015.

Plat of the City of Zion, Circa Early June. https://www.josephsmithpapers.org /paper-summary/plat-of-the-city-of-zion-circa-early-june-25-june-1833/1. Accessed March 17, 2021.

Proceedings of Inauguration of City Government. Pittsfield, Massachusetts, January 5, 1891.

Rabbat, Nasser O. *The Citadel of Cairo: A New Interpretation of Royal Mamluk Architecture*. E. J. Brill, 1995.

Ramadan, Ashraf, et al. 'Total SO_2 Emissions from Power Stations and Evaluation of Their Impact in Kuwait Using a Gaussian Plume Dispersion Model'. *American Journal of Environmental Sciences,* January 2008, vol. 4, no. 1, 1–12.

Raunkiær, Barclay. *Through Wahhabiland on Camelback*. Routledge & K. Paul, 1969.

Regan, Bob. *The Bridges of Pittsburgh*. Local History Company, 2006.

Ribeiro, Gustavo Lins. *O Capital Da Esperança: A Experiência Dos Trabalhadores Na Construção De Brasília*. UNB, 2008.

Rink, Bradley. 'The Aeromobile Tourist Gaze: Understanding Tourism "From Above"'. *Tourism Geographies,* 2017, vol. 19, 878–96.

Rodgers, Daniel T. *As a City on a Hill: The Story of America's Most Famous Lay Sermon*. Princeton University Press, 2018.

Rooke, Henry. *Travels to the Coast of Arabia Felix: And from Thence by the Red-Sea and Egypt, to Europe*. London, 1784.

Rush, Alan. *Al-Sabah: History & Genealogy of Kuwait's Ruling Family, 1752–1987*. Ithaca Press, 1987.

Saint-Exupéry, Antoine de. *The Little Prince*. Translated by Richard Howard. Mariner, 2000.

Schmidt-Biggemann, Wilhelm. *Philosophia Perennis: Historical Outlines of Western Spirituality in Ancient, Medieval and Early Modern Thought*. Springer, 2004.

Schuyler, George Washington. *Colonial New York: Philip Schuyler and His Family*. New York, 1885.

Schwartz, Lloyd, and Robert Giroux, editors. *Elizabeth Bishop: Poems, Prose, and Letters*. Library of America, 2008.

SCVTV. https://scvhistory.com/scvhistory/costanso-diary.htm. Accessed June 3, 2021.

Sexton, Anne. *The Complete Poems*. Open Road Media, 2016.

Sharma, Ajai. *The Culinary Epic of Jeddah: The Tale of an Arabian Gateway*. Notion Press, 2018.

Sharma, S. R. *Ahwal-e-Mir: Life, Times and Poetry of Mir-Taqi-Mir*. Partridge Publishing, 2014.

Shiga, Naoya. Lane Dunlop, translator. 'At Kinosaki', *Prairie Schooner* 56, no. 1 (1982): 47–54.

Simon, Carly. 'Let the River Run'. 1988.

Singh, Kushwant, editor. *City Improbable: An Anthology of Writings on Delhi*. Penguin, 2010.

Singh, Patwant. 'The Ninth Delhi'. *Journal of the Royal Society of Arts,* vol. 119, no. 5179, 1971, 461–75.

Singh, Upinder, editor. *Delhi: Ancient History*. Social Science Press, 2006.

Sjoholm, Barbara. '"Things to Be Marveled at Rather than Examined": Olaus Magnus and "A Description of the Northern Peoples"'. *Antioch Review,* vol. 62, no. 2, 2004, 245–54.

Skidmore, Thomas E. *Brazil: Five Centuries of Change*. Oxford University Press, 2010.

Sklair, Leslie. *The Icon Project: Architecture, Cities, and Capitalist Globalization.* Oxford University Press, 2017.

Smith, J. E. A. *The History of Pittsfield, (Berkshire County,) Massachusetts, from the Year 1734 to the Year 1800.* Boston, 1869.

———. *The History of Pittsfield, (Berkshire County,) Massachusetts, from the Year 1800 to the Year 1876.* Springfield, 1876.

———. *The Poet Among the Hills: Oliver Wendell Holmes in Berkshire.* Pittsfield, Mass., 1895.

Smith, Joseph, and Smith, Heman C. *History of the Church of Jesus Christ of Latter Day Saints.* Lamoni, Iowa, 1897.

Smith, Richard Norton. *On His Own Terms: A Life of Nelson Rockefeller.* Random House, 2014.

Soucek, Gayle. *Marshall Field's: The Store That Helped Build Chicago.* Arcadia Publishing, 2013.

Springer, Carolyn. 'Textual Geography: The Role of the Reader in "Invisible Cities"'. *Modern Language Studies,* Autumn 1985, vol. 15, no. 4, 289–99.

Stamp, Gavin. 'The Rise and Fall and Rise of Edwin Lutyens'. *Architecture Review,* November 19, 1981.

Stark, Freya. *Baghdad Sketches: Journeys Through Iraq.* I. B. Tauris, 2011.

Starr, Kevin. *Golden Gate: The Life and Times of America's Greatest Bridge.* Bloomsbury, 2010.

———. *Material Dreams: Southern California Through the 1920s.* Oxford University Press, 1991.

Steinbeck, John. *The Grapes of Wrath.* Penguin Books, 2006.

Stephen, Carr. *The Archaeology and Monumental Remains of Delhi.* Simla, 1876.

Stierli, Martino. 'Building No Place: Oscar Niemeyer and the Utopias of Brasília', *Journal of Architectural Education,* vol. 67, no. 1, March 2013, 8–16.

Stockbridge-Munsee Community. https://www.mohican.com/origin-early-history/. Accessed August 16, 2021.

Suh, H. Anna, editor. *Leonardo's Notebooks: Writing and Art of the Great Master.* Running Press, 2013.

Swanton, John Reed. *The Indian Tribes of North America.* Genealogical Publishing Company, 2003.

Tan, Tai Yong, and Gyanesh Kudaisya. *The Aftermath of Partition in South Asia.* Taylor & Francis, 2004.

Tauxe, Caroline S. 'Mystics, Modernists, and Constructions of Brasília'. *Ecumene,* vol. 3, no. 1, 1996, 43–61.

Thompson, Leonard. *A History of South Africa.* Fourth edition, revised and updated by Lynn Berat. Yale University Press, 2014.

Thornes, John E. *John Constable's Skies: A Fusion of Art and Science*. University of Birmingham, University Press, 1999.

Tombs, Robert. *The English and Their History*. Knopf Doubleday, 2015.

Toye, Hugh. *The Springing Tiger: A Study of the Indian National Army and of Netaji Subhas Chandra Bose*. Allied Publishers, 2009.

Tracy, William. 'A Talk with Violet Dickson'. *Aramco World*, November/December 1972.

Trevelyan, George Macaulay. *Garibaldi's Defence of the Roman Catholic Republic*. T. Nelson, 1920.

Ummid. https://www.ummid.com/news/2016/February/15.02.2016/ghalib-is-delhi-and-delhi-is-ghalib.html. Accessed September 4, 2021.

UNESCO City of Design. http://www.unesco.org/new/fileadmin/MULTIMEDIA/HQ/CLT/images/CNN_Seoul_Application_Annex.pdf. Accessed August 17, 2021.

United Nations. https://www.un.org/en/events/citiesday/assets/pdf/the_worlds_cities_in_2018_data_booklet.pdf. Accessed August 31, 2021.

University of Texas at Arlington. https://texashistory.unt.edu/ark:/67531/metapth231670/m1/1/. Accessed September 5, 2021.

USCDornsife. https://dornsife.usc.edu/uscseagrant/5-why-we-have-two-major-sea ports-in-san-pedro-bay/. Accessed June 5, 2021.

US Department of Transportation, Federal Highway Administration. https://www.fhwa.dot.gov/infrastructure/longest.cfm. Accessed June 3, 2021.

US Department of Transportation, Federal Highway Administration. *Manual on Uniform Traffic Control Devices*. Revised edition, 2012.

Van Engen, Abram C. 'Origins and Last Farewells: Bible Wars, Textual Form, and the Making of American History', *The New England Quarterly*, vol. 86, no. 4, 2013, 543–92.

Vanhoenacker, Mark. *Skyfaring: A Journey with a Pilot*. Knopf Doubleday, 2015.

———. 'Four Cities in a Day'. *The Monocle Escapist*, Summer 2015.

Vann, Michael G. 'When the World Came to Southeast Asia: Malacca and the Global Economy'. *Maritime Asia*, vol. 19, no. 2, Fall 2014.

Varma, Pavan K. *Ghalib: The Man, the Times*. Penguin Group, 2008.

Varthema, Lodovico de. *The Travels of Ludovico Di Varthema in Egypt, Syria, Arabia Deserta and Arabia Felix, in Persia, India, and Ethiopia, A.D. 1503 to 1508*. London, 1863.

Vatican News. https://www.vaticannews.va/en/saints/10/12/our-lady-of-aparecida.html. Accessed June 1, 2021.

Villiers, Alan. *Sons of Sindbad: An Account of Sailing with the Arabs*. Hodder & Stoughton, 1940.

WBUR. https://www.wbur.org/radioboston/2016/06/29/ge-and-pittsfield. Accessed August 16, 2021.

Waits, Tom. http://www.tomwaits.com/songs/song/114/Rubys_Arms/. Accessed August 31, 2021.

WCVB.https://www.wcvb.com/article/boston-s-iconic-hancock-tower-renamed/822 5046. Accessed May 25, 2021.

Weaver, William, and Damien Pettigrew. 'Italo Calvino: The Art of Fiction No. 130'. *Paris Review,* no. 124, Fall 1992.

Werner, Morris Robert. *Brigham Young.* Harcourt, Brace, 1925.

White, Sam. *The Climate of Rebellion in the Early Modern Ottoman Empire.* Cambridge University Press, 2011.

Willard, Charles Dwight. *The Herald's History of Los Angeles City.* Kingsley-Barnes & Neuner Company, 1901.

Williams, William Carlos. *Paterson.* Revised Edition. New Directions, 1995.

Willison, George Findlay. *The History of Pittsfield, Massachusetts, 1916–1955.* City of Pittsfield, 1957.

Wilson, Ben. *Metropolis: A History of the City, Humankind's Greatest Invention.* Knopf Doubleday, 2020.

Wilson, Richard Guy. *Re-Creating the American Past: Essays on the Colonial Revival.* University of Virginia Press, 2006.

Wolf, Burkhardt. *Sea Fortune: Literature and Navigation.* De Gruyter, 2020.

Woodruff, David, and Gayle Woodruff. *Tales Along El Camino Sierra.* El Camino Sierra Publishing, 2019.

Woolf, Virginia. *To the Lighthouse.* Harcourt, 1981.

World Travel & Tourism Council. https://wttc.org/Portals/0/Documents/ Reports/2019/City%20Travel%20and%20Tourism%20Impact%20 Extended%20Report%20Dec%202019.pdf?ver=2021-02-25-201322-440. Accessed August 31, 2021.

World Urbanization Prospects: The 2018 Revision. United Nations, Department of Economic and Social Affairs, Population Division, 2018.

WTAE. https://www.wtae.com/article/just-how-many-bridges-are-there-in-pittsburgh /7424896. Accessed September 6, 2021.

Wyler, Marcus. 'The Development of the Brazilian Constitution (1891–1946)'. *Journal of Comparative Legislation and International Law,* vol. 31, no. 3/4, 1949, 53–60.

Yavuz, Vural, et al. 'The Frozen Bosphorus and Its Paleoclimatic Implications Based on a Summary of the Historical Data', 2007.

YouGovAmerica. https://today.yougov.com/topics/international/articles-reports/2015 /05/12/why-blue-worlds-favorite-color. Accessed August 31, 2021.

Permissions